PENGUIN BOOKS

ARNHEM

John Nichol is a former RAF flight lieut   ado bomber was
shot down on a mission over Iraq durir   st Gulf War in 1991. He
was captured and became a prisoner of war. He is the bestselling co-author
of *Tornado Down* and author of five novels. He is also a journalist and widely
quoted military commentator. His website is www.johnnichol.com.

Tony Rennell is the author of *Last Days of Glory: The Death of Queen
Victoria* and co-author of *When Daddy Came Home*, a highly praised study
of demobilization in 1945. He is a former deputy editor of the *Sunday
Times* and writes regularly on historical subjects for the *Daily Mail*.

Together John Nichol and Tony Rennell are the authors of *The Last Escape*,
Tail-End Charlies, *Home Run* and *Medic*, all published by Penguin.

Arnhem

The Battle for Survival

JOHN NICHOL AND TONY RENNELL

PENGUIN BOOKS

PENGUIN BOOKS

Published by the Penguin Group
Penguin Books Ltd, 80 Strand, London WC2R ORL, England
Penguin Group (USA) Inc., 375 Hudson Street, New York, New York 10014, USA
Penguin Group (Canada), 90 Eglinton Avenue East, Suite 700, Toronto, Ontario, Canada M4P 2Y3
(a division of Pearson Penguin Canada Inc.)
Penguin Ireland, 25 St Stephen's Green, Dublin 2, Ireland
(a division of Penguin Books Ltd)
Penguin Group (Australia), 250 Camberwell Road,
Camberwell, Victoria 3124, Australia (a division of Pearson Australia Group Pty Ltd)
Penguin Books India Pvt Ltd, 11 Community Centre,
Panchsheel Park, New Delhi – 110 017, India
Penguin Group (NZ), 67 Apollo Drive, Rosedale, Auckland 0632, New Zealand
(a division of Pearson New Zealand Ltd)
Penguin Books (South Africa) (Pty) Ltd, Block D, Rosebank Office Park, 181 Jan Smuts Avenue,
Parktown North, Gauteng 2193, South Africa

Penguin Books Ltd, Registered Offices: 80 Strand, London WC2R ORL, England

www.penguin.com

First published by Viking 2011
Published in Penguin Books 2012
001

Copyright © John Nichol and Tony Rennell, 2011
All rights reserved

The moral right of the authors has been asserted

Typeset by Palimpsest Book Production Limited, Falkirk, Stirlingshire
Printed in Great Britain by Clays Ltd, St Ives plc

ISBN: 978-0-141-04835-2

www.greenpenguin.co.uk

Penguin Books is committed to a sustainable
future for our business, our readers and our planet.
This book is made from Forest Stewardship
Council™ certified paper.

ALWAYS LEARNING   PEARSON

For Sophie and Harry

This book is dedicated to all those Arnhem veterans, military and civilian, who fought with such incredible courage and selfless dedication. Their fortitude in the face of overwhelming odds is an inspiration to us all.

Contents

Illustrations

around Oosterbeek (Airborne Assault, Imperial War Museum, Duxford)

16. RAF pilot Richard Medhurst, who was killed when his aircraft was shot down while dropping supplies at Oosterbeek (Rozanne Colchester)

17. Sergeants Whawell and Turl of the Glider Pilot Regiment search for snipers in the ruins of a destroyed school in Oosterbeek (Airborne Assault, Imperial War Museum, Duxford)

18. Heleen Kernkamp, who witnessed much of the fighting in and around Arnhem (Marga van Lennep-Kernkamp)

19. Soldiers of the 1st Airborne Division in defensive positions around Oosterbeek, 18 September (IWM BU 1143)

20. German infantry probe the perimeter around Oosterbeek, September 1944 (IWM HU 2126)

21. Dutch civilians evacuated from the St Elizabeth Hospital (Airborne Assault, Imperial War Museum, Duxford)

22. *Left*: Kazic Szmid in 1944 (Andrzej Szmid); *right*: at Arnhem in 2009

23. Wounded men of the 1st Parachute Squadron RE, Arnhem (Airborne Assault, Imperial War Museum, Duxford)

24. British paratroopers march into captivity (Airborne Assault, Imperial War Museum, Duxford)

25. An officer of the 1st Airborne Division loses his trousers after crossing the Rhine (Airborne Assault, Imperial War Museum, Duxford)

26. Corporal Ron Mills pays his respects at the grave of Trooper Edmond (IWM BU 1105)

27. A wounded soldier is carried away from the Divisional Administrative area at Oosterbeek, 24 September (IWM BU 1141)

28. *Left*: the letter received by Ron Brooker's mother in October informing her that Ron was missing in action; *right*: the letter she received in November 1944 informing her he was a prisoner of war (Ron Brooker)

29. Aerial view of Arnhem, destroyed during the battle (Airborne Assault, Imperial War Museum, Duxford)

Maps

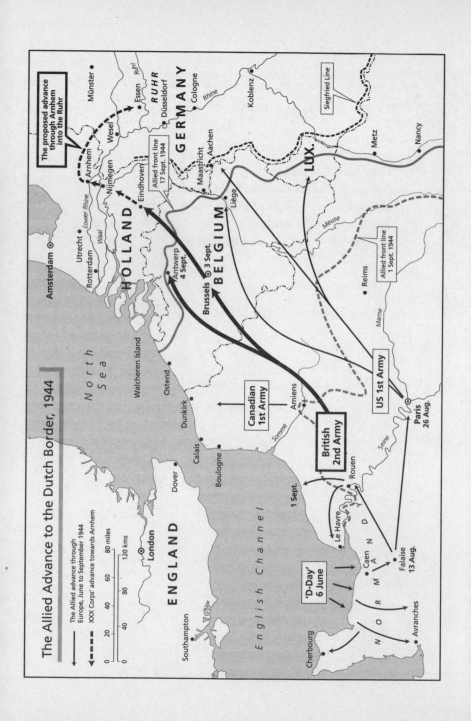

The Allied Advance to the Dutch Border, 1944

→ The Allied advance through Europe, June to September 1944

▪▪▪ XXX Corps' advance towards Arnhem

The proposed advance through Arnhem into the Ruhr

Allied front line 17 Sept. 1944

Allied front line 1 Sept. 1944

Siegfried Line

Canadian 1st Army

British 2nd Army

US 1st Army

'D-Day' 6 June

North Sea

English Channel

GERMANY

HOLLAND

BELGIUM

LUX.

ENGLAND

N O R M A N D Y

RUHR

Amsterdam

Münster

Essen

Düsseldorf

Cologne

Koblenz

Metz

Nancy

Aachen

Maastricht

Liège

Arnhem

Wesel

Nijmegen

Eindhoven

Utrecht

Rotterdam

Brussels ⊙ 3 Sept.

Antwerp 4 Sept.

Reims

Paris 26 Aug.

Ostend

Dunkirk

Calais

Boulogne

Le Havre

Rouen

Falaise 13 Aug.

Caen

Cherbourg

Avranches

Amiens

London

Dover

Southampton

Walcheren Island

Lower Rhine

Waal

Rhine

Meuse

Marne

Seine

Somme

1 Sept.

0   20   40   60   80 miles

0   40   80   120 kms

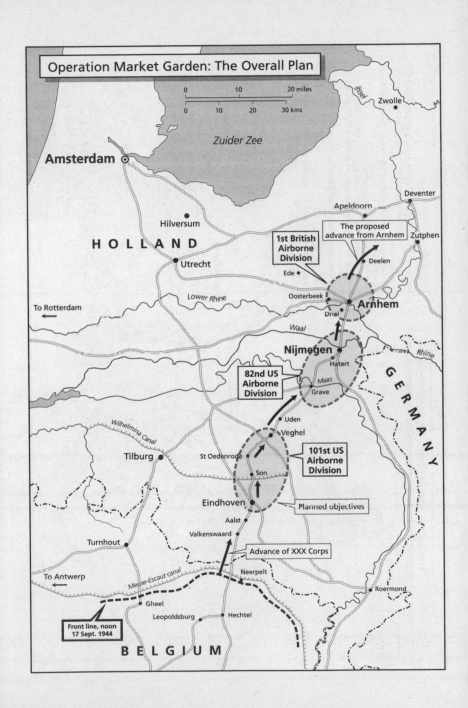

Operation Market Garden: The Overall Plan

Zuider Zee

Amsterdam ⊙

HOLLAND

Hilversum

Utrecht

1st British Airborne Division

The proposed advance from Arnhem

Apeldoorn

Deventer

Zutphen

Deelen

Jssel

Zwolle

Ede

Oosterbeek

Arnhem

Lower Rhine

To Rotterdam ←

Driel

Waal

Nijmegen

82nd US Airborne Division

Hatert

Maas

Grave

GERMANY

Rhine

Uden

Veghel

Tilburg

St Oedenrode

101st US Airborne Division

Son

Wilhelmina Canal

Eindhoven

Planned objectives

Aalst

Valkenswaard

Turnhout

Advance of XXX Corps

To Antwerp ←

Meuse-Escaut canal

Neerpelt

Roermond

Gheel

Leopoldsburg

Hechtel

Front line, noon 17 Sept. 1944

BELGIUM

0   10   20 miles
0   10   20   30 kms

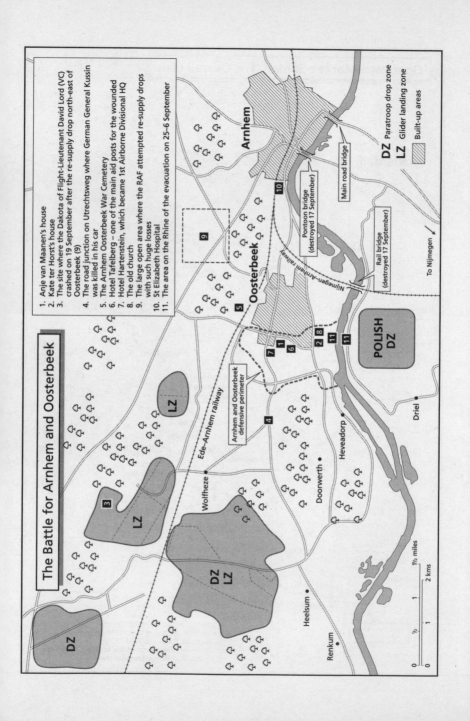

The Battle for Arnhem and Oosterbeek

1. Anje van Maanen's house
2. Kate ter Horst's house
3. The site where the Dakota of Flight-Lieutenant David Lord (VC) crashed on 19 September after the re-supply drop north-east of Oosterbeek (9)
4. The road junction on Utrechtseweg where German General Kussin was killed in his car
5. The Arnhem Oosterbeek War Cemetery
6. Hotel Tafelberg – one of the main aid posts for the wounded
7. Hotel Hartenstein, which became 1st Airborne Divisional HQ
8. The old church
9. The large open area where the RAF attempted re-supply drops with such huge losses
10. St Elizabeth Hospital
11. The area on the Rhine of the evacuation on 25–6 September

DZ Paratroop drop zone
LZ Glider landing zone
Built-up areas

Arnhem

Oosterbeek

POLISH DZ

Pontoon bridge (destroyed 17 September)

Main road bridge

Rail bridge (destroyed 17 September)

To Nijmegen

Nijmegen–Arnhem railway

Arnhem and Oosterbeek defensive perimeter

Ede–Arnhem railway

Wolfheze

Doorwerth

Heveadorp

Driel

Heelsum

Renkum

0   ½   1   1½ miles
0   1   2 kms

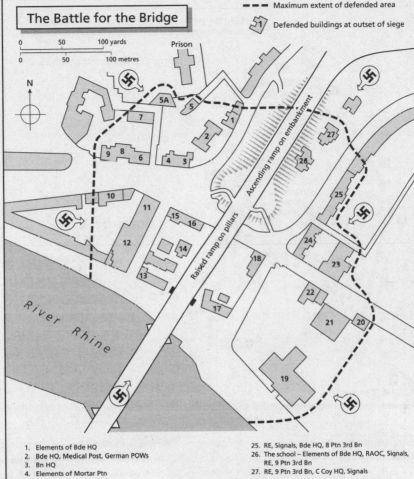

The Battle for the Bridge

- - - Maximum extent of defended area

Defended buildings at outset of siege

| 0 | 50 | 100 yards |
| 0 | 50 | 100 metres |

N

Prison

Ascending ramp on embankment

Raised ramp on pillars

River Rhine

5A
5
1
7
2
9 8 6
4 3
27
26
10
11
25
15 16
12
14
24
23
13
18
22
17
21 20
19

1. Elements of Bde HQ
2. Bde HQ, Medical Post, German POWs
3. Bn HQ
4. Elements of Mortar Ptn
5. Royal Army Service Corps
5A. Mortuary
6,7,8. Elements of Bn HQ & Support Coy, Glider Pilots, 9th Field Coy
9. Anti-tank Battery HQ (from Tuesday)
10. Mixed party
11. B Coy and mixed party
12. 1 Ptn
13. 1 Ptn and Machine-gun Ptn
14. Anti-tank Battery HQ, 9th Field Coy and parts of Machine-gun Ptn
15. A Coy HQ and RE
16. 2 Ptn and 9th Field Coy
17. Elements of B Coy, A Coy HQ, 2 Ptn, RE
18. 3 Ptn
19, 20, 21, 22. Elements of 8 Ptn 3rd Bn, 2 Ptn, Bde HQ
23. Elements of Bde HQ
24. Elements of Bde HQ, RAOC, Signals units

25. RE, Signals, Bde HQ, 8 Ptn 3rd Bn
26. The school – Elements of Bde HQ, RAOC, Signals, RE, 9 Ptn 3rd Bn
27. RE, 9 Ptn 3rd Bn, C Coy HQ, Signals

Key:
Bde – Brigade
Bn – Battalion
Coy – Company
Ptn – Platoon
RAOC – Royal Army Ordnance Corps
RE – Royal Engineers

This map is an indication of the many units involved in this close-quarter, 'house-to-house' fighting around the north end of the bridge. The positions changed regularly over the course of the battle. All units are 2nd Battalion unless otherwise shown.

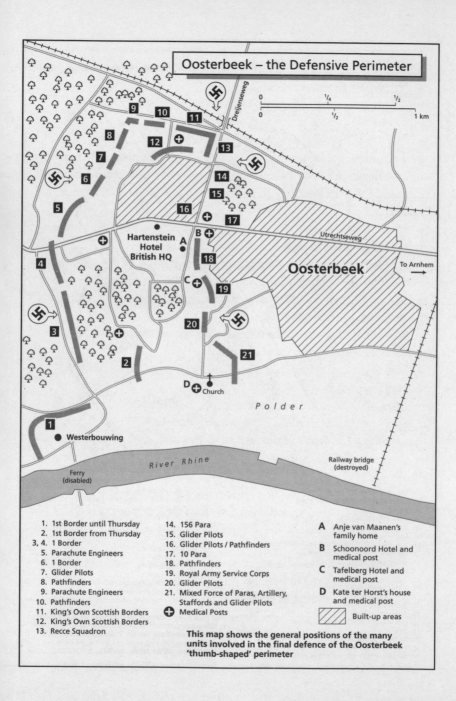

Oosterbeek – the Defensive Perimeter

Dreijenseweg

Utrechtseweg

Oosterbeek

To Arnhem →

Hartenstein
Hotel
British HQ

A

B

C

D Church

Polder

Westerbouwing

River Rhine

Ferry
(disabled)

Railway bridge
(destroyed)

1. 1st Border until Thursday
2. 1st Border from Thursday
3, 4. 1 Border
5. Parachute Engineers
6. 1 Border
7. Glider Pilots
8. Pathfinders
9. Parachute Engineers
10. Pathfinders
11. King's Own Scottish Borders
12. King's Own Scottish Borders
13. Recce Squadron

14. 156 Para
15. Glider Pilots
16. Glider Pilots / Pathfinders
17. 10 Para
18. Pathfinders
19. Royal Army Service Corps
20. Glider Pilots
21. Mixed Force of Paras, Artillery,
    Staffords and Glider Pilots
✛ Medical Posts

A Anje van Maanen's
  family home
B Schoonoord Hotel and
  medical post
C Tafelberg Hotel and
  medical post
D Kate ter Horst's house
  and medical post

Built-up areas

**This map shows the general positions of the many
units involved in the final defence of the Oosterbeek
'thumb-shaped' perimeter**

Acknowledgements

There are many people who willingly gave us their time and expertise while we wrote this book. It is impossible to mention every individual, but we are truly grateful to them all. Our heartfelt thanks also go to:

Major Mike Peters of the Army Air Corps, who sourced countless accounts and pictures and proofread the manuscript.

Mr Jonathan Baker, Curator of Airborne Assault at the Imperial War Museum, Duxford. Jon also proofread the manuscript, and he and Becks Skinner provided unstinting assistance during our visits to the museum's incredible archive.

Sarah Standeven at OfficeOffice, who transcribed our countless interviews with amazing skill and speed.

Our agent, Mark Lucas, and everyone at Penguin who edits, produces and markets our books.

Mike Collins, National Secretary of the Parachute Regimental Association; Alan Hartley, Chairman of the RAF Down Ampney Association; Lieutenant Colonel David Reynolds, editor of *Pegasus* magazine; Niall Cherry of the Society of Friends of the Airborne Museum; Mark Hickman, creator of www.pegasusarchive.org; Cathy Pugh of the Second World War Experience Centre; Martin Mace, editor of *Britain at War* magazine; Air Commodore Graham Pitchfork of the Aircrew Association; and Peter Elliot from the Royal Air Force Museum.

Countless authors and researchers with an unparalleled knowledge of Arnhem contacted us offering their assistance. Again, it is impossible to name them all, but the following went 'above and beyond' in their efforts to help us: Derek Armitage, David Blake, David Brook, Luuk Buist, Tom Buttress, Philip Chinnery, George F. Cholewczynski, Derek Duncan, Bob Gerritsen, Chris Gryzelka, John Howes, Dick Jansen, John Jolly, Gary Jucha, Steve McLoughlin, John

O'Reilly, Mark Pitt, Paul Reed, Mark Roberts, James Semple, Roger Stanton, Graham Stow, Andrzej Szmid, Arie-Jan van Hees and Steve Wright.

Our wives, Suzannah and Sarah, for their unconditional love, support and advice.

Finally, to the many Arnhem veterans and their families who related their personal accounts of the battle, often reliving traumatic events long since buried; we are incredibly grateful. Sadly, we could only use a fraction of the stories we read and heard, but we hope we have done justice to you all.

'I will not say that Arnhem was a defeat. Such men as they can never be defeated. They fought till they had nothing left to fight with – and then fought on.'

– Dick Ennis, glider pilot

Preface

The well-manicured lawn runs down to the Thames near Abingdon. Pleasure boats cruise by and families are out enjoying the sunshine on this glorious midsummer day in tranquil southern England. But the thoughts of 89-year-old Peter Clarke – whose home this is – are of a different river and a different, troubled time. As he remembers faces and places, his eyes mist and he is on the banks of the Lower Rhine in the Netherlands, two thirds of a century ago. He is back among the brave and the bellicose, the wounded and the weary, the dead and the dying, in Arnhem. It was here that in September 1944 a shock force of British troops dropped from the skies into enemy-occupied Holland in what was hoped would be the decisive final battle of the Second World War. It was the most daring of raids behind German lines. If all went well, the war would be over by Christmas.

The strategy was simple enough. In an effort to speed up the defeat of Hitler's already retreating armies, twelve thousand British and Polish airborne troops flew many miles into Nazi-held Europe and descended from planes and gliders on the Dutch city of Arnhem, close to the German border, to capture and defend its vital bridge over the Rhine. Within forty-eight hours, a fast-moving column of armour from the British Second Army would arrive overland along a corridor it carved through the German lines, sweep over that bridge and on into Germany through what was in effect the open back door. That was the plan. But the mission went wrong, the reinforcements never arrived and the airborne forces were left isolated. What began as an audacious masterstroke to end the war became a desperate struggle for survival itself. Surrounded, outgunned and running out of supplies, these brave men fought for a week and more in Arnhem and in Oosterbeek, a pretty village in wooded countryside nearby.

Every street was a war zone, every stand of trees a fortress. Every inch was contested; casualties were enormous, on both sides. But in this furnace a legend was forged – of bravery and endurance far beyond the simple call of duty. Even the remorseless enemy admired what the Red Devils of the Airborne Division did at Arnhem. 'You fought well, Tommy,' many a German soldier told the six and a half thousand who were finally forced to capitulate, long past the point when they could have honourably surrendered and only when they could fight no more.

Here, in the company of the thoughtful and gentle Peter Clarke, a retired solicitor, it is a leap of the imagination to see him as a young staff sergeant fighting for his life and for those of his comrades as they huddled inside their diminishing redoubts. He is uneasy as we gently tap his memories. 'I remember very little of that time, nothing almost,' he says at first. But it's impossible to hold back the past, especially events that were so brutal and so intense, so grand in scale and yet so deeply personal that they can never be erased. There are long pauses in our conversation as if he is reloading the tape, revisiting the horrors and finding himself as affected now as he was sixty-six years ago. 'Everything melded into one,' he says. 'There are no separate days, no separate nights. I don't remember morning or afternoon or evening.'

The images come tumbling out. 'I recall a haystack that caught fire, throwing light all around the darkness and giving our position away. I was in a slit trench on the edge of a wood. There were trees behind and to the sides but in front it was wide open. I felt completely vulnerable. And then the German mortars were screaming in and all you can do is crouch down in your dug-out and hope and pray. Oh, I was scared when they were mortaring us. I remember my knees knocking. You're under constant attack. I don't remember any times of respite. But we just got on with it. There were no orders, there was nobody running from trench to trench saying do this, look in this direction. You were out there on your own, you made your own rules, you made your own decisions.' And yet, for all he had to endure, he feels privileged to have played a part and to have given so much of himself for a cause he passionately believed in – the defeat of Hitler and Nazism.

Time is taking its toll on his unique generation of fighting men. Ron Brooker, the same age as Peter Clarke, was a sharp-shooter in his

Arnhem days. Now his eyes are dimming. 'I used to be quite a marks-man,' he laments, 'but I can't see a bloody thing these days.' He's a cheery soul, neighbours pop in all the time, and, as with Peter Clarke, we have to remind ourselves that this is a man who stood toe to toe with SS soldiers. 'This was close-quarter killing with bullet and bay-onet,' he says. 'It was brutal. I think I had every six-foot soldier in the German army coming through the windows!' He draws a map of Arnhem on a scrap of paper to illustrate where he was at this moment or that. He has precious mementoes to share – the letters his mother sent to him and the ones he wrote to her from a prisoner-of-war camp in Germany, the War Office telegram his parents received tell-ing them he was missing in action. As he shoves them back into a battered brown envelope, his eyes look damp with emotion.

On his walls are paintings that depict those glory days – 'the best time of my life'. In one, a figure is standing amidst shattered build-ings, and he can recall with photographic clarity how he was firing his rifle across that very scene. He is still haunted by the possibility that he accidentally shot one of his own side. It was all too easy in the chaos of intense and isolated actions along the constantly shifting and re-shaping front line. That chaos makes it hard to unravel the com-plex manoeuvrings of the twin and concurrent actions at Arnhem and Oosterbeek, and we have not attempted to reconstruct the battle in this way. Besides, one of the significant features of Arnhem was how the tidy pieces of military organization – the brigade, company and platoon structures – were swept aside by events and men fought shoulder to shoulder with those next to them, whatever the colour of their beret or the badge on their smock. This was no orderly set-piece battle, no neat chessboard of attack and defence. Rather it was a maze and a muddle, the confusing interweaving of a myriad of sep-arate actions. Times and places merged and plotting one's way can be as difficult as navigating the currents of the Rhine proved to be. It is easy to drown in detail.

But here, in this book, it is the grander and more glorious picture we re-create – the drama of individual men fighting on when all seemed lost, glued together by hope and comradeship. Those who led and directed them – the politicians, the generals, the brigadiers,

even the colonels – are bit players in our narrative. They are the context (and important for that) but not the content. This is essentially
the story of ordinary men – the likes of Peter Clarke and Ron
Brooker, heroes all, though, with the modesty typical of their generation, they deny the very suggestion. You will also find here not
only the battle-hardened professional infantrymen of the parachute
brigades but others whose contributions are often overlooked – the
sappers and the signallers, the pilots and the medics, the padres and
the Poles. To those readers steeped in the Arnhem story, some of
these figures will be familiar, but others are new, with untold tales to
tell. What they have in common is that they can all say with hand on
heart, 'I was there.'

Being there was crucial. It is strongly felt by Arnhem men – more
so perhaps than in any other Second World War battle – that to have
any real grasp of what it was like to live and die in that cauldron, you
had to have experienced it. That is why their own accounts are at the
heart of this narrative and much of this story is rightly in their words.
What we hear is the authentic voice of Arnhem and Oosterbeek,
with all the horror laid bare and the heroism revealed. That goes for
the brave Dutch people too, men, women and children risking the
Gestapo knock on the door to try to protect the Tommies who had
come to free them. One of the often overlooked tragedies of Arnhem
is that they were left to make the best of a bad job when the mission
failed and suffered grievously for it.

Courage apart, what also makes the Arnhem story so enduring is
its resonance. It echoes many of the memorable battles of history. A
small band of elite soldiers defies immensely superior odds, just as the
Spartans did at Thermopylae and the English at Agincourt. There is
all the do-or-die drama of the sieges at the Alamo and Rorke's Drift,
plus gruesome trench warfare in the rain and mud that has hints of
the Somme and Ypres. As for the fierce hand-to-hand fighting house
by house, this was nothing short of a mini-Stalingrad. Those nine
concentrated days at Arnhem had all those elements and more. They
also encompassed every shade of human emotion – hope, fear, love,
loyalty, disappointment, grief, regret. But never – and this is what
was remarkable – despair.

Yes, Arnhem was a defeat. What many trusted would be a simple operation turned into a brutal losing battle with terrible losses. Of those airborne soldiers sent on this ill-fated mission, 1,500 died and 6,500 were taken prisoner. The vital bridge at Arnhem that they had come to capture stayed resolutely in German hands. The war was not over by Christmas. In the end, as one anonymous paratrooper put it, 'Courage was not enough.'

But undefeated courage is what we record here – the courage of the blood-soaked, bandaged para who, when asked how he was, replied, 'Except for shrapnel in my arm, a leg missing and a splitting headache, I think I'm okay.' And it is the unbroken human spirit that we celebrate – the mortar sergeant who, with a wry smile, declared to his mates on their way into captivity, 'Look, chaps, we may have lost the battle but we did come in second.'

1. 'Where are the Tommies!'

As Arthur Ayers slipped into a fitful sleep in his army billet in eastern England in September 1944, he tried not to think about tomorrow. Reveille would sound at 5.30 a.m., and then he would be going into action with thousands of other British soldiers of the 1st Airborne Division. Weighed down with weapons and supplies, they would cram into hundreds of planes and gliders already lined up at a dozen airfields, fly 200 miles from the safe shores of England, and land 70 miles behind enemy lines in Nazi-occupied northern Europe. Ayers, a sapper, was philosophical about his own survival, as most fighting men are on the eve of battle. 'If you're going to die, there's nothing you can do about it,' he told himself, 'so there's no point worrying.'

Instead, he directed his mind to loving thoughts of Lola. She was his wife of just a few weeks, theirs one of those 'marry me quick' romances that the special circumstances of wartime encouraged. He had spotted the vivacious eighteen-year-old redhead in her smart ATS uniform at the tea bar in a Woolworth store and knew instantly she was the one for him. His mates had gone over to chat while he held back, too shy to speak. But he wrote to her, his first letter a complete shot in the dark – he sent it care of that Woolworth's tea bar, where a friend of hers was working. Lola got sick – a bout of TB – Arthur came to her hospital bedside, love blossomed. They didn't wait. In those days, it was important to seize the moment, especially since he knew that, for airborne troops like him, a big military operation was in the offing and had been since D-Day in June. He got special permission from his CO for the wedding and the honeymoon, short and sweet in a bungalow near Brighton. 'We didn't talk about the possibility of me being killed. We just enjoyed life while we had it.'[1] After five days as a husband he was back with his unit and now about to head over the North Sea to the Netherlands.

There was something of that same *carpe diem* spirit about the ambitious military operation he was embarking on. Field Marshal Bernard Montgomery, the British army commander, had spotted an opportunity to end the war quickly and seized it. Fired up with optimism, he conceived this bold plan to deliver a surprise 'left hook' – his phrase – by-passing Germany's static defences along the fortified Siegfried Line and punching into the heartland of the Nazi nation. Already on the run, the German army would be sent reeling; resistance would crumble. One big push now and the war Britain had been fighting and its weary citizens enduring since September 1939 could be over in a matter of weeks. A huge air armada had been hurriedly assembled, the biggest of the war, and the objective of the heavily armed strike force it was ferrying into battle was the German-held road bridge over the Rhine at the historic Dutch city of Arnhem, close to the border between the Netherlands and Germany. Win it and hold it until reinforcements arrived en masse over land and they would be striking a massive and decisive blow in the war to defeat Hitler.

Victory was within the Allies' grasp, and soon. If all went well, there would be peace at last. Ayers would be reunited with his bride. The last-minute briefing at camp was reassuring. 'From intelligence reports we have received,' his company captain informed the eager young paratroopers lined up in ranks before him, 'it seems there will be very little opposition at Arnhem, just a German brigade group and a few light tanks.' In reality, what lay ahead was one of the toughest and hardest-fought battles of the Second World War. Ayers was one of the lucky ones. He would survive. But it would be a long time before he returned home.

*

Just hours before Ayers went to war, on a grassy water meadow beside the River Rhine, Anje van Maanen, a teenage Dutch girl from Oosterbeek, a well-to-do village just a few miles west of Arnhem, was playing hockey with her friends. It was the weekend. The day was sunny and warm. They were unaware of the hope and then the horror that were about to descend on them, changing their lives for ever. Finn, Anje's dog, a lively Belgian Shepherd, was on the loose and interrupting their game with his antics. He grabbed the ball and ran off. Seventeen-year-old Anje, the local doctor's daughter from the big house just off Oosterbeek's main street, shrieked in irritation and delight as she chased after him, and wrestled the ball from his teeth. She tickled his black ears and stroked his head, and everyone laughed as the game got under way again. Such a nice day – friends, fun, fine weather, Finn. For a few precious moments you could almost forget about the hated *Moffen*, the German soldiers who had been holding sway over Holland for four years and four months.

There were constant reminders of the harsh, humiliating realities of being a conquered nation – the fact that the hockey game was girls only, for example. Where were the boys? Most of those in their teens and twenties had gone into hiding – living 'underwater', as the flood-prone Dutch put it – to avoid being rounded up and transported in cattle trucks to Germany to work in tank and aircraft factories: slave labour to fuel Hitler's increasingly overstretched war machine. Anje's three brothers had disappeared into the ether to avoid being deported. Two had gone away, 'but my youngest brother Paul, who was a medical student, was hiding in our house, up in a room in the attic. We had to be careful and not talk about him, even to friends. We couldn't really trust other people.'[2] Suspicion ruled everyone's lives. A whispered word praising the Allies, a V-for-victory sign flashed with furtive fingers – such acts could be dangerous. Safety, survival even, lay in silence and invisibility.

Beneath their apparent acquiescence, the vast majority of the nation fumed. The total lack of freedom under the Nazi occupiers weighed heavily on Heleen Kernkamp, a trainee nurse working in an Amsterdam hospital. 'What is allowed – but especially what is *not* allowed – is dictated by the authorities,' she noted with bitterness. Food and clothing, curfew, the blackout were all minutely regulated and enforced. Wireless sets were strictly forbidden, bicycles confiscated, 'to say nothing of arbitrary punishments and reprisals'.[3]

In Oosterbeek, in the eastern part of the Netherlands, the German presence was minimal compared with the occupied cities in the west of the country. A few soldiers were billeted in requisitioned homes; a heavy hand hardly seemed necessary with the border of the Reich just a dozen or so miles away. Here you could still, to some extent, get on with your life and try to ignore the ugliness of the bigger picture. Anje and her friends from school were free to play in the streets and woods near her home – 'hide and seek, that sort of thing, football, tennis and hockey, of course, normal children's games, amidst the war'. Yet the occupation was still an unforgivable affront. Older people might be more accommodating, playing a longer, subtler game, but young people like her were deeply resentful of the Germans. 'We'd hear the soldiers singing in the streets – *our* streets – and that made me very angry. I thought they were monsters. We couldn't go to the cinema, to the theatre or to concerts because that's where the Germans were. The films, everything, were in German. I hated it.'

There were more *Moffen* encamped just a mile or so along the road to the east in neighbouring Arnhem – of which affluent Oosterbeek and its handful of streets and comfortable hotels was increasingly an overspill, a suburb. Centuries-old Arnhem, with its pretty squares, parks and large houses, was a solid place, rooted in the past but with a purpose in the present as the provincial capital and administrative centre of Gelderland.[4] It had thrived in the Middle Ages as a trading city, been fought over by dukes and emperors and was, by the twentieth century, established as a quiet, genteel place among whose magnificent greenery Dutch merchants liked to retire to live out their old age in comfortable, bourgeois splendour. It possessed the refined atmosphere of Richmond or Bath, but with the strategic importance of its position on the Rhine.

The Rhine was many things: a vital line of communication, a border, a barrier, a battleground. But, more than anything, this ancient waterway was a potent German symbol. It fed myths and legends of gods and maidens and Teutonic knights as it rose in the Swiss Alps some 750 miles away, passed through wooded gorges, beneath clifftop castles and by medieval trading towns, then poured through industrial cities such as Cologne and Düsseldorf. Berlin was Germany's capital, Bavaria its spiritual home, but the Rhineland was its heart and its powerhouse. Along the way the river picked up tributaries

– the Neckar, the Main, the Mosel, the Ruhr – before, wide and fast flowing, it crossed out of Germany and into the Netherlands.

There, it divided for the last leg to the North Sea. The main river took a southerly route and, renamed the Waal, rushed towards Nijmegen and on towards the coast. The lesser stream meandered to the north, into Arnhem, under the town's massive road bridge – the only one for miles – and then past Oosterbeek's wide, grassy banks, where locals came to swim in its muddy waters, before rolling down to the estuary at Rotterdam. This was the Neder Rijn, the Lower Rhine, and to Anje and her friends it was their adolescent playground. 'We would bathe in the Rhine or paddle around in canoes. I swam all the way across' – it was a quarter of a mile there and back at this point – 'a couple of times because there was an orchard on the other side where we could pick cherries.' In the autumn of 1944, though, it would be the scene of an epic battle that would add a new chapter of courage and self-sacrifice to the rolling Rhine's neverending story.

*

Back in 1940, the Netherlands had fallen quickly to the invading Germans. Without warning, the Third Reich's paratroopers had dropped from the skies to grab vital bridges over the country's extensive rivers and canals, its panzer divisions poured across the border and its Stuka dive-bombers flattened Rotterdam. Flooding the country, the Netherlanders' traditional defence against invaders, didn't work. It was all over in six days. There was little comfort for the Dutch as Belgium and France also succumbed to the Nazi juggernaut. The swastika flew unchallenged over northern Europe, leaving Britain huddling behind the Channel to stand alone. British defiance then and over the coming years was an inspiration, especially when the RAF began taking the fight to Berlin, Hamburg, Cologne and a host of other German cities. Squadrons of bomb-laden Wellingtons and Lancasters flew high over Holland on their way eastwards. Below, the Dutch would peep from behind locked doors and shuttered windows and hug themselves with delight. 'At night, we'd hear the bombers overhead and just be pleased to know that someone at least was trying to fight the Germans,' Anje recalled. 'Those planes were a sound of hope from overseas.' But they put lives at risk if the raids came too close to home. 'I was at school in Arnhem, right next to the bridge, when one day Nijmegen, 10 miles to the south of us, was bombed. We all hid under the tables. The noise was incredible and we were really scared.' It was a sign that, though liberation would come for certain one day, it might not be won easily or without pain.

The successful D-Day landings in Normandy in June 1944 – news of which the Dutch heard as they crouched around illicit wirelesses and crystal sets – raised any flagging spirits. Then, after weeks of tough fighting to crack stiff enemy resistance to their advance, the Allies broke through and roared across France and Belgium, chasing the German army 'like a hunt after a fox on a glorious spring day', as one historian put it.⁵ Paris was liberated, then Brussels. The Germans were in full retreat, whole armies speeding eastwards for the safety of the Rhine and the fortified Siegfried Line. The Netherlanders waited for their turn, anxious to be free too. September came, full of hope, speculation, expectation. But *anticipation* was to be avoided at all costs. Defy the jittery occupying Germans too openly and too early, and disaster could strike. Rumour was deadly dangerous if it ran too far ahead of reality. But defiance was undoubtedly growing, and an encouraging message was passed by radio from London that Prince Bernhard, son-in-law of the exiled Queen Wilhelmina, had been appointed commander-in-chief of the so-called 'Dutch Forces of the Interior', the Resistance army. With this came a plea for everyone to stay calm. 'We have to wait for the prince's orders,' fifteen-year-old Marie-Anne, another of Oosterbeek's young inhabitants, confided to her diary.⁶

For all this apparent caution, early in September the nation lost its patience and its self-control in what was ever after known as *Dolle Dinsdag* – Mad Tuesday. The word spread that Antwerp, the Belgian port on the Scheldt estuary, had fallen to the Allies. The door into Holland had been flung open, or so it seemed. 'We're next' was the thought in everyone's mind. In the cities, patriotic orange flags appeared in windows and crowds gathered in the streets, encouraged by the sight of the German military hurriedly packing. Bonfires blazed in the courtyards of official buildings as the occupiers destroyed piles of secret documents, a precursor, it seemed, to leaving. Members of the NSB, the SS force formed from Dutch Nazis, prepared to disappear before they paid for their collaborating misdeeds at the end of a lynch mob's rope. At Oosterbeek, an excited Anje was swept along by the tide of hope. 'I talked to my friends about how we'd soon be free. And the boys would come home – my brothers and my boyfriend Rob, who was in hiding in the north and whom I hadn't seen for two years.' She climbed with her family to the roof of their house and stared into the distance, straining to see British soldiers. 'Where are the Tommies?' they asked each other.

*

The answer – though, on that Oosterbeek rooftop, the van Maanens had no means of knowing it – was that the Allied ground forces were between 60 and 70 miles away. The British Second Army – commanded by General Miles Dempsey and part of Montgomery's 21st Army Corps – was strung out along the southern bank of the Meuse-Escaut canal, which formed the border between liberated Belgium and the still-occupied Netherlands. It had come to a halt. After the breakneck canter from Normandy, it had run out of steam – steam and, more importantly, supplies. The port of Antwerp was in Allied hands all right, as all those wildfire Dutch rumours had said. But the rest of the Scheldt estuary giving access to the North Sea was not. The shores continued to be held by the Germans, and there was no way for relief ships to get into the docks and wharves of Antwerp past their big guns. The over-extended Allies were left still tied umbilically to the French port of Cherbourg, 350 miles away, as the sole entry point into Europe for desperately needed re-supplies of equipment, guns, ammunition, food: everything. Thousands of laden trucks – the Red Ball Express, as the largely American drivers called themselves – trundled northwards from Cherbourg in convoy, moving as fast as they could to feed the front line, then turned round and went back for more. But the distances were getting longer and the logistics tougher all the time. The onward rush was grinding to a halt, and serious consideration was given to the next step.

The obvious military move was to backtrack, go west not east, crush the Germans dug in along the Scheldt, open up Antwerp to shipping, ease the supply chain, then resume the drive eastwards to Germany. But that would be costly, in manpower and time. And the impetus would be lost. On the other hand, standing there on the Meuse-Escaut canal and looking at a map of what lay ahead, the German border seemed tantalizingly near, almost within reach. And wide open. If only the Allied armies could race through Holland as they had raced through France and Belgium, then they would be round the enemy's line of fortifications, in by the back door and on their way to Berlin. There was a problem, of course, with all those Low Countries waterways. If each canal, stream and river had to be assaulted one by one, the Allies might end up stalled and stymied as they had been for so long by the narrow lanes and high hedges of Normandy. Control of the bridges would be crucial, making sure they were captured intact before the retreating Germans demolished them. Allied commanders paused for thought.

Meanwhile, in the Netherlands, life for the locals became harder and more dangerous as the occupying German forces reacted to the enemy at the gate not by running – as, for a while, everyone had thought certain – but by regaining their nerve and cracking down on every hint of opposition. After Mad Tuesday, a state of emergency was proclaimed and a dire warning given that groups of more than five people gathering in the streets were liable to be shot. Curfew was brought forward to 8 p.m. Normal life virtually ceased. Trains stopped running, the mail didn't get through, the phones went dead. Food was scarce, ration books pointless. Individuals were grabbed at gunpoint in the cities to dig shelters and defensive trenches. Even worse, men were routinely abducted for transportation to be slave labour in Germany. Now it was not just the young and the fit with reason to fear the round-up. All males under fifty were at risk, picked up at random on the streets or winkled out from their homes in brutal house-to-house searches. Suddenly, liberation was more desperately needed than ever.

At Oosterbeek, the once quiet village was filling up with retreating German soldiers demanding billets in people's homes, requisitioning the school for a depot, erecting anti-aircraft guns in the meadows. Their manners were brusque and threatening. Marie-Anne thought them 'tiresome' and 'vulgar'. A *Feldwebel* [sergeant] marched into her garden and demanded to inspect her father's bicycle workshop. When she got back from a trip to the shops – 'You queue for hours and then at the butcher's I get 5ozs of meat, for the six of us! We won't grow fat on that lot' – he was not only still there but had taken charge. The workshop had been cleared out and converted into a field kitchen for his platoon. She wanted to object, 'but the time has not yet come that we can ignore what the "*Herren*" order us to do.' Everywhere there were signs that the situation was worsening. 'In the afternoon I went across the river to get some pears. The ferry is now guarded by the SS.'

Confrontation and hostility were in the air and violence not far behind, as the 22-year-old Heleen Kernkamp discovered. She had left her job in Amsterdam and was in Arnhem, her home town, staying with friends from her schooldays. Two of them had jobs in a large local plastics factory, the biggest employer in the town, whose bosses were ordered by the Germans to provide a workforce to dig trenches. The patriotic Dutch directors bravely refused to comply. Instead, they shut down the factory and gave their workers six weeks' pay, enough for those who felt threatened to go into hiding. 'The tension in Arnhem was tremendous,' she recalled. People locked themselves away at home, trying to hide their menfolk. The streets were deserted, except for the Germans stripping the factory. Massive machines were dismantled to be carted off to Germany. The Dutch were dismayed. Their loss would be a terrible blow to the local economy, to jobs and livelihoods. But what could they do to prevent this ransacking of the town's assets? On the night of 15 September, a local resistance group blew up a railway viaduct to delay the machinery being taken away. The Germans retaliated. Posters appeared warning that if the perpetrators were not found, an unspecified number of civilians would be taken hostage and summarily executed. 'We discussed these reprisals all day long. Who would they take? How many?' The deadline was noon on 17 September. Arnhem and its people were desperate and afraid. A massacre seemed unavoidable. 'We hardly slept that night, fearing what the next day would bring.' The salvation they dreamt of was to come from a totally unexpected direction – out of the sky.

*

Two hundred miles away, across the North Sea, thousands of men were preparing to liberate Arnhem. The training was behind them, the briefings had been given. Now it was a case of maintaining morale and comradeship at a pitch where they would go into battle without flinching. Bombardier Leo Hall, a radio signaller, and his mates were let out of camp in Lincolnshire to go to the cinema. He could never recall anything about the film they saw, not even its name or who was in it, but the blistering march back to barracks, with full-throated voices belting out the bawdy words of 'The Big Flywheel' in unison like naughty boys – 'Round and round went the bloody great wheel/ In and out went the p**** of steel' – released some of the tension, took their thoughts away from what lay ahead. Paratrooper James Sims, on the other hand, well remembered what he'd watched on the silver screen that night – *Hellzapoppin'*, an American song-and-dance funny starring comedians Ole Olsen and Chic Johnson – and thought it 'the funniest film I'd ever seen'.[7] He also remembered the rows of military police lining the auditorium to make sure no one got cold feet and tried to do a runner. Near his base, another paratrooper, Andy Milbourne, downed pints in the pub as his platoon went through the extensive repertoire of ghoulish para songs, from 'He Ain't Gonna Jump No More' to 'Three Cheers for the Next Man to Die'. Beer and bravado steadied the nerves as the 1st Airborne Division prepared to leapfrog into Europe.

Airborne troops represented one of the Second World War's ground-breaking new weapons. Technologically, this global conflict was revolutionary in many ways – the long-distance bomber, submarines, rockets and the atom bomb among them. But the one device that really came into its own was the parachute, floating down from the skies with an armed, aggressive infantryman on the end of it. Germany led the way with its *Fallschirmjäger*, parachutists dropping behind the lines to great effect in Denmark, Norway, the Netherlands and Crete. Ironically, the heavy losses sustained in Crete persuaded Hitler that airborne attacks were over-extravagant and unnecessary and he put a stop to their widespread use. But Britain, by then, had seized on the airborne idea, egged on by the personal intervention of prime minister Winston Churchill, who delighted in shock tactics to bamboozle an enemy and take him by surprise.

The Parachute Regiment was founded as a small, elite force to carry out hit-and-run raids, then expanded (though still very much an elite) to become a full-on attacking force, a spearhead to thrust into the heart of the enemy, ahead of the main force. The training was tough, the risk and adrenaline levels high. Only the bravest need apply. Only the best were recruited. To be qualified to wear the red beret set a man apart. 'We were lauded as super-fit and super-daring,' recalled Leo Hall. 'We turned heads in our comings and goings. Though generally from working-class backgrounds, we became an aristocracy.' As Allied paras,[8] both British and American, led the invasions of North Africa, Sicily and Italy, they proved their worth as impact players, making a vital difference to the outcome of battle. They also had back-up in the 1st Airlanding Brigade, whose gliders provided an additional means of back-door entry into enemy territory. Towed to enemy air space by 'tugs' and then cut loose to coast down, they could carry not only infantry but heavy equipment as well, including jeeps and small tanks. Once on the ground, paratroopers generally had just their own two feet for transport. Gliders were a means to increased mobility – to hitting further and faster. The men and machines they carried were, in effect, the airborne cavalry.

At the D-Day landings, troops of the 6th Airborne, one of the British army's two airborne divisions, were in the vanguard. Just before the Allied infantry stormed on to the beaches of Normandy, parachutists dropped inland to knock out the gun batteries which dominated the cliff-tops. Meanwhile, brilliantly flown gliders landed just yards from a canal bridge vital to the advance inland, enabling the troops on board to capture it. Strategically, these were vital missions. If either had failed, so too might the entire enterprise. There was every chance of the Allied army being pushed back into the sea. The men of the 6th demonstrated in full the impact of airborne on the modern battlefield. Three and a half months later, there seemed no reason to doubt that a similar smash-and-grab operation could be repeated, with equally devastating results, this time to seize bridges over the wide and muddy waters of the Rhine in the Netherlands.

The plan was the brainchild of Montgomery – the hero of El Alamein and the Western Desert – and was remarkably daring for this habitually meticulous military planner. But he had a point to prove. His recent promotion from general to field marshal was the clue to his state of mind – the enhanced rank was a personal and political sop concocted by Churchill and the king to divert attention from the fact that he had lost overall control of the land forces in Europe to the American supreme commander, General Dwight 'Ike' Eisenhower. He was also losing the argument among the Allies about how best to defeat Hitler. Eisenhower wanted a broad-front attack on Germany, his armies ranged from north to south and advancing in tandem as they pushed towards the Rhine, sweeping all before them. But Monty, contemptuous of the Americans – he thought Eisenhower pedestrian and unfit to command – believed this approach slow and cumbersome. Every yard would be a battle. The Germans would have time and opportunity to re-group their defences. Certain of his own pre-eminence as a military leader, his preference now was for a single rapid strike, concentrating forces on one weak spot and thundering through the enemy lines. 'One really powerful and full-blooded thrust towards Berlin is likely to get there and thus end the German war,' he lectured Eisenhower in a communiqué at the beginning of September. '[But] if we attempt a compromise solution and split our resources so that no thrust is full-blooded, we will prolong the war.'[9]

It was not just his belief in the superiority of his own military prowess that led him to this conclusion. He picked up on the sense of urgency that had developed among the Allies, and especially the British public, since the euphoria of D-Day. With hindsight, we know that final victory over Germany was close, just seven months away in fact. It didn't feel that way at the time. For war-weary armies and civilians back home, the desire to see a glimmer of light was immense. Britain had been at war since September 1939, and the conflict had already outdistanced the 1914–18 War to End All Wars, by many months. London was under intense aerial bombardment again; sirens wailed and for the first time since the Blitz of 1940–41, women and children were dying in the rubble of their own homes, first from doodlebugs, Hitler's revenge weapons, and then, the latest horror, V2 rockets. Morale – which should have been sky-high with the victories in Europe – was lower than it had been for years. An exhausted air hung over the country.

The thought of another new year opening with the country still at war was almost intolerable. But wishful thinking would not win battles and hasten victory. Privately, Churchill admitted that neither the German army nor the German people were about to roll over. 'It is as likely that Hitler will be fighting on January 1 as that he will collapse before then,' he wrote in a memo on 8 September. Nonetheless, to counter the gloomy prognostications, there was an outbreak of wild, 'if only' optimism that it could indeed all be over by Christmas, particularly among the men now briefed for the major assault they were led to believe would do the job – Operation Market Garden. 'We thought the Germans were on their way out,' one recalled. 'They were being pushed back so fast that we would be that final little pin that opened everything up.'[10]

The belligerent Monty had finally got his way – well, partly, at least. At a meeting in Brussels, Eisenhower, weary himself not so much of the war but of his warring generals and their constant bickering and backbiting, agreed that Monty's Second Army should mount a thrust of its own. This 'left hook' would sweep northwards through the Netherlands to try to outflank the German defences. Then it would descend on the industrial powerhouse of the Ruhr valley. His battle-plan – described by him with characteristic immodesty as 'certainly a bold one' – was for the Allied forces to drive hard and fast towards the Rhine and grab a bridgehead on the other side 'before the enemy reorganized sufficiently to stop us'. That would mean first getting over numerous rivers and canals in the Netherlands, notably the River Maas at the town of Grave and the River Waal at Nijmegen. Each would be taken by storm from the air.

To the American airborne divisions he gave the task of securing Eindhoven (20 miles behind enemy lines) and the bridges at Grave and Nijmegen (40 miles behind the lines), while to the British airborne division fell the hardest part – capturing the Arnhem bridge, 64 miles into enemy territory. Meanwhile, XXX Corps, the spearhead of the Second Army, commanded by Lieutenant-General Brian Horrocks with the Guards Armoured Division in pole position, would set out from the Meuse-Escaut canal and race by land over the captured 'carpet' laid down by the Allied airborne troops to reinforce them and consolidate what they had captured. Within forty-eight hours, he was confident that XXX Corps would have linked up with the 1st British Airborne Division at Arnhem and secured a substantial bridgehead on the German side of the Lower Rhine. With that in place, more reinforcements would head eastwards and the Second Army would 'establish itself in the general area between Arnhem and the Zuider Zee, facing east, so as to be able to develop operations against the northern flank of the Ruhr'.[11] Next stop: Berlin. It was a plan intended to make the Führer tremble, demoralize his armies and undermine the will of the German people to continue a war they were now certain to lose.

Pride of place in the operation was reserved for the British forces. Their objective – Arnhem – was at the furthest end of the line, their attack the deepest inside enemy territory. But it was a fight that the British 1st Airborne were up for. They had been seriously disappointed and even affronted at missing out on the Normandy landings. The 6th were dropped into France while the 1st were held in reserve and never used. There had been numerous schemes to deploy them in the advance through France and Belgium but, when German resistance collapsed in late August, the front line moved forward so fast that they never had the chance to drop behind it. At the headquarters of the Airborne Corps in the plush surroundings of the exclusive Moor Park Golf Club in Hertfordshire, detailed operations were drawn up by Major-General Roy Urquhart, commander of the 1st

Airborne Division, and his staff, intensively trained for, then abandoned without a ripcord pulled or a shot fired. Gliders were loaded for action, then unloaded. 'Order, counter-order and consequent disorder are the order of the day,' Major Ian Toler, commanding officer of a glider squadron, noted ruefully in his diary, stuck with the unenviable task of keeping his men focused while stifling his own growing despair. 'We just sit back and laugh, as always.' But the joke was wearing thin.[12]

Sixteen times in three months the airborne forces had been on the brink of going into action, on Op Transfigure, Op Wild Oats, Op Comet, or some such fancy name. They should have liberated Paris. Sometimes they got as far as boarding the plane before the order to stand down came, more often than not because their target had already been overrun by the advancing land forces. 'The suspense was killing us,' said Sergeant Ron Kent, a pathfinder para, whose job would be to go in just ahead of the main force and secure the drop zone. 'The only fighting we were getting was with the Yanks in the pubs of Salisbury, Newark and Huddersfield!'[13] Constant squarebashing, route marches and weapons training were meant to keep the men alert and ready but, as Kent explained, 'We were like boxers, in danger of becoming over-trained, afraid of passing our peak.' Each time they were stood down, they got a 48-hour pass to go to London to make up for having been confined to barracks in the run-up to the aborted mission. But each time, too, more puff went out of their sails and the sharp edges the fighting man depended on were blunted.

Even the commander was losing patience and perhaps even some of his edge. 'By the time we went on Market Garden we couldn't have cared less,' Urquhart conceded in an interview after the war.[14] 'We became callous. Every operation was planned to the best of our ability in every way. But we got so bored, and the troops were more bored than we were. We had approached the state of mind when we weren't thinking as hard about the risks as possibly we had done earlier.' Ironically, given all the delays and the hanging about, when Market Garden was conceived, it all came in a rush. It was 10 September before Urquhart was made privy to Monty's master plan and two days later before he was in a position to brief his brigadiers and their staff officers for what was, in effect, a hurriedly revised version of Comet, the last cancelled operation. He didn't like some of the conditions imposed on him, in particular the choice of drop and landing zones. They were too far from the centre of Arnhem in his opinion, a view many others shared. But this was the RAF's call, and the judgement of its planners was that, if the planes flew in any closer, the German flak and the unsuitability of the soft, riverside ground for gliders to land would be major difficulties. Urquhart didn't have time to win the argument, even if such a thing were possible. There were just five days to the off. And, anyway, after so many false starts, he was raring to go. He remembered 'the euphoria which existed across the Channel and in the Airborne Corps that the war was nearly over and any new operations would be the final nudge to complete German defeat'.

If the men themselves greeted the latest operation with scepticism, it was hardly surprising. The briefing Ron Kent was called to on Saturday 16 September seemed, at first, little more than a repeat of the one a fortnight earlier for Comet. 'We were going to Arnhem. The dropping zone was about five and a half miles west of the town, well inside Holland and almost into Germany. If we could take and hold the bridge long enough we might be in Berlin by Christmas.' That's if they ever got off the ground. 'What's the betting we'll be in London on a pass tomorrow?' one cynic called out.

Briefings were lengthy and thorough, poring over area maps, street maps, sand-tables, models and aerial photographs 'until we felt as if we were almost natives of Arnhem', as one para recalled.[15] Dutch guilders were doled out, five per man, for use once on the ground and, optimistically, a few Deutschmarks as well. For many of the lads, the foreign money burnt a hole in their pockets and they quickly got the playing cards out. Medic Les Davison ended the equivalent of £56 up after a marathon game of brag in his hut. 'Whether I would ever get a chance to spend it remained to be seen,' he noted.[16] But, for others, it was a much bigger gamble that occupied their thoughts that night. Some men were baffled and not a little worried by what they were told in the briefings. Wireless man Leo Hall was concerned whether the radios essential for coordinating this complex operation would have the range to work over the long distances involved. He also thought it 'crazy' to land and drop so far from the bridge, with a long slog to the target, during which the element of surprise might well be lost. On the other hand, they were assured that the opposition they faced would be light: 'Only third-rate enemy troops in the area.' Events would show this to be an awful error. So too was another part of the briefing – 'Don't trust the Dutch. Arnhem is close to the German border. They are probably Nazi sympathizers and Quislings.' Nothing, as it turned out, could be further from the truth.

That night, thousands of men in camps and airfields from Dorset to Lincolnshire and Gloucestershire to Kent passed the time as best they could. Some played football and darts noisily, others read quietly, lost in their own thoughts. In one barracks, a soldier with a pleasing baritone voice (and a heavy note of sarcasm) sang, 'What a Lovely Way to Spend an Evening', the new hit song from the United States. Many wrote letters, to be left behind and delivered home to wives, sweethearts, mums and dads if they did not return. These were hard words to think let alone put down in writing, even harder when biting back the tears and trying to disguise the fear and the regret. 'Dear Mam,' one young soldier of the South Staffordshire Regiment began. 'Tomorrow we go into action. No doubt it will be dangerous and many lives will be lost – maybe mine. I am not afraid to die. I like this life, yes – for the past two years I have planned and dreamt and mapped out a perfect future for myself. I would have liked that to materialize but it is not what I will but what God wills, and if by sacrificing my life I leave the world a slightly better place, then I am perfectly willing to make that sacrifice. Don't get me wrong. I am no flag-waving patriot nor do I fancy myself in the role of a gallant crusader fighting for the liberation of Europe. No, Mam, my little world is centred around you, Dad, everyone at home, my friends. That *is* worth fighting for – and if by doing so it improves your lot in any way, then it is worth dying for too.'[17] He folded the pages, slipped them into an envelope and handed it to his platoon leader for safekeeping. With a bit of luck, he told himself, it would never be read.

2. 'A Piece of Cake'

The morning of Sunday 17 September was beautiful, a surprise after a night of heavy rain. Now the late-summer air was filled with a high-octane scent of excitement, tension, fear and diesel fumes as thousands of trucks and planes kicked into life – and huge optimism. In the years of recrimination that followed, the unspoken misgivings of that morning would come to the fore. The plan was hasty and misconceived, a hurried bolt-on of previous abandoned ops. The drop zones were too far away; there were perfectly usable polders (river meadows) much closer to the target. The spreading of the drops over three consecutive days rather than in rapid and immediate succession meant the assault was too slow and left the initial strike force undermanned. The enemy strength was woefully underestimated, and intelligence to the contrary deliberately overruled. The ease and speed with which the relieving XXX Corps was expected to travel along a single narrow road to get to Arnhem in just forty-eight hours was unrealistic. All in all, it would be said, Market Garden was over-optimistic to the point of lunacy, a 'bridge too far', in the neat tag that will always be attached to it. And all this, it would be suggested, was as clear as day before the first glider pilot hitched up his tow rope.

Except that it wasn't like that. Every military plan has flaws; every commander has doubts and uncertainties he must overcome. Nothing is ever perfect. The days before the Normandy landings were fraught with worry. Eisenhower, by his own admission, was a nervous wreck – fearing the weather wasn't right, that the enemy was stronger than he imagined, that his men might not even get off the beaches. He had prepared a sombre communiqué taking the blame in the event of failure and defeat. At some point, as Eisenhower did, you have to swallow the misgivings before they choke you. In that crude but telling Americanism which first became current among the cigar-chewing transatlantic military at around this time, it's a case of piss or get off the pot.

It was the same with Market Garden. For all the operation's inherent faults, the archive of personal memoirs makes it clear that the men embarked on their mission that day with a remarkable fervour and an unshakeable belief in themselves. To Major Tony Hibbert, the gung-ho spirit was such that 'if somebody had offered to drop us in the middle of Berlin we'd have been as happy as sand boys.'[1] The fact that they had been stood down so often thus far added to their keenness to get on with it. Leo Hall was 'excited at the prospect of making our mark on the war'. Ron Kent was proud not dismayed that the 1st Airborne had been given the toughest assignment of all, to get to the Arnhem bridge and hold it. He knew the Americans were getting the easier ride, to Eindhoven and Nijmegen, and didn't mind. 'We felt it right and proper that the hardest task should be handed to us,' he said. Heads held high, he and thousands like him went willingly and eagerly to win the war. 'We were invincible, weren't we?' recalled one man. 'Completely confident that it was all going to go to plan.'[2]

They were not scheduled to take off until 10 a.m. but, in Kent's recollection, 'we were woken up at some unearthly hour. We'd drawn our parachutes the night before and slept with them alongside us in our tents. Because of the rain, the camp was a quagmire and we queued in the mud to draw our breakfast in mess tins. Then we sloshed our way back to our bivouacs to consume the salted porridge, bacon and baked beans, a thick slice of bread and hot strong tea.' It was still pitch dark as section commanders like him lined up their 'sticks' – the technical term for a section of paratroopers – and checked each man's equipment by torchlight. 'We'd been through it all so often before we could have done it blindfold.' With dawn breaking clear and bright, they clambered on board trucks to take them to the airfield, the canvas backs lashed down to conceal them and their mission from the prying eyes of civilians. They had got this far and further before and been stood down at the last minute, but he felt certain this time they would go. 'By 7.15 we were on the road to Fairford [in Gloucestershire]. Our parachutes, pre-fitted and chalk marked, followed in trucks behind. As we rolled round the perimeter of the airfield, we could see twelve big black Stirling bombers lined up at the end of the runway.' Their taxis were waiting.

At more than a dozen airfields, trucks filled with troops were arriving. In some, men sat in silence, pondering what lay ahead. In others, noisy chatter covered nerves or one soldier would begin to hum and the rest joined in until, as they careered at speed through sleeping villages, everyone was roaring out some reassuring ditty: 'That's my brother Sylvest/ Gawt a row of bloody medals on his chest, big chest/ 'E fought forty soldiers in the west/ That's my brother Sylvest.' At some airfields, they were welcomed with a rare treat – ham sandwiches, handed out by ladies of the WRVS. 'I hadn't seen boiled ham for five years,' Leo Hall recalled. Each aerodrome bustled with intense activity around the planes, parked nose to tail, engines ticking over. Each 'stick' made its way to its allotted plane and sat down on the grass to wait. Not that sitting was easy. At Barkston Heath in Lincolnshire, Reg Curtis of 1 Para – feeling at one moment like 'a stuffed duck' and then 'a well overdue pregnant hippo!' – checked off his gear: 'One Gammon bomb, two hand grenades, combined pick and shovel, web equipment with small pack, two ammunition pouches, a canvas bandolier with 303 rifle ammo, a water bottle, mess tin, iron ration, emergency chocolate, field dressing, a camouflage net scarf, triangle-shape air-recognition bright yellow silk scarf which was tied around the neck ready for instant use, one rifle, an ingenious escape outfit comprising a silk map of Europe, a button compass about half an inch in diameter, a strong file as big as a nail file. That was about it, except for a kit bag strapped to my leg and parachute, plus Mae West life jacket in case we finished up in the drink. I also had a couple of hundred cigarettes and two bars of chocolate and some boiled sweets.'[3] One para officer calculated his jumping weight at 22 stone, not including the folding bike he was carrying.

Curtis was in the main pack that day, but leading the way – twenty minutes ahead of everyone else – would be Ron Kent's company. As the pathfinders on this mission, they had to pinpoint the right landing zone, and he and the navigator of his allotted plane stood on the runway checking maps against recent aerial photographs. 'I pointed out the long rectangular shape of a barn near the centre of our DZ and asked if he could put us down within a hundred yards. He saw no problem.' The time came to board. With a casualness he did not feel inside, Kent called his seventeen-man stick to attention and wished them luck. 'Then, I took my place in the line, at number six.' Within ten minutes they were airborne, climbing and circling to get into formation with the other planes in the advance party. 'Flying in these conditions was boring and uncomfortable. We were seated on the bare floor of the fuselage facing one another but the noise of the engines made normal conversation impossible. The British never designed an aircraft specifically for parachuting, and we often thought this was deliberate. It meant we were always glad to jump when the moment came.'

Time dragged. Anxiety about what lay ahead constantly threatened to get the better of even the toughest. 'After an hour or so in the air I found myself looking at my watch rather too often and beginning to yawn. Signs of nervousness.' Kent's every move was being watched and he must not let his feelings show – fear, though understandable, was contagious, especially in the claustrophobic confines of a plane. 'I stood up and moved down the line nodding, winking and grinning, I hope, reassuringly.' His corporal, who would be jumping last and whose job was to hustle the rest of the stick out in double-quick time to ensure a tight formation on the ground, beckoned him over. 'How long to go, Sarge?' he mouthed through the din. Kent cupped his mouth to the man's ear. 'About half an hour. It can't be too soon for me.' The corporal nodded in agreement. 'I gave his shoulder a friendly thump and made my way back to my place.'

A sign from a crewman prompted Kent to plug in his intercom. The pilot's voice flooded calmly into his earpiece: 'We'll be crossing the Dutch coast in a few minutes. Then we'll open up the hatches to give your chaps a blow of fresh air. We alter course soon after, and begin our run-in in about twenty minutes. It's a lovely day up front, and your drop should be a piece of cake. I should get your chaps hooked up now and then stand by. Good luck and cheerio.'

On Kent's command, the stick of hunched, thoughtful men came to life. Heavily laden with their equipment, they scrambled to a semi-crouch position. An RAF dispatcher moved methodically between the two shuffling and swaying lines, checking that parachutes were properly hooked to the static line which ran the length of the fuselage and automatically triggered the canopy as each man exited the plane. The twin flaps of the large jump hatch – coffinshaped, Kent noted – opened, and sunlight and fresh air streamed in. The word was passed – ten minutes to go. 'We all stood up and, taking care that our static lines did not become snarled up round someone's ankle, we eased our way closer to the hole. I began to sweat. Weighted down with the parachute pack on my back and full battle order on my chest, my helmet (the top of which was stuffed with half a pound of pipe tobacco) on my head and securely strapped with its chin piece in place, I waited my place in the queue.' This was always a moment unlike any other, as each man struggled with his thoughts – the fear of jumping, the fear of the humiliating consequences of *not* jumping.[4] 'Then the engines throttled back. We started to lose height. Through the hole, I could now see the ground. We were beginning the run-in.'

If they had hoped to sneak in totally unnoticed, they were disappointed. Kent heard 'pinging noises, metal on metal, and I guessed we were coming under small-arms fire from the ground. In the roof above the hole, a red light flashed on. The men at the front poised on the edge and the rest of us pressed forward, practically on each other's backs. The red changed to green and, as if by magic, the men before me disappeared and I was at the aperture and through it and into the slipstream.' He struggled in the rushing air. His parachute did not completely fill. He was falling too fast. He only had seconds to jerk and twist his body to untangle the lines. He managed this in time to slow his descent and drop gently on to a ploughed field, just yards away from that long barn he had been aiming at. The first men were down on the heath between the villages of Renkum and Wolfheze, five miles to the east of the bridge they had come to capture. The Battle of Arnhem was under way.

★

Ron Kent was still tangled up in the rigging of his parachute and struggling to free himself when, across the heath where he'd landed, he saw someone rushing towards him. The sergeant, in the advance party of parachutists dropping to secure the landing zone on Renkum Heath, reached for his revolver, a Colt automatic. But this was no hostile reception, no Nazi soldier with his finger on the trigger of a Schmeisser. Quite the opposite. The man, a Dutch civilian, was thrusting out his hand and excitedly greeting Kent as if he were a long-lost friend. 'You are American?' he asked, a suggestion that made Kent bristle. He'd had more than one dust-up with pushy, self-opinionated Yank soldiers in pubs back home acting as if they were the only ones who could win the war. Being mistaken for one now was galling. 'No, we are British,' he snapped, and turned to get on with the job of supervising his section, now that they were all down in one piece. Men were already spreading out panels on the ground in the shape of an 'X'[5] to mark the dropping point for the main force, just minutes behind now. A Eureka radio homing beacon was deployed and smoke candles lit to check the wind drift. The bulk of the troop fanned out and took up defensive positions around the drop zone. Then the men waited for the rest of 1st Airborne to arrive. Kent pulled a pack of tobacco from the stash inside his helmet, filled his pipe, lit up and relaxed. 'It was a beautiful day, all too perfect to be true. If this was German-held territory, where were the Germans?'

By now, the main force was on its way to Arnhem, heading out over the Suffolk coast at Aldeburgh and due east across the North Sea. At the same time, a separate stream was passing over Kent and the English Channel with the American airborne divisions en route to Eindhoven and Nijmegen. In all the subsequent inquests into what went wrong with the mission, the triumph of logistics in getting this huge armada – the 'Market' part of Market Garden – assembled in the air was often overlooked.[6] An airborne operation of this magnitude – three thousand aircraft over two days – had never been attempted before, not in North Africa, Sicily, Italy, not in Normandy. It took meticulous flight planning – take-off time, route, height, speed, and so on – to get each plane to its rendezvous point. Iron discipline was then needed to move this vast swarm in the same direction without planes knocking each other out of the sky. The sheer numbers took away the breath of those who witnessed it, whether Sunday worshippers down below returning home from church, or people on their way to the pub and looking up in awe from the ground, or those in the air right in the middle of it all. At home in Essex, a fourteen-year-old schoolboy leaned out of an upstairs window and checked off the Dakotas, Stirlings, Horsas and Hamilcars against an aircraft recognition chart on his bedroom wall. 'It was the most wonderful sight I had ever seen, a never-ending stream of planes and gliders.' Though he cannot have known what mission they were embarked on, he remembered thinking, 'Jerry's going to get a real pasting. That's it. This lot will win us the war!'[7]

Reg Curtis was one of those up there and, like the vast majority of those jumping that day, in an American Dakota, which was much more comfortable than the RAF planes that Kent and his pathfinder paras had travelled in. It had benches to sit on rather than the cold metal of the floor and porthole views of the skies around them as they circled around for an hour manoeuvring into the mass formation. He was inspired. 'I have never seen so many planes in the air at one time. And not just transporters but Typhoons, Spitfires and Mustangs weaving between us, as protection against enemy fighters. I wondered where the heck all these men and machines had come from. It was a far cry from the Dunkirk days when we had no paras and were lucky to scrape up a few fighter planes.' Ted Mordecai, flying in the heart of this 'mighty air armada', felt the planes were so close that if he stretched out his hand he could almost touch the wing of the nearest one.[8] The sheer weight of numbers swelled his confidence.

Others on that journey were less enthusiastic. Seeing the sun shining off the clouds, James Sims felt he was in heaven, the view was so beautiful, but the thoughts inside his head were far from serene. 'What if we ran into flak or enemy fighters? And even if we got safely to the other side, what German reception committee was waiting for us? Cannon fire? Machine guns? Tanks? Cold steel? "What the hell am I doing here?" I asked myself. "I must be bloody mad!"' A glance around the aircraft at the coolness of his comrades was reassuring, though he was almost certainly not alone in his sense of dread. To distract himself he buried his head in a copy of the Reader's Digest but then his mind wandered to the 'cocktail' of comrades-in-arms seated beside him – 'English, Irish, Scots and Welsh, Geordies, Scousers, Cockneys, men from the Midlands, men from Cambridge, Kent and Sussex. Some of us had been shop assistants, others salesmen, farmers, and barrow boys. There was even a poacher.' But where they had come from was irrelevant now. Only the immediate future mattered, where they were going and what they would do when they got there.

'Nearing the Dutch coast, we were warned to brace ourselves as the aircraft dived down through the clouds to about 2,000 feet.' Stomachs churned. 'From below a German naval vessel opened fire at us with a machine gun. The pilot took instant evasive action and the plane banked alarmingly. We watched fascinated as a stream of tracer bullets arched towards us, whipping past the open doorway like angry hornets. Some of our fighter escort peeled off and swept down to attack the German vessel, which vanished in a storm of rocket fire. We were undamaged and quickly resumed our position in the armada, but quite a number of us had to make use of the brown paper bags issued for sickness. Fancy giving people bacon sandwiches before take-off!'

Now, those who dared to look out could see Holland below and, ahead of them, the route to Arnhem marked out by blazing anti-aircraft-gun emplacements taken out by the fighters and low-level bombers. Time to go. As they stood up and edged towards the exit, a wisecracker called out 'Pass right down the bus, please!', but any laughter was now stifled by the rushing wind outside as they dropped to 700 feet for the run-in. Etched in Sims's memory would be the split-second sight of his platoon commander, Lieutenant Woods, standing framed in the doorway, 'the slipstream plucking impatiently at the scrim netting on his helmet', before he was gone. Sims went too and 'found myself in the middle of a blizzard of silk. I was exhilarated, conscious of taking part in one of the greatest airborne descents in the history of warfare.' In his plane, Reg Curtis, a veteran of North Africa, Sicily and Italy, felt a slight pat on his back and then he too tumbled out of the doorway 'into that familiar open void again. My chute once more obediently opened.'

Down on the ground, Ron Kent heard the murmur of aircraft engines away to the south, turning to a steady low roar, and snapped back into action. 'Wave after wave of transport planes came into sight. I had never seen so many low-flying aircraft in a single formation before. I could see gliders among the armada, black, long-nosed Horsas, which began to cast off, turn gracefully, then dive at incredibly steep angles. They were beautiful to watch but what really caught the eye was the spectacle of the mass parachute drop directly over us as the sky blossomed forth with flower-like patterns, brilliant in the sunlight.' To a puzzled German artillery officer who happened to glance out of the window at his unit's base in a school in Arnhem, it seemed at first that, in the distance, snowflakes were falling from the sky. Then he realized that 'it never snows in September. They must be parachutists.'[9]

Whatever they looked like, whether 'flowers' or 'snowflakes', the men arriving were more like a whirlwind or a dust storm. As they fell, they called out to each other, coordinating their descents with the usual banter of an elite corps, then hit the ground, gathered up their parachutes and marched to the edge of the drop zone to re-form into their platoons and companies. For Reg Curtis it suddenly hit home that he was now actually behind the lines, in enemy-occupied territory. But he was reassured as he looked around at the busy, purposeful chaos of the landing site. Until moments before it had been just a deserted piece of anonymous Dutch countryside. Now it teemed 'like a giant crossroads, with jeeps calmly bouncing over the ploughed earth, gliders coming in to land like an inter-city air service, soldiers collecting equipment from containers, then sprinting off sharply to join up with their units, earmarked by various coloured smoke canisters.'

For those still descending, like James Sims, the view below resembled a nest of ants. He spotted a yellow flare marking his battalion's rendezvous point and tried to steer towards it. 'The ground, which a moment before had seemed so far beneath me, came spinning up at an alarming rate. My right leg was dangling helplessly below me, with my kitbag, which I'd been unable to haul up, on the end of it. We'd been warned that to land in this way would almost certainly break a leg. Any second now I was going to find out. *Wham!* I hit the deck with a terrific jolt. But fortunately I was all in one piece. I sliced through the cords that held my kitbag and pulled out my rifle. In the distance delayed-action time-bombs exploded, sending up great fountains of earth. They had been dropped twenty-four hours previously in an effort to persuade the Germans that this was just another bombing raid. Some hopes! Something glinted in the sun not 30 yards away. A rifle was levelled straight at me. To my relief a very Cockney voice shouted, "What battalion, mate?" "Second," I croaked. "Over to your right about 200 yards. OK?" "Thanks a lot," I shouted, and I hoisted my 60lbs of mortar bombs on to my back, together with the pick, shovel, rifle and small pack. Looking like a Christmas tree, I set off in search of my mates.'

*

Less than a mile away from the drop zone where Curtis and the parachutists were landing, Horsa and Hamilcar gliders laden with men, vehicles and equipment were already down on the ground. As he bumped across the grass of the landing zone and brought his glider to a halt, pilot Sergeant Alan Kettley was relaxed and not a little pleased with himself. Job done. The take-off, he had to admit, had been nerve-wracking – 160 gliders and their Dakota tugs at Fairford in a continual stream to get airborne. 'One aircraft was halfway down the strip and the next one was already rolling. Very difficult to do. You had to practise it.' Careering down the runway, correct the trim, watch the airspeed indicator head to 80mph, wait for the nose wheel to judder, heave back on the stick to get the weight off the nose, then ease it forward again to keep the other wheels on the ground until the tug is airborne and you're both up and away. Those in the back felt every bump along the ground, then the silent surge into the air. Once up there and joined by gliders from other airfields, it was 'a magnificent, amazing sight' in the sky over the English countryside, the glider force, six abreast, stretching as far as the eye could see, each little speck signifying between a dozen and thirty men, guns and vehicles, all heading into battle.

In the cockpit Kettley was blasé about the dangers, but they were real enough. He later discovered that his best friend was piloting a glider carrying a jeep and a trailer of ammunition in the back, 'and the silly buggers didn't tie them down hard enough. He took off and the jeep came straight through the front and killed him.' On the way over, a glider was seen to explode over the sea and bodies and equipment tumble out. But Kettley's own flight was uneventful. 'The fighters had done a wonderful job and I didn't see any flak at all, none. It was an easy trip into Arnhem – a piece of cake. We could see the landing zone from way out – no navigation problems.' He lifted up into the 'high tow' position above the tug, shouted his thanks to the tow pilot down the intercom and dropped the rope. 'I think we were one of the first to land because it was an empty field down there.'

Also quickly down from his release point was glider pilot and squadron commander Major Ian Toler. 'Speed back to 90,' he logged. 'Half flap. Almost up to the LZ. Full flap and nose down. Terrific juddering as if we are stalling, but we are dropping fast. I aim a little short of some trees and pull up over them to get rid of surplus speed. The landing is okay and well short of the overshoot boundary. Take off the flap to run on. Halfway across we run into soft plough and we come to a rest.'

Waves of gliders were now careering in for their controlled crash-landings. Up in the air and waiting his turn, army driver and mechanic Ron Brooker glimpsed the hundreds of gliders already on the ground, some of them upside down or on their side after bad landings. 'It was so crowded I couldn't see any room to get in,' he recalled. 'I worried a bit, knowing we'd got no engine. I was more afraid of flying than the enemy. How I wished then that I was parachuting in.' The ground rushed up, he braced and he held his breath as they hit the earth hard and the skidding glider flashed past those already parked before coming to a halt in the far corner of the LZ. 'No straps – you just hold on and hope for the best!' After the bumping and shaking stopped, relief washed over him. 'We're down, we're here.'[10]

Staff Sergeant Peter Clarke was also relieved. He had been with the Glider Pilot Regiment since it was first formed back in 1942 but had not seen action. To his disgust, he missed out on the D-Day campaign because his co-pilot went down with glandular fever. 'My frustration was building up. I wanted to contribute to the actual fighting.' His wish was granted, though he found piloting a glider was not the easy job some people took it for. The controls were notoriously heavy 'and, though you're being towed, you can't just sit back. You must stay directly behind the tow and in the right position above or below the slipstream. You can't let your attention go for a second. It's tough physical and mental work and a real test of pilot skills. We were flying for over three hours on tow behind a Dakota. I'd never flown that long before.' Added to which there was the responsibility. In the back he had a mortar platoon – eight men and three handcarts loaded with shells. He felt an affinity to them, an intense loyalty. 'You don't meet the people you're carrying until that day and you may never see them again. But you feel a massive sense of responsibility to get them there in one piece. These are men who will go on to fight and possibly die and they are placing their utmost faith in you.'[11]

As the tug released him, he dropped steeply towards the ground and made a textbook landing on a flat, harvested field, slamming on the wheel brakes and running to the end of it before coming to a halt just short of the woods. To his right he could see another glider in trouble. 'It hit the top of the trees and disintegrated. In seconds, all those lives were wiped out. It was absolutely devastating to see but I didn't have time to dwell on it. I was just glad I'd got my damn'd thing down intact.' In an instant, the mortar platoon in the back was out through the door and away. 'It was the last time I saw them.' Around him, bolts were unfastened on scores of other gliders and their tails crashed to the ground. The engines of the jeeps inside fired up and they roared off, trailing anti-tank guns, ammunition and supplies behind them. Next stop the bridge at Arnhem, 5 miles away! Around the landing zone, platoons were already in defensive positions, protecting this inland beachhead from an as yet unseen enemy. Unseen but, it would all too quickly be apparent, not absent at all.

3. 'Home by the Weekend'

Earlier that bright Sunday morning in Oosterbeek, the biggest village between the airborne landing zones and Arnhem itself, the sound of the organ could be heard from the church, its rich notes wafting out over the river bank and down to the Rhine. Anje van Maanen was still in bed. It was 11 a.m. and she was not getting up, she told herself. 'We are not going to church today so I have all the time in the world.' Through the window of her bedroom she could see the sun glinting on the garden. Suddenly the roar of aircraft shattered her peaceful reverie. She was used to fleets of bombers overhead, en route to and from the Ruhr Valley or some other target in Germany, the RAF at night and the B-17s of the US airforce in the daytime. But this seemed different. 'Gosh, quite a lot of them,' she thought. 'They're busy today!' She heard footsteps on the stairs, and her brother Paul – the one in hiding – rushed into her bedroom. 'Bombs are dropping from the planes,' he called out, and together they rushed to the top of the house and poked their heads through the attic window. Mosquitoes were racing across the sky, guns blazing. In the distance to the west, smoke and flames were spiralling upwards from Wolfheze. In the other direction, the barracks at Arnhem were on fire too, along with electric, gas and water works. To the north, the airfield at Deelen was under attack. 'German anti-aircraft guns in the field behind our house start to bark. We see more fighter planes coming over. It's looking pretty dangerous so we head back downstairs. Outside on the street, the Germans are nervous. They shout and they fire their pistols at the planes. How silly!'

Many Dutch families took to the air-raid shelters that morning as the Allies' pre-invasion action to knock out German ground defences intensified, but others ignored the danger in their excitement. In Arnhem, Heleen Kernkamp could not drag herself away from the window, her eyes fixed on the 'fantastic' dogfights up among the thin clouds: 'I felt no fear.' But at the home of Piet Huisman in the north of the town, bomb fragments and bullets flying around outside came too close for comfort and interrupted the birthday celebrations for his four-year-old son. The family hastily retreated from the drawing room to mattresses in the cellar. At her house close to the river at Oosterbeek, an anxious Kate ter Horst bundled her children inside from the apple orchard where they had been playing when the *rik-atik-atik* of machine guns broke the quiet of the morning. Seven children and three adults crowded under the staircase as bullets skittered across the slate roof. The little ones clung to their mother's side. From the church just across the way came a new sound – the congregation, on their feet apparently, and defiantly singing the Wilhelmus, the Dutch national anthem. Gingerly, the family assembled outside and marvelled at the seemingly endless waves of Allied planes.

At the van Maanen house, a neighbour poked his head round the front door, bringing news, but stopped in amazement as he caught sight of Paul. Paul, in turn, went white. He wasn't meant to be seen by anyone, indeed, had *not* been seen for months, even by this friend from next door. With lives at stake, secrets were best kept if nobody outside the house knew. But now, it appeared, the days of secrecy might well be over. The neighbour came with incredible tidings: 'He tells us he has seen parachutists dropping from the skies. Something big is clearly happening. It's the invasion! We go crazy. We jump and dance around. We shout with joy. This is IT . . .' The telephone rang, and their doctor-father came on the line from the police station, where he was manning a casualty post. Excitedly, he told them to go to the roof and look to the west. 'We rush up the stairs and on to the flat roof. We see aeroplanes with gliders, a glorious sight. When the gliders drop their tow ropes, they dive down into the bushes while the planes that have been towing them come right on towards us, turn above our heads and go back towards England. We wave at them enthusiastically. Planes and more planes are coming from the misty horizon. Freedom is coming from the skies. It really is fantastic. The war is over now. By tomorrow, we could be FREE!' The moment they and millions of other Dutch people had prayed for and dreamt of for so long was here. 'Out in the street, people are singing and dancing.' It seemed almost too good to be true. 'Is this the long-awaited release from our misery?' Kate ter Horst asked herself. 'Can it be true?'[1]

Back in Arnhem, Piet Huisman eventually emerged from the cellar and watched in wonder the array of red, green and blue parachutes floating down in the distance. (The different colours identified the type of supplies slung underneath – ammunition, food or medical.) His son whooped with joy, under the impression that all the colour and commotion was in celebration of his birthday. There were so many parachutists dropping, so big an army, that Huisman wondered 'if the British will liberate us today'.[2]

The answer to his question came sooner than anyone expected. A friend from Wolfheze rang Heleen Kernkamp to say that she'd come home from church to find a British officer, fifteen men and two jeeps in her garden. Most amazingly, he had saluted her and said, 'Good morning, madam,' as nonchalantly and politely as if he had come to deliver the groceries. That afternoon, young Marie-Anne stood at her garden gate and watched a stream of retreating German soldiers heading into Oosterbeek from the direction of Wolfheze. 'A sergeant had been shot in the leg and he could hardly walk. Some other German soldiers were standing along the road and one would think that they would hasten to help their wounded comrade. But no, the dirty swine just stand there, hands in pockets, watching him. And I thought that soldiers could always rely on their comrades to help them!' Meanwhile, the German platoon who had been billeted on her family was preparing to leave. They clambered on to trucks and went, calling out, '*Auf Wiedersehen*! Till we meet again!' It was not a sentiment she could return. 'I hope I'll never have to look at another German again,' she thought to herself.

Now only the platoon's cooks remained, getting more and more agitated as they waited for transport to arrive to haul away their mobile kitchen. Nothing came, and they paced up and down anxiously, until the local vet happened by in his car to inspect horses and cows wounded by the bombing. The Germans forced him to halt and at gunpoint ordered him to drive them to the German border. Marie-Anne watched as the Germans piled in, 'but at the last moment one of them goes back to the house for some bread and cheese. Suddenly two other soldiers come down the street shouting, "*Die Engländer, die Engländer!*" and they all start running away towards Arnhem. With the Germans gone, we go inside, and I am standing in the corridor when I hear voices. I peer around the door and see soldiers, lots of them. They are English. The Tommies have come. They're here!'

★

Leo Hall felt like a crusader. He had only just avoided disaster when he landed, missing the open space of the DZ and coming down in a tree. 'I was left dangling 6 feet from Dutch soil.' A helping hand to cut him down, followed by a reviving swig of grog from someone's flask, got him on his way. His morale was sky-high as, in battle order, he and his platoon moved off the drop zone towards Arnhem, along a leafy tree-lined track until they came to a narrow road. 'This was the day we'd waited so long for.'[3] Those they had come to liberate were pouring out of their houses to cheer them. 'I passed an elderly man, tears streaming down his face as, eyes closed, he sang "God Save the King" in English. Young men were urging us on, wanting to help, bringing hijacked trucks, wearing their orange armbands with the sort of patriotic pride I'd never seen before in all my twenty-three years. Bang goes number-one bit of briefing, I thought. Where on earth did that "probably Nazi" rubbish originate? A "play safe" bit of intelligence, I guessed. I'll trust these people any day.' But he worried that their joy might be premature, that they may have underestimated the determination of the German army. 'Did they realize how much havoc the enemy could cause with a couple of snipers, a machine gun and a light field gun? I wanted to tell them that it wasn't over, by any means. There would be killing, devastation, even if all went according to plan.' As if to confirm such fears, James Sims met his first Dutchman — smartly dressed in a tweed suit and a felt hat — who warned him that there were six German armoured cars in the area. 'As he spoke, we could hear their powerful engines revving up.' The enemy were here already.

Nonetheless, after landing, most men set off full of optimism.

Despite the impressive sight they had made as they dropped, in truth they were a smallish force for such a large and important task, with just five thousand parachutists and glider troops landing that first day. But more would come in the second and third lifts, enough to hold off the Germans for the couple of days necessary until XXX Corps could get there overland. And there seemed no real opposition to worry about. The bigger danger in fact was heavy supply canisters or kitbags dropping on the heads of the unwary. Those who had been on earlier airborne missions were amazed at the ease of it all. Compared, for example, with a fiercely opposed night-time landing in Sicily – the memory of which had lodged uneasily in the minds of some veterans before they dropped – this was more like a practice jump than the real thing. There was some sporadic firing to be heard from around the DZ, but very little. A few German soldiers who happened to be in the area – some, apparently, out for a Sunday picnic on the heath with their girlfriends – were quickly dealt with by the advance guard. For many arriving in enemy country that day, their first sight of the actual enemy was either a dead one lying on the ground or those who, taken by surprise, had surrendered. Hands in the air and looking very frightened because they thought they were about to be summarily shot, they were being marched to a temporary compound. It was a heartening sight and augured well.

Fred Moore thought the rest was a formality – 'a quick advance to Arnhem, overcoming any slight resistance from demoralized groups of second-class enemy soldiers, secure the bridge, then just wait for the British armoured divisions to relieve us within forty-eight hours'.[4] They might even be home by the weekend. Ron Kent, left behind to protect the landing zone, saw a mate, Sergeant Billy Watts, on his way and wished him luck. 'We promised to meet for a beer in Arnhem once we'd got the bridge and the Second Army boys were here. Watching those battalions forming up and streaming off the DZ in the direction of Arnhem, I had no reason to doubt that we would do just that in a few days' time.'

But not all the omens were good. When machine-gunner Andy Milbourne got to his rendezvous point in a wood, the kettle was on for a brew-up. He'd been tasked to bring the tea and now, to his horror – 'my dismay and undying shame', as he described it later – he realized he had left his haversack crammed with tea and sugar with his discarded parachute. 'Bloody well go and get it,' his mates roared when he told them. 'Sheepishly, I turned and retraced my steps. I hadn't gone far when a burst of machine-gun fire made me dive for cover. Hot lead raised spouts in the earth around me.' Clearly not all the Germans around the drop zone had been dealt with. 'I wormed deeper into the ground, cursing like mad at my predicament. Tea, the most important thing to the British Tommy. I swore that if I got away from those bullets, I would never drink tea again.' He was pinned down for what seemed like an age. He could not see his attackers, only the bullets pitter-patter around whenever he tried to move. When another gun opened on him, he simply threw caution to the wind and ran for the cover of the trees. Tea forgotten, his section was moving out. 'Where the hell have you been?' an irritated sergeant demanded to know. Didn't he know there was a war on?

*

At the now almost empty landing zone, Ron Kent heard shooting in the distance. 'What opposition there was must have woken up to the fact that they had Sunday-afternoon visitors,' he surmised. He wasn't worried. A few crews remained, struggling to offload jeeps, trailers and light artillery from gliders that had landed awkwardly, but otherwise 'our job was done. Everyone and everything was moving eastward towards Wolfheze, en route for Arnhem.' He and his men set off for their own company rendezvous a mile away. 'We left behind our parachutes, and already the villagers from Heelsum were out collecting them. One enterprising soul had a horse-drawn cart out and was stacking it high with rolled-up chutes. I have no doubt that a great many Dutch girls were wearing silk and nylon underwear that winter.'

For those Dutch girls, the prospect of silk next to their skin was a minor luxury compared with the pleasure they felt at what was happening before their very eyes. From her bedroom window in Oosterbeek, Anje van Maanen could now see German soldiers taking to their heels in full retreat. She caught sight of the monocled army commander Field Marshal Walter Model in the back of his car fleeing for his life. She recognized him by the wide red stripes down his grey trousers and the red flashes of rank on his uniform. He had recently set himself up with his headquarters staff at the Tafelberg Hotel in Oosterbeek to plot the defence of Germany's borders against the oncoming Allies, far enough away from the front line, or so he believed, for them to carry out their planning undisturbed. The news of the landings shattered his Sunday lunch at the hotel. His first reaction was that this was a commando raid to capture him. In reality, the Market Garden planners did not even know he was there. As he fled to safety, it became clear from the numbers involved that something much bigger was under way. Anje watched his convoy of staff cars accelerate out of Oosterbeek and race off down the road towards Arnhem. 'We wave a cheerful goodbye to them. Terribly happy never to see them again . . .'

By mid-afternoon, Oosterbeek seemed pretty well a German-free zone, though Anje, peeping out of the window, could see a soldier sitting in a neighbour's garden hiding behind a bush, a gun in his hand. 'He doesn't move. Perhaps he is dead.' The tension of waiting and not knowing for sure that this really was liberation was almost unbearable. Friends rang from Wolfheze. Yes, they were free 'and smoking the Players cigarettes and eating the chocolate the Tommies gave us'. A few hours later, another call, this time from within Oosterbeek itself, with the same message. 'They're coming our way too. We hear the shooting getting nearer and nearer, and we are very excited.' But as night began to fall they were still waiting. Desperate for information, they decided to risk the street and go to the house of a neighbour they knew had a clandestine radio. 'We hear shots nearby and move carefully, one by one, dressed in dark clothes because we know both sides, the Germans and the English, will fire at anything they see or hear. On the neighbour's wireless the announcer talks about parachute landings at Eindhoven and Nijmegen, but there is no mention of Arnhem.' This made her anxious. 'So is it not true? Are the Tommies not coming after all?' Prince Bernhard's sonorous voice was now coming from the loudspeaker with another call to his countrymen to stay calm, 'and then, all of a sudden, there is more news. Landings at Arnhem are confirmed! The Wilhelmus rings out from the radio and we are all deeply moved. We have a drink and raise our glasses to victory.'

Not surprisingly, the van Maanen household spent a restless night, wondering about tomorrow. Anje woke early. 'At 6 a.m. I hear my brother sneaking down the stairs and I get out of my bed and follow him into the spare room, which has a view over the road outside. Have the Tommies come? Or are the Germans still here? We can't see properly because it is still dark but we can just make out a line of soldiers shuffling very quickly beneath the trees. We think they must be Tommies but we don't want to call out because if they are Germans we are sure to be shot.' Suddenly her Aunt Anke put an end to the uncertainty. She flung open her bedroom window and shouted out cheerfully to the men outside, 'Good morning,' in English. Back came a hissed answer, 'Good morning to you too.' Anje thrilled to the greeting from what was an advance patrol, scouting ahead of the main pack. 'These whispering figures in the darkness are Tommies. We are free, free, free!' Many years later, she would try to put into words the elation she felt in that moment, but there were none in her vocabulary or anyone else's to do the occasion justice. 'Seeing the Tommies was just so wonderful. Here were our saviours. To see their friendly faces was just overwhelming. After four years, our ordeal was over. We were free at last.'

Impulsively, she didn't wait to dress but pulled a coat over her dressing gown and rushed down to the street. 'Aunt Anke and I walk along beside a British soldier and we ask him all sorts of questions. I dash back home and down to the cellar to pick up a basket of food, fruits and sweets. I go back up to the street, where it is now a little lighter, and crowds of people in their pyjamas are coming out with cups of tea and coffee, bread, pears, apples to welcome our liberators. I offer fruit to the soldiers and try to say something but I am terribly shy and no words come out so I just smile at them. When my basket is empty I hurry home and get some more. All of us are so excited and we hand out everything we have. And then we go home to dress up in our smartest clothes because today is a feast day and a celebration. At home, I find Aunt Anke dusting her room. She must be mad. Who can dust on a day like this?'

The centre of Oosterbeek was now filling with British troops. What impressed Marie-Anne as she joined the crowds welcoming them was the sheer number of the soldiers and how well equipped they were, not just arriving on foot but with jeeps and tracked vehicles. 'All the jeeps have radios, the long aerials swishing behind.' Kate ter Horst marvelled at the 'impossible, incredible' sight of the British on the streets of her town, 'like a long green serpent, a couple of yards between each of them. One gives a jolly laugh from under his helmet and spreads out his arms. "Give me a kiss!" he says and then he is gone. Behind him they come in endless files, with a rhythmical movement.' The steady march of the paras was an eye-opener to a people weary of jackboots. 'We are so accustomed to the noisy marching of the Germans that we stare and stare at soldiers who are not marching and yet proceed in perfect order. Big fellows in khaki coats with countless pockets, which absorb the apples and tomatoes we offer them. Orange streamers and flags, flowers and cheering, people embracing each other in joy.' A church bell, which the Germans had missed when they were seizing metal to be sent back to the weapons factories in the Ruhr, began to ring, pushed to and fro by two villagers with their feet because there was no rope.

For the soldiers, the heroes' welcome they received that day was unforgettable, though tinged with the realization that they still had a job to do. Ted Mordecai would have relished the mugs of beer that a joyful innkeeper was handing out but he was ordered to refuse and settle for a cup of ersatz coffee instead. A clear head was needed for the march to Arnhem. But this was still a moment to savour. A soldier bent down and beckoned Anje to come up and sit on top of his tank. Embarrassed and shy though she was, she did. 'We all shout and dance and we are so gay, all of us. A woman is running backwards and forwards getting the signatures of all the English soldiers for her guest book. She takes pictures of everybody. A friend of my mother's comes along, her arms full of orange flags, which she distributes to us, and we wave them and laugh and are so happy. But still . . .' She could hear shooting, some of it quite close. Ignore it, she told herself. 'We don't think about taking cover or going away. Why should we? The jubilation grows and grows.' For now, the Oosterbeekers could sleep easily, for the first time in four years, 'calmly and quietly and without appre-hension', as Kate ter Horst put it. In her house the secret trapdoor to a hiding place did not have to be left open, ready for a hasty retreat. 'No raids to fear. We need not sleep with half an ear open for the ring at the door. Tonight my husband is safe. There are no Huns any more.'

*

No Huns any more? That was not Andy Milbourne's experience as he tried to make progress towards Arnhem through the woods and country roads north of Oosterbeek. Things hadn't got much better since he had fled from some unexpected and frighteningly accurate machine-gun fire on the edge of the landing zone. Now more machine-gun nests and hidden snipers were blocking the way for-ward. The airborne battalions had a number of designated routes into Arnhem but some were proving far from easy to progress along. What had begun as a confident march to a quick victory was, for the likes of Milbourne, turning into a crawl, down on the ground 'Indian style and cursing furiously at the grenades and other imple-ments of war hanging from my belt and digging into my flesh'. It was all he could do to erect the tripod he was dragging behind him, clamp the legs tight and mount his machine gun. He let off a burst of bullets – 'my first at Arnhem' – and ducked as it was returned, with interest. 'The very blades of grass were being nipped in two.' He gave the rest of the platoon covering fire as it charged and silenced the enemy gun.

But this was just one obstacle of many in their way. It was becom-ing evident that virtually every bush and clump of trees would have to be cleared – and all the time the minutes were ticking away if they were to get even close to Arnhem and their objective. Success in this operation had always depended on everything going like clockwork. There was little margin for error. Yet right from the start it was going wrong. They were also taking casualties. He saw two medics bending over the body of 'one of our boys' prone in the middle of a crossroads. He was beyond help, and all they could do was remove his ID tag and leave the body. As dusk fell, the fighting in those nightmarish woods continued, getting fiercer all the time. 'Groans and shrieks of pain filled the air. Everywhere we turned or moved, we were swept with a withering fire. Dead lay all around, wounded were crying for water. As best we could we attended to the wounded, at the same time pumping everything we had into a determined and reckless foe.' Nor were the Germans simply digging in and defending what they held. They were also coming out aggressively on the attack. 'Time and again they overran our positions and had to be driven out with bayonets.' His gun got so hot that he burnt himself when his bare flesh accidentally touched it.

Fred Moore's progress was less bloody but just as slow. Fits and starts. Taking cover. The sound of furious gun battles ahead. 'This was not according to plan.' He looked at his watch and realized they were already behind schedule. 'We should by now be advancing rapidly through the outskirts of Arnhem and joining up with the other battalions as we neared the objective.' Instead they were stuck in the woods – and woods, moreover, in which there was no clear battle-front but different bodies of men, some German, some British, moving uncertainly through the darkness. He saw and heard the enemy in the undergrowth to his left, but made the wise decision to let them go. To engage them would sacrifice precious time and lives – the two elements on which the Battle of Arnhem, now beginning to be fought in real earnest, would pivot.

The crucial development causing all this was that, after exiting Oosterbeek at high speed, his abandoned lunch still on the table at the Tafelberg, Model, the German commander, had passed through Arnhem and established his headquarters 20 miles to the east of the city. There he rallied his forces and drew up plans. He had realized that the aim of the operation was not to grab him but the bridge at Arnhem, and this was confirmed as reports came in of an intelligence coup. The singed remains of written orders outlining part of the Market Garden air operation had been found on the body of a dead American officer pulled from the wreckage of a glider shot down not long after it passed over the Dutch coast on its way to Nijmegen. The Germans had no trouble recognizing the Allies' plan to lay down an airborne carpet over rivers and canals. It was the same one that the

Wehrmacht had employed when invading the Netherlands four years earlier, except from the opposite direction.

Model took overall charge. The Prussian-born soldier was in his element. He was not from the same mould as field marshals like Rommel, never happier than when on the offensive. But Model was unsurpassed when it came to defence strategy. He had proved this on the eastern front, where his leadership and unshakeable confidence that he could turn around any situation had avoided a complete rout and, for the time being, slowed if not stopped the advance of Stalin's Red Army. This achievement made him Hitler's most favoured fire-fighter, and the Führer sent him west to perform the same feat against the British and the Americans. Noted for his ability to instil *Kampf-willen* – the resolve to fight – into his men, Model called on all that resolve now to stop the Allies' attempt to snatch control of the Netherlands. He sent troops to counter the American landings at Eindhoven and Nijmegen. But his crucial strategic decision was to concentrate his efforts on Arnhem. Whatever the cost, the bridge there must not be lost to the Allies, nor must the XXX Corps relief column be allowed to get through to it.

Model was the master of the counter-attack, which, with two crack SS panzer divisions fortuitously on his patch to recuperate and refit after Normandy, he was now mounting. So much for the briefings to the likes of Ron Brooker that they would be up against old men and second-rate troops. The reality, as he was now discovering amid the deafening sound of explosions and the scream of mortar shells, was 'unexpectedly heavy resistance'. It was coming from one of those SS battalions that had been on a training exercise in the woods around Wolfheze when the landings began. Guessing before everyone else that the Arnhem bridge was the target, its commander deployed his machine guns and heavy guns in the woods and on the key roads to slow the British advance almost before it had begun. With more troops and tanks soon on the way, a crucial blocking line was beginning to be established between Oosterbeek and Arnhem.

Reg Curtis ran into it as he and his company nosed their way forward. 'Suddenly there was a loud explosion up ahead and sporadic machine-gun fire as our lead company came under hit-and-run jabs from the enemy. Mortar bombs whined and bullets slashed the undergrowth. The smell of war was in my nostrils.' The whole battalion was forced to lie up in woods 'for what seemed like hours, pushing on occasionally but cautiously'. The dismaying fact, as he now realized, was that the enemy were all around. He could even see their vehicles from time to time. Any advance was 'rough, tedious, plodding along winding lanes and woods'. Hope soared when scouts reported that the main road into Arnhem was just ahead. But then, disaster. Cruising up and down the road were lines of heavily armed German half-tracks. 'We lay doggo beneath the trees not 80 feet away and watched this display of enemy armour. We had no choice. To take on this little lot would have been slaughter for us.' There was going to be no quick march into Arnhem. It was back to groping their way slowly through the woods.

*

For one group of men, the battle now developing was a particular challenge. The glider pilots had done their ferrying job and done it well. But unlike the airmen who flew the tugs or the transporters that offloaded the parachute troops, they did not have the luxury of turning round and cruising home to a beer and a sing-song in the pub. They were grounded alongside the troops they had carried, and with a new job to do. They were trained to be soldiers as well as pilots: 'We were flying infantrymen,' as 27-year-old Alan Kettley put it. He had been called up as a soldier back in 1940 and, in the aftermath of the Battle of Britain, applied to the RAF. He passed the tests, was told he was too old to be a pilot but could be a navigator, 'and I thought, "Great," and waited and waited and never heard another word. I discovered my CO didn't want to lose me so had blocked my transfer.' But flying was in his blood so, when in 1942 appeals were made for men to train as glider pilots, he volunteered and was accepted. 'In the run-up to Arnhem we didn't think how tough it was going to be or how bad it was going to get. I thought, "We'll get there, hold the area and then XXX Corps will arrive. Four or five days, that was it."' So, after expertly landing his glider, he reported for general duties. 'You're on the ground, you're in enemy territory, but nothing to worry about. You go from a glider pilot to a fighting soldier but that's what we were trained to do. And as I had been in the infantry I knew about rifles, Bren guns, Sten guns, mortars and so on. Everything was going perfectly as far as I was concerned. Our orders were to defend the landing zone until the next day, then to make for the bridge with the trailer and the ammunition.' As he settled down for the night on the edge of the landing zone, he was relaxed. 'I had no idea how things were going to change over the coming days!'

Peter Clarke joined his group of glider pilots at their rendezvous point at a school building near the end of the field where they'd landed. Outside, some fellows were lolling under trees, just as if they were on leave and waiting for the pub to open. They were elated at their success so far, but their buzz of chatter was overlaid with some anxiety. They could hear gunfire, 'and when you first hear gunshots and mortar you suddenly realize where you are and the danger you might be in.' He wasn't too concerned, still confident that the bridge would be taken in no time 'and then we would move back to England ready for the next operation. We'd be out of there within a few days.' He was relaxed about doing his bit as an auxiliary soldier. 'If you had an infantry background, as I did, you were prepared for this sort of thing. I'd learned to shoot on a Lee Enfield.' But there were – as he later came to realize – big gaps in his training. 'I hadn't done any actual infantry exercises and never been taught how to go on patrol. Nor had I been briefed on what to do if I was captured.' Before becoming a pilot, he had been a medic. This, though he didn't know it yet, was the experience that would stand him and his comrades in the greatest stead in the days ahead.

Of the glider pilots, Major Ian Toler was more wary than most, but then he had the burden of command. 'It is all too quiet,' he noted after landing, 'ominously so.' He got his men to dig in and showed the way so vigorously with his spade that his hand came up in blisters. He logged his casualties. Four men missing and two wounded. 'They were unlucky enough to land within a few yards of an enemy machine gun, which opened up, killing some and wounding others before it was liquidated.' That night he took the advice of an infantry officer and piled up more earth around his trench. He slept fitfully and then, when he stood his watch, heard spasmodic gunfire coming from the direction of Arnhem. Another of the men on sentry duty recalled the 'fearsome' whine of 'Moaning Minnie' mortars in the distance. But the next morning, the weather clear and sunny and after a breakfast of porridge, meat tablets and biscuits from his ration pack, the major felt better. 'Everyone is strolling about and it is just like an exercise, only we see the padre burying one of our men who has died in the night. Perhaps this is the real thing after all.'

For some pilots, there was no 'perhaps' about it. Staff Sergeant Ronald Gibson, one of the last to link up with his regiment because it took so long to get the bolts out of his glider's tail to release the contents, went from bus driver and delivery boy to infantryman with scarcely time to catch his breath. No sooner had he caught up with his column than they were heading east, down a tree-lined track and into a village. There was a fulsome welcome. Children ran to them with apples. He was especially moved by an old man in a blue cap who saluted them as they passed. 'Suddenly there was the loud crack of a gun and a cloud of earth burst up from the pavement. We dived headlong for the bank of leaves at the foot of the trees.'[5] When they got up, all those happy villagers had vanished and there was a huge shell-hole in a fence. There was no sign of the enemy. He discovered that the shell had come from a German armoured car which had fired as it crossed a road junction just ahead and then disappeared. The British soldiers took cover again.

'I lay down beside a woodshed and peered forward through a screen of grass and nettles over a field where some dappled cows were cropping the grass. A chilly silence had followed the crack of the gun and I could hear the sound of their munching. I felt a hand touch my shoulder. I turned to see the old, blue-capped Dutchman standing with a jug of milk in one hand and a cup in the other. "You here, we free," he said. I thought what a farcical war this was. We were crouching in a garden, waiting for the enemy to show his head, while an old man was pottering about, quite unconcerned, attending to our comfort. I had seen a similar instance in Normandy – a crowded village street, with British infantry filing along the shadow of a wall after a German sniper hiding in the churchyard, while old women hobbled over the stones with baskets under their arms on the way to the baker's shop. The old man then brought us a bowl of plums, crawling round the corner of the shed on all fours so as to avoid revealing our position.' This intermingling of soldiers and civilians would be repeated throughout the Arnhem campaign and be one of its most distinctive features, a triumph of trust and solidarity between two nations fighting very different types of war but against a common enemy.

Progress was not only slow but patchy. There was a minor breakthrough in one sector and a way ahead now seemed to open up alongside the Ede–Arnhem railway line that ran to the north of Oosterbeek. But as the troops trudged beside it they encountered increasing evidence of the ferocious German defence. Wolfheze station was a shelled wreck. A broken cycle lay in a ditch beside a dead German. From the heathland to their right, the perfume of heather and pine mingled with the sour smell of cordite. The crackle of Bren-gun fire sent them hurtling to the ground, searching for cover. The advance on this particular route was completely stalled, and Gibson's squadron was ordered to dig in. 'On the edge of a wood, I chose a level patch between two trees, stacked my rucksack and rifle against a trunk and began to dig a foxhole in the needle-covered sand.' As he finally put his head down for some much-needed sleep, he took one last look around him and could see in the distance that a line of gorse was blazing. 'The noise of firing continued till dawn. The wind chilled my back and I passed a sleepless night.'

Another glider pilot, Sergeant Eric Webbley, was also at a standstill. He had left the landing zone with the jeep, the gun and the men he had just brought in and joined another line of infantry advancing towards Arnhem. A German mobile gun barred the way. 'We crouched near our gun waiting to get a shot at it when there was suddenly a terrific explosion as Jerry fired along the road. He missed us but hit another jeep, which caught fire. With illumination from the blaze, he sent in more rounds and machine-gun fire.'[6] Then the Germans put up a star shell, catching Webbley out in the open. 'I dived into a ditch as a shell passed just yards away. I felt damned scared as Jerry swept the road with machine-gun fire.' There was nothing else to do but keep their heads down. A decision was now made to divert around the German gun, and the infantry company left the road and headed out across fields and through hedges. It was tough going. Webbley's jeep towed the gun but 'we couldn't use the lights and, the night being pitch black, I walked ahead with my left sleeve rolled up and my arm behind my back, so that our driver could see the luminous dial of my wrist watch. When the column in front stopped, I put my arm down and the jeep stopped too.' The outflanking movement didn't work. They halted and dug in for the night but in the morning they could see German soldiers advancing through the trees towards their position. They were as far from Arnhem as ever.

But not everyone in the airborne division was at a standstill. The leading strike force had found a reasonably open route into Arnhem and, with luck and good speed, had the bridge well in their sights. For them at least, the main objective of Market Garden was within reach.

4. 'Are We on Overtime Now?'

Ron Brooker was in the so-called *coup de main* striking force, which was tasked to race ahead in jeeps the 5 miles or so to the bridge at Arnhem and seize it, hopefully before the Germans realized what was happening and could react. There were three routes designated for the invading force to converge on the city, and his 200-strong reconnaissance squadron, a mixture of paras and glider troops, started out on the northern one, only to find a strong enemy force in its way. Its job was not to stop and fight but to skirt around trouble and keep going. Brooker was driving the squadron's commanding officer, Major Freddie Gough, and they now swung south away from the trouble and congestion, to take the centre route. 'We passed the wrecked car of a high-ranking German officer. His body lay half in, half out of the vehicle; a pool of blood covered the area around his body.'

This was Major-General Friedrich Kussin, the military governor of Arnhem and the man ultimately responsible for the defence of the bridge. When the parachutists and gliders were spotted landing he had driven out to see what was happening. His car had run into a forward airborne patrol and been raked with machine-gun fire before the driver could turn and flee. Numerous soldiers recalled the sight of that high-ranking body and being encouraged that they had the enemy on the run. 'Must have been a severe blow to them,' concluded para James Sims, stretching out his hand to trace a cross on the dead man's cold forehead. It was the first corpse he had ever seen, and his mother had told him that if he did that it would never come back to haunt him. But a mother's soothing words had no currency here. 'What are you doing?' yelled a sergeant. 'Get mobile. You'll see plenty more like him before you're much older.'

But this line of advance was soon blocked too, running into more and better armed opposition. Pressing forward, Brooker found himself almost deafened by the sound of small arms and heavier weapons and the high-pitched screams of mortars. 'We passed several bodies, both the enemy and our own.' It was time to switch routes. Once again, the way ahead was blocked, and he headed for the southern route, following the north bank of the Rhine. This was the one already taken by Lieutenant-Colonel John Frost of 2 Para, leading the only group making real progress towards the target that day, though also taking losses. 'Hairy' was how, with typical army understatement, Brooker would one day describe what now lay ahead: a hellish advance on Arnhem through a series of ambushes and obstacles. He kept his head down and his foot on the accelerator as the major, sitting beside him, gripped the Vickers K4 machine gun mounted on the front and swivelled to meet each attack and rattle out his response. 'Bullets were whizzing back and forth but I just pointed the jeep and kept going. I felt remote from everything, just concentrating on driving. I had absolutely no control over my own destiny.'

The grey-haired, ruddy-faced Gough – 'a marvellous man, a perfect gentleman' – was, he noticed, having the time of his life. 'He was loving it. He was normally a benign, calm person, but he was different in action. You couldn't have wished for a better bloke beside you.' The enemy were popping up all over the place. 'We turned a sharp bend in the road and almost ran into a group of Germans marching in file down the road, heading in the same direction as ourselves.' With Brooker's foot on the pedal, the paras just sailed past without a shot being fired, by either side. 'I don't know who was the more surprised. We were sitting ducks and I was half expecting the bullets to start flying into our backs, but nothing happened. It was almost like an Ealing comedy.' Further back in the line, Leo Hall was startled to see a German patrol coming towards him on a side road from the river. They were on bicycles. 'I walked towards them with my Sten. With rifles slung, they were helpless, so off their bikes they tumbled and quickly surrendered to me. Their panniers contained stick grenades. I felt chuffed. Easy!'

By now, the countryside was petering out and the frontmarkers were moving into the increasingly built-up area on the outskirts of Arnhem. Brooker was astonished to see civilians coming out from their houses. 'Old men, kids and women threw flowers, right in the middle of the battle.' He was concerned that this joyous welcome was slowing them up. James Sims felt the same as, the deeper they penetrated into Arnhem, the more crowded the street became. 'One young Dutchman was charging about on a bike completely drunk and offering swigs of gin to one and all. Our officer lost his temper and threatened to shoot him and any of us who touched a drop. We were losing time and he realized that this semi-triumphal entry into Arnhem was not going to last.' To the right now lay the railway bridge across the Rhine, which the battalion had hoped to capture on the way – the more bridges the merrier. As riflemen approached it, the Germans defending it opened fire. A fierce fight began, which was punctuated by a huge explosion. 'Jerry had blown up its southern end, so denying us its use.' Passing by the spot a few minutes later, Sims saw a young British soldier propped up against a wooden seat where, on a different Sunday, strollers might stop for a stunning view of the river. 'His legs were buckled under him and his helmet removed. His battle-blouse was soaked with blood. Out of a waxen face his eyes stared past us into eternity. We crept by as quietly as possible as though afraid of waking him from that dread sleep.'

Up front, the head of the advancing column was meeting ever stiffer opposition. A cry of 'Tanks!' went up, and the thought of panzers in their path produced a shiver of fear among the infantrymen. But a jeep filled with anti-tank specialists came roaring up from the rear of the column, whooping and cheering as they brandished their trademark PIAT[1] weapons. 'They vanished round a bend in the road and there followed a succession of shots and shouts, then a single loud explosion. The menace had been dealt with.' But whatever element of surprise the column had hoped to have on its side was all but gone. From the other bank of the river, German heavy machine guns opened up and, though, over that distance, the salvoes were pretty harmless, they signified that the chances of an easy, unopposed seizure of the bridge were diminishing with every minute. Ahead of him, Sims could hear more firing as the riflemen leading the advance fought for possession of a pontoon bridge across the river, until a loud explosion announced that it had gone the same way as the railway bridge. 'Once again, Jerry had beaten us to it.' The dead and dying from the contact were lying at the northern end of the pontoon and, as he passed, Sims got the chance to stare his enemy in the face for the first time. He was not impressed. 'Some of the German casualties were SS. 'I was curious to see what these supermen looked like but, apart from their distinctive uniform, they were just like us. One was badly wounded and terrified we were going to shoot him. He was screaming and carrying on something shocking. Our lieutenant waved a .45 at him and that shut him up.'

Now – with the railway bridge and the pontoon bridge gone – the last unblown crossing over the Rhine was the Arnhem road bridge itself, still half a mile away. Sims could see the top of its huge single span and the strutted frame underneath. The sight of it had the same impact on Lancashire-born Leo Hall as seeing Blackpool Tower when he was a boy on his holidays: 'a special memory of my childhood'. He was as excited now as he was then, 'seeing the thing that we'd come to capture'.

The column halted to prepare for the final assault and Sims was not alone in suddenly feeling overcome with exhaustion. 'It was growing dark and we had been in action for several hours. When joining the Parachute Regiment we were told that one parachute jump was equal to eight hours' manual labour; by now I could believe it.' Out on the river, a small German patrol boat was sighted, its crew seemingly unaware that anything unusual was happening in Arnhem that Sunday. 'A soldier was leaning over the stern smoking a pipe, at peace with the world. Commands rang out and our machine-gun platoon pulverized the boat. The pipe-smoker toppled over the guard rail into the Rhine. I don't suppose he knew what hit him. The boat heeled over and sank in seconds.' The machine-gunners were exultant, though Sims noted rather sarcastically that, 'from the fuss they were making you would have thought they had sunk the battleship *Scharnhorst*.' But the real task was to get to the bridge in time. 'We knew the Germans must be working feverishly to set charges to blow it up. We set off on the last lap.' Sims ducked and dived from one piece of cover to the next. 'We pressed on, flitting from door to door. All of a sudden I got the fleeting impression of grey behind me, and I stiffened, expecting either a bayonet or a burst of Schmeisser fire. Nothing happened and I spun round, lunged with my bayonet and narrowly missed a young Dutch girl, no more than sixteen and wearing a grey jumper. My relief turned to anger at the fright she had given me and I bundled her back inside her front door.'

As they neared the bridge, its size and extent became apparent. It was massive, lifted high above the surface of the water on huge piers and accessed on its northern side by a long and high road ramp that loomed over the surrounding buildings. Sims's platoon veered away from the river and headed into the town to find a way up. 'People looked down on us from their windows and waved, but without huge enthusiasm. Perhaps they could foresee that their beautiful town would be laid in ruins before long. Even so, some of these Dutch civilians took quite extraordinary risks to warn us of enemy activity or snipers.' A burst of fire as Sims was crossing a road sent him dashing for cover, until help arrived in the shape of a Bren-gun carrier. 'An officer jumped aboard and ordered the driver to head straight for the enemy machine-gun nest. When he got there he fired straight down their throats while we dodged past the back of the carrier to gain the shelter of the houses beyond.'

A last effort was needed. From up ahead came jubilant shouts of 'Whoa Mahomet!'² the battle cry the paras had picked up and adopted as their own when fighting in North Africa. They were coming from Frost's men, already on the approach to the bridge. Inspired, Sims's patrol raced forward, throwing caution to the wind. 'We ran on past an SS police barracks, which was now on fire. Several of Hitler's black-uniformed thugs lay dead on the path outside. In the gutter lay two more dead in Luftwaffe blue. They were a boy and a girl of about my own age. The boy was slumped across a light machine-gun with the girl beside him, the ammunition belt threaded through her fingers. The girl's blonde hair was stained with blood; they had died quickly and violently.' He could only guess at who they were and what they were doing there. 'Brother and sister? Lovers? It was just another of those wartime incidents that make a mockery of fiction.' The bridge was now just a hundred yards ahead and he could see that the riflemen in the front of the column were swarming over its northern end and engaged in a fierce fight with German defenders holed up in pill boxes. Flame-throwers were sent forward to deal with them and, suddenly, with German soldiers on the retreat, running for their lives, it was over. The northern end of the bridge was captured and, though the other end was still in enemy hands and attempts to storm it repulsed, the German sappers laying explosive charges underneath had been chased off.

The Arnhem bridge was intact. Stage one of Market Garden was nearly complete. Wearily, the British troops moved into the buildings around the end of the bridge and to either side of the road ramp, set up their positions and settled down to wait for stage two: the arrival of reinforcements, firstly from the other airborne columns on their way from the drop zone and then, in a day or so – tomorrow even if things went really well – from the heavy armour of XXX Corps racing to Arnhem from their start point on the Dutch–Belgian border.

Fires from burning German vehicles which had tried to escape across the bridge lit up the night. Abandoned guns littered the road, and the men of the strike force took great cheer from this visible proof of their triumph. 'We felt pleased with ourselves,' Sims said, 'for we had dropped many miles behind the enemy lines, fought our way into a large town and captured the northern end of our main objective, the road bridge.' Para Major Tony Hibbert acknowledged feeling 'pretty cocky. We'd achieved the first part of our operation order in taking the bridge. Now all we had to do was hold it for forty-eight hours.'[3] It was to be a task easier said than done.

*

What the paras held – and that precariously – was, in fact, not the actual bridge but the tiniest slice of Arnhem at its northern end. Even at its greatest extent, it was the size of just a dozen football pitches and in the end would shrink to the equivalent of barely one. From their various vantage points, Frost's men covered the approach road to the bridge and a few streets around it, but the span itself was a lethal no-man's land. The other end was resolutely in German hands,

as was the rest of the city. As backmarkers from the strike force continued to arrive, they had to fight their way through enemy lines.
Ted Mordecai hugged walls and crawled in the gutter to reach the
archway under the road ramp. 'Lead was flying all over the place and
we couldn't make out who was firing at whom. The sound of shot
and shell was deafening.' He wasn't supposed to be here in the heat of
battle. An ordnance man, his role on the Arnhem mission was a logis-
tical one, rooting out petrol supplies and commandeering vehicles,
but he was ordered to forget about that now. Foraging could wait;
every hand was needed for fighting. His platoon scurried across a
road to a large house and banged on the door for entry. After a long
delay, it was opened by a Dutchman. The soldiers apologized for
having to occupy his home and advised him to leave with his family
while he still could. 'He fetched his wife and small daughter from the
cellar, packed a small suitcase and they left, walking down the middle
of the street away from the bridge. I thought to myself, "I hope they
don't get shot by the Germans." I also wondered where on earth they
could go.' As he watched the civilians trudge away, the house came
under mortar fire.

By now, Ron Brooker had been at the bridge for some time and
was guarding brigade headquarters, which had been set up in a large
building on the near side of the road ramp. An orderly recalled how
beautifully furnished the house was, with shelves of books and a fine
china tea service laid out on a table. (A sergeant-major, sensitive to the
need not to upset the owners, threatened retribution on anyone who
damaged the china. Later, when things hotted up, he was seen to
sweep it all away when the table was urgently needed for a barricade.)
The entrance was through a gateway into a courtyard and Brooker
positioned his jeep in the gateway with his Vickers machine gun pointing out. He was chatting to a comrade about home, family, football
– anything to distract them from the present situation – when a lorry
came meandering slowly down the road. It was full of German troops
and it looked as if the driver, far from leading an attack, had taken a
wrong turn in the confusion. But Brooker was taking no chances. He
opened fire – the first time he had pulled the trigger since arriving in
the Netherlands – and brought it to a halt. The driver and passengers

were dead, but what was a shock to him was what they were wearing: the uniforms of SS panzer troops. 'Until then we'd thought we were up against old men and boys. We didn't expect crack front-line troops and tanks, and we'd got nothing to fight them with.'

Brooker was then ordered to the top of the building, where, in a large attic room, Frost, Major Gough and other officers were planning their defence strategy. A window looked out over the ramp, but to see the actual bridge meant climbing on to a chair and peering through one of two dormer windows. Brooker stood at the larger window, his rifle at the ready. There was a radio operator in the room too, but, amid mounting frustration among the officers, he couldn't get through to anyone else in the brigade to find out where they were or what was happening. In a neighbouring building, Major Hibbert was having the same problem, despite antennae sticking out of every window. 'My first job was to inform Division that we were on the bridge. But not one of our wirelesses could pick up the faintest whisper from anyone in northern Europe except John Frost, who was all of 50 yards away.'

At this point, command of the entire operation was becoming an issue of serious concern, and not wholly because of faulty communications. The British end of Garden was theoretically being run by the commander of the Airborne Corps, the aloof and upper-crust Lieutenant-General Frederick 'Boy' Browning. Guards-trained as well as a qualified glider pilot, he was better known generally for being the impossibly handsome husband of best-selling novelist Daphne du Maurier, whose *Rebecca* and *Frenchman's Creek* were huge cinema hits in wartime Britain. In military circles he was renowned for introducing the Sandhurst tradition in which the adjutant rode his horse up the steps and in through the college doors after the cadets' passing-out parade. He chose to set up his tactical headquarters near Nijmegen and dropped in there by glider, alongside the US 82nd Airborne Division, with his headquarters staff of two hundred. This in itself was unwise – the thirty-eight gliders needed to get them there might have been more usefully employed ferrying extra fighting men into Arnhem. But even more of a problem was that, a dozen miles distant from the action at Arnhem and with almost zero radio contact, he was hardly ever in touch with the brigades it was his job to direct.

Meanwhile, his commander on the ground, Roy Urquhart, had gone missing. He had set up his divisional headquarters close to the Wolfheze landing zone and then, frustrated by the radio problems and anxious to keep the advance moving, jumped into a jeep to hare frantically around his various battalions and squadrons to gee them along. He was in such a hurry that he took no protection squad with him and was helpless when, on the outskirts of Arnhem, he ran into the enemy. Forced to take shelter in a civilian house surrounded by German soldiers, he hid in the attic and was out of contact with his staff officers for a day and a half. What's more, his designated number two was wounded and also out of action. Twin crises of command and communication were a military man's worst nightmare, but this was the scenario now unfolding.

At the bridge, Frost, desperate not only to report his position but also to establish what was going on, sent out a four-man patrol to try to make contact with the other columns supposedly on their way from the drop zone. Brooker, one of the four, had difficulty just getting out on to the street, because the yard was in the firing line of German snipers perched high on a nearby church. Once outside, they ducked through the darkening streets until they came to a square. Peering round a corner, they could see German infantry assembling and digging in. Of their own reinforcements, there was not a glimmer. Unable to go any further, the patrol made its way back to HQ, 'having achieved nothing'. Other forays proved equally unproductive. Frost sent out a thirty-man platoon to forage for a boat, cross the Rhine and come up on the bridge from the other side. 'We set off along the bank but couldn't find a boat,' its leader, Lieutenant Pat Barnett, recalled.[4] After a gun battle with the enemy, they withdrew. More attempts to rush the bridge and seize a foothold on the other bank were repulsed and incurred heavy casualties. No one, it was rapidly becoming clear, was going anywhere. As a day of enterprise, courage and shifting fortunes came to an end, the paras at the bridge dug in while the Germans called for reinforcements to winkle them out. A stalemate had been reached, for now.

Sims took up position on a large, grassed traffic island in the middle of a five-way road junction between the road ramp and the river.

He set about digging mortar pits and slit trenches in the sandy soil. This would be the first line of defence for the houses and warehouses behind, most now occupied by various British platoons and turned into strongholds. He moaned that it was tiring work, and did they really have to go so deep? His mate, digging alongside, told him to get on with it: 'Two or three hours from now and it won't seem half deep enough.' All around, parachutists were making similar burrows for themselves in the earth, like a colony of sexton beetles, Sims thought. Finally, he settled into his hole, took out some army fruit-cake from his pack and munched on it. It was dry but good and very welcome. 'Up on the bridge itself, vehicles were still burning. One was an ammunition lorry and, every now and again, it shuddered as the fire reached another box of bullets or shells and they exploded in a fantastic firework display.' Sims started to doze off. 'It was like drifting into sleep after a particularly good Bonfire Night when the last squibs are being thrown on a dying fire.'

There was no sleep for Ted Mordecai, however. In the house his company occupied, he knocked the glass out of a window on the top floor and took up a position a yard or so back behind a makeshift bar-ricade, facing the bridge. 'Outside, the fires had really taken hold and lit up the whole area.' He worked out his line of fire and pulled the scrim netting from his helmet down over his face so he couldn't be seen. As the night wore on and the flames and the firing around the bridge died down, he saw a figure outside approach the house and demand to know who was inside. The most extraordinary thing about him was that he was waving a rolled umbrella. It was, it turned out, the brave Major Digby Tatham-Warter, whose stiff-upper-lip calmness under fire would be one of the triumphant images of the whole Arnhem experience. He was casing the area, finding out who was in which building, a death-defying business, since some housed Germans. He wanted six volunteers to come outside and cover him as he reconnoitred a particular building down the road. Mordecai went with him, Sten gun sweeping the windows and doors, as the major stood brazenly in the open and loudly demanded to know who was inside. 'Personally, I thought it was stupid, because if Jerry had been in the house we would have been in for a rough time out there in the open. Fortunately for us, the reply came back that it was occupied by some of our gunners and sappers. This evidently satisfied the major and he strolled off into the darkness, still directing operations with his brolly.' But the commotion had stirred up the enemy and a machine gun opened up on Mordecai as he and the others dashed back to their house. 'Having regained our breath, we resumed positions at the windows until daybreak.'

One of the last to get through to the bridge was Major Eric Mackay of the Royal Engineers. He and his men had a tough time getting there. As they trudged through central Arnhem dragging trolleys loaded with explosives, 'all around us there seemed to be surreptitious movements in the dark. We could hear the enemy moving along parallel streets.'[5] They were ambushed by a German patrol and a 'sharp scrap' ensued. Then they had to brave furious crossfire from either side of a city square and cross 40 yards of open ground, still with their trolleys. Once at the bridge, Mackay was directed to some buildings on the far side of the road ramp and ordered to fortify and hold them. One was a school, the other a house. Ten minutes after they took possession they were attacked from a building just 15 yards away, which turned out to be the headquarters of a company of German soldiers. 'The enemy crept through the bushes and right up to us before we were aware of them. They threw grenades through the window and got a foothold in the basement. Determined hand-to-hand fighting with fists, boots, rifle-butts and bayonets dislodged them. They brought up a machine gun and poked it through a window, spraying everyone in the room. I was beside the window, shot the gunman and turned the gun on the mob outside.'

More grenades were lobbed in. 'Nearly half the force in the house was already wounded and it was apparent that if we stayed any longer we should all become casualties.' They would have to retreat to the school, and to do that meant clearing the enemy out of the garden first. Mackay, his sergeant and six men went out and 'mixed it' in the bushes. The enemy, he recalled, had no stomach for cold steel and retired. 'We pursued them to their building with grenades and gave them a taste of their own medicine. We then kept up hot fire as my corporal got the wounded over a high wall and into the school, where we rejoined the rest of the force.' From this eyeball-to-eyeball duel – the first of many in the days ahead – he had seven wounded men, two of them seriously, and he himself had minor shrapnel wounds and a cut in his head where a bullet had gone through his helmet – 'more messy than painful', as he put it. With his fifty men, six Bren guns and lots of ammunition and grenades, he prepared for a siege. 'We had no anti-tank weapons, very little food, only the water in our water bottles and no medical supplies except morphine and field dressings.' Before dawn, they repelled two attacks – and that was only the start.

★

The citizens of Arnhem, their peaceful town suddenly turned into a battlefield, were understandably in turmoil, unclear about what was happening in the streets not far from their homes. Were they about to be free, or weren't they? Their emotions were taut, like violin strings that could either deliver the sweetest of music or snap apart. They didn't know what to think or who to believe. A jubilant Heleen Kernkamp had watched as panicking German soldiers quit a requisitioned house just across the street from where she was staying. 'In a tearing hurry, they loaded tables, desks, telephones and food into jeeps and drove away.' The departure of black-uniformed SS troops, 'who had been responsible for an incalculable amount of grief and misery', brought the greatest relief and satisfaction. But, as a counterpoint to all this, there was the shelling and the bombing to contend with, getting nearer and nearer all the time, and the terrifying uncertainty about what was happening. The Klompe household where she was staying was filling up as neighbours and friends crowded in, seeking shelter together. The electricity and gas were cut off but the telephone kept ringing. 'All the piecemeal fragments of news we heard only made us more and more excited and nervous. Nobody knew exactly what was going on except that, judging by the noise, there was heavy fighting. We could not leave or go outside, as we could hear bullets hitting trees, walls and streets.'

They wanted desperately to believe the friend who phoned from Oosterbeek to sing the first verse of the Wilhelmus and announce the liberation there. If the people were free in Oosterbeek, then could Arnhem's deliverance be far behind? 'We were all very deeply moved. This was tangible, it was really happening and we became greatly excited.' Though it was late and the day had been exhausting, no one wanted to go to bed. 'The constant shelling made us nervous, and we were much too tense and strung up. We all sat together in a big circle round a candle and talked over the events of the day. Suddenly a loud banging on the front door gave us a terrible fright.'

Years of instinct and discipline kicked in, and they all dashed upstairs to hide two young men in the house who were on the run. In their haste, they forgot one of the many cardinal rules of concealment – they failed to remove the young men's chairs from the circle, and any SS or Gestapo officer entering on a raid would almost certainly have spotted that there were more seats than people and drawn the obvious, calamitous conclusion. As it was, the knock at the door was a false alarm, and they all joined the two men in the attic to stare out over the rooftops of Arnhem. It was 'a truly fantastic' sight, with enormous fires from buildings set alight by the Germans or by the bombing burning all over the town. 'A stiff breeze was blowing sparks along our windows and the whole neighbourhood was lit up by a ghostly reddish glow, through which we could pick out people in the street. One group was sneaking from house to house and peering through windows. We thought that, in spite of everything that was going on, it must be the Germans still hunting out men in hiding. But we were afraid and none of us dared venture outside to check.' The knock on the door, it transpired, was from someone in the town trying without success to get help for a casualty from the bombing, but the Klompes weren't alone in being too scared to open up. The atmosphere had switched from hope to apprehension. 'The fact that we were without light and power for the very first time produced in all of us a sensation of hopelessness. I tried to comfort one woman who was beside herself with terror, but the feeling of being trapped with no means of escape will remain with me for ever. It was one of the most terrible and nerve-wracking experiences of my life.'

Pieter Huisman was another of Arnhem's worried citizens sleeping uneasily in his bed that night, wondering what tomorrow would bring. The family had busied themselves around the house, packing bags in case they suddenly had to flee the city, but now they were down in the cellar again, his small sons on mattresses and he and his wife stretched out in armchairs. 'There is a lot of firing. The boys are very afraid.' A phone call from his nephew in Oosterbeek told him that, there, the people had been liberated and so, he was reassured, would he be, very soon. 'But when I looked out of the window all I could see was Germans manning machine guns.' Where were the British? Rumour had them on the bridge, at police headquarters, in the heart of the city, at the St Elizabeth Hospital. But then counter-rumour said the Germans were hitting back and the British were retreating. There in the candle-lit cellar with his frightened family, he did not did not know what to believe. 'Which is true?' he asked himself. It was a very good question and one to which there was no simple answer. All that Heleen Kernkamp could discern from the noise of machine guns and rifles and bullets slamming into walls was that 'first one side and then the other was advancing, only to be driven back.' It was a fair summary of the developing military situation.

*

As dawn broke on a misty Monday morning and the second day of the Arnhem operation began, a fog swirled over the waters of the Rhine. Those few men of 1st Airborne who had managed to get some sleep in their various buildings and dug-outs around the Arn-hem bridge and road ramp were roused by an encouraging sound. Ron Brooker heard the rattle of tank tracks and the revving of engines. Armour was on its way. It had to be XXX Corps! 'Every-body cheered. Our boys were here. We felt excited and relieved.' Looking back from a distance of sixty-five years, he could see that such optimism was absurd. 'Logically, it couldn't be them. We'd been in Arnhem only a few hours and there was no way they could have got here that quickly. But it's strange how the mind works. We told each other, "Yeah, it's over, they're here." Of course, they weren't.' What was heading their way across from the southern end of the bridge was, they realized by the black crosses painted on the sides, a

German column of half-tracks and armoured cars. The enemy was counter-attacking, and in force, attempting to win back the northern end of the bridge they had lost the night before. Everyone snapped into action. As Leo Hall put it, 'it was as if both sides had been waiting for the referee's dawn whistle in order for play to begin seriously.' For the airborne soldiers, their heroic battle to hang on to the Arnhem bridge was about to begin.

The German armour came on, tanks, lorries and open-topped Opel troop carriers in line astern, 10 yards apart. They were hit by heavy and accurate fire from the paras' positions. There was an explosion as a 6-pounder anti-tank gun fired from just below the ramp and caught one of the cars, which slewed to a halt, blocking the bridge. Ted Mordecai remembered how the others were forced to pull up and presented 'a perfect target for all of us. Everyone in range immediately opened fire and any German soldiers who tried to cut and run were knocked over.' But not all. When a shell halted one half-track, a German leapt from the back and, though half a dozen British rifles fixed on him, he danced out of trouble. Brooker was back up on a chair and leaning out of the dormer window to get in a shot at him when a burst of German machine-gun fire shattered the glass. A shard hurtled down through his beret and sliced a large flap of skin from his head. A glass fragment entered his right eye. 'It was the first time I'd been wounded and I was shocked.' To this day, he carries scars from the thirty-seven stitches needed to patch him up. Staggering down to the basement for treatment, he realized his luck as he caught sight of the bodies of the dead, a dozen or so, piled up in a shed outside. The paras might be holding off the German attackers, but at a growing cost. He took his place among the wounded, sitting on the floor of a long passage. 'The attitude of these men, many quite badly wounded, was truly amazing. They could still manage a laugh and give moral support to each other. The main topic of conversation was "Any news of XXX Corps?"'

In a lull in the fighting, Mordecai went to the kitchen of the house he and his troop were occupying and boiled up some water and Oxo cubes. Breakfast! It was the first hot drink any of them had had for twenty-four hours. 'We all felt better after this and more alert.' He also tried to snatch some sleep, but his mind was racing and he couldn't, despite the luxury of a feather bed in an upstairs room. What relaxation he was getting was then blown apart by a huge explosion. 'A large cloud of smoke and dust came gushing through the bedroom door.' Out on the landing he saw that a shell had hit the house and there was a gaping hole where the back wall and roof had been. 'The worst of it was that three Signals chaps had gone into a small back bedroom to sleep and the one who'd got the bed rather than the floor was now lying under a pile of rubble.' The other two were just stunned, but he was dead, such was the luck of the draw.

Elsewhere on the battlefield, James Sims had left his slit trench in the traffic island by the bridge and climbed through a window into a nearby building – dubbed the White House, though its façade was really more of a light grey – to set up an observation post from which to direct mortar attacks. The house was already under fire, ominously not from the Germans on the other side of the river but from the west. This was the direction from which reinforcements from the drop zone should be arriving, but the shelling indicated that the Germans must still be holding that area and keeping those reinforcements at bay. What if they never got here? What if they couldn't push aside the German forces in their way? He drew the obvious and chilling conclusion 'that we were now in real danger of being completely cut off from the remainder of the 1st Airborne Division'.

He reached a large upstairs room overlooking his traffic island and was forced to dive to the floor as bullets ricocheted around him. 'Snipers,' a badly wounded officer, his jaw set firm but his eyes betraying the pain he was in, informed him. 'You'll find it safer to crawl on your belly.' Up another flight of stairs, and Sims was in the attic, from which he saw German infantry in lorries advancing along a road from the river towards the White House. Evidently, they were unaware that houses they were passing were filled with paratroopers, whose bullets now ripped through them, killing virtually all of them. Sims watched with horrified fascination as one terribly wounded German soldier, shot through both legs, pulled himself hand over hand towards his own lines. 'He was the only creature moving among a carpet of the dead.' With superhuman effort, he managed to drag himself across the road and up the grassy incline leading to the bridge road. He was just about to heave himself over a parapet to safety 'when a rifle barked out next to me and he fell back, shot through the head. To me it was little short of murder but to my companion, one of our best snipers, the German was a legitimate target. When I protested he looked at me as though I was simple.'

If the compassionate Sims felt sorry for his enemy, it was not for long. Shortly afterwards, a white civilian ambulance came hurtling down the same road and a British Bren-gunner opened up on it until he was ordered to stop. 'Can't you see the red cross, you bloody fool?' an angry officer demanded. Just then, the doors of the ambulance opened and several SS troopers rushed out, firing from the hip. Most were cut down before reaching the White House but 'one made it to the front door before collapsing on the steps, riddled with bullets. The road outside was covered with dead and dying Germans. Our medics went out to clear the dead away and treat the wounded.'

For now, frontal assaults ceased, but the barrage of shells continued. From on high, Sims looked down on his comrades in the slit trenches outside. 'Shrapnel was pattering down like a thunderstorm of death but, by some miracle, not one of them was hit.' On the contrary, they were the ones doing the damage, after Sims and his officer trained their binoculars on lorries of German reinforcements arriving at the other end of the bridge and assessed the range and elevation to pass down to the men in the mortar pit. The walkie-talkie wasn't working so Sims leaned out of the window to shout the instructions, withdrawing his head just before the snipers spotted him. The mortar barrage took out two trucks, sending the troops on them scuttling away. 'It must have come as a terrific shock for them to be hit by such devastating fire from the other side of the river.'

Then came a new threat, as a column of light tanks and armoured cars approached. Bravely, soldiers of the Airlanding artillery wheeled out two 6-pounder anti-tank guns into the middle of the street to confront them. Their first shot took out the leading tank. Belching black smoke, it slewed to a halt, blocking the way for those behind. Another attack had been repulsed, but there were more to come and, inch by inch, the Germans' superiority in tanks and manpower began to tell. Yet the British were defiant. They were well dug in, sheltered behind the walls of sturdy buildings, though by now brickwork was crumbling and plaster falling under the constant onslaught. They also had a major consolation to bolster morale. As Sims put it, 'we knew we had only to hang on until the main relieving army arrived.' Their sense of humour was undiminished. Between barrages, the Germans filled the silence with the loud wail of sirens so the Brits would get no peace. 'That must be the knocking-off whistle,' one wag called out. 'Are we on overtime now?'

*

At brigade headquarters, the wounded Ron Brooker found himself called back into action. As the battle outside intensified and the building was pounded by enemy tank shells until the walls shook and broke up, a sergeant-major entered the basement where the casualties were being treated, looking for volunteers to return to the fight. 'There was no hesitation as about a dozen of us followed him. With my right eye covered I was not much use with a rifle or machine gun, so I was given the task of delivering ammo to the gun positions.' The enemy stepped up its attacks. 'They infiltrated our positions, grenades came through windows and snipers in the church steeple ensured we could not safely use the courtyard. On one of my rounds, I passed a stretcher case being carried down the staircase and I held on to his hand and chatted to him. He was very badly wounded and mumbling, talking to his mother. As we reached the ground floor, his grip tightened and he died. I saw many deaths, but this one stands out in my memory. I have no idea who he was but I hope I gave him a little comfort. I still think about him.'

The dying man's conversation with his mother, that instinctive return to the womb, was what seared itself on Brooker's memory. Though he did not know it, at this very moment, back at his home in Brighton, his own mother was snatching a moment to write to her 21-year-old son, wherever he might be. 'Hoping you are safe and well,' she told him as she recounted the movement of family and friends. In this parallel universe, while one son was fighting for his life, she was taking his little brother to the cinema to see Walt Disney's *Snow White*. 'Cheers,' she concluded. 'God bless and keep you safe.' In Arnhem, Brooker needed every prayer.

If things were bad in brigade headquarters, it was in the buildings on the other side of the ramp that Major Mackay and his engineers were fighting off an even fiercer onslaught, and had been all day. From first light, Mackay and his men, barricaded inside the school – Anje van Maanen's school, as it happened – had been coming under attack from Germans in the building next door, just 20 yards away. Outgunned, he had to be clever. He placed a machine gun in one window, which he fired by remote control. 'It drew all the enemy fire and allowed us to open up on the machine-gun crew with our Bren guns and kill them.' For a while, Mackay and his men were holding their own and even got a chance to strike back. German armour advanced across the no-man's land of the bridge and down the road ramp, directly opposite a first-floor window in the school and barely a dozen yards away. 'Five armoured cars went by and there was nothing we could do about them because we had no anti-tank weapons. But then some open-top half-tracks tried to sneak through.' The paras lobbed a grenade into the first and took out the second with a machine gun. 'The crew of six tried to get out and were shot one by one, lying round the half-track as it stood there in the middle of the road.'

More half-tracks came on, guns blazing, but were forced back. Two collided, and 'we poured a hail of fire into the milling mass. The score of bodies was beginning to mount.' Then a half-track got so close that, as it passed the window, Mackay found himself looking into its commander's face. 'His reaction was quicker than mine. With a dirty big grin he loosed off three shots with his Luger. A shot hit me, smashing the binoculars hanging round my neck.' But this attack too was beaten off. 'The boys immediately rallied round, and he and his men were all dead meat in a few seconds as the half-track crashed into a wall.'

There were lulls in the fighting as the enemy, forced back to its side of the bridge, re-grouped. The bridge itself was now completely blocked by burning vehicles, so there would be no more attempts to cross, for now. Mackay counted his casualties. 'They were comparatively light. We were doing well.' Then mortars crashed into the school and, when he stopped to listen, Mackay could hear that the orders to fire them were coming from the other side of the ramp *in English*! 'We were being mortared by our own side. Leaning out of the nearest window, I gave vent to some fruity language at the top of my voice. The mortaring stopped.' His men then let loose with a loud chorus of their 'Whoa Mahomet!' war cry, which was taken up by inmates in all the para-held houses around the bridge. Ted Mordecai heard it in the house he was occupying and went out on to the veranda to wave his green silk recognition scarf. 'The air was ringing with the sound. Morale leapt. Throughout the succeeding days this cry was the only means of telling which buildings were still being held. It was one thing the Germans, with all their cleverness, could not imitate.'

In truth, though, the situation in the school was critical. The men had had little to eat apart from biscuits and boiled sweets since breakfast back in England before take-off. The water was cut off, so they were thirsty too. But when Mackay managed to get through to Frost on the radio, he assured the colonel that 'we were quite happy and could hold out till the following dawn. He said this would not be necessary as help was very near. XXX Corps was only 5 miles south of us, and the rest of our division was battling its way into the town one and a half miles to the west. This news was passed on to the men, which pleased them.' Whether they believed it – and whether it was true (it was not) – was another matter. 'We could hear heavy gunfire away to the south, but still no relief.'

In the White House, James Sims and his men were told that XXX Corps' earliest estimated time of arrival was now midday on Tuesday, twenty-four hours away. 'What had gone wrong? Evidently things were not going quite as planned with the relieving army. But could we hold out that long?' Certainly not without water, the only source of which, Sims discovered, was a tap in the middle of the backyard. He would have to brave the bullets flying overhead to get to it, which he did, heaving himself along the ground until he was underneath it and could reach up to turn it on.

He filled two mess tins and made his way back, pushing the tins in front of him. The riflemen and engineers watching cheered as he made it to the door.

Meanwhile, on the far side of the road ramp, the battle beneath the bridge started up again. This time the enemy had got into a house opposite the school and was pouring in machine-gun fire on the stairs, the only means of moving between floors. Once again, Mackay resorted to guile. One Bren was fired by remote control, while the others eliminated the enemy posts as they fired back. 'After three and a half hours of this we had succeeded in clearing the houses opposite.' But he was running short of fit men and no longer had enough to man all the rooms on the ground floor. So, planning for the night that was fast approaching, he withdrew to just two rooms as a stronghold. Outside lay the crashed German half-tracks, almost certainly with rations, weapons and ammo inside. 'I determined to take out a patrol and recover all this booty.' But renewed machine-gun and mortar fire kept them pinned down and a German flame-thrower deliberately destroyed the half track Sims had had his eyes on. Desperate for ammunition, he sent his corporal across the battlefield to the headquarters building for more supplies.

There, Brooker and three others loaded up with bandoliers and boxes and accompanied the corporal back. They sidled out of the building, dashed for the gate, hugged a wall before crossing the road and scuttling through the tunnel under the ramp. Then there were 300 yards of open land to the school under a hail of bullets. 'How we managed it I just don't know.' As they arrived and unloaded the ammo, the school came under renewed attack as the Germans made a concerted effort to win back all the buildings on that side of the ramp. Someone pushed a Sten into Brooker's hands, 'and I was back on the active list. The Germans had got inside and we were fighting them face to face, close-quarter killing with bullet and bayonet.' Running out of ammo for his machine gun, he picked up a fallen rifle and bayonet and went to work. 'It was brutal. They were coming through the windows, through the door, everywhere. There were so many you couldn't count them. You just do what you have to do.

Thrust with a bayonet, shoot, whatever is required, until we pushed them out. I don't know how we survived against such odds, but we did.' It was all over in ten minutes.

But brutal as the fighting was, there were moments of surprising compassion and even empathy for those on the other side. Brooker left the school to cross back to brigade headquarters. On the way he came across four Germans in the tunnel under the ramp. 'Three of them were wounded, the fourth was very young, just a boy, and he looked petrified. We stopped and looked at them, and they looked at us and we moved on. It didn't seem right to kill them. They were in the same boat as us.' As Brooker re-entered the brigade building, he glanced at the shed by the main gate. The number of bodies had grown to thirty or forty, lying in rows, covered in blankets and curtains or their smocks pulled up over their heads. 'The stench was terrible, the smell of death.' Meanwhile, the enemy seemed closer than ever. 'No more than a few yards separated us.'

That evening, as the light faded, a desperate plan was under discussion for what was called a 'flying column' to rush the German defences on the other side of the bridge in jeeps, break through and keep going until contact was made with the relief column from XXX Corps. It seemed pretty crackpot to Brooker. 'The Jerries were sitting at the other end of the bridge with armoured cars and machine guns and there was no reason to think they would not be manning the miles of road beyond it. I couldn't see how we'd have even got across the bridge.' Nonetheless, when he was asked if he was prepared to drive the lead jeep and give it a go, he said yes.

'I wasn't being brave, but by that time we all had the feeling that we were reaching the end. But that particular plan was crazy, suicidal.' It was sensibly abandoned. But the mood among the men had now switched – from optimism to fatalism. For Brooker, the realization 'that there was no way out, there was no rescue, you've had your lot,' and that there was every chance he would die in Arnhem, surprisingly failed to dent his morale. If in conversation anyone talked about 'tomorrow', then someone would invariably say, 'There won't be any bloody tomorrow.' But that was as far as the despair about the situation went. Here, as in so much that went on at Arnhem, was the triumph of the spirit over the very worst of human experiences.

*

It was getting harder to be hopeful, however, particularly for Arnhem's civilians such as Heleen Kernkamp. That evening, she and those in the house where she was staying – sixteen in all, mainly women – were, in her own words, 'dejected and downhearted. We had no idea what the outcome would be. All that had happened so far could not be in vain . . . could it?' The day had not brought liberation, as they had fully expected. Instead there had been nothing but gunfire all around, 'and not a clue about what was going on'. They had not dared to go out but stayed indoors, 'jumpy and on edge'. Friends rang with worrying news about heavy tanks in the city centre and hard fighting at the bridge. The whereabouts of the main body of the Allied army was a mystery. 'In our neighbourhood the shooting quietened down and eventually stopped. But heavy firing could still be heard down in the city centre and the consequences of that cast a huge damper over our spirits: it meant the Allies were being driven back.'

Not, however, if Eric Mackay had anything to do with it. That night, as if he and his men holding out in the school had not had enough to contend with already, they came under the most intense of attacks in a battle that went on until the middle of the next day. So many bullets crashed through the building that splinters from shattered floorboards caused scores of injuries. This time, too, as well as machine guns and mortars, the enemy brought in flame-throwers, and for three hours the defenders were forced to use their smocks to beat out flames in the roof. But even more havoc was caused by a 20lb anti-tank bomb which demolished a corner of the school and knocked Mackay himself unconscious for a while. His batman was blinded. With many of the men downed or dazed by this ferocious attack, there was an opportunity for the Germans to storm the building against little or no opposition, but they failed to seize the initiative.

'We were given a breathing space,' Mackay noted, 'but not for long.' Clearly, the enemy thought they had just delivered the killer blow because when, twenty minutes later, he looked out of a window, he saw directly below him a dozen of them unhurriedly setting up a machine gun and mortar. He could hear them chatting to each other, 'and they were evidently under the impression that all resistance in the house had ceased.' Limping from shrapnel in his foot, Mackay did a quick room-to-room recce through the school, glancing unseen out of every window, and discovered there was a ring of Germans all around – sixty of them and no more than three or four yards away. 'They were unaware of our existence. It seemed too good to be true.'

Whispered orders sent his men scuttling to every window, grenades ready, the pins out. 'On a signal, they were dropped on the heads below, followed instantly by bursts from all our six Brens and fourteen Stens. Disdaining cover, the boys stood up on the windowsills, firing from the hip. The night dissolved into a hideous din as the heavy crash of the Brens mixed with the high-pitched rattle of the Stens, the cries of wounded men and the sharp explosions of grenades. Swelling above it all was our triumphant war-cry, "Whoa Mahomet!" It was all over in minutes, leaving a carpet of field-grey round the house.' It was 3 a.m. That should keep them quiet until the morning, Mackay told himself with a sense of satisfaction as he went to see his casualties. One had fifteen bullets through the chest and was dying. Another had a stomach wound, often the worst kind and untreatable, but Mackay reckoned that, luckily, no vital organs had been hit. 'I shoved a plug in it.' The rest of the casualties were mainly suffering from shock and fatigue. 'I had plenty of morphia and kept them all well doped.' He could have done with some himself as a medical orderly tried to extract the sharp piece of shrapnel that was painfully pinning his boot to his foot but failed. He radioed a message to Frost, updating the colonel on his current fighting strength and assuring him that 'we are all happy and holding our own.'

The order came back to hold on at all costs. XXX Corps was closing in and relief was imminent, Mackay was assured. The real situation, however, was very different. In the far distance, Model's forces were fatally slowing the advance of the rescue column from the Belgian border while, on the outskirts of Arnhem, the reinforcements from the landing zones were blocked, bogged down and fighting for their own survival in field, forest and street skirmishes. Meanwhile, the men at the bridge were surrounded, isolated and in desperate straits. In odd moments when their radios were picking up signals, they could hear the BBC reporting that everything at Arnhem was going to plan. Some hope, they thought.

5. Stopped in Their Tracks

The advance units under Frost that had managed to reach the bridge desperately needed to be reinforced by the bulk of their comrades, who were still battling against growing opposition to make their way into the town from the landing sites. Quietly and in single file, Reg Curtis and his company of paratroopers crept into a square on the western edge of Arnhem in the darkness just before dawn and were met by eager and excited members of the Dutch Resistance. There were whispered greetings and discussions as the young civilians, proudly displaying their orange armbands, pointed out the quickest way to the bridge. They could be there soon, the young men said, backing up the battalion that had already made it. But the outskirts were as near as Curtis and any other of those relief columns ever got to the object of their mission. The bridge would remain out of reach. Among the houses and along the roads, the Germans had been busy, preparing gun emplacements, taking up vantage points, posting snipers, concealing tanks. 'Machine-gunners shattered the peace of the early morning. I darted for cover in a neatly laid-out garden of a nearby house. I went around the back and fired at two Germans in the shrubbery.' In no time, a prolonged pitched battle was in progress. 'Lunchtime passed but no one stopped for a snack.'

The British troops inched their way forward, taking casualties with each step. 'In every direction I could see the motionless forms of our men cut short in their tracks.' This was street fighting of the toughest kind, with a violent encounter at every turn. In one mad dash, Curtis chased some Germans into a house, slung in a grenade and dashed through the door to finish them off with his Sten. 'Then, as we belted to the back of the house, I tripped over a broken fence and went sprawling. Scrambling up, I heard a whine and dived for cover by a low wall. *Wham!* A mortar bomb landed so close I felt the draught.' On he went. 'Snipers took pot-shots at us as we dodged and weaved through gardens and back yards. I came towards a factory near the river, from which murderous mortar and machine-gun fire was coming. Throwing myself to the ground, I finally came to a stop.'

That factory, with its landmark tall chimneys, figured in the recollections of many airborne soldiers busting a gut to get close to the Arnhem bridge against newly arrived German reinforcements. Lieutenant Eric Davies had lost men getting this far but he was now ordered to launch an immediate frontal assault on the hill the factory stood on. 'I have got about twelve men left and go straight in with them,' he recorded in a fast-moving account that caught the breathlessness of the close-up encounters that were developing all along those access roads to Arnhem.[1] 'We charge straight up the road to the high ground, a good fast advance under sniper and machine-gun fire, and we all got to the top – no casualties. We then took some houses on the hilltop but lost men in the process. Bren-gunner shot in the face as I directed his fire. Little girl about ten years of age came out from one house and was hit, shot in thigh. Our medics attended to her, but we had to hold the mother off as she went berserk. Huns running. Now got eight or nine men left with me. Shells and mortars now descending on the factory. Decided to try and advance further. Had a close shave – bullets struck the wall 6 inches above my head, which made me very cross. Went after machine-gun nest. Getting Bren gun into position on a ridge when I am hit by enemy sniper and then by machine gun. My boys got me down and gave me morphine. Bullet through both legs and also hit in neck. A bit serious. Our lads get "my" sniper – he was up a tree. Handed over command to Sgt Poulton after blacking out once. Received an apple from one of the lads as a parting gift. Good boys, the right spirit.' As he was strapped to a jeep to be taken for treatment, the lieutenant was cross with himself. 'I don't mind being shot but I do resent being out of the battle. I was just beginning to enjoy myself.'

What Reg Curtis was experiencing, however, was anything but enjoyable. In the bedlam around him he could distinguish every sound – bullets cutting the air, the stonk of mortar bombs, the fizz and clatter of hot shrapnel pinging rooftops. One piece struck his helmet and echoed in his head 'like a pea in a drum'. And there were the human – or, rather, the inhuman – noises of battle. 'Men were shouting curses, lobbing grenades through open doors and windows and following up with shrieks of contempt for the enemy.' The wounded groaned, but the dead said nothing. 'They lay motionless in the road and slumped over walls. A pair of feet protruded from the gateway of a Dutch garden.' The battalion, Curtis realized, was taking fire from every direction and being cut to ribbons.

To his right was the factory, and he raced over open ground for the cover of its walls, 'catapulting forward like an Olympic runner, zigzagging for twenty paces, then hitting the ground and rolling sideways to dodge those Jerry snipers'. They were in windows and behind chimney pots. Some had strapped themselves to the branches of trees. He found a position between the factory and the river and began to snipe back at the snipers. Inside the building, a battle to the death was under way. 'Men were scrapping like gangsters, with grenades, Stens, Colts and knives.' From the far side of the Rhine, German artillery shells were crashing in.

Curtis had his sights lined up on a German in the garden of a terraced house and was about to pull the trigger when he felt a sharp pain and an explosion beneath him. 'The lower part of my right leg was in a most unusual position. Blood was oozing out fast. I was placed on a stretcher and carried to a wooden shed a few yards away, where medics cut the boot from the foot of my shattered leg. It looked awful.' A veteran of North Africa, he'd been carrying a field dressing in his blouse for years and in many different parts of the world and never had to use it. He never thought he'd be a casualty. 'Now I lay there and tore it open.' Amid the pandemonium and the noise, a medic kept a steady hand as he drove a morphine injection into the wounded Curtis. 'Then, while he hunted round for a makeshift splint, a young Dutch girl appeared from nowhere and offered me some water. I was feeling cold and clammy, and her help was of great comfort.'

On a stretcher, Curtis was carried away from the battlefront and hidden behind a garden wall. The scene he left was deteriorating all the time. 'Everyone was scattered. There were dead paras in the road, on the pavement, in gardens. Snipers were busy trying to winkle out those still alive.' But the paras were far from beaten. When they saw muzzle flashes from an upper window 20 yards down the road, four of them pressed themselves into a wall as they worked their way stealthily towards where the firing was coming from. They lobbed grenades inside and followed up by charging the door and spraying Sten-gun fire up through the floorboards. 'A Schmeisser automatic fell from the top window, followed by an SS man.'

For Curtis, too, the fighting was over. He was moved to a barn doubling up as an aid post and then, strapped to the bonnet of a jeep, driven to the makeshift field hospital set up in the Tafelberg Hotel at Oosterbeek. As he was carried into the foyer, he saw the mayhem of many wounded comrades and heard the clatter of gunfire from just outside. Clearly, such was the scope of the battle, there were no safe havens in and around Arnhem. 'Ah well,' he told himself, 'we will have to make the best of it.' It was fast becoming the brave and stoical motto of the entire enterprise.[2]

*

The greater part of the British assault on Arnhem may well have been stopped in its tracks short of its target, but its fighting presence bought time for those on the bridge – time perhaps for XXX Corps to get through. Knowing this, the German military command was desperate to destroy Frost's beleaguered force on the bridge's northern approach as quickly as possible and ordered it to be swept away like a nest of irritating ants. But while other ants were swarming around at the edges, the Germans could not focus their military superiority on the siege at the bridge. They had to spread their forces. What spurred on the likes of Fred Moore as they continued their advance into Arnhem was the message filtering through that Frost's paras had indeed reached their objective. 'But we faced a bloody battle through a built-up area against defended positions.' Progress was so slow that his company was ordered to occupy some houses and try to get some rest. As they settled down they were aware that the Germans were camped in nearby houses too, perhaps even next door.

'We made as little noise as possible,' and Moore had angrily to silence the snores of one of his men to avoid alerting the enemy.

They made an early start next morning, hoping to sneak the remaining 2 miles to the bridge under cover of darkness. They kept to one side of the road, ducking low and creeping along at the back of buildings. They made progress – until the dawn revealed that they were fully exposed to a German artillery position on the other side of the river. 'They raked us with a concentrated barrage. We had nowhere to hide.' Moore's three-man machine-gun crew was sent out into the open to try to pin down the German gunners, a near-suicidal position. He could only watch as one of his crew slumped sideways, dead. 'I pushed his body aside and moved into his position. I hoped that he had been hit by an indiscriminate shot rather than a targeted one. A shout from the rear signalled us to pull out and, stopping only to collect the identity disc from our dead comrade, we beat a hasty retreat. We were but one mile from the bridge!'

This was their limit. Any further advance along this line was blocked by armour and there was no alternative but to fall back. As he withdrew, just up the road, Moore came across Andy Milbourne being attended to by a medic. 'He had been manning a machine gun to cover our retreat and had taken a direct hit. His hands were shattered and his face covered in blood.' Milbourne's own recollection was of being in a garden and firing into a wood where the enemy were massing. 'Shells and mortars kept bursting among us. It seemed as if a thousand devils were raging in our midst. Death reared its ugly head on all sides. German SS infantry were trying to rush us.' He heard himself shouting, 'Let the bastards have it,' and there was 'a flash . . . then stars'. When he came to, his hands felt strange – 'no pain but far away'. He asked where the two men who'd been at his side were. They were dead. 'Now, old son,' a voice said, 'let's get these bandages. Just relax while I give you a jab of morphine. Easy does it.' The next voice he heard was a long time later, and it was German. Milbourne's Arnhem experience would leave him with just one eye and no arms.

That morning, Sergeant Bob Quayle also got as far as he was going to get. The day before had been hell, and he had been caught in the

same 'scary' open ground near the factory as Reg Curtis. He and his
unit had tried to find another route but everywhere was carnage. At
a road junction he came upon para jeeps and trailers parked up but
with their drivers and passengers dead, hanging out of the doors at
grotesque angles. 'I decided it was too dangerous to advance along
the street, so took the lads through back gardens and on to a track by
the river bank. We did well for some time but came under heavy
machine-gun fire again. We had to get into the river for cover, and it
was very cold.'³ They spent the night in a house near Arnhem's St
Elizabeth Hospital, down by the river on the town's western edge,
and he got his men up early next day for what he hoped would be the
last leg to the bridge. He was leading them down an alley back to the
river when he heard a noise. A lieutenant with five riflemen emerged
out of the mist and asked him where he was going. 'To the bridge,
where else?' he replied. He was put straight. 'No, you're not.' Things
had moved on, orders changed, realities had to be accepted. 'We've
been sent,' the lieutenant continued, 'to contact as many men as possible and tell them to forget going forward to the bridge. Take up
defensive positions, Sergeant, and hold out as long as you can.'

Forget the bridge – it was official. What had been the primary objective of the mission had just been cancelled, for his unit at least.
Clearly, things were not going well and they were being forced to fall
back. Quayle moved his men into a semi-detached house and waited.
'Very soon the rattle of tanks came up the road and we opened fire,
with little effect.' He had thought he and his men were isolated and
on their own but was reassured at seeing firing coming from other
houses nearby. 'We were not alone, then.' But any semblance of a
battle-plan seemed to be disintegrating. Fred Moore could not help
noticing the total confusion in the para ranks. 'No one seemed to be
in command as we retraced our steps, back towards our starting
point,' he recalled. 'The battalion had, to all intents and purposes,
ceased to exist as a defined unit. We were now a mixed group from
different units and battalions with no clear destination or purpose.'
Some sense of order had to be restored or this could all too easily
turn into an ignominious rout.

That it didn't was because the surviving officers rallied and took hold of the situation. As they urgently conferred on what to do next, Moore nosed round a nearby building and came across a large kitchen with a stove, a frying pan and a supply of eggs. It was too good an opportunity to miss, and he set to work. The eggs were sizzling in the pan, the yolks firming and the whites turning nicely white, his mouth watering . . . and suddenly he had to abandon the feast. There were new orders. German tanks had been sighted. The troops were to evacuate the area immediately and regroup at Oosterbeek, where a defensive perimeter was to be set up. Moore was ordered to stay behind with his machine gun for a quarter of an hour to cover the rear of the retreating column. His appetite was gone. 'I was not altogether thrilled at seeing the last of the column disappear around the bend in the road, leaving us behind. We scanned the approaches to our position and listened for any sound of armour coming my way. I mentally counted each interminably long passing second until the fifteen minutes were up and we set off to catch up with the main body.'

When he reached the column, it was under attack. A low-flying Messerschmitt roared over and scared everyone half to death, but the real danger was from clanking German tanks that could be heard approaching over a hill *in front*. Was their escape route about to be cut off? An anti-tank crew was deployed forward and as the first panzer – 'a huge monster' – came over the crest, they fired and hit it head on. It ground to a halt across the road and there was a cheer from the British ranks. But a second tank followed. This one fired and hit the British anti-tank crew, killing them both, but not before they had managed to unleash a last shell. It struck home, and the second tank burst into flames. The way to Oosterbeek was unblocked. 'We rounded a bend in the road to find a number of houses on each side – a defensible position at last. We occupied the houses and dug slit trenches in the gardens at strategic points.' The bridge at Arnhem was forgotten, an irrelevance now. Here in Oosterbeek, a fresh battle, every bit as fierce and deadly, was about to begin.

*

The Dutch were distraught. Anje van Maanen had been exultant at the arrival of the British soldiers and, when a stranger among the jubilant crowd celebrating on the main street of Oosterbeek had suggested that the Germans might well be coming back, she had dismissed him as drunk or mad. Now she wasn't so sure. She and her brother Paul watched from their attic window as khaki-clad airborne soldiers who earlier had been parading openly through the town began showing signs of nervousness. They were hugging the cover of buildings, avoiding crossing the road: 'All very strange.' Four Tommies, as she called them, had taken up residence in what had been a German slit trench, and she took them some tea. Two were washing and shaving and another was pulling on his pipe. They seemed relaxed enough. 'Is Monty coming soon?' she asked eagerly, and they replied, 'Within the hour. We've just heard it on the radio.' They told her that the Airborne had captured the bridge at Arnhem and were now simply waiting for XXX Corps, the spearhead of the British Second Army, to relieve them. She wasn't totally convinced. 'We can hear guns in the distance. Clearly, the fighting around the bridge is still going on.'

As if to confirm this, she saw wounded soldiers being driven into her street and taken to the Tafelberg Hotel, where she knew her father was running a field hospital to help the British. Earlier she had shuddered and screamed at the sight of German corpses in the street, 'their dead eyes staring at me', and now the carnage was continuing. 'I don't dare to look at the jeeps passing our house carrying the wounded. Suddenly, we hear a whistling noise above our heads. Bullets! We are being fired on and we are scared. It must be a German sniper firing from a tree or a rooftop. We hide.' Her father came home with tales of treating the wounded and urged her to visit one young soldier, whose birthday it was. 'I promise I'll go but I'm embarrassed, and I never do, which is sad because he died.' That night, as evening fell, so did the optimism of the day. 'There is more shooting now and we have a queer feeling that things are not going as well as we hoped. The great army is not here yet.' The family stared into the distance from the rooftop and could make out lights on the road from Nijmegen to Arnhem. 'We think that must be

Monty. But we are also a little bit afraid. Outside, the shooting is louder and getting nearer.'

In the morning, the news was no better and, if anything, worse. Apparently, the Dutch resistance groups had been told to take off their orange armbands. 'The situation is still too dangerous for them to come out in the open. Better to wait until all is safe. We are terribly disappointed. This must mean that things are not going well with the liberation. Are we going to have the Germans back again? *Oh no.*' Anje's anxiety was not allayed when she spotted coming down the street not Germans but 'very strange figures with trolleys, bags and suitcases. They look like beggars. Who are these people?' She went to the front door and was told they were refugees fleeing from Arnhem. 'I think to myself, how ridiculous. They must be out of their minds. But more and more appear – young couples, old tired women and men. And they are all carrying things or pushing prams. There are weeping kids too.' She was gratified to see the Tommies climb out of their trench to help – 'they are such gentlemen.' The stream, though, seemed endless, as now were the jeeps passing on their way to the Tafelberg with wounded lashed in pairs across their bonnets.

The refugee situation hit home when family friends, the Aalbers, arrived in the street with their bags and asked if they could stay. Their house was on the outskirts of Oosterbeek, but there had been fighting and they had taken fright and left. 'They look terrible, exhausted and almost mad with fear. Over tea at the table, they tell us how they had a little British tank in their garden which was firing at Germans on the other side of the railway track. The Germans fired back and set their house ablaze and they had to flee through a rain of bullets, climbing over the gate and creeping through gardens.' All this was a shock for Anje, the more so when she was sent to her room to pack in case she had to flee too. 'I thought we were free, that the war was over. The future had looked so perfect. I just couldn't understand it. I was devastated.' Upstairs, she crammed a cardigan, new black shoes, socks, stockings, underwear and a toothbrush into a small bag. 'I also put in my little box with a few jewels in, but Aunt Anke takes them out and says it's better to put them in the safe.'

At her house in Oosterbeek, Marie-Anne had the dismaying

experience of seeing large numbers of British soldiers heading her way from the direction of Arnhem. 'We cannot be certain what they are doing, but we are afraid they are retreating.' Two asked to come in and went upstairs to set up a look-out post. 'They remain in Mummy and Daddy's bedroom. When they come down again, we ask them if they want to wash. They like that, as they are very dirty. We fry some potatoes for them, with apple sauce. They tell us their names are Len and Gerald. Len is thirty and married with two boys. Gerald is twenty-one, married but has no children. Neither of them has had any sleep for three nights.' The two soldiers passed the word, and soon others came by to refresh themselves. 'They are very grateful for the opportunity. One of them gives me a dark red scarf. They are all very nice boys.'

At the van Maanens', the cellar was prepared for the night with mattresses on the floor and a cushion under the window for the dog. 'We fill the bath, buckets and tins with water. Anything combustible is taken out to the garage.' Suitcases were stowed under the stairs, along with brother Paul's accordion, in case a quick getaway was needed. Anje headed outside with more tea for the soldiers in their slit trench. 'When is Monty coming?' she asked for the umpteenth time. 'In a quarter of an hour,' they say. 'We stop and strain our ears and imagine we can hear the tanks in the distance, but it is not true and the waiting goes on. I help a soldier with a sprained ankle to walk to the hospital. He has come from Arnhem on this foot and collapsed in front of our house. More and more people are arriving from there. They say corpses are lying everywhere and there is fighting all over the place. The bridge is no-man's land. It must be like hell.'

That night, the van Maanens and the Aalbers, a dozen of them in all, crammed into the candle-lit cellar. 'Some of us go to sleep right away, in spite of the stuffiness and the tension. But with such a crowd you cannot expect to be comfortable. Eventually, everyone is settled and sleeps, or at least pretends to. Then, at midnight, we all stir, and some start to toss about. I get up and go upstairs for some fresh air. Outside, I look up at the stars and the scarlet sky. There seems to be fire everywhere around us. Paul and I go to the top of the house and look out hoping to see Monty's army. There are an awful lot of lights out there. That must be Monty now. We rush downstairs to tell everyone the good news and with a feeling of reassurance we go to sleep again.

'From time to time I am woken by funny little sharp cracks outside, around the house, as if someone is throwing gravel on the pavement. Most peculiar. Maybe it's pistol shot. I hear thunder in the distance and shooting. Out there, thousands of men are wide awake, fighting for our freedom . . .'

Liberation still seemed the likely outcome – the Germans would be forced away again and the Allies would win this battle. After all, even if Monty's army was more enquired about than actual, some reinforcements had come. The day before, everyone had thrilled to the sight of more British parachutists and gliders arriving in open ground to the west, a bit further out from where the original landings had been. Anje had noted excitedly 'thousands of aeroplanes filling the sky and all sorts of coloured parachutes dropping – red, blue, white, orange, green, yellow, like a bunch of flowers. We wave and jump around.' Marie-Anne was excited too, as also were the soldiers in her house. 'It is a magnificent sight to see those large gliders landing and red, white, blue and green parachutes bringing more munitions and food.' And men. Surely they would turn the tide back in the Allies' favour? This second 'lift' of parachute and glider troops would make all the difference, wouldn't it?

*

It was always part of the Market Garden plan to drop troops into the Netherlands. There was no other choice. The Allies simply did not have enough transport planes and glider tugs to get a total of 34,000 men, 2,000 vehicles, 568 guns and 5,000 tons of equipment behind enemy lines in one go. If Arnhem had been the sole objective of the operation, then a single lift would have been possible, but the Americans also had to be fed into the Eindhoven and Nijmegen areas on day one in order to secure the 'carpet' for the land forces to get to Arnhem. This, however, restricted the number of planes available to the British for their initial assault and therefore the number of men they got on the ground in the early stages. It was a crucial compromise that, in the event, jeopardized the entire mission. The second lift should have turned the tide of the battle in favour of the Airborne, but it was in trouble before it even began.

It came in on the afternoon of Monday 18 September, hours later than planned because fog over the airfields in England delayed take-off. As he finally boarded his plane, sapper Arthur Ayers, a plasterer by trade before the war but now a parachutist, was, as he freely admitted, 'raring to go'. The last time he had been in Europe was at the time of Dunkirk; he had managed to escape in one of the very last boats home. Going back four years later completed the circle from defeat to what seemed certain to be victory. As he peeped out of the window at the sea below, he got the jitters. 'What the hell was I doing here, waiting to jump into enemy-occupied territory? I must be mad to have joined the paratroopers. Why did I? Was it the glamour of the red beret and the blue wings insignia? Was it the sense of adventure or the challenge of the unknown?' If so, all too quickly the 'unknown' was staring him in the face, and it wasn't nice.

Unlike the 'piece of cake' first lift, when the Germans had been taken by surprise and put up little anti-aircraft fire, now the flak gunners on the ground were all action. Black puffs of smoke filled the sky. As Ayers stood by the door of his Dakota for the run-in, he wondered, 'My God, how can they miss us?' He could see other aircraft in the formation, and one was suddenly lit up by a bright flash. 'It seemed to shudder then banked slowly away. Yellow flames and dirty black smoke trailed from one of the engines as it turned in a half-circle, then with horrible inevitability spiralled earthwards. It dropped out of my vision and I felt sick inside, imagining all too clearly the scene inside – the trapped paratroopers waiting like ourselves for the order to jump. Even if they had the presence of mind to jettison themselves, it would be of no avail because they would be too close to the ground.' Another aircraft came into view, with both engines alight, and he counted five jumpers before the plane erupted in a sheet of flame. 'I stared in disbelief as bits of flaming aircraft and small black objects' – men – 'started to fall to the ground. I felt a desperate urgency to get out of this flying death-trap, and I could see from their strained faces that the others in my stick had the same desire.' The moment the green light flashed, they were out.

Meanwhile, down on the ground, sapper Jo Johanson was relieved to see the mass of Dakotas overhead at last. He was part of the force held back from the advance on Arnhem to protect the drop zones to the west of the town. When the planes were late and the skies remained ominously empty, a terrible thought had passed through his mind that perhaps they had all been shot down or forced to turn back. He considered an optimistic possibility – that Monty's army had already made it to the Arnhem bridge and the second lift had been cancelled as unnecessary – but on second thoughts, 'this seemed too good to be true.'⁴ As the weather-delayed armada winged its way over and the parachutes began to fall like dandelion seeds in the wind, he found himself taking fire from a substantial enemy force hidden in the woods around the heather-topped DZ. Clouds of white smoke were billowing, punctuated by the bright flashes of the recognition flares sent up by the British ground party.

Ayers drifted down, enjoying those few fleeting seconds of tranquillity beneath the canopy that were every paratrooper's special experience. 'The silence was broken by the sound of automatic weapons below. Little red lights were flying up towards me and strange sighing noises going past in the air. It was enemy tracer bullets. They were trying to pick us off as we floated down. I heard a scream nearby and saw a paratrooper, falling parallel with me, clutching his stomach. He had a pained, surprised look on his face and I realized he'd been hit. A shudder went through my body. That could have been me.' As he neared the ground, he felt every German gun around was trained on him.

And then he was down. A clumsy landing, falling on his back, striking his head heavily on the ground, lying there dazed. He grabbed for his kitbag and his Sten gun. It was useless, the barrel bent into a U by the impact with the ground. This was not good, especially when he got to his feet and surveyed the chaos and the menace of the landing zone. Instead of the soft scent of heather, 'a heavy pall of smoke hung over us and I could smell the acrid tang of cordite and burning vegetation.' He was in enemy-occupied territory – and unarmed. 'The sound of rifle fire and the staccato burst of an automatic weapon echoed across the heath.' As he looked for his RV, his rendezvous point, he saw dark figures advancing towards him. 'Friend or foe? I had no idea.' Then he recognized the familiar green camouflage smocks of the British paratrooper. 'It's all right,' one of them called out. 'He's one of *ours*.' The implication was that there were plenty of *theirs* on and around the landing zone that day.

Captain Theo Redman, a para medical officer, ran into *them* the instant he landed. 'They appeared through the trees,' he recalled, 'no more than 20 yards away, firing as they came.' He and two other men with him tried to find cover as bullets kicked up earth around them. One of his companions was shot dead and he himself was hit in the arm. 'There seemed little future in trying to take them on with my revolver so we gave ourselves up.'⁵ Such was the opposition now amassing to fight off the airborne attack, his war was over before it had even begun.

Meanwhile, Arthur Ayers had found his squadron of engineers in a wood and was relieved to be back among friends. 'Considering the reception we had, I was surprised to hear about 80 per cent had reported to the RV.' He was given a replacement Sten, which had belonged to a poor lad 'who wouldn't need it any more'. The troops lined up for what they imagined would be the march towards Arnhem. They looked pretty shambolic – 'like a circus', according to Johansen. 'Every jeep was towing a trolley or a cart with the heavy kit on. Some men were walking, some riding motorcycles, some riding pushbikes and the rest perched on the mountains of kit.'⁶ Already the plan of action was changing. The direct route ahead – the one they had been briefed to take – was impassable due to enemy action, and the men were sent a different way, winding through the woods. Ayers remembered seeing a German soldier lying face up in a ditch with a neat round hole in the centre of his helmet. 'Derogatory remarks were made as we filed by about the only good German being a dead one, but my thoughts were for his mother and father, perhaps a wife and young children.' From the sky came the sound of low-flying aircraft. 'Spitfires,' said a hopeful voice. 'Air cover for us.' He was wrong. 'Jerries!' the shout went up, and they dived for a ditch. Bullets sprayed down the road and through the foliage. Ayers pressed himself into the rich Dutch earth and prayed not to end up like the German he'd just seen. 'They made one more swoop over our position, then made off as quickly as they had come. We clambered out of the ditch, miraculously without any casualties.'

It wasn't supposed to be like this. According to the plan, the bridge should have been secured by now and the men of the second lift having an easy passage along enemy-free roads to reinforce the battalions already there. Instead, the advance slowed to a crawl and then to a stop as they took up defensive positions along the Ede–Arnhem railway line, miles from the bridge. When they set off again, they came under another aerial attack from three Me109s, so low that Ayers could see the black crosses on their fuselages. 'I crouched low, feeling exposed and vulnerable. I heard a man scream out in pain, as a bullet found its mark. A few brave souls returned the fire with their automatic weapons but their efforts were unfruitful.' After the strafing, they advanced a little, then dug in; a pattern, slow and morale-sapping, was setting in. In their latest slit trench in a pretty, wooded valley, Ayers chatted to his mate, a 21-year-old from Leeds with an attractive blonde wife and chubby six-month-old baby son back at home. Photographs were swapped, Ayers pulling a small snap of Lola from his wallet. He wondered what his bride of three weeks was doing. Suddenly, thoughts of home were interrupted by a shout. Black dots had been seen in the distance, advancing their way. Germans! Ayers lay, waiting, for the order to fire. 'My nerves tingled. This was my first encounter with enemy troops. My heart beat faster and there was a tightness in my stomach.' He peeped over the top at the distinctive bucket-shaped helmets, a dozen of them, automatic weapons at the ready, getting closer.

The voice of his sergeant ended the suspense: 'Let 'em have it, lads' – and the troops let loose with everything they had. '"How can we have failed to hit them," I thought, "with that withering field of fire?" But apparently we had, because they were soon returning fire. Bullets streaked by, thudding into the tree trunks and branches just above our trench.' A man nearby screamed in pain, and a gutsy medic dived through a hail of bullets to get to him. The firing stopped, to be followed by an unearthly silence, the sound of men waiting to know if they were about to die or not. But there was no fresh attack. The enemy had gone, leaving two dead bodies behind. 'We conjectured it had been a small patrol scouting the area.' But conjecture was all it was. The bigger picture eluded them, as it did many similar parties of men caught up in skirmishes like this all over the western approaches to Arnhem as the master battle-plan disintegrated in the face of tougher than expected enemy opposition. Over the radio came news confirming that Frost's battalion was at the bridge but under constant attack and fighting to hold on. The second lift had come to reinforce them, but now there was little chance of getting anywhere near them. 'It was becoming a grave possibility that they would soon be cut off from the rest of the division,' Ayers solemnly noted. 'This was disheartening.'

He and his men continued in the direction of Arnhem. What else could they do? The battlefield had descended into confusion. Some units were retreating, others were holding defensive positions, but the bridge still needed reinforcing and, in the absence of any other orders, Ayers and his men went on. 'We marched along a dusty road in files of twelve men on alternating sides, keeping on the alert for any signs of the enemy. The road seemed to stretch for miles.' There were more brushes with the enemy, with more bloody outcomes. Ayers passed lines of the dead – 'some dressed in para-smocks and others in field-grey uniforms. British and German alike, they lay there together, pitiful bundles of rag and blood. Pitiful reminders of the waste and uselessness of war.' At a crossroads, they encountered a British patrol with new instructions. There was still no way ahead and they were to make for a large country mansion on the edge of Oosterbeek and take up defensive positions. It was around this, the Hartenstein Hotel, that the 1st Airborne was re-forming.

Despite this order to pull back, 'we were still in good spirits. There was no thought that it might all end in disaster. We still thought the Second Army would be here in two or three days to relieve us.' But not everyone was so upbeat. A para major who came in on the second lift was appalled by what he saw as a disastrous lack of leadership on the ground. The further he progressed from the drop zone, the more frustrated he became. 'We could hear the sound of heavy fighting not far ahead but no one seemed to know what was going on or why. There was a good deal of speculation among those from whom I tried to obtain information, most of it somewhat defeatist. No one seemed to be in overall command, and the men appeared to have lost confidence in their officers. The euphoria had evaporated and morale had sunk to a dangerously low level.'[7]

*

Gliders dropped in, too, on that second lift, and for those in the back and in the cockpit the ride was not just bumpier than the first lift had experienced but downright dangerous. Captain Harry Roberts, a REME (Royal Electrical and Mechanical Engineers) officer, hated being in a Horsa – 'such a flimsy plywood contraption' – and would much rather have been on the end of a parachute.[8] He was caught short on the trip – too many cups of tea before take-off – and, somewhere past the Dutch coastline, was standing to urinate into the rubber tube that served as the on-board 'facility' when the plane bucked violently. A gaping hole in the fuselage opened up between his legs. Shrapnel from ack-ack shells had raked the plane and nearly robbed him of his manhood. It was only the start of his troubles. The glider pilot slipped the tow rope and nosed downwards, spotted his landing zone, lined up to cruise in . . . but was forced to bank away as the plane in front disintegrated in mid-air and another spun sideways out of control.

This was supposed to be an unopposed landing, protected by the men who had dropped the day before. In fact, a wholesale battle was under way between the perimeter defence force and German troops, and the gliders were coming down plumb in the middle of it. As his glider finally touched down and was sliding to a halt, Roberts threw himself out while it was still moving. A machine-gun burst from point-blank range hit him in the back. His gas-mask, strapped across the small of his back, took the edge off the impact. The bullet chipped his spine and flicked through the muscles in his back before stopping short of a vital organ. He was paralysed from the waist down but alive – unlike his driver, who had jumped beside him, and the two glider pilots.

Dick Ennis, co-pilot of another glider, was also in deep trouble. The minute he dropped the tow-rope and went into free flight near the landing zone, the aircraft was hit by flak. 'A shell burst smashed our port wing-tip and the kite rocked and heeled.'[9] The first pilot was slumped in his seat, blood from his head spreading across the perspex windscreen. Ennis grabbed the controls. 'My one thought was to get down.' But his flaps had gone and parts of the wing were breaking up. It was do or die. 'I pulled the kite into a steep turn, stuck the nose down and headed for a patch of the field. I was over-shooting, without enough height left to turn in. Straight ahead was a wood. I pulled back on the stick in an effort to pancake on top of the trees, but the damaged kite was slow to respond. We hit the trees head-on with well over 100mph on the clock. I should have been killed but I went straight through the perspex instead. I ploughed along the ground and finished up among the trees about 20 yards from the glider.' He came to, still strapped to his seat, and struggled to his feet to find a Dutch woman offering him a drink. 'It may have been port, or sherry or even cocoa,' he recalled, 'but it did pull me together a little.' He dashed back to his plane, now virtually matchwood, with a couple of trees lying across it. 'Everything was deadly quiet. I called out the first pilot's name but there was no answer. I made for the tail and heard movements inside. I hammered on the door and forced it open. Our two passengers alighted, very shaken, but quite safe and sound. We found Allan [his first pilot] lying with the jeep and trailer on top of him, but in all probability he was killed in the air before we crashed. I removed his identity disc and we buried him quietly beside the glider.'

One corner of the landing zone was taking a particular battering. The Revd George Pare, a padre with the Glider Pilot Regiment, was with the ground protection force and in a rescue party that rushed to the scene to find that some men from the gliders had managed to make it to shelter but many others were still out in the open, pinned down by enemy gunfire. 'I grasped a red cross flag, beckoned to two stretcher bearers to follow me and, with palpitating heart and waving my flag, set off. Five gliders were heaps of ashes and smouldering. Bodies were stretched out on the grass. They had all been shot in the back as they tried to reach the shelter of the trees. I was wearing my clerical collar and I sent up a prayer. We reached the first body and the soldier was dead. I moved to the next, and he groaned in thankfulness. I told the bearers to do no more than apply a very quick dressing, and then, since the shooting had stopped, waved my hand for a jeep to come out of the wood and get him. The last man I came to was beside a dead body. To my astonishment, he was not wounded, but prostrate with grief at the death of his friend.' Still waving his red cross flag, Pare now made his way slowly back to cover. 'No sooner was I there than a fusillade of shots crashed into the trees. For the first time I thought well of the enemy. We had been in his view all the time, and his fire had been deliberately withheld.'[10]

Meanwhile, with bullets flying over his head, the paralysed Harry Roberts had somehow managed to haul himself into a shallow gully. He saw a figure at the end and laboriously edged towards it, only to realize that the man was a German. He turned as best he could on legs that would not move and headed in the opposite direction, towards his own lines, he hoped, but the gully petered out. He was stuck in no-man's land, shattered and physically drained. Lying there, 'my brain went into overdrive. I could not face up to the prospect of spending the rest of my life in a wheelchair and I considered ending it all with a Mills grenade. But I still had my much-loved Lee-Enfield rifle. If I could only get a German in my sights, it would be more in keeping with my character than suicide.' He lined up all his spare cartridges in a neat row, checked he had a round in the breech and waited. 'I found myself studying the beautiful wood grain on the butt and breathing in the faint smell of oil, as if it was an aphrodisiac. I reckoned I would have time to get off the best part of a magazine before the enemy located the source of fire. Then, with a bit of luck I would never feel the head or heart shot that killed me.'

He spotted a German behind a nearby bush and levered himself up into a firing position. 'He was so close it was impossible to miss.' One shot and the man fell, but Roberts continued to pump bullets into the undergrowth. Then another German ran across in front of him, but Roberts was too slow to react and cursed himself. 'The object of the exercise was to take as many of the enemy with me as possible. I had evened up the score a little, but to blaze away like that was pathetic.' He needed to be cold and clinical. 'It was difficult to repress thoughts of home and family, but it was necessary. There was no place for love, hope or beauty in my life, just bloody revenge.' He flattened himself against the ground, 'snug in the security of my gully', and discarded his red beret and brass cap badge, which might attract the enemy's eyes to him. He took snap shots, like a sniper, at the enemy until he was so exhausted he could barely move his arms and shoulders. 'The end came quite suddenly. I sighted three clear targets setting up a machine gun. I could not believe my luck, and I forgot all basic self-preservation, especially the old soldier's superstition of never lighting three cigarettes from one match. The first shot was easy. Bullets were whizzing round me as I took the second, but what happened to the third will forever remain a mystery. I can vaguely recall a blow to my head and then everything blacked out.'

He came to with blood pouring from his face. A German bullet had hit the metal bolt of his rifle and sent it crashing into his head. He was not seriously injured by it, but the rifle was now useless. 'My private war was over.' He lay there and toyed with the Mills grenade again as a solution to his predicament. His contemplation was shattered by a bullet crashing into his shoulder. 'I was now immobilized, with blood flowing from three areas of my body, none of which I could reach. There was nothing else to do except leave it to fate and hope that our side won the battle still raging above my head.' He was lucky. The paras won this particular skirmish. A stretcher party found him and took him to a first-aid post and then to the field hospital in Oosterbeek. 'They discovered seventeen bullet holes in my smock.'[11] And he hadn't even got off the landing zone. The second lift – flown in to reinforce the first – was getting nowhere fast.

By now, Dick Ennis, after taking time to bury his pilot, had managed to escape the LZ, though it hadn't been easy. The jeep he had carried in the back of his glider was a wreck, and it was a while before he hooked up with the other glider pilots. The squadron had set up headquarters in an asylum for the blind. 'The patients were seated quietly in the grounds with their nurses looking after them. They kept asking if the Germans would return. We told them the British had arrived to stay, and they need have no more fear of Germans. At that time, we were still confident that everything would be a walk-over.' The pilots – now transformed into foot soldiers – were ordered to join a column heading not for Arnhem, as they might have expected, but somewhere called Oosterbeek, which had never figured in anyone's plans.

*

The odds were moving against a successful mission with almost every development. The bulk of the airborne forces advancing on Arnhem were being driven back. The second lift bringing reinforcements had been ambushed. With an advance party of Polish troops and light armour coming in gliders, Ron Kent's reconnaissance platoon was dispatched to try to defend the landing zone in the hotly contested area north of Oosterbeek.[12] Once they disembarked, Kent was also to pass on orders that, instead of making its way to Arnhem, his platoon should head for Oosterbeek. Messerschmitts gave them trouble again, strafing their defensive positions in the woods around the LZ. When the noise stopped and he looked up, leaves, twigs and even whole branches littered the ground. Protecting the incoming planes was going to be virtually impossible, if they ever got here. They were late, 'damn gliders'. Finally, they appeared overhead, 'long and broad-winged Horsas, moving in the air like graceful black swans', in Kent's view. A hail of flak went up to greet them and they were suddenly swans no more but sitting ducks. The Messerschmitts were having a field day too, and observers on the ground watched in horror as one glider was hit by cannon-fire on its approach and broke apart 'like a matchbox'.[13] A jeep, a gun and people fell out, looking like toys as they tumbled through the air.

Kent was helpless as German mortars and machine guns raked the landing zone. 'As the gliders came into land, some crashed into one another as pilots, riddled by bullets or hit by flak, lost control. Some made beautiful landings, only to be cut to pieces on the ground.' Their thin plywood walls were no protection. 'I saw one literally torn in two on landing. Few of the men inside survived and those who did emerged staggering and collapsed immediately after.'

Kent left the safety of his position, ran out into the open field and dashed from plane to plane, trying to help. 'From the body of one poor Pole, I snatched a fighting knife and used it to hack my way into a glider that was riddled like a sieve with bullet holes. But no one emerged.' He went to the next glider and the one after that, all the way down the line. Stunned troops were scrambling out, and he pointed them towards cover. As he got closer to the woods he came under fire himself from Germans hidden in the trees. 'I turned and fired a burst of Sten-gun fire in the general direction from which I was being shot at, then, wheeling, crouching and zig-zagging, I hared my way back to the platoon position across half a mile of ploughed land. Thank God I was fit.' The chaos on the landing site was such that, in one corner, British soldiers mistook Poles running for cover for Germans and opened fire on them. Panicked Poles fired back at British soldiers helping to unload gliders.

That wasn't the end of it. Kent's platoon was now under attack from German infantry moving through the trees towards them, under the cover of smoke. 'Glider pilots and Poles were crammed inside our perimeter, and one or two fell, shot where they stood. They had expected nothing like this and seemed to take time grasping the situation. I imagined I would too if I'd been dumped into this turmoil just two and a half hours after leaving England. They had not yet learned to keep close to the ground as we had.' The Germans were still coming on through the woods, closing in. 'We could hear their voices as they tried to infiltrate through the woods. I caught sight of an officer with white piping on his epaulettes, chivvying his men on. He was 25 yards away. I squinted down the sights of my Sten gun and squeezed the trigger. He went down, and our Bren-gunner cut the rest of the party to pieces as they tried to rush across the open ground to get behind us.' But this could only be a temporary reprieve. More Germans appeared. The paras' position was hopeless. 'We fell back.'

It was a tortuous withdrawal back to the perimeter line around Oosterbeek. The sounds of battle were everywhere but the actual fighting must have been in small pockets, because large tracts of the countryside and even the roads were deserted. The atmosphere was eerie in the extreme as they walked in fear and expectation of a deadly burst of gunfire from every bush and around every corner. A jeep shot down the road, stopped, and a red-bereted officer pointed them in the direction of divisional headquarters. 'We marched on, slowly and carefully towards Oosterbeek.' Back behind his own lines, safe for the time being at least, Kent took stock as once more he dug into a new defensive position and placed his section's Bren-gun, mortar and rifle men among some pine trees. 'We had been on the move nearly sixty hours with little rest and only makeshift meals. We knew that some of the Division were holding the bridge at Arnhem, while we were now forming this defensive circle at Oosterbeek.' At least he could see some military point to what was happening, some light in the confusion and chaos. 'Being where we are is diverting the enemy from an all-out attack on the force holding the bridge,' he told himself, and he was right. For all concerned, it was a case of hanging on.

6. 'If You Knows a Better 'Ole'

Every British soldier knew who Old Bill was, and his wisecracks from 1914–18 could still raise a knowing smile among them. With his tin hat and walrus moustache, he was the quintessential cartoon Cockney squaddie, created and immortalized in ink by artist and First World War army captain Bruce Bairnsfather. His most famous drawing had the veteran sharing with a much younger infantryman the sort of filthy, rain-sodden Flanders trench that Bairnsfather had known only too well. The bedraggled youngster's complaint about the conditions was met with Old Bill's most memorable riposte, a catchphrase from 1915 that could have been invented for what was now happening in and around Arnhem – 'If you knows a better 'ole, go to it.'[1] The strung-out men of the 1st Airborne, spread out in pockets of differing sizes from Oosterbeek to Arnhem itself, were finding themselves in some pretty fancy 'oles, as well as some downright awful ones.

In the defensive perimeter now forming piecemeal around Oosterbeek, Arthur Ayers gazed in admiration at the Sonnenberg, a grand house that could have passed for a little piece of gentrified old England. 'It was a large building, very similar to a Victorian country mansion,' he said. 'There were several outbuildings, and a tall tower stood at one side. On one side was a covered veranda, with chairs placed here and there. The green lawns reached down to a wooded area, which nearly surrounded the building, apart from a gap where a driveway led out to the road.' They were clearly not its first military occupiers. 'It was obvious that it had been a billet for German soldiers, who, judging by the remnants, had left in a hurry.' The question was how far they had gone – not very far, probably – and whether they would be back, which increasingly looked a certainty. Ayers took his place in the semicircle of slit trenches outside while others in his company climbed to the top floors as lookouts.

He was sent out in a jeep on a scouting mission to find out what was happening at another house not far away from which reports were coming of a mortar attack. He and an officer drove along a met-alled road for half a mile, then turned into a narrow track between a wood and an open field. Suddenly, several paratroopers appeared among the trees, shouting and gesticulating. 'We took this as a greet-ing and waved back.' In fact, the paras in the distance were frantically calling out a warning: Germans! 'A hail of bullets came flying from the field, pinging on the side of the jeep and throwing up clouds of dust as they hit the ground.' Ayers and the officer had wandered into the middle of a fight and were in no-man's land, something that was all too easy to do in such a fluid situation. It would be all too easy to die as well, and they would have done if they had not thrown them-selves into cover. They didn't hang around long. 'With covering fire from our chaps, we then dived simultaneously back into the jeep. With the engine roaring, we shot off up the track, heads well down as the enemy opened up at us again. At a sharp bend, the vehicle skid-ded towards a large tree. I tensed myself for the pile-up, but the lieutenant swung the steering wheel and we missed the tree by inches.' Here was another lesson that Old Bill would have relished. If the bullets didn't get you, desperate driving to escape them might.

*

In this increasingly chaotic situation, reliable battlefield information was hard to come by. With almost all the radios down because of technical malfunctions and problems of range, did anyone have a clear overall picture? Almost certainly not. Practically speaking, the Arnhem bridge was now a separate and increasingly desperate battle of its own. But beyond the city limits there were many soldiers in the dark about what was happening and, while most of those who had tried and failed to get to the bridge were now in a fighting retreat through the town's suburbs and outskirts and heading back to Oost-erbeek, there were others still making valiant attempts to get through to the main objective. Glider pilot Alan Kettley was one of them. He had come in on the second lift and was with his squadron near the church at Oosterbeek when his commander's frustrations got the better of him. All communications had broken down and no one had any idea what was happening up ahead. The commander sent Kettley on a one-man mission to get to the bridge and report back. The staff sergeant set off on foot, a lonely figure trudging down what was now an empty road to Arnhem. There was virtually no opposition. If it was all as easy as this he would soon be able to whistle up reinforcements.

That was until he got to the outskirts of the main town, 'and suddenly some bugger's shooting at me.' It was a shock – 'a wake-up call' – because, in his pre-war life as a stock clerk for Sainsbury's and in four and a half years of military service, he'd never had someone trying to kill him. 'I knew it wasn't personal but I didn't like being a target.' He dived behind the wall of someone's front garden to get out of the sniper's way. Then he worked his way round the enemy positions as best he could, 'and continued my way forward towards the bridge'. But heavy machine-gun fire stopped his progress. There was a road he had to cross but, every time he tried, he was met by bursts of fire. He had to face up to it – the bridge was out of reach, a conclusion that was confirmed when half a dozen jeeps and trailers came crawling towards him with wounded men hanging off the backs. One told him, just in case he missed the signs, that it was 'hell at the bridge'; they'd had to get out and he'd be wise to do the same.

By now it wasn't just snipers who were blocking the way into the town. When glider pilot Eric Webbley had 'another bash' at getting through to the bridge, he was to be faced with the weapon the infantry most feared – tanks. He was at a crossroads next to a park where a large number of British soldiers were installed and trying to fight back. Anti-tank guns were lined up to blast the enemy positions and the troops lined up to follow in with a rifle and bayonet charge. 'Suddenly a Jerry Tiger nosed its way around the corner at the end of the street. A cry of "Tanks!" went up and folk began to move to cover.' One of the guns roared and spat out a shell meant for the Tiger. But, as Webbley wrote sarcastically in his memoirs, 'The gods who sit up above and watch all these things must have decided that the odds against us weren't great enough.' From nowhere, a British jeep accidentally backed into the line of fire and took the full impact. 'Both the jeep and the gun blew up and the blast hurled people right and left. Pieces of stone and metal ripped past us and ugly red patches showed up all over the road. Everyone began to panic and move back.' And then, as if enough damage had not been self-inflicted, the Tiger opened up. 'Once again the air was filled with flying stones and the groans and cries of the fellows who'd been hit.' What staggered Webbley was the speed at which a carefully planned attack had turned into complete chaos. Sniping from top-floor windows and a strafing from some passing German fighter planes completed the 'bloody shambles'.

Morale was shattered as well as bodies. There was still one anti-tank gun operational, and Webbley deployed it for the next time the Tiger might appear. He was, he admitted, 'utterly scared' as he crouched against a tiny hedge and waited. He could do with some back-up and discovered that there were thirty or so troopers sheltering in a nearby building. His plea for help was turned down flat. They were shell-shocked and immovable. 'An officer told us that nothing would shift the fellows at that moment and the best thing we could do would be to look after our own necks.' He and his mates stood their ground for a while, taking a few pot shots at enemy snipers, then they were ordered to retire. 'We regretted having to pull back. It meant leaving ground we had fought for. But we were so terribly small a force in the face of much greater numbers. This turned out to be our last attempt to break through to Arnhem.'

*

As units pulled back, there were inevitably those left behind. Medic Les Davison was nursing seventeen wounded men in the basement of a house on the outskirts of Arnhem. His battalion had done its best to penetrate the German defences but, like so many others, got only so far before being fought to a standstill. The decision was made to withdraw. 'We need a volunteer to stay with the wounded,' a sergeant intoned, 'and that's you, Davison.' On the night before they'd left England, Davison had cleaned up in a marathon game of three-card

brag using the Dutch money doled out for the troops' use in the Netherlands. But the odds were stacked against him now. 'I resigned myself
to the fact that I would probably be a prisoner of war in the very near
future.' With the battalion gone, he waited down there in the cellar.
He had plenty of drugs to do his job – morphine ampoules, antiseptic
dressings and bandages – and a good supply of food rations, though he
didn't feel hungry. He sucked on a boiled sweet as a battle raged outside. 'The wounded kept pretty quiet, wrapped up in their own
thoughts as to their fate.' He sedated them with the morphine. Not far
away, he knew, was the St Elizabeth Hospital. It was staffed by doctors from both sides and taking casualties from both sides. Control of
the area around it fluctuated. It was, to all intents and purposes, right
in the middle of no-man's land. And his plan was to get all his patients
there as soon as he could.

The prospects did not look good. Through a grating at street level
he could hear the clatter of boots, and he caught sight of uniforms.
They were field grey, 'obviously not our lot'. He whispered to his
patients to keep very quiet until the Germans had gone. Hours later,
there were more boots, but, when he looked, the uniforms this time
were khaki. These were men of the South Staffs Regiment who had
arrived in the second lift. Somehow they had made their way this far
forward and were planning to advance further still. 'My spirits rose as
I figured by their presence that we must now be getting the upper
hand after all. I informed the patients, who gave a quiet cheer. We
were all thinking that maybe we wouldn't have to go to Germany as
POWs after all.' The optimism didn't last, because the next time Davison saw the same South Staffs, they were coming back. They'd made
an unsuccessful attack and been repelled, and his rollercoaster of
emotions took a downward dive.

The waiting went on in his subterranean casualty ward, hour after
hour, until finally the noise outside turned to a hush and, steeling
himself, he crept upstairs to see what was happening. The swirl of
battle had moved yet again, and the British, it seemed, were back in
control of the area. He skipped down the road to the St Elizabeth
Hospital and asked for help with his patients. He was told that everyone was busy and to bring them himself. Back at the building, there

was a bonus awaiting him – a jeep was parked outside with nobody in it and two stretchers in the back. He didn't stop to ask whose it was or how it had got there. He climbed in and yanked the starter. Nothing. Checking under the bonnet, he could see that the rotor arm of the distributor had been taken off; it was presumably in the pocket of the jeep's driver. Davison grabbed a bike that was lying about and went looking for a spare. He stopped and asked everyone he came upon, with no luck. Then he came upon a jeep wrecked by mortar fire, dug through the metal and the mess and found what he was looking for. 'With a red cross on my helmet and red cross flags on the bicycle, I rode back to the house . . . only to discover that, in my absence, the jeep outside had been completely destroyed. I sat down in the street and cried with frustration.'

Davison pulled himself together. He had no jeep to carry the wounded. He needed alternative transport. 'I cycled down to the hospital and found a gurney, which I wheeled back to the house. Then, taking the most seriously wounded first, I evacuated everybody.' One by one he trundled all seventeen down the street while all around him the battle had recommenced and bullets and shells filled the air. 'It was quite dangerous,' he recalled, with the self-deprecating understatement typical of Arnhem men, 'but I had no option. I had to get them to hospital.' It was a phenomenal act of courage and endurance, and it wasn't over yet. He'd taken sixteen and come back for the last one, 'but as I started down the street I realized the situation ahead had changed, for the worse.' SS men, he could see, were at the hospital door and in a cordon around it. They hadn't spotted him and, before they could, he and his laden gurney quickly veered off course and into an empty house.

The two men, medic and patient, took stock of their situation. It wasn't good, they had to admit. The wounded man needed surgery sometime soon. But for the time being they were still free, and who could tell how the flow of the battle would go next? They decided to hide out, and crawled under a bed to sleep. 'Twice over the next twenty-four hours we were woken by the sound of heavy footsteps as German soldiers tramped through the house. They were clearly hunting out our chaps from all the houses but, amazingly, they never looked under the bed.' The two were finally uncovered by two Dutch doctors from St Elizabeth's who had come to help. 'They said they had seen us go into the house the night before but had been unable to come over until now. They told us the area was now completely under German control. Their plan was to get us into the hospital as if we were dead, otherwise there was a danger the SS on guard might shoot us. They told us to get on the gurney and then covered us with a sheet, and we were wheeled across the road and straight into the hospital chapel, which was being used as a mortuary. There, unseen by the Germans, we hopped off the gurney.' The wounded man joined a long queue for surgery while medic Davison reported to the British army doctors – who had stayed put even though the hospital had changed hands – and went to work in the overcrowded wards and packed corridors that would be his home for the next ten days.

★

For the airborne forces – both those coming from the drop zones in the second lift and those who had been repulsed on the outskirts of Arnhem – the focus was now the area around Oosterbeek, the village itself, the woods immediately outside and a number of large houses and hotels that seemed to afford decent protection. This was a good place to make a stand, to dig in. Glider pilot Dick Ennis and his men were doing just that, and in double-quick time. 'With pick and shovel we dug foxholes and used felled trees to strengthen them. When we felt really secure we lit pocket stoves and prepared porridge from biscuits soaked in water. It was our first meal in Holland.' Digging would become – next to dying, perhaps – the single action that most characterized the Market Garden experience. Ron Kent was sharing roughly the same ground as Dick Ennis and recalled its importance. 'Digging,' he wrote later, 'was the soldier's salvation. However much he loathed it – and I loathed it myself – it kept him active when there was little else to do but wait and think of the things that could happen to him. The simple entrenching tool was a weapon that negated the menace of the high-powered and sophisticated machine-gun carrier. We dug as never before and saved our lives as a result. I had a hole that was 3 feet deep.'

The pressing need for these defences became apparent when thirty Messerschmitts came wheeling in overhead, then dived in, guns blazing. 'We crouched in our slits and listened to the bullets thudding into the trees and ground around us,' Ennis recalled. 'Retaliating with small arms would only have given away our position so we just lay low until the sound of aircraft died away.' The respite was brief. When they raised their heads, they could see grey-uniformed troops approaching, 'advancing through the woods towards us in extended line'. They were clearly unsure where the camouflaged and dug-in British forces were because they kept coming until, at a range of 100 yards, the Brits opened fire with their Brens. 'Jerry dropped flat and wriggled behind trees for cover. We were dug in – they were not – we had the advantage. I killed my first German.' Ennis could see the man's head and shoulders sticking out from behind a tree as he levelled his rifle. 'I took careful aim and squeezed the trigger. He leapt into the air and then slumped forward. I remember thinking to myself, "That's one for Allan [his dead co-pilot]."'

But the line of Germans kept going. 'We gave them everything we had – Brens, grenades and rifle fire – but the first of them had already reached our trenches before our superior firepower began to tell and those who were left fell back.' German casualties were high. There were also forty or so prisoners, all pretty badly wounded. 'For many of us this was our baptism of fire, and flushed with our little victory we immediately set to repairing any damage done to our defences.' There was more strafing from the air to come and more attacks on the perimeter, as the Germans, now out of defensive mode and very much on the attack, probed for weak spots. Enemy motor transport could be heard on nearby roads, never very far away.

The boys, though, were undismayed. They'd had a victory of sorts, they were well dug in, they were confident. 'We were fully expecting relief at any moment.' They had no reason to think that XXX Corps would not show up on time. 'Our officers had no information to give us as to how far away our armies were, but like us they did not think it would be long before they got here.' But the sooner the better, everyone agreed. Rations were running low; ammunition wouldn't last for ever, not at the rate it was being used. Away in the distance, perhaps 20 miles away, they could hear the faint rumblings of an artillery barrage. 'That'll be them,' Ennis remembered the men saying to each other. These must have been the words most often repeated – by fighting men and civilians, inside their heads if not spoken out loud – throughout the entire Arnhem campaign. They were also, for all the good intentions of everyone involved, not true.

Meanwhile, in another part of Oosterbeek, Ronald Gibson was in a park on the Arnhem side of the town and finding it impossible to work out what was going on. Things were moving fast now, and in the fury and flurry as units fell back and regrouped, it was inevitable that many men would become isolated and marooned. For them, the overall picture was a blur at best, more likely a total mystery, as, cut off in circumstances they could never have imagined, they struggled to survive. Gibson furiously fashioned a foxhole for himself close to the park railings. He heard the rumble of tanks along a street but had no idea whether they were British or German. He kept digging until he was 4 feet down. The only activity around was a few locals passing along the street in their clogs. Then, out of nowhere came the sound of running feet in the road followed by a burst of machine-gun fire over his head. The Germans, he guessed, were trying to outflank their position, and he called out to his mate Gordon in the next trench. 'I had heard his spade clinking in the gravel a few minutes before, but now no one answered.' Gibson peered over the top of his foxhole and lined up his grenades. There was scuffling in a nearby allotment, and German voices. 'Two figures dashed across a gap between the rows of peas. Someone fired. Three more figures followed the first. We all fired, and two of them dropped out of sight. I heard one of them groan. A peak-capped head rose from where they had fallen. I fired again, and the head vanished. Someone shouted from a garden on the right of the allotment and a door slammed in the house beyond. Then a motorcycle halted outside the house and there was more shouting, in German.' It was a strange sort of warfare – incoherent, pointless, inconclusive. A smoke canister was thrown, a grenade exploded. Gibson fired at a figure silhouetted in a doorway, and it vanished. Later he would learn that his section had been ordered to withdraw but the message hadn't got through.

Suddenly, there was activity away to his left. The Germans were in the park, running, shouting, shooting, hurling grenades. He looked around for support. Where was everyone? The lieutenant was not answering, and nor were the Bren-gunners by the fence. 'All I saw was a green-clad body sprawling at the foot of a tree. I couldn't tell who it was.' As far as Gibson could tell, he was on his own, and there was only one thing he could do. He ran. 'I grabbed my grenades, bandolier and rifle and dashed across an open glade into some stacks of wood. I ran on, zig-zagging among the trees and the fallen logs. Once I stumbled and nearly fell. The noise of shouting faded as I passed further into the wood. I passed an empty stables and pushed through a hedge into the garden of an empty house. The shutters hung open and the curtains billowed out in the wind.'

He was lost, alone and ill equipped. His rucksack was back in the foxhole. All he had was a rifle and forty rounds, two grenades, a blanket, groundsheet and water bottle – not much to fight a war with. 'I wandered southwards through gardens, looking for a British uniform. I came to a tall, shuttered house with a broken slate roof and gaping windows. The walls were pitted with splinter marks and a few yards from the front door stood a battered jeep. I dashed over to it and nearly tripped over a corpse with his back leaning against the rear wheel, clothes on fire, and lying huddled up like a scarecrow of straw.' But there was life, of sorts, in the house. An exhausted medical orderly was sitting in a window, leaning against the broken sill and staring vacantly into the road. He snapped out of his reverie and pointed Gibson in the direction of British troops further along the road. Gibson caught sight of his commanding officer staring out over a pile of rubble about 50 yards away. He dashed over, sprawled down beside the officer and reported in. 'Our section's been wiped out, sir,' he explained. The major was bemused. 'Didn't you get my runner?' he asked. 'I sent him over to say we were pulling back.'

Later, Gibson thought over his survival in what could well have been a fatal situation. His body tingled, 'half relief, half exultation'.

He was angry that he'd been forced to run in the way he did, 'but confident now that I had survived the baptism of fire'. Like so many men who found themselves with their backs against the wall in the Arnhem campaign – both figuratively and literally – he was determined to make the best he could out of a bad job.

And, after all the fog of war that had earlier engulfed him, he was now to get a clear and honest overview of the situation he and the rest of 1st Airborne were actually in. He was back with the pack and digging in again – his favourite occupation – when an officer came with the 'rather serious' information the men needed to know. 'We were told the paratroops at the bridge had been isolated from the rest of the division. We were hard pressed by large German reinforcements that had been mustered from a wide area during the last three days. The division was falling back to Oosterbeek and concentrating in a horseshoe-shaped perimeter with its base on the river bank. XXX Corps had passed through Nijmegen, but they were held by heavy German fire on the road between the two rivers.' It wasn't good, but at least they knew where they stood now.

*

For the Dutch civilians, hope was turning into horror before their eyes. The sight of planes in the western sky and more paratroopers and more gliders arriving from England had lifted their spirits, but the sounds they could hear around them now were a death knell. Waking up to another day in the cellar beneath the family's home on Wednesday morning, Anje van Maanen's head was filled with a shrieking, whistling noise coming nearer and growing louder. 'We huddle together like scared chickens.' Not far away from her house was the stately Hartenstein Hotel, now commandeered by the Airborne as its divisional headquarters, and its white stucco walls and immaculate lawns were coming under heavy shellfire. 'We look at each other with large, frightened eyes.' This must mean the Germans were bringing in their big guns. There was a lull, and she was about to take morning tea to the Tommies outside her house when the shrieks started up again. 'We hear the thundering of shells, about ten of them. It's just awful.'

The prospects were no better after her father returned from a long and hard night's work in the field hospital at the Tafelberg. 'He tells us the fighting is terrible everywhere. Cars can hardly get along the street because of all the rubble.' But, surprisingly, Dr van Maanen was not downhearted. 'The British are still optimistic,' he insisted, though it could not have been easy to keep faith in the face of what Anje and her family were actually experiencing. She managed a smile for the Tommies in their trenches outside. 'Their faces are completely black, but as they smile back they show beautiful white teeth.' She could not stop herself from mouthing the agonizing question that never left her mind: 'When will Monty come?' The unspoken thought was that it had better be soon because there was now no let-up in the mayhem around her. On the contrary, it was getting worse by the hour. 'All day long the shells thunder and howl overhead, smashing down into streets and houses. From all sides there is shooting. In the field behind us, British guns start up, which is not good for us. The Germans will be sure to answer with their own shells and then our house will be in peril.' Happily, they were not hit, not even a near miss, but it must have seemed only a matter of time.

In another part of Oosterbeek, teenager Marie-Anne and her family were not so blessed. She was trying to chat to Len, one of the two English soldiers lodged in her house, over the kitchen table – not an easy thing to do, because she found his Cockney accent hard to understand – when there was a loud crash. 'German!' yelled Len – a word she had no trouble in grasping – and flung himself to the ground. She followed suit, as did her mother and Gerald, the other soldier. 'The shells keep on falling. Outside everything is pitch black.' Shrapnel and debris rattled against the windows. When the shelling died down, she found that more soldiers who had been outside had now made their way hurriedly into the house for shelter and were lined up in the corridor and spilling into the rooms. 'There are now thirty soldiers in our house,' she noted nonchalantly. 'They have trenches at the back of the garden but remain mostly indoors, in our back room'.

Family life went on. Her mother cooked potatoes and apples, sparse supplies indeed. The cellar was prepared as a safe haven of sorts, with chairs, foot stools and rugs on the cold floor. The shelling had moved off but, every time he heard a crash, Len was taking no chances and was down those stairs like lightning. The younger Gerald, Marie-Anne noted, was braver and stayed upstairs in the sitting room unless a burst came very near. Increasingly, she was made to stay in the cellar – 'The English are very concerned for our safety' – and all the more so when the word went round that German tanks were coming. But she refused to stay out of harm's way. There was work to do. 'Upstairs, many of the soldiers ask for water and I help them to get it. I lost count of how many flasks I filled.' She stood at the back door with Len, gazing at the red glow in the sky from hundreds of fires. She munched on some biscuits he brought for her and made tea. 'He says he will warn me when the German tanks are coming and I *must* go down to the cellar then.' More airborne soldiers were arriving all the time, so many that Len and Gerald were worried the Germans might begin to take notice. 'They do not want us to risk our lives.' In truth, it was much too late for that. In the mess that was now developing, there were no neutrals. Everywhere was a war zone and no one's life was safe, as Kate ter Horst, more than most, must now have realized.

Overnight, her large house down by the river in Oosterbeek had turned from a tentative first-aid post for the British into a full-blown casualty clearing station. She had emerged from the cellar after a troubled and sleepless night, tossing and turning in the heat generated by the crammed-in bodies of her family and friends, to be 'struck dumb' by the transformation of her splendid home, and not a little alarmed. 'The long corridor is filled with wounded, lying side by side on red-linen stretchers. There is just room between them to put down one foot and I get through to the kitchen with great difficulty. There, the large table is covered with dressings and bandages and a doctor is examining six or seven injured men on the granite floor.' Wounds were bandaged after being treated with penicillin, the new wonder drug which the Allies (but, significantly, not the Germans) had for controlling infection and which had been in use for less than a year. 'There is not much more to be done,' Kate noted, 'for there are no surgeons here. Orderlies give the patients morphine injections and write on their forehead the dose and the time.'

She continued her tour. 'Wounded everywhere, in the dining room, in the study and the garden room, in the side corridor and even under the stairs and in the lavatory. There is not a single corner free of them.' Every windowpane was smashed and every room unrecognizable because all the furniture had been hurled outside to make more space. But all she could think was that she needed to do more to help them, to be a better 'hostess', as she put it, in their hour of need. Despite protests from the army medics that they did not want to spoil her fine things, she insisted they strip the untouched family beds upstairs of mattresses, blankets and linen. Then she directed the padre to the preserved vegetables and meat in the larder. 'Here, take it,' she said. He declined. They wouldn't take her food, he told her, 'You'll need it for the kiddies,' and then he pointed hopefully to the sky to indicate that he was expecting fresh supplies to be arriving soon. She liked his quiet confidence. 'I get a feeling of power and assurance that this army has everything, knows everything, conquers everything.'

It was a brave and optimistic assertion on her part, because there were too many indications of the opposite. Her husband, who had come out of hiding when the British landed and shared her bed for one night of freedom, had reluctantly had to make himself scarce again because of the very real threat that the Germans would soon be back in control. Outside in the village, soldiers were manning a barricade they had strung across the street made of cars, household furniture and even a piano. Now, loud explosions were shaking the walls of Kate's home, and a neighbour's house was on fire. The wounded must have been alarmed, lying there helpless against whatever was happening around them, but there was not a word of complaint. She wanted to stay with them, but other loyalties called. 'I must go down into the cellar, for five little ones are longing for me and trusting I'll remain uninjured in order to protect them.' She went to her children. Later, when the shelling subsided, she came back up. The effect of the German onslaught and the paras' fight-back against it was clear to see, because now it was not just the ground floor that was overrun with wounded but the rest of the house as well. 'The whole top floor is full and so are the stairs and the landing. An orderly tells me they are even lying in the attic.' The only consolation was the gallons of English tea boiling away in the copper kettle on the kitchen stove, some of which was dispatched to the grateful family in the cellar.

That evening, she managed to get to the back door, step outside and breathe in much-needed fresh air. She was revitalized, but not for long. As she cast her eyes around, 'I see them for the first time – the dead. Six or seven of them, perhaps more, with tousled hair over their muddy faces. They lie like forgotten bags which have fallen on the path to the kitchen.' But still she clung on to crumbs of comfort. Monty's boys were 'really quite near', she'd been told. Best of all, 'there are still no Germans in our house!' She read the children a bedtime story, one they knew well and which would take their minds back to better times. As always, they laughed. 'You are very brave,' she told them. 'It won't last much longer and then we shall be free.' For a treat, each got to take a cherry from the bottle of preserved fruit, and then she put out the candle. What tomorrow would bring, she did not dare to contemplate.

*

On that loose and leaky defensive perimeter now establishing itself around Oosterbeek – enclosing a thumb-shaped space roughly a mile long and three quarters of a mile wide with the Lower Rhine at its base – a strong sense of mutual dependence set in. *Esprit de corps* was always a major part of para culture and, significantly, it survived intact when severely tested in the field. Arthur Ayers recalled how a message came to his section, holed up in the northern edge of the enclave, that food was running short at another one not far away. 'The major immediately gave orders that half of our meagre rations should be sent to them.' Casualties were arriving all the time, to be treated at an aid post in the cellar, as were remnants of parties who had tried to make it into Arnhem and been repulsed. But set against this was the heartening sight of more German prisoners. No wonder it was so hard to gauge how the fighting was really going and what the outcome would be. Victory still seemed perfectly feasible – indeed, likely – if you saw, as Ayers did, a large group of captured enemy soldiers being herded to the tennis courts at the Hartenstein Hotel, which were in use as a p-o-w cage. 'The grey of their faces matched the grey of their uniforms,' he noted, and was moved to pity. 'Eyes were sunk deep in tired, battle-weary, dirty and war-grimed faces. They shuffled along, some reeling like drunken men. Their expressions showed the hopelessness of war when the mask is off.'

Ayers waxed lyrical and philosophical at the sight of them. 'For some the trials and tribulations of this world were nearly over, as their heartbeats slowly fade away and they sink into their last sleep. For them a white stone in a war cemetery will mark their last resting place. The others, some maimed for life, will, eventually, return to the country they fought for and probably be forgotten after a few years. Such is war.' He imagined their bewilderment at having come to this. 'Inspired by their leaders and forgetting the reason and cause for their actions, they go into battle intent on killing their fellow men, but the shine is dulled when a bullet rips into their bodies and they feel their life-blood seeping through their fingers. As they lie in the mud, they have time to think, to ask themselves what they are doing there.' It was the soldier's lament from time immemorial, and the truth was that there were thousands echoing it at that moment, on both sides. Perhaps the compassion that welled up in Ayers was a presentiment that, pretty soon, he would face the same fate as them.

Twenty-three-year-old trainee solicitor Peter Clarke was also dug in on that northern flank, and his mind too was mulling over the nature of war, now that, rifle in hand, he was in the very thick of it. He was strongly religious, with a deep Christian belief, and felt torn between that and his desire to do his bit to defeat the evils of Nazism. With pals from his bible class, he had enlisted to train as a medic and was eventually posted to work on ambulances at an RAF station in Kent. He had always wanted to fly and the only thing that had stopped him applying to the RAF in the first instance was that his mother thought it too dangerous, 'and in those days we took notice of what our mothers said.' He also stretched his conscience into convincing himself that 'there was a difference between using a rifle, which might be against my Christian belief, and flying a fighter, which would be killing from a distance.' The lure of the air got the better of him and he applied to switch from medic to aircrew. It was a particularly brave decision, because he of all people knew the risks – he'd picked up the remnants of airmen who crashed on landing or take-off. He was accepted by the RAF for pilot training but then diverted by the army to the Glider Pilot Regiment. Thus he had come to a thicket at the edge of a wood on the outskirts of Oosterbeek and the personal decision of what to do with that rifle he was carrying. 'I didn't want to kill anybody, and certainly not to bayonet anybody.'

In their small sector, he and his unit were not well armed. 'We had mainly rifles and a few Sten guns, but nothing of any significance apart from one paratrooper with a Vickers gun, which he used with tremendously good effect when some light German armour came towards us. He saw off this attack with gusto.' 'Gusto' was what Clarke found it hard to summon up. 'When it appeared necessary, I fired my rifle in certain directions, across this large field in front of us and into the woods, but I was not conscious of hitting anybody.' He remembered the whole experience in the slit trench as like being in a 'tiny little world' of his own, the precise details of which time and trauma have erased from his memory. 'We were in that trench with no idea about what was going on 50 yards away. Not a clue; you are just there on your own amidst this warfare, this battle.' Unusually for men in such tight spots, he couldn't even recall the name of the man beside him in that slit trench, though he thought he was probably a glider pilot like him. But he knew what got him through an ordeal that was to last a week. 'I had a pocket bible with me and I read the 91st Psalm.' Its words were comfort. 'The Lord is my refuge and my fortress. In Him will I trust.' Its resonance with his situation was unmistakable. 'Thou shalt not be afraid for the terror by night; nor for the arrow that flieth by day; nor for the pestilence that walketh in darkness; nor for the destruction that wasteth at noonday.' His faith would not let him down. 'A thousand shall fall at thy side, and ten thousand at thy right hand; but it shall not come nigh thee . . . For He shall give His angels charge over thee, to keep thee in all thy ways. They shall bear thee up in their hands, lest thou dash thy foot against a stone . . .With long life will I satisfy Him, and show Him my salvation.'

When he looked back years later, Clarke was certain that his belief was vital to his survival. 'I relied on my faith. I didn't know what was going to happen but I felt that, whatever happened to me, my future was assured in the context of eternity. I think it would be much worse to be in that situation without any well-rounded faith to draw on. There was a very real sense that we might die or get seriously injured in that trench. You struggle to understand how you could come out unscathed.' The other saving grace was that he found work that he could do wholeheartedly. Drawing on his earlier training as a medic, he organized a first-aid post for his sector. 'I wouldn't have been any good if they'd sent me out on patrol because I wasn't trained for that sort of infantry work. But I did know how to treat the wounded, even if it was as much a padre's job as a medical one.' His memory failed him on how many people he treated. 'Ten or a hundred? I haven't a clue. Nor do I remember sleeping, though I must have done at some point. I was on my own with some basic first-aid equipment plus sheets, blankets, towels and a little food I found in a house. I could do only simple stuff like apply field dressings. Then the casualties were evacuated by jeep to a field hospital.' So intense was this experience, so focused in on itself, that he was never sure where that field hospital was, though it must have been quite close. Orderlies would come to pick up his patients, though he didn't know on whose orders. 'I haven't a clue how they knew where to come and collect them but at some point my unofficial aid post must have become an official one.' Head down, concentrating on what had to be done, he managed to stay at his post until the bitter end.

Ron Kent, meanwhile, on the western edge of the Oosterbeek perimeter, was running out of rations. All the company cook could come up with for breakfast was a dixie of boiling tea. He searched his pockets vainly in the hope of finding an overlooked scrap of food, half a biscuit maybe. Action took his mind off the emptiness of his stomach as the first shots and shells of the day hummed from a wood opposite. It was half-hearted to begin with, but the pace stepped up when a German mobile gun set up in the corner of the 'killing field' directly in front of the perimeter and lobbed in shells from a frighteningly short range. The paras replied with mortars, but they fell short. Kent watched in admiration as a comrade edged around the wood with a PIAT anti-tank weapon on his back. 'He stalked that gun until he scored a direct hit and kept going until he could get in another shot to make certain it was out of action.' The man picked up a bad stomach wound for his pains and, though he survived, would later become a prisoner of war. But, this apart, the dug-in defenders did very little. Kent ordered his men to conserve their energy and their ammunition. 'My orders to the riflemen of my section were simple: "Fire at will if, and only if, you have a clear target." The Bren would fire only on my command.'

With the British firing largely at a standstill, an uneasy peace settled over the immediate area. When the German mortar fire ceased too, there was a blessed silence, a stillness in the eye of the storm. It was broken by a strange tinkling noise, an amplified sound that Kent likened to the tinny music he'd heard from ice-cream carts in his childhood. This unreal jingle gave way to a message from a loudspeaker somewhere in the distance. 'Men of the 1st Airborne Division,' said a man's voice in halting English. 'The game is over. Your comrades are being slaughtered. Your tanks will never reach you. Surrender now. Come out waving a white handkerchief. You have two minutes to decide whether you live or die. Surrender or tonight will be your last night on earth. You will never see your wives and sweethearts again.'

Some paras replied with obscenities. 'Go f*** yourself, Jerry,' they chorused, with suggestions on where the man on the loudspeaker could shove his own white handkerchief. But Kent was not alone in feeling perturbed by what he had just heard. 'Something turned over in my stomach and quietly died,' he admitted. He felt calm rather than distressed, 'calmer in fact than I had felt for days', but this, paradoxically, was because the threat of what was to come seemed very real. Resigned to his fate, if that was what it would be, he told himself, 'This is it. This is where your death or glory stuff gets you.' But then the defiance snapped back in, the pride asserted itself. He wasn't going down without a fight. If the enemy thought they could just walk over him, well, let them try it. The bluff was called, and rightly so. 'We expected all hell to be let loose at us after that but, apart from renewed mortar fire, to which we had become accustomed, nothing happened.'

However, although the perimeter was holding here, elsewhere it was creaking. It had to be tightened, and Kent received orders to fall back closer to divisional headquarters in the Hartenstein. The move was to be made in the dead of night. 'We were also warned that the Germans had some of our smocks and parachute helmets and might attempt to infiltrate our position. They had already tried it in another sector.' As he waited in his trench to begin the pull-back with his platoon, his spirits plummeted. 'Curled up in that hole, I suddenly felt deathly tired and terribly alone.' That day he had lost two of his best mates. One, a fellow sergeant, took bullets in both legs. 'I knew his wife was expecting a baby in a month and I only hoped he would get back to her.' Then there was the soldier he had been sharing his foxhole with, who had been hit and fallen back into Kent's arms. 'His eyes were wide and staring vacantly. His face took on a ghastly grey hue. I thought he had been killed outright.' Kent had got him to a casualty station but then had to leave him, uncertain of his fate.

Now, alone in the trench, he missed his companion. He dozed and dreamt, a terrible dream of being buried alive, while that disembodied German voice from earlier in the day sounded in his ears. An officer came by and hissed at him to stay awake. 'Oh, how I knew it,' he said, recalling the moment years later. 'As I write these words, I can feel the battle between my willpower and nature all over again.' His willpower won, and he moved along his section's foxholes with a quiet word of encouragement to all his men.

The company gathered in the dark for its tactical withdrawal. 'A quiet roll call was made. One of my men was missing. I fumbled my way in the dark to find him still in his foxhole. I had to force him out of it. He was all for staying there and taking his chance when daylight came.' The man was Jewish and a refugee from Germany, and was showing extraordinary courage just by being there with the Allied forces. Kent knew of a number of men with the same background and had enormous respect for them. Although they had Anglicized their names as a precaution in case of capture, some had faltering English and heavy accents that would have soon given their ethnic identity away. But this one particular man had lost his nerve or his reason because, against everyone else's better judgement, he was bent on giving himself up. 'I had no intention of letting him do so and I finally persuaded him he would be better off staying with us. Part of the persuasion was the cold metal of my Colt pressed against his ear and my promise that I personally would see him off before any German could do so. When the withdrawal started I kept him directly in front of me so that he could not slip away in the dark.'

That night march, as Kent called it, was more of a nightmare. They shuffled along in the pitch black over rough and unfamiliar ground, constantly in danger of losing touch with the man in front and wandering off course. It was a nerve-wracking hour of stopping and starting before they made it into the grounds of the Hartenstein and settled down to rest. 'We lay in section lines among the leaves,' Kent recalled, 'which had already fallen from the trees. It seemed to me that autumn came early that year. I eased off my pack, lay my Sten close to hand, ready for use, and put my head down for a nap. As I did so I felt something soft and yielding beside me but thought no more of it. As dawn broke, we roused ourselves and I discovered I had spent the night alongside a dead German soldier. He was barely covered with a few inches of earth and leaves, and it was his hand, sticking out from his resting place, that I had touched. He cannot have been long dead, for there was hardly any of the stench of putrefaction which was to become so familiar to me in the days to come.'

He was glad to move on when his company relocated again in the early-morning half-light to a group of houses at a crossroads on the main Oosterbeek–Arnhem road. They were now on the more vulnerable eastern side of the perimeter. Surprisingly, Kent was positive, more so than he had been for a while. Strangely, he was closer now to Arnhem itself than he ever had been – or ever would get – and, paradoxically, he interpreted this as a sign of progress rather than the desperate shoring-up that it actually was. 'Maybe in a day or so,' he told himself, 'we'll hear that the Second Army have reached the bridge, that German resistance has ceased and that I can have that beer with my mate Bill Watts, promised back at the drop zone, after all.'

In his sector, glider pilot Dick Ennis was indulging in that fantasy too, imagining in his head the arrival of the Second Army. 'We had visions of the relief reaching us. We saw ourselves running towards the tanks, cheering, kissing them, climbing all over them. We would joke with the tank crews about them keeping us waiting.' Such thoughts were a triumph of hope over experience, because the previous twenty-four hours had been horrific. Sniped at, bombarded with 'Moaning Minnies', constantly ducking shrapnel while still trying to keep an eye above the parapet for signs of an enemy attack – that was life in a foxhole on the Oosterbeek perimeter. When that attack came, it was a closely grouped frontal assault, designed to sweep them aside. 'We saw a continuous line of field grey advancing straight upon us and gave them our all. Phrases learnt at battle school were running through my head – "You will kill the Boche. You will kill the Boche." We did. We killed them. But still they came on, until they were close enough to exchange grenades. The air was thick with curses, bullets and smoke. Will they break? Will they break?' And, this time, the enemy did, faltering first, then pulling back but firing all the while. 'There was a lull, then they were on us again with an assault as furious as the first.' Ennis had no idea how any of his side survived that second attack, but, slowly, the enemy once more withdrew.

The cost in casualties was high. A third onslaught would overwhelm them. Ennis and the men around him made the manoeuvre that was being repeated along much of the perimeter: they withdrew to a new line of dug-in defences further back. They barely made it. 'We moved our wounded back under cover of fire, and then, just as the rest of us prepared to move, Jerry attacked again. They literally chased us into our new defences and were firing into our backs as we ran. We reached our new line and jumped into foxholes, which were already occupied. With us out of the way, the occupiers of those foxholes had a clear view before them. They now knew that everyone in front of them was a German and they set to in tremendous style and repelled this attack.'

1. (*top*) Paratroopers of the 1st Airborne Division in their aircraft during the flight to Arnhem, Sunday 17 September

2. (*left*) Glider pilot Staff Sergeant Peter Clarke, who set up an improvised dressing station during the battle around Oosterbeek

3. (*right*) Glider pilot Sergeant Alan Kettley in 1945. Kettley was captured at Oosterbeek but managed to escape and return to the UK. In late October 1944 he flew back to occupied Holland to assist in the rescue of other evaders

4. (*top*) Paratroopers of the 1st Airlanding
Reconnaissance Squadron gathering their
parachutes, Arnhem, 17 September

5. (*left*) Arthur and Lola Ayers on their wedding
day in August 1944, just before Arnhem; (*right*)
they celebrate their sixtieth wedding
anniversary in 2004

6. Horsa and Hamilcar gliders at Landing Zone Z near Wolfheze Woods, west-north-west of Arnhem. A number of gliders have run on into the trees and bushes, and some are clearly damaged

7. (*top*) 1st Parachute Brigade at Drop Zone X Ray at 2.30 p.m. on 17 September after gliders have landed

8. (*left*) Ron Brooker on joining the army in 1939; (*right*) at his home in 2010

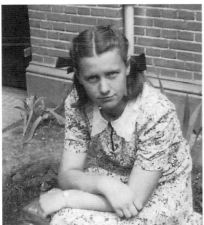

9. (*top*) Paratroopers pose with Dutch civilians after landing near Arnhem

10. (*left*) Anje van Maanen, aged sixteen in 1943. Anje helped to treat many of the airborne soldiers wounded in the fighting; (*right*) Anje outside her home in 2011, aged eighty-four

11. (*top*) An aerial photograph shows the many German vehicles destroyed during the battle at the ramp approach to the north end of the bridge at Arnhem, *c.* 19 September

12. (*bottom*) Soldiers of the 1st Parachute Battalion utilize a large shell hole as a defensive position in Oosterbeek. Corporal Alfred Reynolds, *left*, was killed soon after this photograph was taken

13. (*top*) Major-General Roy Urquhart, commander of the 1st British Airborne Division, plants the Airborne flag outside his headquarters at the Hartenstein Hotel

14. (*bottom*) A paratrooper fires from the shell-damaged Hartenstein Hotel

15. (*top*) RAF Stirlings drop supplies to the beleaguered airborne forces around Oosterbeek – smoke from bursting flak shells can clearly be seen

16. (*right*) RAF pilot Richard Medhurst, who was killed when his aircraft was shot down while dropping supplies at Oosterbeek. The aircraft captain, Flight Lieutenant David Lord, was awarded a posthumous Victoria Cross

The problem was that each time the enemy were halted, they re-grouped and came again, as relentlessly and as strongly as before. In their foxholes, the British soldiers could now tell when an attack was about to be launched. 'We'd hear the German NCOs screaming at their men,' Ennis recalled. 'This would go on for some time and would then be followed by a few "*Sieg Heil*"s. When the "*Sieg Heil*"s were over, the attack would commence. As the enemy carried out this procedure before each assault, we were able to prepare a recep-tion for him.' But, standing against this tide, cold, wet and hungry British troops were in danger of losing heart, the more so when it became clear that their plight was not fully appreciated in the outside world. In a lull after his unit's hand-to-hand combat with enemy infiltrators who got within a yard or two of their trenches, Jo Johan-son managed to get his wireless set going and tuned in to the BBC. He was furious at what he heard, and perplexed. 'Someone was talk-ing about Holland and saying, once we had it, it would be an easy matter to go straight through to Berlin.' The complacency riled him. 'It was all too obvious to me from where I was standing that we did not have it.' The BBC voice went on to say that the 1st Airborne were 'surrounded but undismayed'. It was such a glib phrase that he switched off. Undismayed? He sat for a while and pondered unhap-pily what the commentator was really trying to say.

Then, however, he and thousands of others on the Oosterbeek perimeter got the encouragement they needed, with the sudden real-ization that they were not alone after all. Help was coming. Dick Ennis remembered hearing the sound of aircraft, 'and I looked up to see the sky black with transport planes bringing our first airborne supplies.' Running out of food and ammunition, the men cheered and cheered at this blessed relief. Here was a cause for renewed opti-mism. 'But our cheers,' Ennis recalled, 'mingled with the thump of enemy ack-ack being thrown up to meet them. The barrage was of a ferocity that I have never before experienced.' Up in the skies, a new chapter in Arnhem's brave tale was being written.

7. 'He was Engaged on a Very Important Airborne Mission'

At the age of nineteen, Pilot Officer Dick Medhurst was one of those flowers of British youth for whom the war was both a duty and a great adventure. He was exceptional in many ways – tall, boyishly handsome, clever, funny. He was also madly in love with a girl he had just met, and threw himself as wholeheartedly into the romance as he did into the war. His older sister, Rozanne, idolized him. 'He was my little brother and I was very close to him,' she recalled.[1] 'He had a great sense of humour, but he was also interested in philosophy and religion. As a little boy he was always going off to think about things.' In keeping with this, after leaving school, he squeezed in a six-month history course at Corpus Christi, Cambridge. Flying, though, was his passion, inherited from their father, a First World War pilot who in 1944 was an air vice-marshal commanding an RAF staff college in Buckinghamshire. From his father's stories, the youngster learnt the lesson that, in a modern war, the place to be was in the air, not down on the ground. 'Father told us about flying low over the trenches and seeing the wretched men stuck on the wire,' Rozanne recalled. 'If you were in the RAF, you were one of the lucky ones.'

Like most of his generation, Dick was desperate to play an active part in the war, to test himself, to earn his badge of courage. His biggest fear was that the fighting would end too soon and he might miss out on action. Given his youth, this seemed increasingly likely. He joined the RAF and was shipped across the Atlantic to Canada and the United States for pilot training. On his return in 1944 he was qualified, but with nothing for him to do. Fighter Command and Bomber Command were full. 'There was such a glut of pilots that some were reduced to driving trains.' Determined to fly, he got his high-ranking father to pull strings and secure him a posting to Transport Command, based at Down Ampney in the Cotswolds.

There was that special girl in his life, though like many wartime romances, the love affair was impulsive and fired by the uncertainty of the times. 'She was eighteen, awfully sweet and very pretty. They met at a dinner party and he fell full flat in love with her. They had one date together in a pub and he was absolutely convinced this was the girl he would marry, though they hardly had time to think about the future.' Rozanne, meanwhile, was on the staff at Bletchley Park, on top-secret Enigma work with codes and cipher, and it was here that her brother came to visit her, just before Arnhem. 'I remember being very proud of him, because he'd grown into a man, and I wanted to show him off to all the girls I worked with. He came for lunch and in the evening there was a party given by a WAAF, and he was very popular. Then he had to go back to Down Ampney that night.' She gave him a hug and a kiss as he got into the tiny open-top Austin he'd just bought from somebody on his station. 'See you again soon,' she called out, and he waved back at her as he disappeared into the night. 'That was the last time I saw him.'

She was not to know that he was about to carve his name in history as one of the heroic airmen who risked – and lost – their lives to run supplies to the beleaguered Allied soldiers in and around Arnhem. He was – in the words of the official next-of-kin letter which arrived a fortnight or so later – 'engaged on a very important airborne mission'.

*

It takes a hero to recognize true courage, and for the men on the ground fighting to stay alive at Oosterbeek, there was no doubt who deserved the greatest acclaim. Dick Ennis, dug in on that hard-pressed perimeter, had had neither the time nor the inclination to ponder the concept of heroism. 'Up to then, I don't think I had ever met a hero,' he recalled, 'and had never found any cause to define the word.' But as he watched the supply planes wheeling in a few hundred feet above him and, through the deadly curtain of anti-aircraft fire, drop their panniers on the end of brightly coloured parachutes, his mouth opened wide in amazement. These were supplies desperately needed by him and all the other beleaguered men on the ground. Continuing the fight depended on them. But the risks the pilots and their crews were taking to deliver them were almost superhuman. 'The men dropping those supplies for us were real heroes, although even that definition is really inadequate for what they did.' As they circled at little more than 500 feet, every German ack-ack gun in the area seemed to be homing in on them and trying, in Ennis's graphic word, to 'claw' them to the ground. He remembered Dakotas flying so low that he could make out the figure of a dispatcher in the fuselage doorway pushing out the containers and baskets, and continuing to do so even when his plane was a mass of flames from wing tip to wing tip. 'He kept on until the plane spiralled to the ground and all that was left was a column of black smoke reaching high into the sky.' Their courage in not pulling out or pulling away until the job was done was what impressed him. 'Yes, the crew could have baled out, but instead they gave us our supplies. They indeed died that we might live. Their lives brought us – some of us – back from Arnhem.' The drops came in day after day, with similar acts of self-sacrifice. 'We will never forget,' Ennis wrote, with a gratitude and an admiration that was beyond words.

Arthur Ayers could not believe how the lines of Dakota transporters and four-engine Stirling bombers stuck to their course as the black puffs of ack-ack shells exploded all around them. In the eight days that the planes kept coming, they dropped close on fifteen thousand panniers in more than six hundred sorties. The sight of the sky filled with planes and parachutes was mesmerizing. It was impossible not to stare in awe and horror at the dramas being played out up there. 'One aircraft, its starboard engine on fire, circled once before discharging its cargo of supplies. Then, as it started to gain altitude, the fire spread to the wing and it immediately lost height before spiralling into a wood.' The rest, their job done, turned and slowly disappeared into the distance, some with black smoke trailing from them. Ayers wished them luck. Though he was stuck far away from home in a situation growing more and more threatening by the hour, he forgot about his own plight for a moment. 'I wondered how many of those brave men would get safely back home to England.'

Some drops hit their target well enough. Sonnenberg House, across from the Hartenstein, got a direct 'hit' on its lawns and gardens, and Ayers was out there to grab the wicker containers almost the moment they landed. 'Those that were within easy reach, we collected straight away. The others, which had fallen some distance away, were left to be collected after dark.' Some swung high in trees after their parachutes snagged on branches, and men had to climb to retrieve them. Others were buried quite deep in the ground, because the parachute had been shot away on the way down.

Once the harvest from the skies was gathered in, it proved to be a mixed blessing. 'We got a supply of ammunition, two new radio sets, which unfortunately were damaged on landing, and some new clothing – airborne smocks and red berets. The parachutes were collected and used to keep the wounded warm in the cellar. But of the commodity we were most short of – food – there was very little. We were having to ration ourselves to a few biscuits and half a tin of meat per day.' The berets became a paratroop myth – one of those stories that convinces squaddies that their affairs are ordered by idiots. But it was real enough. A major and his men, desperate for food and ammunition, opened a fallen container to find 'serried ranks of brand-new red berets'. He and his men doubled up with laughter, which quickly and understandably turned to exasperation.[2]

By far the largest part of the new supplies, however – more than 90 per cent, according to some estimates – fell beyond the reach of those they were intended for. Wind, weather and flak didn't help anyone's accuracy, but the principal problem was that the supply runs were planned on the assumption that the paras would be holding the ground below. And the fact – which it was not always possible to communicate back to the supply airfields in England – was that the area in para hands had never been that extensive and now was shrinking all the time. Inside the Oosterbeek perimeter, Eureka radio beacons were set up on a water tower to try to guide the supply planes in, but, for technical reasons, their signal had a 2-mile margin of error, a fatal discrepancy when the enemy was in the next bush or house. Their batteries were also running low. Soldiers took their lives in their hands to stand out in the open with Very pistols to try to indicate their position, but with little success. Because of the tree screen, the flares could not be seen from above until the planes were directly overhead, and by then it was too late. And, anyway, it later transpired that, for security reasons, aircrew on the drops were specifically ordered to ignore lights from below because they couldn't be sure whose they were. The Germans gleefully swept up the mass of supplies that dropped into their lines – aware that each container that came their way was important not so much for its contents but because it was vitally needed supplies denied to the British, as were the ones that fell into no-man's land. These lay out in the open, often visible and tempting but, as Ron Kent noted, 'it was as much as one's life was worth to go and get them.'

Where the supplies got through, they brought fuller bellies and fresh hope. Ennis's men couldn't get out into no-man's land to collect stray containers because the Germans flooded the area with lights from flares and were poised with machine guns and snipers to drop anyone who tried. But they had enough to be going on with. 'They put new vigour into us as we repelled the enemy attack,' he said. Each man received one tin of foodstuff and about ten cigarettes. The smokes went down well – they always did – but even hungry men turned their noses up at the awful tinned peas and a weird kind of Christmas pudding. Ennis, however, managed to find 'one tin of tomatoes which contained more liquid than substance, but, when heated up, made a very tasty meal. We practically licked the lining off the tins.'

*

Dick Medhurst's role in all this was as the co-pilot of perhaps the most famous aircraft to take part in the entire re-supply mission, sitting up front in the cockpit of Dakota KG374 alongside Flight Lieutenant David 'Lumme' Lord. What happened on the morning of Tuesday 19 September would cost the lives of all but one of the eight-man team on board – four crew and four army dispatchers[3] whose job was to throw out the cargo. It would also win Lord a posthumous Victoria Cross.[4] Lord was an unusual figure, in his early thirties and an old man compared with the young tyros around him. He was known as 'Lumme' after the mild expletive[5] that he, a man who had once considered training for the priesthood, tended to use rather than the coarser four-letter swear words that were common among the boys in blue. He'd had a pretty varied life – born in Ireland, raised in India, schooled in Wales and Spain, then jobs as a chemist and a writer of short stories. He was a hugely experienced flyer who enlisted long before the outbreak of war and, as a sergeant pilot, flew old biplanes in missions against Pathan tribesmen in India. War service in North Africa and the Far East saw him promoted from the ranks to officer status and the Dakota squadron at Down Ampney.

He carried paratroopers into France on D-Day, was hit by flak and got home without flaps, then flew continuous supply missions to the Normandy beachhead for several months before preparing for Market Garden. He was non-operational on the first day, but piloted a tug for a glider in the 'second lift' on 18 September. It was a bumpy journey, with trouble in the Dakota's starboard engine and flak peppering the tail, but the experienced Lord reached his designated cast-off point and released the Horsa he was towing. And now, the next day, he was off on a supply mission. In the second pilot's seat of KG374 was Medhurst, this keen but totally green young man. Fresh out of training, he had arrived on squadron just two weeks earlier and had never flown in anger before. Thus are the random pairings of wartime. Also new to Lord's team was his old friend Flying Officer Henry King, borrowed from another crew and brought in at the last minute as a one-off replacement for his regular navigator, who had gone on leave to get married.

With sixteen panniers of food[6] in the back and a briefing beforehand that as much as possible had to get through, they took off five hours later than planned, delayed from the morning to the afternoon by mist over the airfields and low cloud blanketing the approaches to the Netherlands. Even when they got into the air there was 10/10 cloud and visibility was down to half a mile for most of the journey, which meant there was no fighter escort cover. The weather cleared a little as they and the other 162 planes in the supply fleet that day got nearer their target, but the tidy, tight formations that had set off from English air space were all over the place. On the run-in, at low level for greater accuracy despite heavy flak, it was going to be each plane for itself. Given the murky conditions, flying had to be on instruments and, on King's instruction, KG374 dropped to 1,500 feet. Emerging through the last of the hazy cloud, the cockpit crew got a visual on the town of Nijmegen below, 10 miles south of Arnhem. 'Spot on, Harry,' called the pilot.

In the back, the four dispatchers belted on their safety straps and got ready to propel the containers along the length of the fuselage and out of the door, a riskier business than it sounded, involving strength, speed and precise timing, while a howling gale from the open hatch threatened to blow them away. There was also the flak, coming up fast and furious from the ground now while the plane itself dropped steadily lower every second, right into the cauldron. There were 7 miles to go to the drop point when the starboard wing was hit twice. Black smoke trailed from the engine, followed by flames. From the cockpit, Lord checked that everyone was okay. Then he asked how far it was to the drop zone. 'Three minutes' flying time,' King told him. He could have pulled out of the stream and abandoned both the drop and the ship by baling out. Accepted opinion among experienced airmen later was that Lord would have been fully justified in doing so. But, aware, one presumes, of how badly needed these supplies were, he made his decision – they were so close he was going in. He told the crew to prepare to jump while he battled to keep the crippled plane, listing heavily to the right and losing height, upright and on course. He could see his target and, not needing King to guide him in, he sent the navigator to help the dispatchers.

King scrambled back to a scene of horror. The engine, glimpsed through a porthole, was an inferno, and the flames were licking along the wing towards the fuel tank. The green-for-go light was on and the dispatchers were frantically at work, unshackling the tied-down panniers and kicking them along a metal roller track towards the door. Bundled in pairs, the panniers should have rolled smoothly out, one after the other, but the first one stuck on the flak-damaged track. They would have to be moved by hand, physically pushed and

shoved into position. The dispatchers threw off their parachute har-
nesses to free themselves up to move in the confined space of the
fuselage. Heaving and shoving, with King at the door giving the
panniers a last kick, they dispatched twelve. But then the red light
was flicked on from the cockpit. They were past the DZ and had to
stop. Two pairs of baskets were left, King told Lord over the intercom. The pilot took another momentous decision. He wasn't going
home with a quarter of his load of desperately needed supplies for
the fighting men below still on board. He was going back in, he
announced. He was not to know that the drop zone below that he
had just resupplied was in enemy hands and, in reality, it was the
Germans, not his own troops, that he was risking his life, his plane
and his crew to feed.

Lord told the dispatchers to hang on tight and, with the door still
open, banked sharply to the left to line up for a second run. To do
this he needed full power from both engines. Experts say that if he
had shut down the burning engine and feathered the propeller, the
fire might well have blown out and he could have headed home with
a reasonable chance of making it. But that was not what he chose to
do. On fire or not, he had to keep both engines going if KG374 was
to complete her mission. He came round in a half-circle and joined
the flight path again, alongside another Dakota, carrying ammunition and medical supplies, that was about to make its first run. The
wireless operator on this plane, Flight Lieutenant Stan Lee, was
standing in the astrodome, horrified as he caught sight of this new
companion, just a wing tip away and on fire. 'At this point we were
over the river and we banked right over the top of the bridge to turn
to the drop zone. The other aircraft [Lord's] stuck to our wing tip as
if by glue and I became alarmed. The fire was out of control and I
could see that it would not be able to continue to fly for much longer.
I was worried that in its final moments it might swerve and take us
down with it. I almost wished it would go away. I couldn't understand why the pilot didn't force-land the aircraft while he still had
some control.'[7]

There was now another change of course. The pilot of the Dakota
that Lord was shadowing deduced from the amount of flak coming

up from his designated DZ that it must be in enemy hands, and he switched to an alternative. Lord followed suit until both planes, still side by side, dropped their loads at the same time. Inside the cockpit of KG374, Lord flashed on the green light for the panniers to go. An observer below could make out the uniforms of the dispatchers and noted how they stuck to their task, though they must have known that, with every second, they were getting too low to jump. Their job done, Lord ordered everyone out. King, who would be the only survivor, remembered the captain calling, 'For God's sake, bale out!' In the back cabin, King saw the fresh-faced Medhurst coming towards him from the cockpit, his hand raised in a thumbs-up that the mission was accomplished.

The plane, barely 500 feet in the air, lurched. King already had his parachute on and was turning to help the dispatchers don theirs when there was a tremendous *whoosh* as the starboard fuel tank exploded. The blast flung him out of the aircraft. 'Suddenly I was in space with the ground racing up at tremendous speed. I felt a jerk and I found I was now floating down. Seconds later I landed heavily on my back.' The radio operator in the parallel Dakota spotted King's white parachute among the coloured ones dropping with cargo, but his eyes were then drawn to the disaster in the air as Lord lost his battle to save KG374 and her crew. 'Its nose dropped sharply, the wheels started to come down. It lost some forward speed and fell behind us. Then it slowly folded in two. The wing tips came up to meet each other and, just as they touched, the starboard wing broke off and floated down like a leaf.' The bulk of the plane, now upside down, nosedived into the ground, ending up a ball of fire followed by a plume of black smoke. Survival was impossible.

On the ground, many soldiers watched in awe as Lord's flaming Dakota dived and died. They would never forget the sight. Roy Urquhart, commander of 1st Airborne, remembered 'the eyes of hundreds and probably thousands of careworn soldiers gazing upwards through the battle haze. We were spellbound and speechless.' Even the Germans stopped. 'An army commander reported that 'a hush came over the battlefield and for two minutes all fighting ceased as German SS and British paratroopers spontaneously saluted in silence the great courage of the men who had just died.' Lord was awarded a posthumous VC, but that badge of courage was, in many ways, earned by the whole of Transport Command for its deeds over Arnhem.

*

Many others met the same fate as Lord in the skies over Arnhem and Oosterbeek.[8] Wing Commander Peter Davis's Stirling was carrying petrol in containers in its bomb bay and, just as the doors were opened for the drop north of Arnhem, the load took a direct hit from an ack-ack shell. Fire exploded in the belly of the aircraft. Davis called calmly down the intercom, 'Don't panic chaps,' followed swiftly by the order to 'Abandon aircraft,' an instruction that he himself ignored. In the rear turret, all the gunner could hear from the body of the plane was the roar of flames. He jumped. The co-pilot glanced down, saw the navigation table on fire and a box of Very cartridges igniting in showers of light, and baled out too. The skipper stayed. He gripped the controls, fighting to keep the plane steady for long enough to give the others a chance. Five made it, four did not, and he was one of them. He must have known that, by staying with his plane, he had no chance himself, one survivor said. Davis, he noted sadly, was getting married in a few week's time, and they'd all been invited to the wedding.

Watching the wing commander's plane fall from the sky that day was Kenneth Darling, an up-and-coming army officer[9] who had gone along for the ride in another supply plane – an extraordinary thing to do but, in those first few days, before the realities hit home, these flights to Arnhem were thought of in some quarters as 'milk runs'. Darling was recovering from D-Day battle injuries and fancied a trip to see some action. He used his contacts to hitch a lift and was allotted a place in Davis's ship, but there was a change of plan at the last moment. Davis had been ordered to carry another passenger, a scientist from Boscombe Down who had some secret equipment to test during the flight, and Darling was shifted to a different plane. From his vantage point there, he saw Davis's

Stirling go down, the one he should have been in. 'We were hit too,' Darling recalled, 'and limped home on three engines. I realized how foolhardy my swanning about had been. I was dressed in plain battledress, not even a water bottle or a parachute. Worse still, my right arm was still in plaster and if we had to make a forced landing I would have been an infernal nuisance to everyone.' He counted his blessings in having been moved from Davis's plane. The scientist who took his place died.

Heavy casualties – 89 planes down and 232 men dead in the whole supply operation – were hardly surprising, given that, from Sergeant Eddie Leslie's position in the cockpit, 'we were sitting ducks really.' He was just twenty, though his papers said he was a year older. He'd lied to join up early, claiming that his birth certificate had gone missing in an air raid. The raid was real enough. He was bombed out of his parents' East End home in the Blitz. It was a close call – 'another couple of feet and none of us would have made it' – and he had to be dug out of the rubble. He never forgot the whistle of the bomb and the might of the explosion, yet here he was, just three weeks out of training, at the sharp end again. Bullets from the ground raked his plane as it passed over at what he remembered as 300 feet. 'I simply couldn't understand why we were being shot at. If the drop zone was meant to be secure, where was all this damn machine-gun and tracer fire coming from? It didn't make any sense.' It made an impact, though. 'Streams of fire were shooting past the window and hitting the aircraft. They formed an arch across the DZ which we had to fly through. I didn't have time to feel scared. I was too busy concentrating on what we were doing, flying straight so the dispatchers could get the panniers out. After the drop, we banked hard left and all I could see was the ground. As we got out of the area I just said, "Well done, Jimmy," to my pilot.'[10]

Like David Lord in his fatal flight, Pilot Officer Neville Hicks also took his plane round twice. His navigator, Gordon Frost, recalled how pumped up the entire crew was for the mission, determined to outfox the German anti-aircraft gunners by coming in very low and weaving from side to side. But they were rattled – literally – by gunfire against the underside of the aircraft even before they got to

Arnhem. 'The shells came up through the floor in a dead-straight line down the full length of the fuselage, and I watched mesmerized as they came towards me. I couldn't have moved out of their way even if I had had the will to do so. They caught a dispatcher in the leg, went behind my seat, struck the armour plating behind the pilot and ricocheted back over my head. Some dropped on to my table as I sat frozen to the spot – and, miraculously, unscathed.'[11]

Undaunted by this early brush with danger, they flew on, to see ahead 'a tunnel of murderous fire. Around us every accompanying aeroplane was taking hits. Stirlings and Dakotas went down, but we kept tight-lipped and did not shout out or even comment. Seconds later our turn came, as a shell removed most of the port aileron. The tailplane was hit, the rudder took a blow, and pieces of our Stirling whizzed away behind us. But we flew on weaving and ducking like a prize-fighter. The scene at the DZ was an inferno, with aircraft turning and diving in all directions to drop their loads and avoid the flak.'

They came in at tree-top level, the panniers went out of the back and pilot 'Nev' piled on the power to gain height and depart. 'At that point, Mike in the rear turret, who had been counting the parachutes as they dropped, shouted out that only two thirds of our containers had gone.' The electrics on the release mechanism had been damaged in the earlier mêlée. A big decision had to be made, 'but there was no way we were going to take containers back. There was nothing else for it but to go round again. We did a low sweep, rejoined the stream and approached the DZ again.' They took more hits as they flew into position, used a manual override to dump the rest of the load and scooted away, having pushed their luck to the limit and, unlike Lord's plane, got away with it. Back at base at RAF Harwell, ground crew crawled over the Stirling and marvelled at its survival. The rear turret was pockmarked with bullet holes. Every one of its fourteen self-sealing fuel tanks was holed. The plane was a write-off and towed away to the scrapyard.

Not all damage was inflicted by the enemy. Navigator Chris Frenchum was in a plane in the stream going in on one of the later supply drops on 21 September, carrying panniers of desperately needed anti-tank mines. He'd been to Arnhem twice already, and nobody was kidding themselves any more that these were 'milk runs'. He cadged a couple of American bulletproof jackets, one for the pilot and one for himself. This, he recalled, was his most dangerous mission. They were up against not just intense flak but attacks by German fighter planes too. As they battled their way in, 200 yards ahead was another Dakota, which suddenly was struck by a free-falling pannier dropped prematurely and disastrously from a plane hundreds of feet above. 'The heavy load landed on the starboard wing of this aircraft we were following, its wing completely broke off and it plunged to its death. The poor devils had no chance whatsoever.' What they had just witnessed was so shocking that Frenchum's pilot had a panic attack. 'The skipper let go of the controls and crouched on the floor.'

Frenchum was a navigator, not a trained pilot, but he had no choice. 'I grabbed the controls and righted our aircraft. By this time we were almost at the DZ and I gave the green light for our own panniers to be dropped. Once we'd got rid of them, I asked for a course to fly back to base.' For much of the return flight, the pilot just sat on the floor in a state of shock, and the crew began to worry that he would not be in a fit state to land the Dakota. Frenchum might well have to perform this manoeuvre himself, a tricky order for a novice. 'I was not a qualified pilot, but I knew all the correct procedures and would have landed the aircraft if it had been necessary.' It wasn't. After crossing the North Sea, the pilot was recovered enough to take control again and landed perfectly. Frenchum, who had already completed a tour with Bomber Command and knew the mental strain, felt great compassion for his skipper. 'He never flew again, but he was an excellent pilot apart from this one incident which, happening right in front of our eyes, shattered his nerves.'

*

In the roll call of courage, the Royal Army Service Corps (RASC) dispatchers in those supply planes are often overlooked. It was a thankless task, involving just as much risk to life and limb as the boys in RAF blue underwent, but without the kudos. The dispatchers were often not even told where they were going or why. Harry King, the sole survivor of David Lord's plane, was fulsome in his praise for the four who went down with his ship. They were 29-year-old Corporal Philip Nixon from Oldham, a former PT instructor, and three drivers, Len Harper, also 29, from Middlesex, James Ricketts, 27, a haulier from Tyneside, and 27-year-old Arthur Rowbotham, a former baker's deliveryman from Lancashire. 'These men,' he said, 'were not volunteers like aircrew, they received no flying pay, yet were superb in fulfilment of their duty, even though their plane was on fire. They were magnificent throughout the operation.'

A dispatcher had no control over his own destiny. His life was in the hands of fate and the flight deck, as 21-year-old Geoff Gamgee was to discover. A clerk in civilian life, he opted to be a driver when he was called up. His postings were all at home, until the 1st Airborne was formed, 'and I ended up in a maroon beret'. After service as a driver in Italy, he volunteered for air dispatch. He knew it involved flying over enemy territory, but 'I tried not to think about being shot down or crashing.' Arnhem was his first trip. 'We knew very little about the operation – as RASC we didn't get much information at all. I knew we were to drop supplies but I had no idea about the state of the battle.' Or even where precisely they were going. He remembered going over 'a dull, dreary-looking sea', 300 feet above the water, followed by 'land mostly flooded except for houses and trees'. Then the flak began. 'You could see the black puffs around the aircraft and occasionally feel a shudder when one came a bit close.'[12]

Nearing the DZ, the dispatchers opened the trapdoor and stood by for the signal to push the panniers out one by one as quickly as possible. 'We watched the 'chutes below us developing.' Time to go home. 'It was then that we ran into trouble. The ack-ack was coming up pretty hot and thick and holes were appearing in the sides and floor of the plane – and there's nothing you can do about that.' Suddenly, a pipe was severed and oil was gushing out over the floor. One engine was hit and cut out and, shortly afterwards, a second engine went. 'With just two engines, the pilot could not make height. He told us to prepare for a crash landing. 'That was a bit of a shock. We'd had no instruction or briefing about crash-landing! He told us to lie down and brace ourselves against something on the fuselage. We lay on the floor with our arms folded at the back of our heads and hoped for the best!'

The landing was a series of horrendous bumps and skids. 'I felt myself being dragged forward as the plane scraped over the ground. Earth was spraying up all around us and coming in through the broken nose. At last we came to a standstill and there was hush for a few seconds before we all scrambled to our feet and got out as quickly as we could in case the plane caught fire. Cows were grazing in the field. After what we'd just been through, it was surreal.' What was horrifyingly real, though, was the realization that they were behind enemy lines. 'There could be Germans behind every tree. I had this sudden fear of coming face to face with them and being captured.' That was not what he had signed up for.

The RAF crew set about destroying maps and documents as figures began to appear across the fields – 'young people in clogs, waving handkerchiefs and shouting, and others in typical Dutch country dress, all running towards us. They stared at us, and we at them.' Gamgee managed to ask – in broken French, of all languages, though they were in the Netherlands – whether there were Germans around, and was told they were a mile or so away in one direction. But in the *other* direction, they were assured, were the Allied lines. 'We made it clear in which direction we wanted to go!' The Dutch villagers provided a car and they set off – eight Englishmen and two Dutchmen all crammed in the same vehicle – to cheers from the villagers. 'They regarded us as liberators and heroes, but we never felt like that. They were so excited to see us and thought the war had come to an end. But it hadn't. They were putting their lives at risk by helping us and I really admired them for that.'

The car took them through the German lines to Grave, now in the hands of American paratroopers after the success of their part in Market Garden, and from there they were taken to Eindhoven. On the way they ran into what all those trapped in Arnhem, paratroopers and Dutch citizens alike, had for so long been desperate to see – the trucks, tanks and armoured cars of the advancing British Second Army. They were way behind schedule and still with a long way to go. It had taken longer than expected for the Americans to clear the bridges in their sectors. Every foot of the road had to be fought for against unexpectedly fierce and concentrated enemy opposition. Indeed, as Gamgee and the rest of the downed crew approached a particular village, they were flagged down by a military policeman and told that a German counter-attack was in progress. Enemy tanks were concealed in a wood and attempting to destroy a road bridge in the village and delay the advance on Arnhem even more. Only when this skirmish was over could they proceed.

When they did get to move on, it was with a convoy of army vehicles picking up German prisoners and taking them to a POW cage. Looking at them, Gamgee couldn't help thinking 'that in slightly different circumstances, it could have been me. The unexpected had happened to them in the same way it had happened to us – but we were still free. For the moment.' That last caveat was significant, because the convoy now came under fire. 'We heard a bang and the sound of a shell exploding. One of our trucks up ahead was burning. I realized we were still in danger, and the Germans could be on us in an instant. Things could still go very badly.' Overhead, he saw the latest flight of supply planes heading north-east towards Arnhem and Oosterbeek. He sympathized with the men inside. He had more than an inkling of what they were about to face. But for Gamgee, the end was in sight. He was home a few days later, though the welcome was hardly ecstatic. The aircrew disappeared to be debriefed, but no one bothered to ask for his report. 'We were left on our own to wait until one of our officers turned up to collect us. He looked at me and my week's growth of beard and dishevelled clothes and suggested I'd better get a shave and clean myself up before I got back to the unit.' Gamgee, though, was just happy to be alive. 'Out of my company of dispatchers we lost twenty-six killed over three days. I was lucky.'

★

Others taking part in the supply runs, however, found themselves in that very situation that Gamgee had feared might be his fate – as prisoners of war. Gamgee's plane came down well south of Arnhem and close to the Allied lines, but bomb aimer Joe Brough's Stirling veered off in the opposite direction after dropping its cargo. 'The barrage over the city was intense and as we turned away we were hit several times. Both inner engines were put out of action and we immediately lost flying speed. As we were only at 500 feet anyway, there was no alternative but to crash land.' The pilot, despite shrapnel wounds to his feet, belly-flopped them down in a field in one piece, but that was the end of their good fortune. 'Our landing place couldn't have been worse. A nearby farmhouse was occupied by German troops who began firing at the Stirling even though we had come to a rest and had no chance of retaliating.' He thought the enemy soldiers' behaviour despicable. 'We evacuated through the escape hatch on top of the fuselage under a hail of bullets. We were lucky that only one of us was hit.' The crew crouched beneath the wing, watching the Germans. But there was nowhere to go, no possibility of escape. The pilot got to his feet and, with his hands above his head and shouting '*Kamerad*', led his men towards the farmhouse and the levelled rifles of their captors. 'As we drew nearer,' Brough recalled, 'I noticed the lightning flashes on the collars of their tunics. They were SS.'

What followed was terrifying. 'We were lined up in front of some bushes and two very large soldiers with sub-machine guns came forward and stood menacingly before us, guns pointing at us at chest level. It was the scariest moment of my life.' They all believed they were about to be shot. Brough felt 'fear, despair, helplessness, panic. I had been frightened before. One can't do thirteen ops over enemy territory as I had done and not have been frightened at times. But I had never experienced anything like this before.' The execution scene froze, and what seemed to him to be a lifetime passed before, on the orders of an officer, the two German soldiers lowered their weapons. 'If this was a display of power to intimidate us, it certainly succeeded.' The crew were herded under escort down a tree-lined street, carrying their wounded skipper, to a barracks, where they were put in individual cells. In that time-honoured phrase, their war was over. An oflag lay ahead for the officers, a stalag for the other ranks, and an eight-month wait for deliverance.

But having to ditch didn't necessarily mean stagnation in a POW camp. One of the best-known Arnhem pilots was Flight Lieutenant

Jimmy Edwards, who became a celebrated comedian of post-war radio and the early days of television. He would be Mr Glum in radio's *Take It from Here* and the cane-wielding headmaster in TV's *Whacko*. Few of those watching him and laughing realized that his trademark, a flamboyant handlebar moustache, hid the scarring that resulted from his part in the Arnhem re-supply mission. He was always a funny man, full of loud bonhomie and vintage RAF humour. Before setting off from Down Ampney in the Dakota he had christened 'The Pie-eyed Piper of Barnes'[13] he nipped into the back to scrawl 'Delivered courtesy of Jim Air' on the panniers.[14] But the run-in to Arnhem through heavy flak on what was his fourth sortie must have wiped the smile from his face. This was a more serious business than ever. He was about to give the signal to roll out the panniers over the designated DZ when he caught sight of a single green Very light coming up from the garden of a large house. In defiance of standing orders to ignore such things, he decided this was a bona fide signal from the lads below – and he was right. He was over the Hartenstein Hotel at Oosterbeek, and he dropped his cargo on the tennis courts.[15] Then it was feet up for a leisurely cruise home. 'I engaged George [the autopilot], and called for coffee and sandwiches.'

A German fighter plane spoiled his day. 'I saw it approaching rapidly, and at our level. There were little sparkles of light on its wings, which could only mean it was firing at us.' As it flashed by, he grabbed back control and tried to manoeuvre away. He was cross, as he later explained. He had a variety show to do that evening at camp, for which he'd specially written some new sketches, and there was now a danger he wouldn't get the chance to air them. The Focke-Wulf 190 came charging in again. Edwards responded, as he had been trained, by turning in towards the attacker, who veered away. Then he sought safety in broken clouds below, but the fighter followed him in and was now dead astern. 'He hit us time and time again until the wings were full of holes.'

Edwards twisted and turned in an ever tighter corkscrew. 'My flying instruments were spinning crazily and I lost all track of time and sense of our whereabouts. It was amazing that the plane was still flying we had been hit so often.' Not long after, it wasn't. The propellers suddenly spun madly, their traction lost, and the starboard engine burst into flames. 'We'd had it. I yelled for everyone to bale out.' His co-pilot and navigator were gone, and he was about to grab his parachute and join them when he saw three of the dispatchers huddled in the back and making no attempt to exit. He roared at them to get out and, amid the raging noise and panic, he saw they were badly injured and unable to move. They had been hit by bullets and were in a bad way.

This was a moment for real grit, which Edwards had. 'There was nothing for it but to try for a crash landing. I yanked open the escape hatch in the roof above my head, and stuck my head out to avoid the flames which were now enveloping the cockpit. With one hand on the wheel of the steering-column and the other held in front of my face for protection, I managed to keep her fairly level as we plunged down towards the ground. I instinctively pulled out of the dive at tree-top height and held the nose up as best I could while the speed dropped off. Then, with a rending and crashing, we plunged into the forest.' The Dakota smashed through a plantation of young trees, which slowed it down instead of tearing it apart. Finally, the nose dug into the ground, and the tail came up in the air. 'We hung poised for a split second, with the fuselage almost vertical, and then, with a sickening crash, the tail came down again, and with the impact I was shot out of the hatch like a cork from a bottle.' He came back to earth alongside the now blazing aircraft. The three wounded dispatchers were still inside, and would never emerge from this funeral pyre.

Edwards was bereft. He had just two of his crew left – the radio operator and one of the dispatchers – and 'moaning and cursing' they stumbled to the shelter of a ditch among the trees. 'We lay there, panting and trembling, and waited to see what would happen to us next. I had absolutely no idea where we were, except that it must be Holland. I didn't really care much, for my hands were now shaking with shock, and the left side of my face was taut and stinging where I had been thrown through the flames.' He'd 'had it', he admitted. If the Germans arrived, he would give himself up.

But it was Dutch people who found them. There was a language mix-up when he thought they were German and, forgetting his decision that he would surrender, he reached for his revolver. 'They seemed to be civilians, but in my state of shock I couldn't work out the situation.' They calmed and reassured him. The area was full of Germans but their rescuers would look after them, which they duly did. The three were smuggled under cover of darkness to a farmhouse, and from there driven across the shifting front line to a British field hospital at Grave for treatment. It had been an epic flight, even in the astonishing annals of the Arnhem re-supply saga. Three men were dead in the wreckage of The Pie-Eyed Piper – ironically, the ones whose lives Edwards had tried to save with his crash landing. Three got home in one piece, though Edwards would need reconstructive plastic surgery for his badly burnt face. The two who baled out went into captivity for the rest of the war.

★

Air Vice-Marshal Charles Medhurst may have been a high-ranking RAF officer with huge wartime responsibilities, but he was a father first and foremost, and he was desperate to know what had happened to his son, Dick, as was the young man's sister, Rozanne. She was in her office at Bletchley Park when the phone rang. 'It was my father, and he said, "Terrible news, Dick is missing." He had been told straight away. As soon as the squadron found out, they must have called him.' She was stunned. 'I'd read about Arnhem in the papers and heard it mentioned on the radio. We knew that Dick was going over with supplies because that was what Down Ampney, where he was based, was mainly for. But we had no idea he was flying into the battle area, no concept that he was anywhere in danger. My mother always imagined he was behind the scenes.' And now he was, in that dreadful word, 'missing'. That KG374 had gone down was a certainty, but the precise fate of its crew was unknown, though those in the trenches around Arnhem who had seen it fall in flames could have had little doubt. But back in England, families could only wonder and wait. Rozanne was in agony. 'Missing is worse than death. You're in limbo. Was he alive? Was he dead? Or terribly badly wounded? Had he lost his memory? All sorts of things go through your mind.

And though you're in the middle of a war, it's still a shock. You never think it'll happen to you or your family. Masses of friends of ours in the RAF had been killed or were missing. But it's different when it's one of your own.'

She managed to get compassionate leave and took a train to the family home in Yorkshire. 'My mother and father were there, along with my sister, who'd just had a baby and whose husband was on active service with his regiment in France. We just kept going over it, that he might be injured somewhere or captured, that we might hear.' But she and her father had to swallow their grief. Duty called, and they both went back to their war work. A week later, Dick's suitcase with his personal effects was sent back from his station. 'I'd never seen my father cry before but now he did. He couldn't open the case. "I just can't," he said, and asked me to. So I opened it and it was just unbearable. It makes me cry still to think about it. All his unfinished letters to June, his new girlfriend, saying how he'd miss her and how he was so in love with her. His little Air Force prayer book, family pictures, his clothes, his log books. Here was his life in a suitcase.'

The waiting to know went on. 'Many people were missing for six, seven, eight months, a lot longer even, and still turned up. But there was no one to ask. We didn't know then that Harry King had survived.' In truth, few people knew that. After being blown out of the exploding KG374, King had landed in a field, never knowing how his parachute had opened, except that it had. 'I had no recollection of pulling the release key but I must have done it instinctively.' On the ground, he met up with a group of paras and was involved with them in a furious scrap with an SS regiment, at the end of which he was taken prisoner, along with sixty-one paratroopers the Germans rooted out of woods and houses. In Stalag Luft 1, he received a letter from Charles Medhurst, who had since heard he was a prisoner, asking 'what you think may have happened to the remainder of the crew, particularly whether they were wounded and whether the aircraft was under control when you left it'. King, who had tried to find out from other POWs what happened to his plane and failed, could be of no help.

There was a postscript. In January 1945, Rozanne's father, now Sir

Charles, was posted abroad as Commander-in-Chief Middle East. Rozanne got a compassionate posting from Bletchley to a Secret Intelligence Service office in Cairo to be with her mother and father. The family was still on tenterhooks, not knowing what had happened to Dick but increasingly anxious as the months went by and there was no news of him. They veered from optimism to despair and back again, stuck in some awful emotional no-man's land. It was in May and the war was over when the news they dreaded finally came. 'My parents were hosting an enormous cocktail party for the whole command. Three hundred people were coming to Air House, where we lived. Just before it started, a message came through from the Air Ministry that Dick's body had been found on a farm near Arnhem by an RAF investigation team.' It was utterly shattering all over again. 'He'd been found but he was dead and so that was that. Up to that point there had been a glimmer of hope and we'd talked about him all the time. But now the waiting and wondering were over at last. And the even more terrible thing was that we had to carry on with this cocktail party and look happy and pleased to see everybody. You could almost go mad. But my father was commander-in-chief and he had to get on with it. He didn't cry then, but he was absolutely white as a sheet and looked ghastly.'

She reckons, though, that he was never the same. 'He was a changed man after losing his only son. It's a dreadful thing, but in reality we were going through what so many hundreds of thousands of families had been and still were going through. And that made it possible for us to carry on too. You know you're not special because you've lost a son or a brother. We had to get rid of Hitler and everyone was making these sacrifices.' Dick is not forgotten. 'I still think about him,' she says, 'and wonder what he would have been, what he would have become, whether he would have married June. I think about him as he was as I last saw him – full of fun, full of life, full of enterprise. I know he would have gone on to do some good somewhere.

'When he came down to Bletchley, the last time I saw him, he told me how when he was training in America he was flying in the Grand Canyon and his engine cut out. "And the funny thing was," he said to me, "that I wasn't remotely frightened. I knew if I didn't get my engine going again, I was going straight into the side of the canyon and I was going to die. But I felt no fear whatsoever, just this intense interest as to what was going to happen next." It was very curious but we found that very comforting. I'm sure he would have felt the same in that aeroplane over Arnhem. He was really philosophical, he'd thought about life and death. At the end, I hope he wasn't scared as he faced his death.'

But had any of this been worth it? So little of the re-supplies that men gave their lives to deliver actually got through that many men questioned what, if anything, had been achieved. It is reckoned that 14,500 panniers were dropped but, at best, 13 per cent got through; at worst, little over half that. Significantly, the total tonnage over 8 days was around 300 tons – when the amount needed to sustain the entire 1st Airborne was a minimum of 270 tons per day, every day. We know where the rest went. When Dakota navigator Harry King joined up with the paras on the ground after being blown out of his plane, they offered him a cup of tea and a bar of chocolate. 'That's all we've got,' they told him. 'What do you mean, that's all you've got?' he exclaimed indignantly. 'We've just dropped supplies to you!' The reply choked him. 'Sure, you dropped sardines, but the Huns got them. We got nothing.'

8. At the Bridge – A Desperate Battle for Survival

As the sun rose on Tuesday 19 September, the mood among the besieged British contingent clustered precariously at the northern end of the Arnhem bridge was reminiscent of the Alamo. Brave men – cut off from the main airborne force, which had retreated to Oosterbeek, and surrounded by overwhelming enemy forces – kept doggedly to their task. There was no well-defined defence perimeter around their positions. Instead, they were scattered in shell-battered and bullet-pitted buildings – houses, warehouses, a school – on either side of the road ramp leading to the bridge. It was not just one Alamo, in fact, but half a dozen or so – to begin with. Over the next thirty-six hours, each stronghold would be eliminated one by one by unrelenting enemy mortar, gun and tank bombardments and constant probing by well-trained and determined SS infantrymen.

It would be romantic folly to think the defenders were undaunted. The roars coming from all directions as the diesel engines of yet more German tanks fired up were chilling indications of the firepower assembling to crush them. To Private James Sims, it sounded like the start of a Grand Prix, and he imagined the enemy drivers playfully jockeying for pole position on the grid. But many of the paras still clung tenaciously to the belief that reinforcements would arrive, eventually, though their faith was being sorely tried. That morning, a wireless operator at brigade headquarters in one of the buildings finally managed to overcome the problems of limited range and high buildings to get a radio message through to corps headquarters. He was able to report for the first time to Montgomery's army that 2 Para were holding the bridge and 'were looking forward to their early arrival'; a wry understatement. The reply was enigmatic and not encouraging. For security reasons, officers at the other end couldn't say on air precisely where they were, but Major Tony Hibbert, who was listening in, got the distinct and unwelcome impression that XXX Corps was still the wrong side of Nijmegen. 'Still a long way to go,' he noted.

The news filtered down the line. Ted Mordecai remembered an officer returning from brigade headquarters to brief the men that XXX Corps was being held up by enemy opposition and it would be 'some time' before they were anywhere near. 'In the meantime, we had to hang on to our end of the bridge end for as long as possible.' Even now, Mordecai and his mates kept the faith. They had no doubt the rescuers would reach them, given time, and they would just have to be patient. 'We settled down once again to wait.' From time to time, the 'Whoa Mahomet!' battle cry would sound from one of the para-held buildings, and the resulting chorus was a spirited confirmation of continuing defiance. It also told Frost and his fellow commanders which buildings the British were still managing to hold. No reply meant that another outpost had been overrun or abandoned.

Sims, though, had no four walls to protect him. He was out in the open, still in his mortar trench in the middle of a traffic island at a crucial crossroads a few hundred yards from the bridge. Suddenly, the Grand Prix traffic he had envisaged was hurtling his way. 'Some damned fool must have dropped the starting flag because tanks and armoured cars came tearing down the road towards us, their machine guns going full blast, raking our position with fire.' Behind him, airborne anti-tank gunners responded. 'Though completely without cover, these magnificent men brought their 6-pounders into action and the leading armoured car ground to a flaming halt, while those that followed either piled into it or fell victim to the heavy fire that poured from airborne-held houses. What was left of the German team beat a hasty retreat.' But only to come again. 'Despite the fact that we had won every action,' mused Sims, 'the pressure never went away. Jerry still had us pinned down.' He guessed correctly that the Germans were taking heavy losses. The crucial difference was that the enemy had reinforcements pouring in. In the end, this was attrition, a numbers game that the isolated and under-strength paras could not win.

Their enclave of resistance was visibly and audibly shrinking. Separate explosions now merged into one almost continuous rolling detonation, Sims recalled, 'and the earth shook as if it was alive. My head sang and I was numb to any feeling beyond the basic instinct to survive.' He could only watch from his slit trench as houses held by paratroopers were set alight by incendiary shells. He was a witness to courage on a grand scale. 'Airborne soldiers kept on firing from the tops of blazing buildings, even with the roof fallen in. Then they moved down to the second floor, then to the first, finally to the basement. Only when this was alight did they evacuate the building and take over another. As each hour passed we were driven into a smaller and smaller area.'

Even in intact strongholds, conditions were deteriorating rapidly. Mordecai was in need of tea but the taps were dry and he was down to his last half-bottle of water. The men pooled what little they had for a brew, knowing there would be no replenishment. But woe betide any Germans expecting a quick, clean sweep to victory. A party of enemy sappers was spotted clambering through the girders beneath the bridge. It looked as if they were attempting to reconnect the explosive charges, the ones they had been laying just before the paras arrived and chased them off. One big bang would destroy both the bridge and any remaining prospect of the Market Garden mission succeeding. A long burst from a Bren gun foiled the German engineers again. The bridge was still in one piece, still viable, still a prize worth fighting for, if ever XXX Corps managed to get here.

Expectation of those reinforcements could all too easily morph into overzealous – and dangerous – outbreaks of optimism. In the schoolhouse, one of two remaining British-held strongholds on the far side of the road ramp, Major Eric Mackay was fighting off a German infantry assault on one wall when an exultant cry went up from the other end of the building. 'We're all right!' came a loud and gleeful shout. 'A couple of Churchills' – British tanks – 'are outside!' Could it be true? Had XXX Corps broken through, finally made it? Mackay dashed through the building – to find himself staring at German Mark IIIs. The air must have turned blue as 'I held a short course in tank recognition.' At that time, the enemy tanks were concentrating their firepower on the other para-occupied building in the area. As German soldiers followed in on foot behind the tanks, Mackay's men caught them in crossfire. The tanks swivelled menacingly, turning their attention to the school, and the defenders inside could do nothing but keep their heads down until the barrage of shells was over. But when advancing German infantry appeared again, the paras popped back up to pick them off with their rifles. The battle lasted five hours, at the end of which the neighbouring house was lost, 'in spite of all our efforts'.

Although the overall flow of the battle was decisively in one direction, there was plenty of ebb, too, as every inch of headway was fiercely fought over. German soldiers who had set up positions in a building next to the school came under such intense fire from Mackay and his men that they came out under a white flag. He refused to accept their surrender and sent them back. 'We could take no prisoners, as we had no food or water,' he explained, 'so we told them to get back in there and fight it out. This they did. Soon they tried to make a break, and were eliminated.' It was a small victory but good for morale at a time when the odds against the occupiers were lengthening. 'Tanks were coming up in relays from the waterfront. The next-door house was gone, as was the one on the opposite side. The only other position besides ourselves was holding out with difficulty.' At midday, Mackay radioed battalion commander Frost with a revised situation report. If attacks continued on this scale, he told the colonel, he no longer thought he could last another night. Frost's reply was unequivocal: he must hold on at all cost.

That cost was fearful already, and rising all the time. When the German tanks took a break – for lunch, perhaps, the laconic Mackay imagined – heavy mortar took over so that, as one soldier put it, 'the very air seemed to wail and sigh with the number of projectiles passing through it.' A shell came through the roof of Mackay's command post, killing one man where he stood and wounding all the others. Meanwhile, the Germans had reclaimed the house whose occupiers had tried to surrender and were pouring a hail of bullets into the side of the school so that movement between floors was impossible. The advantage was firmly with the attackers. For the Airborne, defending what they held was about to become even more desperate.

*

There was no respite on the nearside of the road ramp either. In brigade headquarters, Ron Brooker's spirits spiralled upwards on a rumour that back-up elements of 1st Airborne had broken through from the direction of the drop zones – 'There's hope in sight, a chance we might actually make it through' – then spiralled downwards when it turned out not to be true and instead the building came under renewed attack. Snipers kept the defenders pinned down while SS troops stormed the walls and windows. 'It took close contact, hard fighting to hold them out,' he noted, but he was being modest. In fact, contact couldn't get any closer than this toe-to-toe warfare as the two sides slugged it out. Casualties were heavy on both sides. 'We were tired, hungry, exhausted, injured. We suffered from lack of food, water and sleep. Because we were running out of ammunition, we were under new orders to fire our weapons only when there was a reasonable chance of hitting a target. Our basement area was packed with wounded men, most of them too badly hurt to carry a weapon. All walking wounded had returned to the fight, many of them to be hit again, sometimes with a fatal wound. Everybody knew it was the endgame. But we still had our chests out and our heads up.' There was a moment of relief when a Messerschmitt pilot mistimed his strafing run and crashed into the church spire, from which one of his own side had been sniping and causing havoc. Both pilot and sniper were killed. Two in one! 'There was plenty of cheering when that happened.'

Not everyone was a hero or able to summon up the willpower to continue the fight. Corporal Leo Hall remembered a fellow signaller who lost his nerve and refused to do his stint on the radios up in the attic, which was an increasing target for enemy fire. 'You can shoot me if you want, but I'm not going,' the man replied when Hall pointed to his stripes and said it was an order. The NCO backed off, remembering that this particular soldier had come close to being killed in Italy and still bore the scars, both physical and, as he now realized, mental. But such examples were notable for their rarity. By and large and by most accounts, there was no despondency among the beleaguered. Para humour survived. One man, standing down from the windows to take a breather, sat on the floor strumming a banjo. When enemy shelling started up again, a mate indicated the banjo player and said, 'Well, you can hardly blame them, can you?' In some houses, the phones still worked and a story went round that one wag got through to the Arnhem exchange and asked to be connected to a Winston Churchill in Downing Street, London. Another paratrooper, spotting a German patrol entering the garden, apparently rang the Arnhem police station to complain of 'intruders'.

There was one very real communication, however, that was not a hoax or a joke. It came from the enemy and was a message that the defenders were completely surrounded and should surrender. Frost's reply became a legend of Arnhem defiance – he told the Germans they were the ones who should come out with their hands up. And in a semi-comical moment, it looked as if they were doing just that. Outside in the street, a white flag was seen waving, greeted by cheers from weary British soldiers behind their barricades. 'Regrettably, our jubilation was very short-lived,' one recalled, 'as we spotted a pathetic band of Dutch civilians desperately trying to reach German lines.' Though he himself was in great pain from a bad chest wound and prevented from getting to a casualty station for treatment by the intensity of the fighting, it was the Dutch he felt sorry for. 'Three days earlier these poor people had greeted us with joy and gratitude. I prayed that they would make it.'

Inside the headquarters building, anyone who could still hold a weapon was drafted to the wall. Despite a blinding eye injury, Ron Brooker took over a Bren gun, lay well back from a window and pointed it roughly in the right direction. 'My vision was very blurred, but I knew if anyone tried to enter the window he would be out of luck.' But what he then found himself facing was terrifying. A Tiger tank rattled down the road ramp and came to a halt directly opposite him. 'The turret turned until the 88mm gun was aiming straight at me. I knew at that moment what it was like to be scared! The gun fired. As the shell came through the top right-hand corner of the room, it made a sound like an express train rushing through a railway station. Then there was another crash as it exited through the back wall. I was covered in dust and debris, but unharmed.' He had no idea how he had survived. 'Was it a dud? Was it an armour-piercing projectile?' As the turret turned to a new target, he was just glad to be in one piece. But for how long? 'Word reached us that the situation on the other side of the ramp was desperate and the perimeter there could soon be lost. Our positions too could not hold on much longer. Our casualties were mounting by the hour. The makeshift mortuary was full, and the dead and dying had to be left where they fell because there was no time to move them or anywhere to put them.'

★

James Sims was still in his slit trench in the middle of that cross-roads, where, somehow, not a single bomb or splinter hit him. 'With each successive salvo of mortar bombs I screwed my steel helmet further into the earth and clawed at the silty soil. I kept repeating to myself, "Hold on . . . hold on . . . you must hold on."' Lying there all alone felt to him 'like being in a newly dug grave waiting to be buried alive. Each fresh explosion sent rivulets of earth crumbling around my helmet and into my mouth. I started praying, and really meaning it, for the first time in my life.' His was a rabbit's-eye view of the battle, popping his head out from time to time to see wave after wave of German attacks repelled. 'One German soldier fell just outside the White House. Two airborne medics, unarmed, wearing Red Cross armbands and carrying a stretcher, ran out from our battalion headquarters building to aid him. Their mission must have been obvious to everyone, but I heard the ripping fire of a German machine gun and saw the front man crumple into the gutter. The man at the rear sprinted for safety, pursued by a hail of bullets. A howl of rage went up from the watching paratroopers at this act of murder.' The body of the dead medic lay 10 yards from Sims, next to the corpse of the German he had died trying to save. 'Debris from a burning house began to fall on them. The flames got hold of the uniform of the medic and licked hungrily along his spine. I looked away.'

If Sims felt all alone out there on the island, that was because, by now, he really was. He heard a shout from the window of a building. 'Blimey,' said a voice, 'there's someone still down there. Eh, you! Come inside out of it.' Sims remonstrated. He'd been ordered to stay there. The voice enlightened him. 'There's no one out there any more except you. Now come on in.' He was appalled and affronted. 'How had I been overlooked when everyone had been recalled?' He surmised that he must have been so far down in his slit trench that he had been missed. 'Gathering my gear and rifle, I slid out of the trench and made for the nearest house. A fusillade of shots rang out, one of which hit the pack I was carrying and spun it round in my hand, but I got there safely.'

Once inside the house, Sims went upstairs. 'I sat down and took off my steel helmet for the first time in nearly three days and rested my head in my hands for a moment. Then I wandered into one of the front bedrooms which overlooked the northern end of the bridge.' A defender lying prone behind a window urged him to get down. 'There's no one out there,' Sims whispered. The other soldier nodded to a still figure lying in the corner. 'That's what *he* thought,' he said. There was a blood-stained rag over the dead man's face but a jolted Sims recognized him by his unusual height. 'A couple of weeks ago he'd got me to forge a sleeping-out pass that he had liberated from some adjutant's desk so that he could stay the night with a girl in Nottingham. Now he was asleep for good.' Sims also discovered that his best mate, a Cockney known as Slapsie, had also bought it, blown in half by a shell. 'I was stunned. It was hardly possible. An ex-Commando, veteran of Norway, Tunisia, Sicily and Italy, Slapsie always seemed indestructible. We had shared the same billet, eaten together, drunk together, taken the mickey out of each other, and mucked in together. Now he was gone. A sergeant saw how distressed I was and gave me a swig of cherry brandy. I was really grateful for it.'

That evening, the White House fell. Sims recalled it first being sprayed with enemy tracer, which the Germans used as a warning that this was the next target for their big guns. It was a last chance for those inside to flee. No one did, and five minutes later a shell from a self-propelled gun burst against the wall from no more than a hundred yards away, point-blank range. 'It hit the top floor and the entire building seemed to shake itself like a dog. We could plainly see the riflemen and airborne engineers inside, caution thrown to the wind, kneeling openly at the blasted windows and pouring fire down at the Germans as though determined to take as many as possible with them to death.' The big gun came even closer and fired a second shell. 'The walls of the White House appeared to breathe out before the whole structure collapsed, floors fell inside and a towering column of flame shot into the sky. A cut-off scream marked the end of many gallant riflemen and engineers.' The destruction of the imposing and seemingly rock-solid White House was a blow to morale. 'Its sudden collapse was a terrific shock for us all.'

The skittles were falling one by one to overwhelming force. Another forward position was lost when Mordecai's unit was ordered to evacuate the building it was in and pull back. 'We picked our way out of the wreckage and out through the back door into a small garden, then over a high wall into the next one.' It was a risky manoeuvre, involving one set of lads sitting on the top – an easy target for snipers – to heave up those on the ground. Fortunately, they managed it without being spotted and scrambled inside the house. Here, fellow paras were trying to fashion a safer escape route by 'mouse-holing'. They were using their bayonets and spades to knock through the dividing wall into the next house in the terrace. 'It was better than going out along the street and being met by machine-gun fire.' But going out into the open could not be put off indefinitely. Two houses away, the building was on fire and the flames were spreading their way at a rate of knots. Staying put was no longer an option. 'The heat was already terrific and we knew we had to get out or be burnt alive.'

Choking from the black smoke now creeping around them, they prepared to dash through the twilight for the cover of an archway under the bridge itself. Jittery men lined up in a back alley, blackening their faces with mud as camouflage in the darkening Arnhem night. It was a pointless precaution because, with flames taking hold all around them, the whole area was illuminated. A road had to be crossed, although it was as bright as day out there. Mordecai steeled himself and went in the first group, head down, hell for leather, and just made it to safety when a machine gun opened up. The next dice with death was a race across a patch of waste ground before flopping down in a ditch alongside a hedge. 'As we lay there, we heard the clank of a tank moving towards us, getting nearer every minute. We hugged the ground, not daring to lift our heads in case the Germans spotted our faces. The clanking came nearer until I could see the shape of the tank through the hedge about 3 feet away. I prayed that it wouldn't swivel in my direction.' Not a muscle moved as the tank went off down the road, then turned and came back, making another pass by the hidden British troops. 'We knew better than to fire at it. Sten guns weren't much use against armour, and we'd only have given ourselves away.' Finally, it moved off, and the men breathed sighs of relief.

But the obstacle race was not over. In another mad dash towards the archway under the bridge, they were silhouetted against the flames of a burning building and spotted. German machine-gunners let rip. 'We put on a spurt and dived for cover behind a low wall.' They were now right down by the river, and it occurred to Mordecai that there might be a way out of all this. He turned to his mate Harry with a radical suggestion. 'Look,' he said, 'it seems obvious to me that we're not going to be relieved. Why don't we swim across the river and make our way towards our own lines?' It was clearly a very long shot that they would make it, but even so the odds might be better than the ones facing them if they didn't try. Stick or twist? But Harry said no. 'We should stick together with everyone else and hope for the best,' he replied. The moment passed.

'By now, we were almost under the bridge,' Mordecai recalled, 'so we ran across the remaining distance and linked up with a unit already there.' Beneath the span they built up a barricade with anything they could find. A party of sappers mined the ground 75 yards ahead, 'then we took up position and waited to see what would happen next. We were all exhausted and thankful just to lie on the ground to rest. But it was now quite obvious that we were on our own, completely hemmed in and gradually being compressed into an ever decreasing circle.'

*

For many of the men at the bridge at this time, the suspicion that had always nagged away at the back of their minds – that XXX Corps was never going to arrive – was turning into a certainty. Not for the first time, the sound of tanks' tracks on the bridge brought a moment of joy that the relieving column was here. Every time, the reality was more German tanks, which inched forward cautiously, though their commanders might have been braver if they had realized, as Sims did, that 'by now we had nothing with which to oppose them except a few hand grenades.' He was, for the first time, downhearted. 'The great thrust by the Second Army to join up with us had failed. We had had it, and we felt bitter and betrayed.' A silence of men contemplating no future settled over the group, broken by the 19-year-old Sims wondering out loud 'what it's going to be like to die'. 'Don't know, kid,' a veteran replied with a grin. 'Never tried it.' Sims lay stretched out on a couch near a window, pointing his rifle out at the smoke and fire beyond. His chin rested on the butt and his helmet was tilted over his eyes. 'I was terrified of being blinded.' His hand dipped into a 'liberated' box of chocolate liqueurs and the silky touch of the packaging set his mind racing. 'I wondered if my fingers would ever feel the soft skin of a girl again. As I munched the rich Dutch chocolates, I thought of the seeming inevitability of death when, at just nineteen, I had seen so very little of life.'

Years later, in his memoirs of Arnhem, he would write movingly about the nobility of the comrades around him as their lives hung by a thread. 'It was as though they grew in stature and all the small, irritating quirks of character disappeared. Ennobled in some strange way by this physical and spiritual auto-da-fé, each man appeared more concerned for his neighbour than for himself. All seemed prepared for the end and ready to face it. The word "surrender" was not mentioned and I doubt if it was even thought of.'

That night, in the school on the far side of the ramp, a weary Mackay was also taking stock as he stared out at flames from burning houses mingling with a pall of smoke to create an eerie sense of doom. He knew how close he and his men had just come to defeat, saved only when two rampaging Tigers opted to withdraw rather than press home their advantage. 'They left not a moment too soon. Two more shots would have finished us.' He considered taking the fight to the enemy, leading out a patrol to sneak up on tanks parked up for the night and blowing them up with improvised bombs. Discretion won the argument in his head. 'We remained in our positions on the first floor.' His defensive situation was not so bad, he convinced himself. The breaches made by shells from the Tigers gave him and his men plenty of holes to shoot through, while the light from the burning buildings illuminated the no-man's land outside so no one could sneak up on them. 'We could hold our own,' he concluded. What worried him most was the condition of his men. He totted up his casualties – out of his original fifty men, four were dead and twenty-seven wounded. Only nineteen were fighting fit, and they were beginning to show signs of fatigue. He issued Benzedrine pills. The stimulants were not a total success. 'Some men got double vision and others saw things that were non-existent' – though whether the imaginary horrors in their heads could be worse than the real ones around them must be debatable. 'We stood by all night, but were not attacked. There were one or two skirmishes as German patrols tried to get by. These were suitably dealt with.' The real problem was that 'no one could afford to go to sleep as we were few in numbers. So ended the third day.'

But in the darkness of that night, it was hard to see much hope, if any. 'We knew our situation was hopeless,' admitted a paratrooper in the headquarters building.[1] 'The whole of the battalion was under ceaseless fire. Supplies of everything were extremely low, casualties continued to mount and we were desperately in need of relief. Paratroopers, once so full of optimism, were being driven out of one position after another with machine-like German proficiency. But, totally weary and most in pain, we fought on.' Tomorrow would show, however, that 'courage alone was not enough.'

★

It was a common theme among men of Arnhem that to have any ink-ling of its true horrors, you had to be there. The same, though, went for different parts of the battlefield. The paras making their last stand at the bridge came to realize that their comrades just a few miles away in Oosterbeek had no grasp of what they were enduring. This came home to Major Tony Hibbert on Wednesday morning when, in the brigade headquarters building, a rare radio signal over the faltering and faulty comms system got through to divisional headquarters at the Harten-stein Hotel. Frost was summoned to take the call and made his way up through the shattered building facing the bridge and into the attic to speak to Urquhart, the 1st Airborne commander, for the first time since Market Garden began. The general was now back with his head-quarters staff after managing to escape from the Arnhem outskirts where, for many vital hours, he had been forced to hide from the enemy to avoid capture. Urquhart was full of admiration and encour-agement, congratulating 2 Para for holding the bridge. 'We're all proud of you, John. Just hang on and the Second Army will be through any moment now,' he declared, not totally truthfully. Frost wasn't going to fall for the flannel. 'But we need reinforcements if we're to continue the battle,' he stated politely through the crackle of the static. 'We need ammunition, and it wouldn't be bad if we had some food either.'

It was then that Urquhart came up with a strange suggestion, under the circumstances: they should organize local civilians to go out and bring in food, ammunition and stores from some of the para-chuted re-supply containers which had gone astray the day before. Frost put the general straight. As Hibbert recalled the encounter: 'The colonel told him that it wouldn't be very sensible to go out for-aging since we were fighting in a devastated area, there were no civilians and we were surrounded in a perimeter of only 200 yards by a superior and somewhat aggressive enemy force. In any case, there were no containers nearby.' Hibbert turned away to observe reality rather than the commander's mistaken conjecture of conditions at the bridge. 'I scanned the road leading from the bridge with my binoculars. Buildings were exploding, with chunks of masonry flying in all directions, bullets were ricocheting from the walls and the road was covered in glass and debris.'

For Ron Brooker, overhearing this conversation between his superiors, the message was clear. They were on their own. Fears that, back at Oosterbeek, the rest of the division was in its own battle to survive were confirmed. 'It was now certain that there would be no help from them.' Here on the northern approach to the bridge they had got so close to conquering, their options were running out. 'The enemy seemed to have unlimited manpower, and they were willing and able to take heavy casualties to finish us off. Tanks arrived on the ramp again, and systematically blew more of our buildings to pieces. No food, no water, no ammo, unwashed and covered in dust and blood, we were a sorry sight.'

But still they were defiant. The school was now the only para-held building on the far side of the road ramp. None of its defenders had slept for three days. Here, too, water and food had long run out. Mackay and his men drove off three attacks in two hours, but the walls now resembled a sieve. 'Wherever you looked, you could see daylight,' he recalled. 'Rubble was piled high on the floors, laths hung down from the ceilings, a fine white dust of plaster covered everything. Splattered everywhere was blood – in pools on the floor, running down the stairs, on our smocks.' Eyes red-rimmed from lack of sleep peered out from blackened faces as the men huddled in twos and threes at their positions. The major was overwhelmed by their courage and pride, as even now they seemed to bask in a sense of their innate superiority. 'Around them lay four times their number of enemy dead.'

Meanwhile, Ted Mordecai was with sixty or so other men in a blocked-off yard full of old building materials in an archway of the bridge. He crouched behind a large iron boiler filled with tar and ate three hard-tack biscuits and two bars of chocolate, swilled down with the last of his water. He jettisoned the empty bottle. It was excess baggage now. So too were the maps he had been given for the operation, and he took them from their case and burnt them. Overhead, a flight of six light-blue Messerschmitts cruised – not Spitfires, as, for a fleeting moment, the men had hoped. Nervous paras fixed bayonets, pulled on their cigarettes and settled down to wait for the inevitable enemy assault on their position. Mordecai noticed a signaller with a small cage strapped to his back, inside which a carrier pigeon was cooing contentedly. He envied the bird its unawareness of what was going on – and its wings to fly from this death trap. When the attack came, Mordecai was deployed to a position in a nearby gutted house. 'To reach it we had to cross a little road, clear a 6-foot wall and then dash across an opening. Firing was now coming at us from all angles and we set off in batches between bursts of machine-gun fire.' He made a flying roll over the wall and landed next to the burnt-out corpse of a German soldier. 'At first glance I thought it was a tailor's dummy, and by the time I'd worked out what it was, the chaps in front of me had disappeared. I'd become separated from my pals' – an increasing occurrence as the pockets of resistance began to fall and the men became strung out.

Alone now, Mordecai reached the shelter of a building and turned to see a bomb explode among the men he'd just left under the bridge. 'I saw a stream of tracer emerging from some bushes and sprayed them with a full magazine from my Sten. The firing stopped.' Over the rubble he then went looking for his mates. 'Crouching low down on a pile of bricks behind the cover of a wall, I noticed that I was sweating and my feet were getting hot. Looking down, I saw wisps of smoke and smelt singeing leather. I was being cooked on bricks still red hot from the fire.' He stood up and ran to the next building. From there he looked out on the main street, a desolate scene of destruction. There was a badly battered tram with its cables dangling down and the grassy island pitted with foxholes, one of which Sims had buried himself in for so long and only lately left. Mordecai could see the bridge, the object of all this effort and fighting, pain and dying, just 200 impossible yards away.

The Germans were closing in all the time, patrolling the streets, slipping in and out of the ruined houses, squeezing the remnants of

2 Para into a smaller and smaller space. A new sound filled the air – loud whistle blasts as SS officers directed their troops in and out of buildings. A machine-gun patrol came Mordecai's way, each SS soldier festooned with ammunition belts. 'As they passed by an open gateway I gave them a burst from my Sten gun.' There was one house that still seemed to be offering organized resistance – brigade headquarters – and he decided that was where he wanted to be. 'I jumped out of a window of the house I was in and headed across the street, joined by some more of our chaps who emerged from another house.' Ducking and dodging, they dashed through well-directed machine-gun fire until they reached the headquarters building and were pulled inside. Here he was given a drink from a bottle of wine, allowed to rest for a short while, and then he was back in the fight behind a Bren gun, the very last, he would later realize, in what would soon be the last bastion in the Battle of the Bridge.

Mordecai was in a small room with half a dozen other soldiers, four of whom were dead or wounded, slumped with their backs to the wall. 'From my position in the window I could see we were completely surrounded.' He duelled with an enemy machine-gunner in bushes outside. 'The German was good and his aim was excellent. Every time I pushed the barrel of the Bren out of the window he let fly and bullets spattered off the outside wall. But by ducking below the window ledge and putting the Bren to one side I managed to silence him.' There were, however, hundreds outside to take the dead German soldier's place.

That Wednesday afternoon, the situation went into a rapid decline. Mackay and his men were finally forced out of the school on the far side of the road ramp when a Tiger tank and large self-propelled gun came in close. Their first salvo collapsed what little was left of the main wall. The dwindling band of survivors took to the cellar as more shells came hurtling in and flames poured down from the roof. Mackay counted his depleted force – fourteen able-bodied men, thirty-one wounded, five dead. 'I considered it necessary to evacuate,' he calmly recorded. They broke out in a group, heading northwards away from the bridge, taking their wounded with them on stretchers. 'Tanks were roaming up and down the roads 15 yards on either side of us.' But it was fierce crossfire from German-held houses that stopped them, ripping through the fleeing pack. Eight of the able-bodied fell; one of the wounded was shot dead. The situation was impossible, especially for the wounded. 'They would be massacred if we held out any longer,' Mackay concluded, and gave the order for them to surrender. But he wasn't yet ready to give up himself. With his six remaining men and the same number of machine guns, he determined to make a last stand.

*

In the building housing brigade headquarters, there was the same gritty air of defiance among its diminishing front line of defenders, though conditions were dire. How much longer could they hope to hold out? Most of the surrounding buildings had been demolished and anything left standing was burning. A mortar scored a direct hit on the room Mordecai was in and sent him flying. As he struggled to his feet, all he could see through the cloud of dust was 'a gaping hole where four of our chaps had been'. The attrition was awful and took no account of rank. Frost was badly wounded, struck on both legs by mortar fire, and out of action. Command of the shrinking redoubt passed to Major Freddie Gough, though, as Ron Brooker, who had been the major's driver on that helter-skelter jeep ride from the landing zone four days earlier, observed, there was very little he could do except hold on as long as possible, in case XXX Corps arrived.

James Sims was down in the basement, a casualty. After the fall of the White House, the German batteries had started on the building he was in and he had been sent into the garden to dig slit trenches, a task he was by now well versed in. He raised his pick and was hit by a blast of hot air from an exploding mortar. Lumps of metal tore into his leg, and he blacked out. He came to as two medics bent over him and 'two sets of brawny arms hauled me upright. They hooked my arms round their necks and heaved me along, my feet dragging on the ground. A shell exploded against a wall on our left and the blast brought us down, but by some miracle none of the splinters hit us. We continued to the back door of the headquarters building.' Inside, he caught sight of dozens of fellow paras at their posts, among whom morale seemed amazingly high. 'Men winked at me and shouted encouragement as I was borne below to the cellar.'

The makeshift casualty station here was a grim sight. 'The floors were carpeted in dead and badly wounded airborne soldiers, with more being brought in every minute. Many of the medics and order-lies had already been killed attempting to rescue the wounded, and the survivors of this brave band of men were out on their feet with exhaustion. A doctor examined me, his eyes lost in deep sockets and his face haggard from lack of sleep. Yet his voice was quiet and sym-pathetic, his hands capable and gentle. The wound was cleaned and I was given an injection.' Sims was curious to know how badly he was hurt. 'The medics had cut off my trouser leg, and my fingers groped gingerly towards my left thigh. There was a large carnation of shat-tered flesh, two holes at the back of the knee and another in my calf. I passed out again.'

He regained consciousness in the dim light of a tiny vault off the main cellar, his head and feet against the brickwork. He was lying between two other casualties. One of them was a dying officer, his body riddled with machine-gun bullets. He was muttering inces-santly, re-living, Sims surmised, his last patrol, because he kept shouting out a warning – 'Look out, Peter' – time and time again. 'Then he seemed to be at home and was talking to his wife and chil-dren.' Sims turned to the man on his other side and saw that his face had been completely shot away. 'A shell dressing covered what had been his eyes and nose, and a large piece of gauze mercifully veiled what had once been his jaws. A slight movement of the head and a bubbling sound from the gauze told me that this shell-torn fragment of humanity was still alive.' In this company, it must have crossed Sims's mind that he'd been laid with the dying and that he must therefore be dying too.

He slipped into a dream that became a nightmare, a twilight zone where he saw the faces of comrades he knew were dead. 'They seemed to be calling to me, "Thought you'd never get here. What took you so long? You're safe now.''' A terrified Sims woke to find a medic shaking him. 'You OK, matey? Blimey, you weren't half creating.' He was hauled out of the vault to the main cellar, over the bodies of the delirious officer and the faceless man, both now dead. He was grateful to be back in the land of the living. But for how long? Through the walls, the dull boom of big guns could be heard from outside. Inside, masonry fell, covering the casualties in dust. Eventually, the helpless Sims realized, 'this building too will collapse, and then what will become of us?' He didn't rate his chances much, 'wounded, losing blood and in a building already ablaze'. 'Any sign of the army?' he asked the orderly. 'No, mate,' the fellow replied. 'Looks like we've had it.'

But no one gave the appearance of being defeated. Wounded paras joked, cussed and shouted among themselves as they were passed information on the state of the fighting from those upstairs still manning the ramparts. 'As far as we knew, this was the last building we held, and it was already on fire. Food, water and ammunition were nearly all gone. But no one complained, and the only moans came from the seriously wounded in great pain. There was no talk of surrender. We still clung to the hope of an eleventh-hour miracle, trusting that our sacrifice was not to be in vain.'

Above, the desperate fight went on, as Sims saw when he dragged himself up the stairs to use the WC. He left the cellar, now so tightly packed with around three hundred bodies that the orderlies had almost no room to step between them. A Tiger tank was at the front door and control of the yard outside was constantly changing hands as the Germans wormed their way in, only to be repulsed. He marvelled that defenders he passed were still firing out of holes in the wall or through shattered windows. 'They turned and grinned at me, shouting encouragement and making ribald jokes at my expense. I noticed several paratroopers counting their rounds of ammo. One man had just a clip of five bullets left.' He overheard an officer talking earnestly into a radio and repeating the message over and over again: 'Our position is desperate. Please hurry.'

Returning to the cellar, Sims had no alternative but to lie with the wounded, and wait for whatever fate had in store. 'By 4 p.m. it was obvious that our position was hopeless. We could hear the crackle of burning wood upstairs and it was becoming painful to breathe because of the dense smoke. Something had to be done if they were not to be suffocated or burnt to death.' Upstairs, the crucial command decision was taken to request a ceasefire so that the wounded, packed like sardines in the cellar, could be evacuated. 'We asked the Germans for a two-hour truce and assistance to get them out,' Major Hibbert recalled. The Germans signalled their agreement but didn't back off and instead used the lull in the fighting to gain ground and infiltrate the yard again. A tougher decision was called for. The fit and any of the wounded who could walk would make a break for it. The rest would have to stay put and face as best they could whatever lay in store for them.

It was, in truth, the only option left. 'The whole area was ablaze and we no longer dominated it,' Hibbert said. 'We were down to around a hundred unwounded and walking wounded, with about five rounds of ammunition per head. We knew the Division was fighting 5 miles to the west [in and around Oosterbeek] and I felt we could be of more use back with them. I formed the survivors into patrols of ten men and an officer, with orders to return to the Divisional perimeter.'

As one of those who would be left behind, Sims felt sure it was the only sensible course of action, though some in the cellar were very perturbed. They were aware of the order Hitler had made in 1942 that commandos caught behind the lines were to be summarily executed, and feared, not unreasonably, that the same treatment would be meted out to red-beret forces. 'In their panic,' Sims recalled, 'they tried to drag themselves upstairs, sobbing that they had been abandoned. What they were forgetting was that their own commanding officer, Frost, was wounded too and lying among them.'

With the last of the garrison upstairs gone, a brave medical officer volunteered to act as a go-between with the enemy outside, poised for a final assault. There was a hush in the cellar as he was heard climbing the stairs. He stepped out into the yard, calling out, 'Cease fire!', but a burst from an enemy machine gun sent him hurriedly back inside. He tried again, speaking this time in German – and the firing stopped. A senior German officer came forward. 'We heard the heavy tread of boot,' Sims recalled, 'and then our medical officer rapidly explaining our plight. He stressed the urgency of removing us as soon as possible from the burning building, which was in imminent danger of collapse. Then came the sound of those hobnailed jackboots approaching the top of the stairs and starting to descend . . .'

9. Hands in the Air . . . but Heads Held High

The endgame was about to play out all over the shrunken battlefield at the Arnhem bridge as brave men, still trying to carry on the fight, were forced to bow to the inevitable. Major Eric Mackay, fleeing from the wreckage of the school that his men had held against all odds for so long, never got to make the defiant last stand he had intended. Having ordered his many wounded to surrender, he and his half-dozen remaining able-bodied paras could find nowhere in that shattered moonscape to hide, nowhere to dig in to mount a rear-guard action. The rubble was too hot from the fires for them to kneel down and find any sort of cover. All they could do was keep running, dodging from wrecked house to wrecked house, pitted garden to pitted garden and across rubbish-strewn streets that were alleys of instant death. All of a sudden, fifty Germans and a tank were blocking their way. 'We stood in a line, firing our machine guns from the hip, pressing the triggers until the ammunition ran out.' Then he and his men – now down to four – dashed to re-group in the gardens. 'We were now completely unarmed.' They split up, assuming that individuals would have a better chance of avoiding detection. 'I told them to rendezvous with me at nightfall and we would try and contact our main forces.' Anger spurred him on. 'It had taken me two years to train my troop of men and I was furious at having lost practically all of them.' Amazingly, he kept the faith that this fight could be turned round even now. 'I was still confident that the Second Army would be up to us by dark, and we'd get some of our own back.'

Exhausted, he lay down in a bush to sleep, to recover some energy to hold out longer, which was his clear intention, whatever the consequences. He was prepared to sell his life dearly, but he also took precautions in case of capture. He took off his officer's pips and destroyed his identity card. Shortly afterwards, seven German soldiers came his way, combing the gardens like beaters at a game shoot. 'They came up to me and I simulated death. A corporal gave me a kick in the ribs, which I received as if I were a newly dead corpse. They were evidently not satisfied and a private ran a bayonet into me. It came to rest against my pelvis and, as he pulled it out, I got to my feet.' As he raised his hands, Mackay glanced at his watch. It was 4.39 on Wednesday 20 September, and for him Operation Market Garden was over, as it would soon be for many others who had fought so valiantly to hold the bridge at Arnhem.

In the overcrowded cellar beneath what had been brigade head-quarters, lines of wounded paras lay waiting, helpless as the crunch of jackboots came down the stairs towards them. One man uncov-ered a Sten gun that he had kept hidden for this moment, intending to go out with a bang. His injuries were severe and there was a chance he wasn't going to make it anyway. He seemed set on taking as many of the enemy as possible with him. Those paras around him moved quickly to stop him. One man's self-sacrifice would condemn all three hundred of them to instant death. 'He sobbed furiously,' James Sims, who was among the wounded, recalled. 'He was fanatical in his hatred of the enemy, but the rest of us knew that if he'd been allowed to shoot, the Germans would have slung in grenades and been quite justified in doing so.' Not that offering no resistance held any guar-antees. The wounded in the cellar had no idea how the Germans planned to treat them. It must have gone through every man's mind, not just the one with the Sten, that there was a real chance they would simply be hauled out and shot or slaughtered where they lay. Some, like Sims, however, were past caring. They had been through so much, 'I was just relieved that it was all over.'

The moment of crisis came. A German officer in a grey greatcoat and helmet stooped his head beneath the low ceiling and stepped into the semi-dark, fetid cellar that reeked with the blood and sweat of hundreds of men. He had an Iron Cross at his neck and an automatic carbine in his right hand. Sims thought the German looked 'tired and drawn' rather than triumphant. Clearly, he was taken aback by the sight before him, and he stared in disbelief. Then he acted. 'He rapped out orders, which were instantly obeyed. More Germans appeared and picked up the wounded with great care as they began to clear the cellar. Fortunately, we had fallen into the hands of regular soldiers of the Wehrmacht, and not, thank God, into the clutches of the SS.'

Sims was carried up the stairs and, as he reached the top, he saw how close they had all come to a trapped and fiery death. The ground floor was ablaze and the building on its last legs. Flaming timbers were falling from what was left of the roof. Bricks and concrete showered down on heads. They had surrendered and were being evacuated only just in time. Outside at last in the fresh air – fresh compared with the cellar, despite the smoke and fumes of battle – a smashed and burnt-out airborne anti-tank gun lay in the courtyard, surrounded by empty cartridge cases. The scene reminded Sims of 'one of those oil paintings you see in regimental museums entitled "The Last Stand"'.

Laid on a grass bank, he cast his eyes around the now shattered landscape they had battled over for the past seventy-two hours. 'All the houses and warehouses we had held were completely destroyed.' Behind him, two German machine-gunners were dug in with a clear line of fire in case anything kicked off. The Germans were clearly still nervous – and rightly so. From the ruins of a nearby building came the chatter of a Bren gun, and the guards scattered. 'Stop! Cease fire!' the prisoners shouted out anxiously, 'British wounded!'; and the firing stopped. 'But we wondered what lone gunner was still fighting on.'

The Germans, even more nervous than before, marshalled their prisoners. Some of the victorious enemy soldiers were amenable, handing out coffee and food. One gave Sims sausage and biscuits from his own rations. Then another thrust his bayonet into the top of a tin of British condensed milk – purloined without doubt from one of those many British supply panniers that had dropped into the wrong lines – and, as he drank, Sims asked for a swig. 'He was a most surly-looking individual but he wiped the tin clean with his sleeve and handed it to me.' There was a discussion going on about the war, military matters, veterans swapping stories. A German soldier covered in campaign ribbons said he had been in Normandy, and there was nodded agreement, almost admiration, from both sides about how stubborn the German resistance had been at Caen before the French town fell to the Allies. The man smiled a broad smile, 'pleased as Punch,' Sims thought, 'to be on the winning side again so late in the war'.

Amid this bonhomie between enemies, British anxieties eased. But they were not totally allayed and, as the prisoners were escorted away from the bridge, Sims was offered a stretcher. 'I could see that all the stretcher cases were being carried down a road leading to the river, so I declined the offer. I was afraid I might be dumped in the Rhine. I don't know if the Germans disposed of any of our wounded in this way, but I was not taking any chances.' He made up a threesome with two other wounded paras and, his arms round their necks and teeth gritted against the pain, they struggled slowly along the road, through an arch under the much fought over bridge and up towards the centre of town. This took them for the first time into what had been enemy-held territory. 'We were amazed at the large number of German dead in the street. It was a shocking sight but also grimly gratifying to see the punishment we had meted out.' It was a delight to have it confirmed that 'we gave them as good as they gave us.' Some German soldiers they passed shook their fists angrily, but others offered, surprisingly, congratulations. From dozens of tanks parked nose to tail – which had been on stand-by to go in and obliterate them if they had not surrendered – voices called out, 'Well fought, Tommy. Good fight, eh?'

Sims was a little bemused – 'they seemed to regard war in much the same way as the British regard football' – but he took the compliment. If there was any glory to bask in, however, it soon looked hollow. In a side road, captured British troops were being assembled, the fit on their feet and the wounded lying on the pavement. The Germans hauled out of the line a young Dutchman, a member of the Resistance who had fought alongside the British. His hands and arms were heavily bandaged. He had been badly burnt when he tried to pick up and jettison a German phosphorus bomb that came through the window. The lad was pushed to his knees and shot in the back of the head. For a shocked Sims the image was indelible and awful. As the boy slumped forward, the unravelling bandages spilled out from his hands and lay on the ground, 'like two grotesque paddles'. 'That's how we deal with traitors in the Third Reich,' announced the executioner. The mood among the prisoners switched to sombre and fearful.

A German soldier went along the line of wounded, searching each man for arms, ammunition, knives, maps, and so on. He pulled a wallet from one paratrooper's smock, but the man resisted, demanding it back. 'It's mine . . .' he was yelling as the German pulled out his pistol and shot him dead. 'There was a stupefied gasp from the British. War was one thing, but casual murder was another.' But Sims made sure that, by the time the soldier got to him, his pockets were emptied and his possessions were out on his lap for inspection. The German turned them over and said curtly, 'You do not appear to have anything of military value, but if you are searched again and such items are then found on you, you will be shot.' His quiet menace – and his track record, just witnessed – left Sims in no doubt that this was a warning to be taken very seriously. When he realized a while later that he still had some maps in his bloodied battledress that he should have surrendered, he surreptitiously disposed of them.

The wounded were now forced to their feet to make their way to an assembly point in a church on the outskirts of Arnhem. That night, 'we were hungry and parched with thirst but neither food nor water was forthcoming. Sleep was difficult, as Jerry kept all the lights on. More and more wounded were carried in. My leg ached and smarted but I just felt relieved to be in one piece. Finally, my head fell forward on my chest and I dropped off into the dreamless sleep of complete physical exhaustion.'

*

Some men were still at large. The fit and able had not been forced to surrender, and around a hundred – split into patrols of ten – slipped quietly away from the last redoubt at brigade headquarters. Ron Brooker was one of them, and he made it to the back door of a church in the town centre. He noted ruefully that the route he was taking was back the same way he had come on Sunday, just three days ago.

Then their expectations had been sky-high. Now they would be lucky just to stay alive. Stumbling into the church, he found fifty others taking refuge there. 'We sat on the floor in complete silence, not moving, not saying a word, as burning embers from the blazing roof fell upon us. On the other side of the door, we could hear German voices out in the street.' He was done in. 'We were approaching our limit. I was already injured, and more bullets were coming through the wall. It was scary, believe me, a vision of hell.' They couldn't stay. The church was no sanctuary for them. But surrender was still not something they were ready to embrace. Time to move on, to keep out of reach of the encircling Germans. In groups of five now, they left the church and made their way through the streets to a square. Guns opened up from two sides.

'We were caught in crossfire and one of our number fell to the ground. The rest of us picked him up, half carried, half dragged him to a ruined building, the debris still hot from the fire. We tried to stem the flow of blood from his wounded thigh with a couple of shell dressings, but every movement we made disturbed the rubble, bringing down more fire on our position. We all had weapons, but not one round of ammo between us. It was quite dark, and it seemed the enemy was content to leave us until daybreak. We were not going anywhere!'

It ended more quickly than that. 'There was a shout, and two figures almost fell on top of us. One was a lieutenant and, when the firing ceased, he took stock of our circumstances. We were stuck, completely defenceless, and one of our party weak and still losing blood. He decided we must give up. The lieutenant called out in German and, when answered, he got to his feet, arms held high, broke cover and, waving his white handkerchief, walked towards the enemy machine guns. We saw him talking to the Germans, then he shouted out to us, "Drop any arms you've got and come over." And that was it. That was the end of our battle. We entered a large building, we were searched and our equipment and smocks taken from us. We were then told to get some rest. We lay on a tiled floor and just fell asleep. I was glad it was over and I'd survived but the future was very uncertain. What was going to happen to us now?'

Last out of the headquarters building had been Tony Hibbert and his ten-man patrol, but they found progress difficult. Going quietly was impossible because the streets were covered in glass and the crunching could be heard a long way off. He headed south from the ruined headquarters building, hoping to hit the river. But it was soon clear that any movement was problematic. There were Germans everywhere, hunting down paras. 'In whichever direction we moved, we ran into heavy German fire.' The only recourse was to find somewhere to hide and hope to get away some time later – tomorrow, perhaps.

The major found a tiny coal shed and shared it with Anthony Cotterell, a writer and war reporter for the Army Bureau of Affairs. 'It was so small that we hoped it would seem an unlikely place to look for two bodies.' They hadn't allowed for snoring – not theirs, but from another soldier in a nearby hiding place. The Germans, alerted by this loud snuffling, started ferreting around the area it was coming from and came on Hibbert and Cotterell as well. 'We were hauled out, covered in coal dust, feeling very angry and foolish. They marched us off to the cathedral square, where a depressing sight met our eyes. About 20 officers and 130 other ranks were being guarded by a large number of very unfriendly SS guards. This probably represented most of the survivors from the bridge. It was a great shock. We'd felt sure some of them would have got away.'

And indeed some had – for now. Ted Mordecai seemed to have a charmed life. When he evacuated the headquarters building, he didn't go far but took up position in a nearby back garden. He found an old slit trench and sat in there carefully cleaning accumulated dirt from his Bren gun so it would be primed for the next time he needed it. He stopped to dig into a tin of pilchards with his jack-knife. A shell landed nearby. 'The pilchards were gone. And once again I was covered in earth. I was annoyed because I hadn't eaten for ages. On top of that, I had to clean the Bren again.' He could see German shells finishing off what walls remained of the brigade headquarters building, and he reckoned the garden he was in could well be their next target. So he ducked out of it, across an alley and into an orchard, pursued by Germans. 'Jerry was almost on top of us but still being cautious and not coming too close.' That wouldn't last. 'I was behind a wall when Jerry lobbed a potato-masher grenade over the top. One of our guys caught the full impact and later I found a piece of shrapnel in my leg.'

But Mordecai and what was left of his party still had ammunition. As night began to fall, he kept on firing, out into the darkness, trying to pinpoint the flashes of enemy gunfire and return bullet for bullet. When the Bren ammunition ran out, he picked up a Sten. Attack after attack was beaten off, 'then there was a lull in the proceedings and Jerry called on us to surrender. A truce was called whilst a discussion took place between the Germans and our few remaining officers. Jerry agreed to let us hand over our wounded. After the wounded had been evacuated, the Germans again called for us to surrender and were told in Army fashion to "Shove off" (or something much cruder). Hostilities commenced once again.'

But could the end be delayed much longer? Mordecai and his comrades took to changing their positions, dashing backwards and forwards across a street, trying to outwit the enemy gunners. 'On one of these runs Jerry changed his order of fire and dropped two in succession at the same place. Four of us dashed through the hole in the wall into the orchard and, just as we arrived, so did a shell. It exploded right in front of us and the three chaps in front of me went flying into the air. I ducked my head to one side just as the blast reached me. I felt a blow on my face and across my right eye, like being hit with a stick. It lifted me off my feet and knocked me flat out. When I came round I couldn't see anything. I crawled over the ground to try and find cover and eventually found a slit trench up against the wall. I flopped in on top of another chap lying on the bottom.' Mordecai's active resistance was over. And not just his. 'The shelling kept up all night, and I heard no reply from any of our chaps at all. Perhaps they were lying low. Either that or there weren't any left.' Which, sadly, was the truth of it.

He held out until the next day, Thursday. When dawn broke that morning, it was very quiet in Arnhem, uncannily so compared with

the last three mornings of constant shellfire. His left eye was working, but with the right all he could see was a blinding glare. 'The
chap under me stirred, but we both stayed in the trench until it got
lighter.' A German voice carried across to them with an invitation:
'Come on out, Tommy, and you will be treated all right. Come out
and surrender.' Mordecai's companion had had enough. He climbed
up out of the trench, scrambled through a hole in the wall and out
into the street with his arms in the air. Mordecai stood up and looked
around him as best he could with one eye. An unexploded shell was
teetering on the top of the trench, and he manoeuvred past it. 'I
took stock of the situation. I was blinded in one eye. I had a Sten
gun but no ammunition. I was out of cigarettes and water.' But he
was still reluctant to take that step that would mean certain capture
and possible death. He saw a fellow para – one he knew – rise from
a hole in the ground and come limping towards him. This man too
had decided to pack it in and, waving his handkerchief, stepped out
into the street. Mordecai waited and watched. This man's fate would
decide his own. If the Germans harmed him, then Mordecai had
decided he would make one last desperate break for freedom in a
jeep that had been abandoned in the orchard, though he didn't
expect to get far. Meanwhile, he kept his eyes on his comrade as the
man limped up the street to where the Germans were standing. 'I
saw them take him away around a corner. I waited for a while, but
couldn't hear any shooting.' That made up his mind. He too was
going to surrender. He broke down his Bren and Sten guns and
hurled the pieces in different directions so they were unusable.
'Then I took a white towel out of my small pack, took a deep breath
and walked up the street with my arms in the air.'

An enemy officer searched him, then handed him a bottle of wine
to drink from. 'It tasted good!' He was taken to join others who had
surrendered, mainly wounded, and they were marched away to a
British-manned casualty clearing post in the town hall. 'One of our
doctors looked at my eye but said that he couldn't do much. He gave
me eye drops and a black patch to put on.' The next day he was
among the walking wounded who filed on to trucks and were ferried
towards the German border. 'The back of the truck was open and I

was sitting near the end. I considered jumping out but the truck was travelling too fast and I decided against it.' He would have to see out the war behind barbed wire.

*

Prisoners though they now were, the captured paras were not about to kowtow to an enemy they had fought against so bravely. Eric Mackay's spirit was far from broken, even though his wounded foot had gone septic, his head injury was troubling him and so was that sharp bayonet wound he'd received when he was captured. He demanded – and got back – the water flask taken from him when he was first searched. Taken to SS headquarters for interrogation, he quietly reminded his fellow prisoners that it was their duty to escape. By surreptitiously switching queues, he managed to avoid the strip-search that would have uncovered the escape maps he had held on to. He watched the German soldiers at work and noted their regiments and equipment 'for future reference'. When an English-speaking German officer tried to worm his way into the men's confidence, he made sure that all the inquisitor got from any of the captives was back-chat. Then, when the captured paras were bundled on to trucks, they fussed and shuffled around and refused to budge up for two German sentries to sit at the back. Eventually, room was made for just one guard, and Mackay sat opposite him at the back of the truck, with two other men between them. 'As we moved off down the main road to Germany, only 16 miles away, I inched my legs over the tailboard. When the truck slowed for a bend, my two men deliberately lurched into the sentry and smothered his rifle while I jumped.' Mackay rolled twice as he hit the ground, as any good parachutist would, but he had chosen a bad place to attempt his escape. He landed virtually at the feet of a German soldier standing sentry outside a building. There was a desperate tussle. 'He gave a yell as I dived for him. I got him down, and had very nearly knocked him senseless when his pals arrived. There was a battle royal before I was eventually overpowered and thrown back on the truck. I was too dazed to make another attempt.'

But he was still undaunted and, determined to show it, at the first opportunity, he went among the men collecting what little shaving equipment they had managed to hang on to. It was time to smarten up. 'We managed to raise one complete shaving set and, using our steel helmets as bowls, we all had a wash and a shave.' It was a gesture, but gestures were all they had left. The captured Major Freddie Gough told the men he was with, 'Let's show these bastards what real soldiers look like,' and he put them through a fifteen-minute parade drill before they were marched away from Arnhem as prisoners of war. 'This boosted morale and restored our self-confidence,' recalled Tony Hibbert. 'We marched very smartly, and as we went along we gave the local Dutch the Victory sign, as they looked in need of cheering up too. This infuriated our German guards and they threatened to shoot us if we did it again – which we did whenever possible.'

Voices were raised in song, cracked, strained and out of tune but remarkable in the circumstances. Another para recalled lines of British soldiers making their way into captivity, all weary, many in great pain, some limping, others burning with fever from festering wounds that had not been disinfected. Miraculously, someone produced a mouth organ. 'With what we hoped was true British spirit, we joined in singing – though with far more enthusiasm that melodic accuracy. Dutch people peered at us encouragingly from behind their curtains as our pathetic, battered crocodile "marched" by.' Then, when the men were interrogated, they amused each other by giving preposterous peacetime professions to their inquisitors. One man said he was a ballet dancer, another an opera singer and a third a lion-tamer. 'More and more improbable answers were given as we fell into the spirit of the moment.' They were down but not out.

Though there were isolated cases of brutality and even some incidents of cold-blooded murder, generally the Germans treated their Arnhem captives with great respect, a nod of admiration for the fight they had put up. But for some of the captured, the defiance and pride they wanted to exhibit was inevitably hampered by a sense of shame at their defeat. It was the common lot of prisoners of war. The underlying mood in stalags and oflags was always disappointment and regret, and the escape planning, digging and scheming a means of countering the incipient depression. The German soldier who told Ron Brooker, in that time-honoured phrase, that 'For you the war is over,' added, 'and you're the lucky one,' for being spared from any more front-line fighting. Brooker was glad to have survived, but 'I didn't feel lucky, no I bloody didn't,' he recalled. 'I felt ashamed that I'd given up, that I'd let the side down, even though I knew there was nothing more we could have done.' As for what came next, 'we were in limbo; the future was very uncertain.' That immediate future included a glass of schnapps – 'I didn't know what it was at the time; I was a brown-ale man' – and a desultory interview by a German officer who seemed to know more about the paras than they did themselves. He got name, rank and number, as prescribed, but already knew their regiments, date of enlistment, and so on. He was more interested to discover their views on Winston Churchill.

When it came at last to leaving Arnhem, Brooker, like others, was shocked by the sight of the battlefield they now trudged through, in stunned silence. 'The damage to the buildings we had fought in was unbelievable. Just piles of bricks and rubble. Most of the German dead had already been gathered but ours still lay where they had fallen, and there were many of them. Thankfully, some had been covered in ground sheets, blankets, sheets and even coloured curtains by the few remaining Dutch civilians in the area. Hardly a sound came from our group, and I know we were all thinking of comrades we were leaving behind.' Ahead, railway trucks awaited them in a siding, and they were herded inside for a nightmare journey. That weekend – barely a week after the whole operation had begun – he passed through the gates of prisoner-of-war camp Stalag 12A.

Back home in Brighton, his mother, totally unaware of his where-abouts, was writing her latest letter to him. 'Just hoping this will find you safe and well,' she began, though she must have had an inkling that he might not be. Had he seen in the papers that men with five years' service were getting a 14 shillings a week pay rise, she won-dered, and then corrected herself. 'It was rather silly of me to ask if you had seen the papers, as we know something of the time you have had from the wireless.' Like most mothers then, she reined in her fears, masking her anxieties in the comfort of platitudes. 'All our thoughts and prayers are with you, Ron, and we hope to see you again soon.' Life went on. She'd run into Ron's girlfriend, Joan. To everyone's delight, the blackout had just been lifted, and his brother Bobby was thrilled to see the street lights burning at night again. 'It gives some hope of this terrible war ending.' She looked forward to his return. 'Your bed is made up and ready for you and the key is on the gramophone in the window. Write as soon as possible, Ron, or better still just walk in.' It would be a while before she got the War Office letter that he was 'in German hands, location unknown', and eight months before he was through the door of home again.

For all that, to this day Ron Brooker looks back on Arnhem with huge fondness and fierce pride. 'I wouldn't have missed it for the world. They were some of the saddest and most frightening times of my life but also the greatest and the best. I still think it was all well worth doing.' A sergeant-major who fought at the bridge and went with Brooker into captivity echoed this self-belief. 'Whatever went wrong or whatever the strategic outcome,' he wrote after the war, 'from our point of view, we had not failed. Our objective had been to capture and hold Arnhem Bridge until the arrival of link-up troops twenty-four hours later. We held it for four horrific days. I am proud to have been there and to have fought side by side with men of courage and determination, so many of whom did not come back.'[1]

*

For the bewildered and frightened residents of Arnhem, precisely what had happened down by the river in their own city was a mystery, to be guessed at in the absence of hard information. They could only piece together this puzzle by sifting the gossip and the unsubstantiated, garbled reports – that's if they even dared to come out of their houses. While the centre of Arnhem burned, in the north of the town, Pieter Huisman had kept under cover in the basement of his home with his wife and children, in the dark in every sense. He was never sure who was advancing and who retreating. There had been rumours (wrong, as it turned out) of the two armies fighting it out in the market area, the British holed up in the central market and the

Germans — appropriately, everyone sneered — in the flea market. From his house, he'd seen victorious Germans marching red-bereted paras along the street and, on one brief, hurried and dangerous trip into the town for water, he saw the bodies of dead British soldiers lined up on the lawn of the hospital. Then again, British planes had flown over dropping leaflets with a message from Prince Bernhard that the allies were at Nijmegen and would be arriving in force in Arnhem very soon.

But the drift of what he picked up was tending in one direction — that the Germans were still in the driving seat, still the masters. When he heard a strong rumour that the British had retreated to Oosterbeek, it was all too believable — and a horrifying swing of the pendulum for people who had thought themselves liberated from an oppressive and hated occupier. The signs were increasingly unmistakable. The noise of firing in the centre of the city had virtually ceased and shifted to its western edge. 'The Germans are installing more ack-ack batteries on the hill and are shooting towards Oosterbeek,' he noted. 'Fresh German troops have come into the town and a regiment of Tiger tanks has been placed on the street behind our home, under the trees. The tank crews are young SS boys, fanatical seventeen- and eighteen-year-olds. Refugees fleeing from Oosterbeek are now passing by.'

If the war was over for the airborne soldiers who had made it to the bridge — one way or another, dead or captured — then it was about to move up yet another notch for those who had not. With the bridge at last secured — and not before time, according to an incensed German high command, infuriated that the paras had held on to its northern end for so long — the German focus of attack switched to the larger part of the invasion force. From behind its loose perimeter at Oosterbeek, what remained of 1st Airborne was fighting for its very survival. The odds did not look good.

10. In the Mood . . . to Fight until We Drop

As the paras at the bridge in Arnhem trudged off into captivity, 3 miles away in Oosterbeek, their airborne comrades were cocking a snook at the Germans. From the woods opposite one of the many private houses British soldiers were occupying in the thumb-shaped defence perimeter, a familiar saxophone riff sounded, followed by the spirited trombones and trumpets of Glenn Miller's big band swinging into the catchy 'In the Mood'. An amazed Dick Ennis stopped firing. This was weird. 'We could not have been more surprised if the enemy had come dancing towards us spreading flower petals,' he recalled. Still, it made a change from mortar shells, hand grenades and the chatter of machine guns. Officially, the Nazi regime banned jazz – Hitler deemed it decadent, the music of *Untermenschen* – which is why it was doubly surprising to hear Miller's signature tune blasting out loud and clear from German loudspeakers. Back in Britain, boys in khaki had been boogying to it with their girls in dance halls and back parlours since the start of the war. It was a poignant reminder of home and better times – as the Germans playing the record well knew. This was the hook. When the last bar had died away came the sell.

'Gentlemen of the 1st Airborne Division,' a soft siren voice intoned in what Arthur Ayers remembered as 'near-perfect' English, 'think of your wives and sweethearts at home. Your division is nearly wiped out and your position is hopeless. You are completely surrounded and cannot survive. The Second Army is long overdue and will never reach you. At this very moment it is losing its last battle in Nijmegen. We ask you in the interests of humanity to cease fighting. Surrender now and yours will be an honourable surrender. You will be treated . . .'[1] Ayers didn't hear the rest because the German offer was drowned out by hoots, whistles and catcalls from defiant paratroopers.

Ennis was incensed: 'Did Jerry really expect us to lay down our arms and go over to him just like that?' Some men supplemented their angry shouts of 'Eff off, you Prussian bastards' with action, firing derisory shots in the direction the voice was coming from, though it was a waste of precious ammunition. The siren voice spoke again. 'Well, lads, what about it? Just wave your white handkerchiefs and come on over. Think of your wives and families.' More abuse was hurled at him from the British trenches, and the tone changed from cajoling to threats. 'You have rejected our terms,' said the voice. 'We have here two fresh panzer divisions, which we will now use against you. None of you will escape.' Shortly after, the shelling began again.

But the men manning the Oosterbeek perimeter had made their position clear – the only way they would cave in was by force. Bring it on, was their response. 'That call for us to surrender had the opposite effect,' according to Ennis. 'If the enemy had two fresh divisions at hand, why stop the battle and tell us about them? If he had them, why hadn't he used them already? It was just a colossal bluff.' He took heart. 'They must be in a very precarious position to adopt such tactics and try to trick us like that. Very childish!' But when his anger had subsided and he had time to mull over the German broadcast, he had to concede that there was a semblance of truth in it. 'The Second Army was certainly held up somewhere, otherwise it would have reached us by now. It was evident that we would have to hold out a little longer.'

And it could not be denied that conditions were bad, and getting worse all the time. Enemy attacks were intensifying, with persistent, morale-sapping shelling and mortaring followed by infantry probes in strength at all points of the perimeter. The Germans, now that they had crushed the airborne infiltrators at the Arnhem bridge, were turning their firepower on the rest of the invading British force holed up here in Oosterbeek. They were also putting their recaptured road bridge to good use. Columns of panzers were even now crossing it and heading south towards Nijmegen to try to head off the slowly advancing Second Army and snuff out that threat too. For the Airborne, things looked bad. Supplies of food, water and ammunition were running very low, and re-supplying from the air had proved ineffective, for all the skill and heroism of the crews in the supply planes. On the Oosterbeek perimeter, the fighting was fiercer than ever, and the constantly rising toll of casualties left fewer and fewer fit men to man the defences. Ayers, a sapper, recalled how his legs trembled as he stood on guard. 'It was not fear, or so I told myself. Perhaps my body was aware, with a kind of animal sense, that there was a risk of pain, mutilation and death, so it just trembled.'

His mind blotted out what he had to do in what was now a merciless fight to the death. 'A dozen figures in field grey advanced towards us, firing their automatic weapons on the run. I fired back at them indiscriminately and saw several of them fall. I felt no remorse for my actions and no pity. They were the enemy and I had to try and kill them. They felt the same about me. It's the war of the jungle – kill or be killed.' After this attack was beaten off, he saw a small party of paras emerging from the trees and called out to them in greeting. They replied with a deadly burst of bullets. 'It was several seconds before we realized they were Germans dressed in airborne smocks and wearing red berets and we fired back. A few reached our positions and were killed in hand-to-hand fighting.' Ayers guessed that the Germans must have got the uniforms from supply panniers that had dropped into their lines, and he was not best pleased. 'I often wondered who was responsible for sending out berets, when it was food and ammunition we desperately needed.'

But the stress was so great that some on that line were too overwhelmed to carry on. In the cellar, where the dying and the wounded were lying on the cold stone floor, Ayers saw a fellow soldier resting in a corner, apparently unhurt physically. 'Eyes glazed, he stared into space. He could not face the mortars any more and could not sit in the trenches waiting for death. His courage had gone and he was in deep shell-shock. He was a shred of humanity.' This man was beyond help but, even for those whose minds and spirits were intact, there was little to fortify them. What information came their way was universally bad. They learned for certain that the bridge in Arnhem was back in German hands and all resistance there had collapsed. They learned that XXX Corps was past Nijmegen but bogged down on the road well short of Arnhem. They heard the sound of German tanks crashing through the Oosterbeek woods to join the battle against them. No wonder that Ayers put his chances of surviving and getting back to England as 'slim'.

Yet, a greater sense of order was beginning to prevail around the perimeter as, at divisional headquarters in the Hartenstein, Urquhart – returned from his lengthy escapade and enforced isolation in the Arnhem suburbs – took a grip. The Arnhem bridge, he knew, was lost, but Oosterbeek was still a useful bridgehead on the far side of the Rhine. Should XXX Corps and the Second Army ever get here – and that was still everyone's fervent belief – then what remained of 1st Airborne could be well placed to assist them across by some other means. A crossing by boat might be possible. Bailey bridges could be hurried forward. In his eyes, this was not a mission to be given up on. To hold his ground, he had a depleted force of some 3,600 fighting men to defend what, to begin with, was 3 miles of perimeter. Roughly a third of them were infantry – largely from the para battalions and the King's Own Scottish Borderers – a quarter were glider pilots and the rest were artillery, sappers, and so on. He ordered his brigadiers to take charge of individual sectors of the line and to consolidate it where necessary.

Increasingly, the lines of defence were redrawn and tightened into a smaller and smaller area. Some withdrawals were orderly. Ennis and the men around him were warned in advance and, in the dark of night, they fell back, trying not to make a sound. 'We stealthily moved through the wood in single file, and out on to a road. We went along the grass verge for about one and a half miles, then back into the wood to dig in at a new position. The digging could not be done in silence, and we must have made a terrific noise hacking at tree roots and scraping into the earth. The enemy could not fail to have heard us, but we saw nothing of them, neither did we hear anything. It took all night to dig ourselves in properly because, weakened through lack of food, we had to have frequent rests. But two hours before dawn the job was completed and we thankfully took up our new posts.'

Other withdrawals were retreats dictated by the advancing, probing enemy as defenders were forced out of the positions they held or the houses they occupied. Glider pilot Alan Kettley was up in the attic when a shell from a tank came through the roof. 'It took every-thing away from under my feet and I fell down through three floors. Luckily, all I got were bruises and cuts, but it was a damned lucky escape.' He retreated with his men to another house and next day was bombed out of that one too. A fellow pilot was an inspiration – though also, as it turned out, a danger. Though wounded in both legs and an arm, he kept up a cheerful banter. He couldn't fight, so he tackled the Germans with Bing Crosby records, which he played incessantly and loudly on a wind-up player in the direction of the enemy, who were just a few hundred yards away. 'We were right in the front bloody line and he put it on full blast, and I can only assume the Germans don't like Bing Crosby, because the next thing you know there's a Tiger tank at the front door!' The big gun fired, silenc-ing Bing and blasting Kettley out of the house. The experience was pretty traumatic. 'Unless you have experienced being shot at by a Tiger tank, no words can tell you how absolutely terrifying it is,' he recalled. 'The ground shakes and the noise is louder than anything you can possibly imagine. Bricks and slate fall for what seems like an eternity. I was terrified, I won't deny it.'

The blast tumbled him down stairs and into a shallow slit trench. From there, he guided a badly wounded lieutenant, the flesh on his left arm stripped down to the bone by machine-gun fire, to a first-aid post. As he did so, he had no choice but to ignore the shelling around him. 'We were in a built-up area and it was not easy trying to get over garden fences and through doors. But getting help for him was my sole objective.' When he got there, he was shocked by the number of bodies piled up outside. As he stared, one of them, he was certain, moved. 'There was a chap on top of the pile lying face downwards, and his left hand came up and he scratched his nose.' Kettley alerted the medics to have another look at the man, and they took him back inside, though it seems he did not survive. The image, though, lived on in Kettley's head. 'I don't know who he was or which unit he was from but the memory of his hand moving caused me nightmares for ten years. I would wake screaming. I can see it now, clearly. It was terrible.'

For days, his unit of glider pilots, enthusiastically throwing themselves into their secondary role as infantrymen, kept watch on their section of the perimeter, discouraging the enemy from passing along the Arnhem road into Oosterbeek and sniping at those who tried. In the midst of the shelling and the mortaring, he took on responsibility for a dozen of the wounded, reassuring them by his presence that they had not been abandoned in the deteriorating situation. 'I couldn't do anything for them medically, but I found a large jar of bottled peaches and dished them out, two in the morning and two in the evening. It was all we had, but it was the finest food I've ever tasted.' He dragged a wardrobe across a window and took pot-shots at any Germans who showed themselves, though with little ammunition, he had to be sparing in choosing his targets. This became his world. 'We had no news at all, no communications, nothing.'

Pockets like his were typical of the increasingly desperate fight to keep the Germans out of Oosterbeek. Peter Gammon, also a glider pilot, was manning a trench and could hear British troops off to his left. 'But there was no communication with them. Nor did we know who was holding the woods to our right.'² He focused his gaze on the field straight ahead, from which he imagined the enemy attack would come. One new development was that the Germans were now taking the nights off, shutting off their bombardments when darkness fell. It was a welcome relief for the sleep-starved defenders, but also ominous in its implication. It meant the Germans were no longer in any hurry. Having won back the bridge and bottled up the relief column, they could take their time to wear out and whittle down the trapped British army. Unlike the British, the Germans had men to spare and no shortage of weapons and ammunition to hurl at the airborne defences. German industry was churning out tanks, guns, bullets and shells in record quantities. So it was that, come the morning, the mortar and cannon fusillades would start up again, and then enemy infantry would advance, probing for weak spots. Grenades and sheer guts would send them back, but always at a price in lives and injuries. Those left standing were dirty, unshaven and physically and mentally drained. The arithmetic of this battle was clear and pointed to only one outcome.

Yet the battlefield itself remained surprisingly fluid. Though the

Germans had the upper hand, they too were pinned back at times by resolute 1st Airborne counter-attacks. Small patrols would leave the lines to hunt for German tanks and try to disable them. Some even came back with prisoners, who were a nuisance – more than two hundred were kept behind wire in the tennis court in the grounds of the Hartenstein Hotel – but also dangerous. Para Fred Moore was frisking one of them when the man pulled a pin on a grenade. The explosion wounded Moore in his hand, arm and leg, and he was bleeding profusely. He was alive but damaged, which at this stage of the battle was not good. Should it come to 'every man for himself', the wounded would be at a severe disadvantage.

By and large, though, the defensive perimeter had little choice but to take the pounding and try not to flinch. The battering was of such intensity and accuracy that, at the Hartenstein, its walls cracked and scarred and its floors covered with plaster and broken glass, the airborne command had been forced to move into the basement. There was no running water and the lavatories were blocked. In one part, Urquhart and his immediate staff worked and, when they could, snatched sleep, while the rest of the subterranean space was taken up by a first-aid ward for the wounded. Most of the headquarters staff had to take their chances in the circle of trenches outside, dodging inside for conferences and O-groups only when they were sent for.

In one of those trenches, another glider pilot, Sergeant Eric Webbley, was protecting an anti-tank-gun position whose crew was still pumping shells back at the enemy. 'We were under continuous mortar fire every day and seldom ventured out of our foxholes. When the bombardment was at its worst we crouched down with our fingers in our mouths to stop our ear drums bursting.' Here were conditions that conjured up terrible images of the Western Front in the First World War, all the more so when heavy rain began falling. Dick Ennis recalled it 'showering from the trees, seeping through the walls of our trench and forming cold, oozy mud around our feet. It was difficult keeping our ammunition and grenades dry. We wrapped what we could in parachute silk and covered it with our bodies.' The downpours added to Webbley's misery. 'We ate standing up in our soaked foxholes. We dug graves to bury the Jerries we had killed the day before and rested their helmets on top. A lot of mortar stuff was falling around us and we had to keep shovelling out the earth that was shaken down from the walls.'

Danger of death was ever present. If the German mortar crews managed to drop a shell into the middle of a slit trench, there was little hope for the occupants. One officer who survived such a direct hit recalled the appalling concussion and his certainty that he was a dead man. 'The top of the pit fell in, my Sten was blown in the air and we were covered with earth.' Now that the Germans had found their range, more shells were bound to come crashing in. 'I felt as frightened as I ever have been and sure that death was only a second or two away.' He bolted just in time, running for another trench and hurling himself in. 'I was very surprised to be alive.'³ This same officer, having escaped the mortar-men by the skin of his teeth, was then targeted by enemy snipers hidden high in trees and strapped in by their belts. He was leaving the Hartenstein Hotel after a briefing and, at the doorway, tested the hostile air outside by hoisting his steel helmet on the end of a stick. 'Immediately there was a loud crack and a sniper's bullet embedded itself in the door frame.' Exposing your head above the parapet was an invitation to fire rarely declined by the enemy. In his trench, Webbley's mate was standing up and leaning over the front after finishing some tinned stew, and a bullet missed him by inches. 'Whenever we were above ground we had to keep dodging about. I was having a wash behind a jeep when a bullet dug itself into the ground next to me.' It didn't help that some of the men (though probably not all) did their best to keep to what Ennis described as 'the finer points of civilized life'. They would insist on climbing out of their foxholes to urinate, despite the risk and the fact that the trench was half full of mud anyway. Such courtesy could be costly. He saw one man disappear for a leak and take a sniper's bullet in his back.

As well as First World War conditions, there was a moment of First World War melodrama too, when an officer came to warn the men not to abandon their positions. 'He said we had our backs to the wall and if anybody attempted to retreat he would have to shoot them.' It was an unnecessary threat to make to brave men. 'I don't believe any of us knew where to retreat to anyway,' said Webbley. 'I know damn well I didn't. But nor had it ever occurred to me to stop fighting.'

It was hard for the officers, who knew the severity of the situation but until now had felt the need to conceal it from the men for fear of unnerving them. Ronald Gibson, hunkered down around divisional headquarters, was assured by a well-meaning, wishful-thinking captain that the Second Army was still very much on its way and would arrive to relieve them in a day or two. The officer wasn't contradicted or argued with, but he wasn't believed. 'We all doubted this,' Gibson commented. 'We had heard too many rumours in the last few days.' Nor did he believe the reports he read in a copy of the *Daily Express* that was dropped in one of the supply containers, probably slipped into the pannier by a handler back at camp during the packing operation, thinking he was doing the boys at the front a favour. On a map, broad black arrows pointed at Arnhem, 'and the relief of our position was prophesied to occur within a few hours or a day'. It flew in the face of what he could see with his own eyes. Half his own squadron of glider pilots were dead or seriously wounded and, of his own section, he and one other man were all that remained. Shortly afterwards, Gibson overheard that same officer who had been so upbeat about XXX Corps' arrival quietly admit the truth to a sergeant-major. He had just come from a brigade commanders' conference where he'd been told that the division had lost half its strength and the ammunition was running out. 'The commander had warned the Second Army by wireless that we might be overrun within forty-eight hours.' Now *that* was believable. The plain fact was that the German officer who had followed the sounds of Glenn Miller with his seductive invitation to surrender had summed up their situation all too accurately.

★

It wasn't, of course, only soldiers risking their lives inside that Oosterbeek perimeter. There were the local people too – those, that is, who had not fled. Caught in the middle of the mayhem, many were bewildered and afraid. From his trench, Dick Ennis saw an old man in his seventies step out gingerly from a nearby house, carefully close the smashed front door behind him and make his way over. 'He was very neatly dressed. His face, with its finely trimmed goatee beard, struck me as very clean. I had seen nothing but dirty faces for days.' In broken English, the man explained that he and his wife had been forced to take shelter in the cellar of the house he had just emerged from but his own home was actually half a mile down the road in Oosterbeek village itself. He must, he insisted, go there to fetch some things. 'We knew it would be madness for him to walk openly up the road. He wouldn't get more than a few hundred yards without being hit by shell splinters or a bullet. He was in danger even where he was standing now.' Ennis told him to go back to his cellar and wait until the street was safer. The man protested. 'I must go to my house. There's something I need.' He stopped when Ennis once again pointed out the danger, went back to the house and closed the door – but within minutes was out on the street again. 'I must go to my house,' he continued. 'We have not eaten for three days and my poor wife is hurt.' Ennis decided to take a look for himself.

'We went back into the house and he showed me to the cellar stairs. I let him lead the way down – I didn't trust anyone so I wasn't going to go first. At the bottom was a fair-sized room lit by a single, flickering candle. By its light I could see a woman lying on a pile of cushions and blankets. She was about the same age as her husband. The sleeve of her dress had been ripped off and round her forearm was a blood-soaked piece of rag. She spoke no English, but just lay there looking at me with tears running down her cheeks. I removed the bandage, under which was a nasty jagged wound. It had stopped bleeding but she must have lost a lot of blood. I bound up her arm with a field dressing. All the time the old man was standing by saying, "My poor wife, my poor wife." I looked round the cellar. There were no signs of food. We had none either, so it was impossible for me to help them. I told the man to stay with his wife and on no account to leave the house. But when I left, he followed me, practically on my heels, fully determined to go into the centre of Oosterbeek. It was useless trying to stop him, so we let him go.

'We saw him picking his way along the centre of the road, knocking twigs and debris aside with his stick. We didn't expect to see him again but, within an hour, he was back, and very distressed. He came right up to us and stood on the edge of our trench. He was crying, and his hands trembled. He spoke, though he was not looking at us. It was as though he was speaking over our heads. "The Germans," he said, "they won't let me in my 'ome. They say to kill me if I go into my 'ouse. My God! Kill me if I go in my own 'ouse!" He turned away and went back to his cellar and we didn't see him again. I think the civilians suffered as much as we did.'

Ennis was right. For Anje van Maanen, the fear she felt and the horrors she witnessed around her were never erased. Back at the start of the British invasion, she had seen her first dead body, a German soldier, and been shocked. She had been cycling to a farm to get some milk and noticed her neighbours walking around 'queer-looking lumps in the middle of the road'. She shied away from them, 'but my eyes are pulled towards a man lying on his back and staring at me with dead eyes. I scream and move away, only to stumble on another corpse, eyes closed, blood on his temples and his hands stretched backwards. It is all so awful, but other people don't seem to mind.' The reality of war hit her hard, whichever side was suffering. 'These were men who lived and who loved and who did not want their lives to end this way. They are Germans, but I feel sick with misery at what has happened to them and I cry. I feel very subdued. I shall never forget this.' Six days later, it was the British whose deaths she was witness to. As, face pressed up against the window of her house, she watched the hurried burial of a para, she was overwhelmed with sadness. 'Is that what he was fighting for? To be put under the earth while his wife or fiancée far away at home has no idea that he is even dead?' She couldn't stop herself wondering if she was destined for the same fate.

She went out to find bread and on her way home had to take shelter behind a wall. 'A shell hits it and I fall flat on my stomach. When the attack stops I race home like a hurricane with the bread still tucked in my arms. I am completely out of breath when I reach the cellar, just as a really heavy attack begins. We hear an enormous whistle and bangs all around. Everything trembles. Tiles are falling from the roof. All we can do is wait, without moving, for the next attack. We are in the midst of the battle and it is terrifying. Only a few days ago I was running around with friends outside and now I am running for my life. I don't want to die and be put under the earth with all the other pale, dead people. I have so much living still to do, things to see, things to experience.' But she was unstinting in her praise for the paras. 'The British fight like devils in their desperate longing to defend us and themselves. They cry over beautiful Oosterbeek that is ruined by others. They cry over Dutch civilians, wounded and killed. They think of us all the time.'

There was loud knocking at the back door, and everyone's first, fear-filled thought was that it must be the Germans. It turned out to be friends, the Aalbus sisters, who had gone to help at a casualty station. 'They are in an awful state. The shells we heard came down right on top of the school where they were looking after patients. A British doctor shoved them underneath the desk and put himself in front of them to protect them from danger. When the shelling stopped there was just terrible chaos around them, blood everywhere, groaning people, the wounded hit a second time by this bombing and lots of them killed. So the girls tell us. They are broken and have fled to us.' From outside, the thunder of the German bombardment of Oosterbeek started up again, 'a cacophony of devilish noise that goes on and on. The house trembles and things fall down. It is so frightening. It is as if the world has come to an end. I can't bear it any more. I am sure the Devil is outside and I am so scared and I can't think of anything else but the shells and death.'

At night, the claustrophobia of the cellar made sleep difficult. 'Daddy's feet are beside my pillow, so close I could bite his toes. Aunt Anke sits on a chair and dozes off and on. Mr Aalbus lies in a wine rack and snores lightly.' As Anje fretted the night away, she was fortunately unaware of the full extent of the horror unfolding around her as, under relentless German pressure, the Oosterbeek perimeter contracted still more. But she must have had an inkling, because she recalled 'a vague restlessness among us, a worry that something horrible is happening and we can't do anything about it, but sit and wait.

I try to pray and eventually fall asleep next to my daddy's toes. Is this our last night in the house?'

It was. The next morning, the doorbell rang, and outside were dozens of desperate paras needing to barricade themselves in. The Germans were closing in, and they had to turn the Maanens' home into a redoubt. 'We ask if they could go somewhere else? Must our house be used as a fortress? Is it really necessary? They tell us yes. They need it badly. They tell us too that it would be better if we left. There is going to be a fight and if the Germans find out we have stayed hidden in the cellar they may well kill us.' Then came that same old refrain that was supposed to deliver reassurance. 'They say Monty will be here any moment now and we'll be able to come back tomorrow.' But the gloss had worn off this promise. As the family picked up their suitcases, buckets of water, blankets, pillows and coats and trudged down the road to the Tafelberg, the only place left to go, Anje was sceptical. 'I think to myself, Monty can go to hell. He will never come.'

Marie-Anne's Oosterbeek house, meanwhile, was already full of British soldiers and had been for days. When they weren't manning the walls and windows, they were sitting on the stairs and sleeping on top of the potatoes in the cellar, alongside her and her family. They were low on supplies. 'Some parachutes were dropped yesterday. Most fell beyond the English lines and the Germans got them. Some landed in the meadow but the boys dare not go and fetch them because the firing is too heavy.' She had developed a real bond with the men and was worried when one of her favourites, Len the Cockney, was showing signs of exhaustion and battle fatigue. 'The shooting over our heads is very bad and he comes down from upstairs and sits with his head in his hands. I try to distract him by showing him some photographs, and he gives me a snapshot of himself in uniform with his youngest son as a baby in his arms. Mummy makes a place for him and he lies down beside her, holding her hands very firmly. Some time later he is called back upstairs. Another soldier tells us that Len is overwrought and thinks too much about home. Len comes down again and sits beside me on the bed. He is almost asleep. I tell him to lie down and he does so, while I sit at his feet. Then another soldier comes and calls him upstairs again. He rises and goes. I never see him again.' Later, when she asked Gerald, her other favourite, how Len was, he changed the subject.

But there was love as well as loss, affection as well as angst, in that Oosterbeek cellar, a form of bunker mentality brought on by proximity and the shared sense of danger. At twenty-one, Gerald was nearer Marie-Anne's age, and he now sat beside her as she lay down to sleep, trying to soothe and reassure her that 'everything will be all right.' The whistling of shells and the din of battle continued to terrify her, and he stretched out next to her to comfort her, the young man far from home and frightened and the teenager suddenly thrust into the maelstrom of an adult world. 'We lie talking for some time. He starts to nibble at me, so I ask him if he is hungry. He laughs and then falls asleep. At first he wakes up when the noise is very loud, then he sleeps on. He must be very tired. Suddenly he starts talking in his sleep. He starts crying and puts his arms around me. I stroke his head and he quietens down again. He wakes up and smiles at me when he sees me looking at him. We talk for a bit, but he falls asleep again. I must have slept, too, but not for long. The night seems endless.'

With their brother-and-sister intimacy, she and Gerald kept each other going, and if, in that intense atmosphere, there were some more romantic exchanges between them, then she never spoke of them. They laughed and romped around and tickled each other; when he wasn't upstairs manning his post, they sat discussing classical music – 'he knows everything about Mozart, Bach and Haydn.' They shared the bed in the cellar again. 'We both fall asleep. Then he turns round, puts his arms around me and calls, "Georgie, Georgie!" When he wakes up, he tells me that is his wife's name. He falls back asleep with his head on my knees.'

If Marie-Anne was like a sister to the men camped out in her home, then Kate ter Horst – her house now turned into a fortress and a full-scale hospital for wounded airborne troops – was a sainted mother to the hundreds finding refuge there. She would walk the makeshift wards, the vision of an angel, minister to the sick, pray with the dying, give aid and comfort, for all of which she was one of the best-known and most admired heroes of the Arnhem story. But she also had to be a mother to her own five children, terrified by what was happening to them and their home. When the fighting around the house was at its worst, she would draw them around her to sing songs and to look through a picture book by the light of a candle. 'We hear the shrapnel bursting and the splinters rattling against the house. Even down in the cellar, the noise is painful so I put cotton wool in baby's ears.' When a frightened little one announced that she wanted to go back to the nursery to sleep in her own bed, Kate had to calm her while concealing from the child the fact that her bedroom now housed a dozen bloodied and bandaged men.

As for the men, they were invariably anxious about her children, sending down treats of eggs or apples and sweets for them. Those manning the walls would sneak downstairs from time to time to connect with the semblance of family life still going on down there. Kate recalled – with guilt – how one soldier, his face and body black from powder and trench earth, came into the cellar and took her baby on his knee. She grabbed back the child because the man was so dirty – and immediately regretted the deed. 'How could I? Perhaps it was the last time he would look into a child's eyes.' She wished she could have called him back and handed him her baby son to hold, but he was gone, back up the stairs to fight, his helmet on and his Sten gun under his arm, a moment of much-needed humanity lost.

Kate split her time between her children and her patients, between heaven and hell, drawn in both directions, a heartbreaking choice between them on every occasion. 'A little hand pulls at my skirt. "Mother, will you fetch my doll for me?" I risk the trip upstairs.' She crept through the house – her own house – pausing in the corridors to find a way past the wounded on the floors and the rows of defenders at the windows. 'Nowhere is there any glass in the windows, but, in spite of the violent draught, there is an unbearable stench of blood, sweat and dirt and the sweetish smell of the dead.' She had brought a bottle of juice with her to quench the thirst of the wounded lying in rows on the floor of her large living room. 'It is passed from hand to hand along all the stretchers and then comes back to me still half full.'

I am amazed by their selflessness and pass it round again. At the back, somebody gets up and helps his neighbour, who has no hands. "You are brave to be here," one of the men says to me. Wounded and helpless as they are, they still feel themselves soldiers and better able to stand the war than a woman.'

In the kitchen she came across a young doctor, his face pale and grave, who told her that the house itself had taken a direct hit and a wall was collapsing. And that was only the start. 'The Germans are pressing nearer and nearer, and the ring within which the British are crowded near the Rhine is getting smaller and smaller,' he informed her. Kate remembered how, as he delivered this seeming death sentence, 'his hands hung between his knees and there was an expression of melancholy in his dark eyes.' She noted a change of heart among the defenders still standing, a dip in their confidence. 'They crowd together and make no show of going outside again. German tanks have been signalled. Are there many? From what direction are they coming? Nobody knows exactly. But there are tanks and they are approaching and that is enough.'

Back down in the cellar, she felt the heat and stuffiness close in on her. 'There are forty people in this hole and the atmosphere is unbearable. Suddenly the baby vomits in his little cradle. Everything is dirty, even his mattress and cushion. Tired and white, he lies in my arms. Soldiers are snoring on the stone steps. The Germans are all round us and are steadily drawing nearer.' Like Anje van Maanen, she wondered if this would be her last night. The mothering instinct conquered her fears. 'It is three in the morning but I find a basin and some warm water and bring it down to the cellar without waking anyone up. I am on my knees as baby plays in the water, his eyes, which have been so dull during the last few days, brighten up. Then I roll him up in a towel and he plays to his heart's content, naked on my mattress. I give him a few spoonfuls of Ovomaltine,[4] the last of the supplies, and take the basin back upstairs to the medical orderlies from whom I borrowed it. I tell them how happy the little fellow is and that he's the only clean thing in the whole house.'

*

For an operation that had begun in high hopes and the bright sun of autumn, the descent of Market Garden now into rain, mud and cold was a severe damper on morale. Glider pilot Dick Ennis's trench was now a foot deep in liquid mud. Crouching there, the rain running off his helmet and down his neck, he thought he must have died and was in Purgatory, 'and that this would go on and on for ever.' He got to move to another trench, but only because the defenders were now so depleted in numbers they had to spread out to show at least some presence along the over-stretched line. He and another man dashed to what they thought was an empty trench but which turned out to contain the body of the previous occupant, his face buried in the mud. 'We propped him up in a corner. In a pocket of his smock were a few cigarettes in a battered tin. We had one each and passed the tin down the line.' When darkness fell, they took it in turns to creep out and scrape a grave in the earth. 'We buried our comrade beside his own foxhole.'

The next morning, from the woods opposite, they heard a heavy engine start and rev up to a high scream. 'The trees swayed, and then fell straight towards us till they lay flat along the ground. The snub nose of a tank appeared, a Tiger armed with a flame-thrower.' Another trench took the first blast of liquid fire. 'We heard the screams of our men as the flames enveloped their dug-out.' The tank now worked its way along the line, 'vomiting fire'. With no anti-tank mortars to engage it, only rifles, resistance was futile. 'There was nothing we could do. We jumped out of our trenches and ran back into the shelter of some trees.' In reality, Ennis wasn't so much running as just managing to stay upright and walk. 'I had become so weak, my knees could barely support me and my lungs were tearing through my chest.' He would be easy prey for the line of German infantry following in the tank's wake.

He made it to the trees and flopped into a trench in a clearing. The tank came relentlessly on, and he prayed, 'Please, please, dear God help us.' Then he spotted on one side of the clearing the camouflaged remains of a 17-pounder anti-tank gun, covered in branches. Its tyres had been blown off and the barrel was stuck in one position. But could it be made to work? Its crew looked just as battered. One was dead and the other three dispirited, but Ennis managed to rouse them to action as the German tank came closer, its caterpillar tracks clanking into a position – 'by a miracle, definitely a miracle' – directly in line with the otherwise useless airborne gun. The tank was broadside on and just a few yards from the barrel when the gunner fired. 'There was a blinding flash and a sound that killed all sound. The tank heeled over, its side obliterated by a gaping jagged hole. Slowly the turret lid opened, a head and shoulders appeared and then collapsed. The Hun sagged over the edge of his turret, blood gushing from his mouth and running down to the ground.' The infantry following behind it wavered. Then they turned and ran. Ennis leapt from his trench and, despite a bullet wound in his leg, led a charge after them, the British troops firing as they went. He was proud to report that only 'a small proportion' of the enemy got away.

It was, of course, a short-term victory. The Germans came back with more firepower. Mortars and shells thudded into his new position, collapsing the sides of his dug-out. 'My eyes were full of dust and soil and it was impossible to see. The air was heavy with cordite. I thought it was the end.' But he survived this onslaught, though his rifle did not. The latest explosion split the barrel and smashed the stock. He re-armed himself by crawling out into the open, to where the body of a young officer lay. 'I removed the Colt .45 sticking out from his holster, but his ammunition pouch was empty. There were just three rounds in the magazine, but I managed to scrounge some more from two blokes in the next trench. I collected about a hundred rounds of .45. I was now happy.' But this was what it had come to – dead men's weapons and cadged bullets.

Ennis had a new mate alongside him, a man called Billy, into whose trench he had fallen. Heads down as far away from the mortars as they could get, they considered their chances of rescue. 'Billy was the most cheerful fellow I ever met, nothing daunted him, and he was optimistic that the Second Army was not far away. "They won't be long," he said. "Listen, you can hear them now." Indeed we could hear the sound of distant battle, but we had heard it every day, and each day we tried to convince ourselves that it was a little closer. The thought of being relieved at any moment kept us going.' Billy fished out photos of his wife and two little children from his wallet and passed them over for inspection. 'I know he was wondering whether he would ever see them again.' Ennis had no snaps of his own to show, but he did have photos he'd taken from the pocket of his pilot, who had been killed on landing, and which he had promised himself he would return to the man's relatives. 'One was a postcard-size picture of a girl. The leather frame was damp and soggy now and the picture itself was showing a few mud stains. The girl was wearing a nurse's uniform – I felt it was rather appropriate for the occasion.'

The two of them settled down to a meal of corned beef and mushed-up biscuits, washed down with tea made from a tea-tablet. Afterwards Billy pulled two very crumpled cigarettes from his pocket. 'I've been saving these for such an occasion,' he said, and the two pals lit up. It was the finishing touch to what Ennis would describe as 'the best meal I have ever tasted in my life'. In the distance they could hear that dull rumbling of heavy guns that could just be from the relief column, perhaps 15 miles or so away. They lived in hope, still. 'I was certain we would be relieved tomorrow.' And the next day there was a glimmer of light in the gloom. The rain lifted and the clouds that had covered the battlefield for days on end cleared briefly. Fighter aircraft appeared overhead and, to Ennis's joy, they were Typhoons not Messerschmitts. He was worried, however, that the indistinct and indecipherable British lines might be accidentally strafed. 'Our perimeter had shrunk out of all resemblance to its shape and size of a few days before. It must have been very difficult for the pilots to distinguish our positions from those of the enemy. But the Typhoons did a wonderful job. Their rockets streaked down into the German lines with a roar like a Tube train. We heard terrific explosions as they met their targets and sent clouds of black smoke towering high into the sky. It was a heartening sight to us. We wondered if any of the enemy mortar batteries had been knocked out. Whether they had or not, the attack would certainly shake Jerry up and make him realize that he wasn't going to have everything his own way.' Yet, once the Allied planes had gone, the enemy shelling continued, as relentlessly as before, and Ennis felt his patience and his morale wearing thin. 'I had to keep a tight hold on myself now. I felt that if I relaxed my grip on myself in the slightest degree, my nerve would snap.' His prayers for the relief column to come were more extreme than ever. He offered a deal to the heavens. 'Oh, please, dear, dear God, send the Second Army tonight and I will never, never sin again.'

But, divine intervention apart, it was Billy's cheerfulness that kept Ennis going. 'Every time a shell landed close and showered us with dirt, he would sing out "Yah, yer missed me – try a bit nearer." I felt that was pushing our luck and told him to shut up. He then started to sing, out of tune. I realized that this was his way of preventing himself from thinking too much about the pickle we were in, and so let him carry on.' Ennis knew that each man had to get through the hell of battle as best he could, and if that meant laughing and singing uproariously in the face of fear, then so be it. The limited number of cigarettes they managed to scrounge also acted as a diversion from the reality of their situation. They would debate for hours when to have the next one, then test their willpower against the clock until the agreed time. 'The moment I said it was okay to light up, the cigarette was between Billy's lips. He took two puffs and passed it over to me. Inhaling was positively glorious. I felt my whole being lift up. I passed it back. It was burning away too quickly. Very soon it was completely finished. It glowed feebly on the bottom of the trench. I hesitated for a few minutes and then squashed it into the earth.'

But his spirits were about to get a huge boost. Billy went to try to find water in one of the nearby airborne houses and returned with an empty bottle but brimming with excitement. He had met some troops from the Signals section and been told by them that advance elements of the Second Army were 5 miles away. The only real obstacle standing between them and the depleted force at Oosterbeek was the river and, said Billy enthusiastically, that very night they were going to assault and cross it further downstream. Help was at hand. As if on cue, the background noise of artillery rose to a crescendo and bright-coloured flares shot up into the air over in the direction of the river. 'This would be the Second Army coming to relieve us, at last,' Ennis assured himself, and muttered a prayer of thanks. 'With a bit of luck we *would* see our homes again.'

He slept with that cheery thought, yet, when the morning came, the German mortaring of the British positions started up again. Of Monty's men, there was no sign. Billy dodged over to the Signals section for an update. He returned dejected, refusing to look Ennis in the face. 'Come on,' demanded Ennis, his heart sinking, 'Tell me. Where are they?' Billy looked down at the steel helmet he was carrying in his hand, as if suddenly it contained something of deep interest that needed his attention. 'They're not here,' he muttered finally. 'They couldn't get across the river.' Ennis lost his cool. 'Of course they're here,' he shouted, seizing and squeezing Billy's shoulder. 'We heard them last night. I know they're here . . . somewhere.' Later he conceded that 'I didn't sound convincing, not even to myself.' The usually irrepressible Billy gave a miserable little laugh. 'I think they got one battalion across,' he said, 'but they landed further down the river. God knows where they are now.'

Both men were gutted, and stood in silence, speechless. 'I couldn't trust myself to speak,' Ennis recalled of this crushing moment of truth. 'I think I would have screamed had I opened my mouth. Oh God, why hadn't they reached us? For how much longer had we to suffer like this? How long had we been here now? A year . . . two years? No, longer than that. My eyes misted over, and I began to sob. Billy hit me and told me to shut up. I pulled myself together. After all, we would be all right. Things could be a lot worse.'

The fact is that the reinforcements they and all the others in the Oosterbeek enclave so desperately needed *had* come, both from the air and overland. The problem was that they were massively delayed, there weren't enough of them and they were on the wrong side of the heavily defended Lower Rhine. Some of them had come an extraordinarily long way to get here.

17. (*top*) Sergeants Whawell and Turl of the Glider Pilot Regiment search for snipers in the ruins of a destroyed school in Oosterbeek. Turl was killed a few days after the photograph was taken

18. (*right*) Heleen Kernkamp, who witnessed much of the fighting in and around Arnhem, and helped treat many of the Allied wounded

19. (*top*) Soldiers of the 1st Airborne Division in defensive positions around Oosterbeek, 18 September

20. (*bottom*) German infantry probe the perimeter around Oosterbeek, September 1944

21. (*top*) Dutch civilians evacuated from St Elizabeth's Hospital escorted by a medic with white flag

22. (*left*) Kazic Szmid in 1944, shortly after the fighting at Arnhem; (*right*) at Arnhem in 2009

23. (*left*) Wounded men of the 1st Parachute Squadron, Royal Engineers, at Arnhem

24. (*below*) British paratroopers march into captivity

25. An officer of the 1st Airborne Division loses his trousers after crossing the Rhine

26. (*top*) Corporal Ron Mills pays his respects at the grave of Trooper Edmond, who was killed on 17 September after landing by glider

27. (*bottom*) A wounded soldier is carried away from the Divisional Administrative area at Oosterbeek, 24 September. Stocks of ammunition and fuel can just be seen in the background

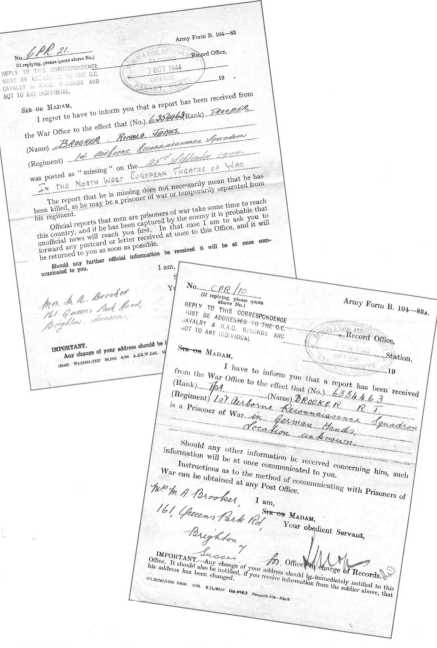

28. (top) The letter received by Ron Brooker's mother in October informing her that Ron was missing in action; (bottom) the letter she received in November 1944 informing her he was a prisoner of war

29. Aerial view of Arnhem, destroyed during the battle

11. A Long, Long Way from Warsaw

For nineteen-year-old Private Kazic Szmid of the 1st Independent Polish Parachute Brigade, the journey that brought him to the Netherlands and face to face with German soldiers for what was, surprisingly, the very first time was a 4-year, 16,000-mile odyssey. The hardship and inhumanity he endured along the way – persecution, deportation and exploitation – were of a severity and magnitude that surpassed anything that British soldiers had had to endure in their comparatively cosseted lives, even those who grew up in tough, poverty-stricken inner cities. It is often overlooked that a major loser in the Second World War was a free Poland, squeezed mercilessly by and between Nazi Germany and the communist Soviet Union. The country whose invasion in 1939 by Hitler's forces sparked the outbreak of the conflict was rolled over by tanks, planes and dictators from all directions, dismembered, disfigured and finally betrayed by a superpower agreement which dropped it into the grasping hands of Josef Stalin in 1945. Half of the 6 million Jews who died in the Holocaust were Polish; a further 3 million of its people were also eliminated. Yet those who escaped to the West and took up arms with the Allies were often mistrusted by higher authority for no good reason, under-appreciated and, as in the Arnhem campaign, allotted a secondary role, then unfairly blamed for failures beyond their control. In fact, they fought with a wild tenacity born of the gruelling experiences that Szmid and thousands like him had undergone.

When war broke out, Szmid was a barefoot, backwoods farmer's boy in the remote and impoverished countryside of eastern Poland, just a few miles from the border with the Soviet Union. Existence was hand to mouth in a house with an earth floor shared with the chickens and pigs. He barely noticed the German invasion 400 miles away on the other side of his country. He never even saw a German soldier. What impacted on him were the Russians. As part of Stalin's secret pact with Hitler to partition Poland, each of them land-grabbing whatever he wanted, it was the Red Army that seized the area he lived in, bringing in its wake the secret policemen of the feared NKVD. Poor though Szmid's father was, he was deemed a landowner and an enemy of the people. Forced from their home at the point of a bayonet, the family was deported to Siberia, along with hundreds of thousands of other Poles. 'I was fifteen,' he recalled seventy years later, 'and I knew that I would never see my home again.'[1]

The 1,200-mile, 3-week journey in cattle trucks to the wastelands of Siberia and winter temperatures of minus 40°C weeded out the old and the weak, their bodies simply thrown out on to the side of the track. In Siberia – greeted by a work camp commandant in the endless forest with the promise that, 'As a pig will never see heaven, neither will you see Poland again' – the family worked as slave labourers, twelve hours a day, seven days a week. The genocidal Soviet authorities were happy for the Poles to die from malnutrition, cold, disease and exhaustion, and a million did.[2] Szmid survived only because his mother sold her wedding ring for potatoes to keep him alive through a deadly bout of dysentery.

Moscow's curse on its captive Poles was lifted temporarily in the summer of 1941. Hitler turned on his erstwhile ally, Stalin, and invaded the Soviet Union. Stalin needed soldiers to die for Mother Russia and, in his mind, Poles were good at dying. He granted them an 'amnesty' – which begged the question of what so-called crime they were being forgiven for – if they would fight. The young Szmid and his family travelled by train to the southernmost reaches of the Soviet Union, where a Polish army was assembling for training. This was another nightmare journey of 2,000 miles in overcrowded, death-trap wagons. He remembered 'mothers abandoning the bodies of their own children to be devoured by the wolves in the woods and the jackals in the desert. Who can count how many Poles were left by the railroad tracks in Russia during this trip to freedom?' He lost his own mother and sister when the train they were on departed without warning and he failed to jump on in time. His father died from typhoid in Tashkent, and the teenager was on his own.

He was fifteen and alone in a savage world. 'Stranded, penniless, hungry and alone, my father dead and my mother and sister God knows where, this was the worst time of my life. I had one boot only and just rags on my other foot. I was filthy and full of lice.' To survive he became virtually feral. 'At night I used to find a hole, nook or cranny and crawl into it for safety. I begged for food, I stole, I even ate dog. Eventually I joined up with about twenty other youths like myself and we operated as a gang, stealing, scrounging and scavenging. We'd pick up anything from the ground that looked edible, even if it wasn't clean. Once I was sleeping rough at the railway station and huddling up to another person for warmth. We chatted until we fell asleep. In the morning I attempted to wake him, but he was dead. I examined his boots, and they were better than mine, so I took them. His coat was warmer than mine, and had roughly the same amount of lice, so I took that too. Life was cheap. The most important thing was survival.'

It was at that same railway station that he was rescued. A train came in with members of the Polish army on board. 'I told them I was Polish too and they hauled me on.' They took him to their training camp, deep in Kazakhstan in Soviet Central Asia, where he lied about his age – he was seventeen now – and joined the Polish 5th Infantry, as much from desperation as patriotism. His lice-riddled rags were replaced with a clean uniform, size seven boots (he was small) and a cap with the white eagle of Poland on it. He may have been at a desert-hot, scorpion-infested and fever-prone camp in a far-flung region not so far from the Soviet border with China, but he had food in his belly from three meals a day, a roof over his head at night (albeit a canvas one) and friendship. And a purpose – even if the distrustful Russians supplied the Polish soldiers with wooden rifles for drilling rather than the real thing.

He learned to fight. But against whom would he go to war? Knowing the Poles were deeply antagonistic to them, the paranoid Stalin and his Soviet military authorities became suspicious of these potential vipers they had taken into their nest. They resolved to get rid of them, one way or another. Butchering them was an option – as it had been in the massacre in the Katyn Forest back in 1940. Instead they did a deal to move them to British command in neighbouring Iran. The

Poles, to their delight, were to be allowed to leave Stalin's inhuman empire, though not without another hellish journey. This ragbag Polish army, accompanied by thousands of family members and dependants, many of them old and sick, were taken by truck hundreds of miles to a port on the Caspian Sea.[3] There, stripped of all their equipment by brutal secret policemen, they were pressed on board a cargo ship and set sail, many still fearing that a Russian submarine might be waiting to sink them with a torpedo in one last act of Stalinist revenge. The boat went unhindered, but was so overcrowded that there was every chance it might sink under the weight of its human cargo as it ploughed its way across 300 miles of open water. 'People were lying so thickly on the deck you could not move,' Szmid recalled. 'In the heat, dysentery forced many to relieve themselves over the railings or on the floor. Those who died were tossed overboard and their bodies followed us, pulled along in the ship's wake. But when we arrived at our destination and disembarked in Iran, many of us were so happy to be out of the Soviet Union that we kissed the ground.'

Tehran was the next staging post, reached after a treacherous truck-drive through single-track mountain passes and across precarious wooden bridges over ravines. Then they moved west to the sandstorms and dry heat of the deserts of northern Iraq to defend its oilfields from possible attack. 'We had gone from one extreme of climate to another – from snow and minus 40°C in Siberia to cloudless blue skies and temperatures of plus 40°C.' From there, Szmid volunteered for the Polish parachute brigade being formed in Britain. The pay, he would later admit, was his main reason. By a miracle, he had managed to locate his mother and sister, who, victims of those chaotic times, had somehow wound up in the British colony of Uganda in East Africa, penniless refugees. He needed money to send to them, and a paratrooper was paid £2 extra a week. For a boy-man who had stared danger and death in the face for so long, the extra risk involved must have seemed of little consequence. Another long journey now ensued – via Palestine and the Red Sea, down one side of Africa, round the Cape, across to Buenos Aires, back to West Africa and then up to the North Atlantic and the British Isles. Travelling in the liner *Ile de France*, which was converted to a troop ship, was a more comfortable passage than any of those before, even sleeping in hammocks twenty to a room, and safer, too, despite the constant alerts for enemy submarines. Eventually, he arrived in cold, bleak but welcoming Scotland.

★

The brigade with which Szmid now went into rigorous fitness training was an elite outfit under its founder and commander, Major-General Stanislaw Sosabowski – known to his men as 'Pops' – a tough and charismatic Polish officer who had fought against the Germans in the defence of Warsaw but managed to escape to the West when his country surrendered.[4] 'He was like a father,' Szmid soon discovered as he came under this man's wing. 'He would not let you down, and we had complete trust in him.' He felt at home in this company of peasants and nobles, barely literate labourers and university professors, men of differing backgrounds but with their Polish patriotism in common. 'This was my place and I felt good about it. I knew that these men around me would help in an hour of need and I was prepared to help them. There was not the severe strictness as in the British army. Our officers were firm but fair. They were extremely sympathetic because of what we had all been through.'

But the brigade was something of an anomaly and its role hazy. It had 'independent' in its name because it was not integrated into the British army but was a self-contained unit responsible to the Polish government in exile in London. The men wore grey berets (in contrast to the maroon of British paratroopers) and a badge with the Polish white eagle diving into attack, its talons extended. The brigade's motto was '*Tobie Ojczyzno*' – 'For the Motherland' – and the exiled politicians saw its principal function as training for the mission they had set their hearts on: parachuting into occupied Warsaw, Poland's capital, when the right time came, and linking up with the 35,000-strong underground army there to kick out the Germans. 'From the beginning of our training,' Szmid recalled, 'we were always told we'd be used to liberate our country.' This, however, was not an idea that ever commended itself to the Allied high command. And though the idea of bringing freedom to their homeland from the air was still the flame that burned brightest among the troops of the Polish Brigade, Szmid's insticts told him that this was unrealistic and would never happen. His private opinion was that 'we were too far away from Poland to be able to help. Nor did the Allies have the planes to get us there. And even if they had, how would lightly armed paratroopers operate against German heavy armour and how would we be re-supplied? It was impossible.'

His assessment was correct. When the disastrous uprising began in Warsaw at the beginning of August 1944, the brigade had no choice but to sit on its hands in England, unable to save its brave country-men and women from systematic destruction by the SS. They had sat on their hands, too, for the Normandy landings two months before and, like the other airborne brigades, spent much of that summer winding up for missions that were then cancelled at the last minute. Now they sat in enforced idleness again while, a thousand miles away, Warsaw burned, and they could do nothing about it. Emotions ran high as call after call came from the partisans for international help, particularly from their own countrymen in exile. 'Many of us wanted to go,' said Szmid, 'even though it might well be a suicide mission and we would be completely wiped out. But we were not allowed.' Allied assistance was confined to dropping weapons and supplies. Then, while Warsaw was being brutally re-taken district by district by the Waffen SS, its buildings wrecked and its people put to the sword, along came the Arnhem mission to distract the Polish paras from the rape of their capital city. It would be the brigade's baptism, their first time into action. 'Some of us were especially keen to go, to take revenge on the Germans,' he recalled.

Their role, however, was never planned to be heroic or even cen-tral to the mission. They would be a back-up force primarily, going in as the third and last wave when, if the Market Garden timetable was met, the fighting might well be over and the job virtually done. They were to drop just a mile directly south of the bridge at Arnhem and link up with the British paras of the 1st Airborne on the north bank, who hopefully by then would already have captured it. In an ideal world, at precisely that moment, the advance troops and tanks of the Second Army streaming along the corridor from the Belgian border would arrive, sweep over the Rhine without stopping and plough on into Germany, leaving the Poles the pedestrian job of digging into defensive positions. That was the theory. Szmid's Polish commanders were doubtful that it would be that simple, and the outspoken 'Pop' Sosabowski annoyed the British by expressing his misgivings. 'What will the Germans be doing while all this is going on?' he asked, not bothering to conceal his sarcasm.

Such thoughts were anathema to those high-ranking strategists convinced that Market Garden would bring a quick end to the war, and his opinions were ignored as negative and defeatist. 'My dear Sosabowski,' said a patronizing Major-General 'Boy' Browning, the Airborne Corps commander, 'the Red Devils and the gallant Poles can do *anything*.' And when he queried whether the bridge would really have been captured by the time the Poles got there, he was told to stop worrying. 'We'll be waiting for you with buses and cups of tea,' a dismissive British staff officer suggested. Unconvinced, Sosabowski briefed his own men to expect hard and bitter fighting, not the predicted picnic.

When the operation began on Sunday 17 September, Szmid stood on the ground at his camp in Lincolnshire and watched in wonder as the first wave of planes passed overhead on their way to Arnhem. He did the same the next day for the second lift. He considered what was to come. 'How will I do when it's our turn? Will I be up to the job? What if the Germans are waiting for us? Will I come back? Will I die?' He would know soon – though not as soon as he imagined. They were due to go on day three, take-off at 10 a.m. from RAF Spanhoe in Northamptonshire. The weather was rotten – fog at ground level and thick cloud up to 10,000 feet, extending out over the North Sea. Three times they climbed on and off the Dakotas, until, by late afternoon it was apparent they weren't going anywhere except back to barracks. The gliders carrying the brigade's heavy equipment and guns had managed to get away, however, from airfields in the south[5] where the visibility was better. They landed in a clearing on the north side of the Lower

Rhine, dropping into the middle of a pitched battle and taking heavy casualties.

Back in England, the Polish paras passed a second day of shredded nerves and frustration as the fog refused to lift. This time they got as far as taxiing down the runway before the take-off was aborted. 'Some of our men wanted to attack the American pilots we were so keyed up. The tension got to one of my comrades, who put his gun to his head, pulled the trigger and blew his head off. Back at the barracks, another man went crazy and crawled under a bed, growling like an animal. He was taken away in an ambulance.' Szmid stayed calm but got through his entire allowance of five hundred cigarettes. There was a technical safety problem, too, to worry about – the uncertain state of their parachutes. 'They were supposed to be packed for a maximum of two days, and we had just gone past that limit.' For Sosabowski, however, more problems were piling up than parachutes past their best. A complete change of plan was dropped on him.

Patchy information was beginning to get through to Second Army command headquarters on the unreliable radio link with the front line. The news from the hemmed-in forces at Arnhem and Oosterbeek was bad. The bridge had not been taken and the 2 Para force there was in desperate straits. The Poles' designated drop zone just south of the bridge was firmly in German hands, and they would be cut to ribbons if they dropped there. From his beleaguered headquarters in Oosterbeek, Urquhart, the 1st Airborne commander, desperate for reinforcements, proposed a new DZ for the Poles – 4 miles to the west of the original one, in fields outside the village of Driel, on the opposite side of the Rhine from Oosterbeek. From there they must hike to the river, cross it on a chain ferry that had hopefully been secured by the British and then link up with the 1st Airborne in Oosterbeek. Sosabowski had, it seemed, been correct in his misgivings, though he got no thanks for his perspicacity. Now he and his brigade staff officers had to jettison all their carefully prepared plans and improvise a landing in terrain they knew virtually nothing about to join a battle on which they had been given virtually no information. It was a tall order, and one which the volatile Sosabowski got very close to refusing on the grounds that he was sending his men to their deaths for no good reason.

In the end, the Poles went into action. The general swallowed his doubts and his anger, and the brigade finally got into the air on the afternoon of their third day on standby and the fifth day of the whole operation – Thursday 21 September. Only then, as they headed to Holland, were the troops told that their drop zone had changed and their mission altered. The new instructions worried Szmid. 'This meant we were parachuting on to a place we didn't know anything about. In the back of the Dakota, no one talked, apart from a few muttered prayers. We sat staring straight ahead, not looking at each other. We were jumping into the unknown.' *If* they got there, that was, because suddenly they were under attack from German fighter planes. The whole element of surprise – the paratrooper's secret weapon – had long gone by the board, and the Luftwaffe was waiting. Szmid looked out to see large bullet holes in the wing. Just then, the green light came on and the troops surged down the fuselage and through the door as fast as they could, dropping free of the enemy fighter planes above but down into the line of fire from German troops on the ground. Below was the paratrooper's worst nightmare – a 'hot' landing zone. They came down into soft farm fields divided by ditches and raked by Spandau heavy machine guns from a nearby railway embankment. 'Fountains of dirt were rising around me as I was fired on. I picked myself up and ran for cover.'

*

The Poles had arrived. Through no fault of their own, they were two days late and their assignment had changed at the last minute, so they were unprepared. But, worst of all, they were, it now turned out, also massively under strength. The take-off from England had been touch and go at best, the weather still uncertain and the light beginning to fade. A third of the 114 planes had turned back after a confusion over messages from base. As the 1st Polish Parachute Brigade re-grouped on the ground in enemy-occupied country, whipped into shape by tongue-lashings from their commander, its fighting strength was down to 950 men. Sosabowski could see the deficiency in numbers but, unable to communicate with headquarters, had no idea what had happened to the rest. The depleted force, a third down, headed towards the river under a storm of shells from enemy artillery and mortar positions on high ground. 'We moved through orchards, pasturelands, climbing over fences, jumping ditches, and other obstacles,' Szmid said. 'I had to throw myself to the ground on several occasions when I heard shells coming towards me.' They were grateful for the armoured vests they had opted to wear under their smocks – unlike the British paras, who rejected them for being heavy and slowing them down. One man had three dents in his, each one a bullet that could have been fatal.

They climbed the last earth embankment and were at the water's edge, staring across the Lower Rhine at the battlefield on the other side they were expected to join. In the distance to the east, black smoke was rising from the centre of pulverized Arnhem, but closer, directly opposite and less than a mile away, was the awesome sight of Oosterbeek, wreathed in orange flames and the white flashes of high-explosive shells. But how were they to get across the fast-flowing river? There was no sign of the British soldiers they had been told would be there to guide them. Thinking they might be waiting on the other side, a Polish officer fired a flare into the air as a signal. The response was a stream of German tracer bullets. There was no ferry boat either. The Dutch ferryman had scuttled it to stop it falling into German hands.

The Poles were not to know that, on the other side, belated efforts were being made to keep this back door into Oosterbeek open. The hard-pressed Urquhart had made an error in his deployment of troops around the perimeter and not paid enough attention to its river end. When patrols were eventually sent down into the open meadows to secure the ferry, they found that the Germans controlled most of the river bank. They were dug in close to the ferry dock and regularly sweeping it with bullets. Not only was the ferry gone, but the dock itself had been reduced to a mass of splintered wood.

A frustrated Sosabowski sent out search parties along the south bank in the gathering dusk to try and find other boats, or any means of flotation at all. They came back empty-handed. The Germans had made sure that this stretch of the river was craft-free. Meanwhile, they kept up their crossfire from the railway embankment and from the other side of the river, pinning down the Poles, who, having found no way over the river, pulled back from the water's edge to the village of Driel for the night. Szmid and his comrades settled down in a barn. 'Suddenly a shell exploded by the window where my friend Wladyslaw was standing. He was blown apart in front of me. He was covered in shrapnel wounds and his hands were hanging off his arms by threads of skin. He was still alive and he was chatting as we gave him some morphine and tried to help him, but I knew it was hopeless. We buried him outside.' Shelling was now constant and frighteningly accurate. 'The Germans were trying to annihilate us,' Szmid recalled, 'anxious to stop us reinforcing the British in Oosterbeek.' But the Poles had the wrong weapons to hit back with. Their heavy equipment had dropped north of the river two days earlier and had largely fallen into enemy hands. They were left with just Sten guns – close-quarter weapons – against German artillery. It was no contest.

This was a grim time, reminiscent of grim times in the past. The frightened villagers of Driel were fleeing, leaving their homes and trudging away into the night carrying whatever they could on their backs. For many of the Poles it was a sadly familiar sight, bringing back memories of when they and their own families were refugees. And, with them gone, Driel was empty, 'except for a lot of our soldiers running back and forth with the wounded on stretchers'. Szmid was scared but philosophical. 'If a bullet came my way, then it came my way. After all, I could so easily have died back there in Siberia or Tashkent or on that ship on the Caspian Sea.' He saw one of his comrades pick up a handful of the soft earth and run it through his fingers, so much darker and richer than the soil of his homeland, he reckoned, and 'so beautiful you almost wouldn't mind being buried in it'.

The next day, two senior British officers from Oosterbeek sneaked past the German positions on the north bank and made it across the river in a rubber dinghy. Urquhart had sent them with a desperate plea for reinforcements, though the sight of their filthy, bedraggled uniforms and haggard, battle-weary faces spoke as persuasively as their words. Any numbers would do, they urged Sosabowski. Even if only five or ten men managed to reach Oosterbeek they would be an incalculable boost to the morale of the exhausted defenders. The British had a handful of rubber dinghies, they said, and they were also making rafts, which they would send over. The Poles got to work themselves, lashing together planks, doors and ladders they found in the village, anything that might float. In the event, all these makeshift rafts sank like stones, but that night the British managed to send over their dinghies from the other side, and the first of the Poles prepared to embark.

They were handicapped from the start. There were no paddles, and the men on board would have to use spades, rifle butts and bare hands to propel themselves through the 10-knot current. They would have to be strong, and any drifting would be deadly. The British held a small patch of the opposite bank. To go off course would mean coming under enemy guns or falling into enemy hands. Nonetheless, the first wave made it over safely and the dinghies came back for more. A second trip was successful too but, on the third time, German flares suddenly lit up the river and bullets churned the surface of the water. Two dinghies sank and the remainder were so shot up they were unusable. In all, fifty men had managed to reach the other side. A rescue force had at last arrived.

As the Poles advanced from the river into Oosterbeek, they could see at once that they had stepped into a nightmare. The place was a shambles, overhung with the stench of burning houses and unburied dead. There were foxholes and graves in what had once been the wealthy suburb's neat lawns and gardens. Hospitals and casualty stations were overflowing with wounded. The enemy bombardment was heavy and constant. They could actually hear German voices, so frighteningly close were the enemy to the defenders of the ever-contracting perimeter. But the newcomers were ecstatically welcomed by the paras who met them. It was a start. If more came, then who knew what might happen? In that desperate place, a little hope was renewed.

*

In Driel too, things began to look up when contact was made with the much-delayed XXX Corps, now at Nijmegen. From there, a reconnaissance patrol of Household Cavalry armoured cars was dispatched northwards at speed and rolled into the village. Over its radios, its men were now able to send on-the-spot reports of the situation back to command centre. New coordinates were passed back for the army's big guns to target the Germans besieging Oosterbeek. Sosabowski was able for the first time to report to Browning, his overall commander, and swap briefings with Horrocks, the XXX Corps commander. An order was issued for twelve assault boats – which the Americans had just used to cross the River Waal under fire and capture the Nijmegen bridge – to be rushed forward through the Second Army traffic gridlock. In a boggy meadow leading to the river, the Poles waited impatiently for them to arrive. The plan was for the whole brigade to cross that night. They had been told each boat would carry eighteen men, and organized themselves into groups of the right size. 'It was dark and raining, and we all got very wet and muddy,' Szmid recalled. 'The Germans suspected something was happening and, after putting up flares, proceeded to shell us.'

It was midnight when the boats arrived – and they turned out to be flimsy, with canvas sides and room for twelve men, not eighteen. A hurried reshuffle took place in the pitch dark, whispered orders, bodies falling over each other: chaos. With space on board now cut back, a third of the men were stood down to wait for a later crossing, Szmid among them. Finally, the boats were hauled across the boggy meadow and over a flood embankment to the river. As they set off into the current, flares popped into the sky, followed by an inferno of shells, bombs and bullets. There were many casualties. But the occupants of those that reached the other side slid overboard into the sticky mud of the north bank and ducked into the reeds. A British officer who stood by to guide them into Oosterbeek noted that they were wet and frightened but very determined. One was seen to pull out a bullet from a flesh wound in his leg with his fingers. These were hardened men and they had accounts to settle with the Germans.

In all, roughly two hundred Poles managed to get across that night to join the fight for Oosterbeek, a token force maybe, but their presence lifted spirits. Moving through the streets, they remembered heads popping out of trenches and wrecked window frames. British paras smiled through swollen lips and pleaded for cigarettes, which were tossed in their direction. The Poles took up defensive positions 600 yards from the Hartenstein in the south-eastern corner of the perimeter, some in houses, others in foxholes. An early-morning mortar attack was a shocking introduction to the realities of the dire military situation they had endured so much to join. Casualties were severe. One man lay dying, whispering for his mother in far-away Lvov. A lieutenant's throat was ripped apart by a shard of shrapnel that found a gap beneath his chin.

Their presence did wonders for the morale of Private Bill Mollett, a bank clerk before the war, who had just spent hours on end at a window in the loft of a house, staring at a gap in the fence 150 yards in front of him and firing at the slightest movement. He was one of eleven men defending an isolated outpost on a crossroads, with orders, he recalled, to 'do or die'. Some were doing the latter. A mate was caught by a sniper's bullet and died quickly, asking that someone tell his mother, and they were down to ten. The owner of the house struggled up from the cellar with a dish of cooked potatoes and spinach for them, and they felt better. Then, as an additional fillip, they saw movement in the abandoned house next door. 'Some strange-looking blokes give me the thumbs-up and victory signs, and we realize they are the Poles, who jumped on the other side of the river and must now have got across. Everyone's spirits rise and we give them covering fire while they move into our house and three other empty ones.' [6]

In one of those other houses was a hard-pressed Ron Kent, his heart in his boots after witnessing another brave but futile supplies drop where the panniers floated to the wrong side of the front line and the Dakota dropping them spiralled in flames into the trees. He turned away from the sight, sickened by war and the waste of good lives. He knew his position was hopeless. 'This was a war of attrition. All the enemy had to do was keep blasting away at us from a distance. We would either die where we were or give up when lack of sleep and starvation forced us to. We were not going to be relieved. Then through a window I saw dim figures of men wearing our smocks and helmets. I was wary. It might be a German trick. My finger on the trigger, I challenged them and the answer came back, "Polish". I could have dropped with relief.' There were eighty of them, he noted, a goodly number to reinforce his 'garrison' of around thirty. But, battle-hardened himself, he was distressed at how un-savvy some of the Poles proved to be, many of them in action for the first time. 'They stood about chattering, quite unaware of the danger of standing in large groups. Some went through the garden to the house next door and took ten casualties in fifteen minutes because they didn't keep low to the ground. Their officer, a captain, was sniped and killed within five minutes of his arrival.'

But they were brave. In the casualty station that her home had become, Kate ter Horst met her first Pole, who was brought to the back door for treatment. He had a metal splinter in his head, lodged above his eye. Eager to get back into the fight, he wanted an orderly to fetch 'a good magnet' and pull it out so he could be on his way. Kate stifled a laugh at his medical naivety but was taken with his bravery – and the sheer fact that he was there. 'Although there are so few, it is a great moral support. The Poles have come according to plan. It is proof that the Supreme Command has not left us in the lurch.' Little did she know that her gladly given and instantly renewed faith that the Allies were coming to the rescue was very soon to be shattered.

*

Polish paratrooper Kazic Szmid was on standby. Denied a place in one of the boats at the last minute, he was rostered to go over to the Oosterbeek shore in the next wave. Then, without warning, he and the others of the Polish Brigade who remained on the south bank of the Lower Rhine were unceremoniously stood down and cast aside. British forces had arrived in Driel, he recorded without comment in his memoirs, 'and we were ordered to give them our boats'. The moment long expected by so many soldiers and civilians on the Arnhem battlefield had come. The overland relief column was here. That desperate question, 'Where's Monty?' had an answer at last, though it was neither encouraging, nor convincing. The field marshal's promised reinforcements had arrived, but there were not many of them and they were woefully behind schedule. By rights, the troops and tanks of XXX Corps should have been roaring up the road from Nijmegen two days into the operation, while the bridge they had come to grab was still graspable. But a week of delays and frustration had gone by, and now they were having to come by the back door, in dribs and drabs rather than the all-out full-frontal drive to glory that had been envisaged.

Lance Corporal Denis Longmate of the Dorset Regiment was in the unit that made its way to the outskirts of Driel on the southern shore of the Rhine on Sunday 24 September, a full week after Operation Market Garden had begun. He himself had been on the move for more than three months now, all the way from the invasion beaches of Normandy. At the age of twenty, he was a veteran, with a busy war already behind him. Aged fifteen, he was an air-raid warden in Derbyshire. He joined the Home Guard at seventeen and applied to the regular army when he turned eighteen. With the South Lancashire Regiment, he went ashore in Normandy on D-Day in June 1944, a searing experience. 'We were one of the first in on Sword Beach at 7.30 in the morning and I was scared half to death as we scrambled down nets into the assault craft. It was terrible on that boat, the deck awash with diarrhoea and vomit. Half of my guts went overboard into the English Channel, what with the shells going over the top of us and the explosions. Then, on the beach, I remember all the bullets, the screaming, the bodies and the body *parts*. As a lance corporal, I was in charge of others and directing some to their deaths. Best part of seventy years on and those things still prey on my mind, even though you don't want to think about them any more.' [7]

Later, as the Allies fought to gain control of the French countryside and push out the Germans, he was caught up in deadly fighting at Falaise, where he and his men were strafed by enemy fighters, and in XXX Corp's costly battle to get across the Seine in amphibious vehicles and assault boats against stiff German opposition.

By now he had transferred to the Dorsets, advancing into Belgium, through liberated Brussels and then to the border with the Netherlands. Arnhem was next on the agenda, not that the men saw any huge significance in that name. They'd been fully briefed for Market Garden's mission to forge a path to the Ruhr, 'and Arnhem as such was not our objective at all. It was just a place with a bridge we would cross on our way through to Germany. The Americans would get the Nijmegen bridge, our Airborne the one at Arnhem and we would sail through both. That's what was meant to happen.' It didn't work out like that. On the contrary, the plan was going wrong from the very start.

On Sunday 17 September, the Dorsets were raring to go. They were assembled in a country road to take their place in the XXX Corps column that would break through the German lines and smash its way to Arnhem and beyond. The area was heavily wooded and very beautiful, Longmate recalled. 'It was a nice day, with just a few puffy clouds in the sky, perfect for a quiet Sunday walk in the country. Around midday we were told to mount up. All of a sudden there was a cheer, as if someone had scored a goal at a football match, followed by applause. Up above us, we could see the sky filled with our planes and gliders heading east. The instruction was immediately given to start engines, and the Armoured Division moved off.' Up ahead, any opposition on the immediate route through enemy-held territory had supposedly been softened up by an hour-long RAF attack and a bombardment of big guns. But enough German anti-tank units were untouched to slow progress almost as soon as it began. Within minutes, nine tanks were knocked out. Those behind took cover and their accompanying infantry flung themselves into ditches. Typhoons had to be called in to rocket enemy pockets and tank-moving equipment brought forward to clear away the wreckage blocking the narrow road, all of which took precious time. When Longmate eventually got to move off, 'the division was so long and the pace so slow that we didn't get more than two miles before we were directed off the road into a wood for the night.' The front of the column had managed to get only halfway to Eindhoven before it too stopped for the night, miles short of its first objective.

But surely the pace would pick up. Lieutenant-General Brian

Horrocks, commander of XXX Corps, reasoned that this tough initial opposition was because the enemy had grouped its forces at the border. Once through this 'crust', as he called it, they would swiftly cut into the meat of the pie. He was wrong. He and his men would have to struggle for every foot of road. 'It wasn't a case of getting in your vehicle and just driving,' Longmate recalled. 'It was a constant battle. We were shelled, and we were mortared, and those at the head of the column got it even worse than we did. As we went through the countryside, houses were burning and we saw dead cattle, dead men.' Even the optimistic Field Marshal Montgomery was beginning to perceive that his master-stroke was already in severe danger of being bogged down. The complex of caravans and tents that had been his mobile tactical headquarters since the Normandy landings was now parked on heathland near the Belgian town of Leopoldburg, just 10 miles from the Dutch border. His band of young liaison officers had been beetling up and down the difficult and traffic-jammed road to Nijmegen and bringing him back their personal assessments. From their reports he could see the problems piling up. 'The advance is being made on a single road,' he noted at the time, 'and movement by wheeled and tracked vehicles off the road is extremely difficult owing to the low-lying nature of the country which is intersected by ditches and dykes and which has been made very wet by recent heavy rain.' Critics of his might well think the state of the terrain was not an unknown factor and should have been added to the equation at the planning stage rather than now, when it was too late.

By mid-afternoon of the next day, Longmate had covered the 12 miles to Eindhoven, to find that American troops who had been parachuted in to clear the bridges there were still fighting to hold the town. German big guns peppered the column with shells. Delay piled on delay, so that British tanks were only just leaving Eindhoven when, according to the plan, they should have been entering Nijmegen, 30 miles further on. A timetable that had been ludicrously over-optimistic to start with was not just being missed, it was crumbling to dust. When the head of the column reached Nijmegen, already the best part of two days late, it was to a town that was proving to be an unexpectedly tough nut to crack. At the start of Market

Garden, American paratroopers had dropped in to seize the crossings over the Waal but they had been denied by a fierce German defence. The Americans were forced to cross the river by assault boat in broad daylight further downstream before they could seize its northern end. It cost many lives and time. Then, when the first of the British tanks arrived and crossed, instead of charging on to Arnhem, they cautiously stopped to wait for their infantry to catch up. Given the uncertain nature of the terrain ahead, this was probably a wise decision, but it meant more delay.

Longmate's recollection was that it was as late as Thursday before his part of the column reached the bridge over the River Maas at Grave, by which time even a humble lance corporal like himself, not privy to the plans of the generals, could tell that they were a disastrously long way behind schedule. 'And we still had 20 miles to go to Arnhem.' There was still fighting going on when he got to Nijmegen. 'Progress was terribly slow. We went round the houses, shelled all the time.' They'd have to jump out of the vehicles and take cover underneath, then back in, move on, out and under again, and so on. They crawled across a railway bridge – 'It was so slow. Shells were bursting everywhere and we were sitting ducks. I looked over the side at the water and it was moving very fast, and I can't swim. I was very frightened. God knows how long it took us, but eventually we got to the other side, and there were dead Jerries and dead Americans everywhere.'

But, once over the Waal at Nijmegen, progress was easier and, for the first time, 'we seemed to motor.' It was a short burst of speed. Near the village of Elst, a German tank came into view and lobbed shells at them. 'A tree in front of us simply shattered.' Longmate and XXX Corps had run into the strong defensive screen of armour and big guns with which the Germans – on the offensive after their victory over the Airborne at the bridge – were blocking the direct route into Arnhem. At the same time, German forces were mounting a counter-attack against the Allies further back down the road, between Eindhoven and Nijmegen, in a pincer movement to split the British column in two. This was a critical moment. In the words of one military expert, Market Garden was now in serious trouble. 'It was being strangled. The Germans had cut off the highways, the route to Arnhem was blocked, XXX Corps had no momentum, the American airborne divisions were being stretched and British 1st Airborne was being systematically destroyed. The Allies struggled on, making it difficult for the Germans to apply the coup de grâce, but they could only do this while they had strength, and that strength was ebbing away.'⁸

Horrocks was forced to change tactics. The bridge that had been his target had gone and was unlikely to be recaptured. His priority had to be reinforcing the beleaguered 1st Airborne in Oosterbeek, or, at the very least, saving it from annihilation. He redirected his front forces to the left flank, down country lanes and across rough, boggy terrain towards the banks of the Lower Rhine, from where they might be able to cross and rescue something from the ashes of Market Garden. Troops from the Household Cavalry were sent ahead to scout a route and make that initial contact with Sosabowski and the Polish Brigade at the village of Driel. A larger force followed.

So it was that Longmate and the Dorsets found themselves staring at the church tower of Driel away in the distance, standing tall above the flat expanse of land, criss-crossed with streams and dykes that led down to the Lower Rhine. As they approached, they could hear the sounds of fighting on the other side but, in all honesty, the lance corporal had no idea what was actually going on. Whether by accident or design, it seemed that the British command was not letting on about the true situation in Oosterbeek, though by this time – Sunday 24 September – it must have known, not least because the abrasive Sosabowski had given Horrocks a thorough rundown of what he knew about the situation on the other side of the river. But the lads who would have to do the dirty work were kept in the dark. 'We didn't know there were people over there who needed rescuing,' Longmate recalled. 'We had no idea about how bad it was for the paras and the Airborne on the other side of the river.'

Late that afternoon, they were told they would be moving off after dark. Though it was late September and 'damn cold', they were, without explanation, told to ditch their greatcoats for what lay ahead. 'We were left wearing battledress, webbing, a small pack and helmet. I had an entrenching tool and my Sten gun.' They were then directed into woods and down a track parallel to the river. 'We came to a junction and were told to stop and rest. We waited and waited and I even fell asleep. Then a cry went up that the 3-tonners had arrived with the boats. 'Boats? What boats, and why? We hadn't been briefed about what we were going to be doing with boats.'

In the dark, with shellfire backwards and forwards in the air above them, the mystified Dorsets unloaded the plywood boats and then lined up for their orders. They were going through the woods, they were told, and down to the river. 'No noise, no talking and watch your step. Then you are to cross to the other side and bring out as many Airborne as you can find.'

*

Behind this decision to send into battle the first British forces to reach the river – albeit with the barest of briefings – lay in-fighting among Allied generals, a battle for command in which Sosabowski was side-lined and the contribution of his brave Polish Brigade, for all the hardships they had endured to get here, disregarded. Earlier that day, the Polish general had been called to a high-powered field conference attended by Browning, the commander of 1st Airborne, and Horrocks, commander of the column whose slow progress, for whatever reason,[9] from the Belgian border had put the Market Garden mission at risk. He arrived to put his considered view – based on long military experience as well as an intimate knowledge of what was happening here and now in the Arnhem cockpit – that only a mass river crossing by Allied forces could stop the Germans wiping out the remnants of 1st Airborne. But nobody wanted to know. He was told a decision had been made. A British battalion would take over the attempt to storm the river and relieve the beleaguered force in Oosterbeek. Sosabowski protested that a battalion was not enough to swing the battle in the Allies' favour. An entire division needed to cross to have any chance of success. Anything less would be 'in vain, for no effect, a pointless sacrifice'. His views were ignored and he was, in effect, relieved of his command of his own brigade. Down at the riverside, Polish sappers preparing for the next batch of their countrymen to cross the Rhine were relieved of their duties too. A British captain flashed his orders, loaded the boats on to Bren-gun carriers and carried them off to the waiting Denis Longmate and the rest of the Dorsets at a spot further downriver.

Longmate would never forget the dramatic events that were about to unfold as he and around three hundred of his comrades made the very last attempt to cross the Rhine and bring some relief to the men in the Oosterbeek redoubt. The view of Kazic Szmid – stood down from the task himself – was that it was a complete and utter failure. 'Not a single pound of supplies, equipment or ammunition reached its destination.' But that was not for want of bravely trying on the part of the Dorsets. 'It was raining and slippery underfoot,' Longmate recalled, 'as we carried the canvas boats on our shoulders down a steep and narrow path through tightly packed trees. We came to dunes of lovely sand and went up and down them until we reached the river. There we fixed the struts inside and got ready to move off. I put one man in the front with a Bren gun and the rest of us arranged ourselves behind him with shovels and rifle butts at the ready because we had only one oar.' He linked up with two other boats, each commanded by an NCO. They lost a man before they even had a chance to push off. A sniper's bullet went clean through his helmet. 'I pulled him out of the water and tested his pulse, but he'd gone. So we dragged him back through the sand dunes and put him against a tree.' It was a terrible loss. 'He was a very good friend and just hours before we'd been sitting talking about his wife and his kid. Now he was gone, just like that.' Grief was suspended as a flare lit the night and they cowered, praying not to be spotted. When its light died, they took off, a sergeant in a neighbouring boat quietly chanting 'In, out, in out,' until they got the rhythm right.

Suddenly, in midstream, the current grabbed them and there was momentary panic. Another flare went up, illuminating a scene of horror. 'Shells screamed overhead, there were explosions on the northern bank, the whine of bullets, the plop of bullets as they hit the water. The guys up front were badly shot up and their bodies were carried past us in the fast-flowing current. There were wounded in the water too, crying out for help, a hand to pull them in, but we couldn't reach them.' Longmate got to the far bank, to discover that it was almost impossible to climb. 'Spandaus peppered us as we dragged ourselves on shore, and just lay there. We daren't even lift our heads to see what lay ahead. We were bogged down, wet, confused and isolated. I don't know how any of us got across in one piece. I think I was just incredibly lucky to survive.' He was. Many of the fifteen boats missed the right landing place and were dragged downstream to where German soldiers were waiting to round them up.

Those who did make it, Longmate among them, found themselves at the foot of a wooded hill, the top of which was held by enemy troops armed with grenades, which they tossed down. But from one pinned-down man to the next went the word that an officer had made it to a building ahead of them. When he blew his whistle, they were to get up and charge to him – easier said than done up a steep, wooded slope under flare-light as bright as day and with grenades landing at your feet. But that's what they did. 'We charged, bayonets fixed, firing away until we eventually got to the top. Once we'd got our breath back, we were ordered around some woods, though every tree seemed to be hiding the enemy – and mortars and grenades were falling, making our force ever smaller.

'Finally, there were just three of us left. It was still raining, all was quiet and there was no movement. And we were debating what we were going to do when a German patrol appeared, about a dozen men coming in our direction. I put a new magazine on my Sten and said to the two lads with me, "Are we going to kill or be killed? It's them or us." It was pretty poor odds with a dozen of them and three of us. But I told the other two to hold their fire and when the patrol came in range I fired the Sten. I'd never killed at such close quarters before, literally seeing the whites of the eyes. I saw the bullets hit, saw them go down, all of them.'

Longmate was changing magazines when he heard a voice say 'Good shooting.' Three figures stood up from a bush and one spoke. 'It's all right. We're Airborne.' They were a sorry sight, Longmate thought – dirty, unshaven and tired, in a much worse state than he was. They'd been told reinforcements were coming and had set out from the Hartenstein to find them, and here, for better or worse, they were, these three at least. Not that there were that many more who made it. The outcome of that disastrous last crossing makes for grim reading. More than three hundred Dorsets clambered into those flimsy boats to make their way over. At least two hundred lost their way and paddled or drifted straight into enemy hands. Many others died in the water or in fighting on the far bank. Only a small number emulated Longmate and linked up with the 1st Airborne inside the shrinking Oosterbeek perimeter. So this was it. The long-awaited relief column – whose expected arrival had been central to the thoughts and hopes of every soldier and civilian in Arnhem and Oosterbeek for days and nights on end and had been invested, in their minds, with almost mythical, battle-turning powers – was here. Just a handful of men. This failure of the Second Army reinforcements to arrive in numbers that could make any difference was a crushing blow.

12. Chaos and Compassion in No man's Land

The thousands of wounded on both sides did not care who treated them as long as it was someone with the skills to ease their pain and keep them alive. British medics ventured out into the woods, the fields and streets to gather in casualties of both sides, protected by no more than a hurriedly waved red cross. The flag of mercy was not always respected as, under fire, they lugged stretchers loaded with shattered bodies over rough terrain back to casualty stations and makeshift field hospitals. These were rare fixed points in the swirl of battle in Oosterbeek and took in all-comers. The fighting went on around them, and they changed hands, sometimes more than once, as the front line shifted. With commendable adherence to the Hippocratic Oath, the doctors, medics and orderlies who manned these places cut, stitched and staunched, irrespective of nationality. This led to bizarre scenes of fraternization in what was otherwise one of the most ruthlessly fought battles on the western front. Padre George Pare remembered a night in the 'hospital' in the Schoonoord Hotel at Oosterbeek where British soldiers, young Dutch civilians and three German SS troopers were mingling in the kitchen, 'a packed throng of humanity', as Pare described it. 'The German boys brought out photographs of their girls, which we politely scrutinized.' One of the Dutch youths was unimpressed. 'I hate German girls,' he whispered in Pare's ear. 'They're too fat.' The talk moved on to Normandy, the Russian Front, Jews. There were exchanges of the 'You started the war. No, you did' type, leading Pare to the conclusion that 'we are all puppets in the game of survival, each believing in his own cause.'

He felt his own survival seriously threatened when he found himself nervously leading a strange procession through the battlefield. Two German soldiers had carried wounded comrades to the Schoonoord under a flag of truce and now they had to be escorted back to their own lines. Heads would have to be put above the parapet, with no certainty that they wouldn't be blown off. Cautiously, Pare set off on foot down Oosterbeek's embattled main street, leading his two enemies and holding aloft a red cross flag. He was in no-man's land and completely exposed. 'Our airborne soldiers were barricaded into houses on one side and German soldiers in houses on the other. We walked between them.' Would they hold fire? They did. 'The battle ceased for a few minutes as we stepped gingerly over a row of mines that lay wired together across the road. Then a German soldier stood up, called the two men and they ran to him. I turned and retraced my steps, with my own men shouting at me and demanding to know what sort of game this was.'

But correct military etiquette could not always be counted on. While Dick Ennis was full of praise for the Germans for respecting Red Cross conventions and allowing free passage for the wounded, Ron Kent wasn't so sure. He suspected the Germans of using the casualty stations as a means of infiltrating snipers into the British lines. He was also saddened at having to watch as 'our wounded, escorted by our own medical orderlies and by Germans, were wheeled, carried or marched off to the dressing stations and into German hands as prisoners of war'. For Ennis, though, there was something moving in the sight of a jeep with three wounded men passing through the battlefield and all firing ceasing to let it through. 'Two, lying stretched out in blood-soaked bandages, were Airborne and the third was a German, who sat with his legs dangling over the tail. He was no more than sixteen, wore horn-rimmed spectacles and looked as though he should have been behind an office desk. His face was covered in tears and sweat. His right arm was shot away at the elbow. He held the stump across his chest, gripping the end of it with his free hand; the blood squirting from between his fingers was leaving a scarlet trail behind the jeep.' He was touched by the boy soldier's distress but did not, he decided after some thought, feel sorry for him. Compassion was different from sentimentality. 'I had seen too many of our own men horribly killed. I had heard the screams of their last agony. How could it be possible to sympathize with the men who had caused all this?'

★

The Tafelberg Hotel also housed a field hospital, and it was here that Anje van Maanen came to shelter when, as the battle for Oosterbeek reached its climax, British soldiers took over her house and advised her family to leave. Her doctor father, Gerrit van Maanen, had based himself in the hotel when the airborne invasion began, intending it to be a first-aid station where he could treat any local people caught in the crossfire. But then British army medics arrived and he worked alongside them. It was a tough business, and getting tougher all the time as the fighting closed in around the hotel. As Anje went in through its gates to find her father, she was shocked first by the dead bodies laid out on the veranda, then by what she saw inside, where every bit of floor space was taken up. 'British soldiers lie everywhere. We have to step over the wounded in the foyer to reach the dining hall where the seriously injured are lying. It is silent. Only occasionally you hear a groan.'

Eric Davies, shot in both legs while trying to get to the bridge at Arnhem, lay prone and defenceless in the Tafelberg. His wounds were going septic despite the anti-infection powder the medics poured into them, and he could smell the onset of gangrene. But of more immediate threat to his life was the shelling from the Germans, especially first thing in the morning, in what the Airborne dubbed the enemy's daily 'hate sessions'. 'Shells hit the roof above us, hell of a noise. I am almost deaf and suffering from slight concussion. On one occasion an explosion lifted me clean off the floor. Dust, dirt, stink and groaning bodies everywhere. Can't move an inch to save my life. Wish I could sit up.' He was a man suffering –'these days are just indescribably, goddamned bloody hell' – but also defiant and ready to fight on. 'I am lying with my Colt .45 on my chest, determined to blast the first Kraut that walks through the door with a gun in his hand. However, this attitude is not popular with the other bods lying in this room. Later I bowed to general consensus of opinion and hid it up the chimney. Oh to be home!'

Anje had no stomach for any of these horrors at first and took shelter in the darkened cellar. Here, there was a terrible personal decision to make. Finn, her dog, was not allowed into this refuge, and her aunt decided it would be better all round if the boisterous animal was disposed of. Anje was distraught. 'I loved that dog. He was such a comfort to have around, to hug and to hold on to. And he hadn't done anything wrong. He didn't understand the war and what was going on, but he trusted me. But Aunt Anke says he must be shot, poor thing. We say goodbye to him and she takes him upstairs to ask some Tommies to put a bullet in him. The Tommies refuse. Such a nice dog, they say, and they tie him to a table up there with them and give him some rugs to lie on. Finn lives on and we are happy.'

But she was not pleased with herself. 'There are many wounded people from Oosterbeek as well as British wounded but I am frightened to go up and help.' She forced herself to do so and sneaked into the kitchen, where she joined two British soldiers peeling apples, about the only food left now. In her shyness, she said not a word to them. But she glanced at them when they weren't looking and liked what she saw. 'Ken is tall, slender, has fair curly hair and blue eyes. The other, Stan, is short with reddish hair and sparkling eyes. At first we are silent. I feel a very silly, little shy girl.' In time she overcame her embarrassment and they began to chat. 'I ask Ken how things are in England and whether he has seen *Gone with the Wind*. We talk for an hour. Stan joins our conversation, and we laugh and chatter and are gay. We almost forget the war. It is jolly nice.'

But then there was another German attack and she took to her heels, rushing back down to the cellar. 'Very cowardly and silly, but I can't help it.' Courage, though, is being afraid and doing the right thing regardless. Having a doctor as a father, Anje had enough knowledge of looking after patients to be able to help, and once again she steeled herself to do so. 'Back upstairs I wander through the rooms being used as wards. You don't hear any complaints at all.' She found it impossible to be dispassionate in treating both sides equally. She had no doubt who was to blame for all the carnage and sorrow around her. 'I see some soldiers carrying away a dead German. His body leaves a wide smear of blood on the white marble floor. He was a sniper and he was killed when he tried to creep inside the Tafelberg. They killed him and I am glad.' Even men of God found it hard to be as compassionate as their calling expected them to be in these circumstances. An airborne padre alarmed himself by how bloodthirsty he became, just as pleased as the next man when Germans were being killed. 'How soon one loses all sense of the grace of peace and Christian charity when in the thick of a battle.'[1]

Anje's anti-German passion was understandable. Others around her, she discovered, were experiencing equally intense emotions, but of a different sort. A Dutch nurse was caught having sex with a British soldier under a blanket – not that shocking given the desperate circumstances with death around every corner. But there was hell to pay. 'Daddy is furious and he sacks the girl. I don't know what has happened to the boy. But I wonder whether they have gone mad. Fancy them making love in a hell like this. They must be mentally disturbed.' Yet it was not so hard to understand and condone such an affirmation of life in what was becoming a charnel house. The British officer in charge sensibly took no action against the soldier, excusing his behaviour as 'an emotional release'.[2] And she herself admitted to 'mild flirting' with Stan and Ken as a distraction from the horror of war. 'We would chat and joke. They were lovely people.' These were fleeting moments, and time was running out fast as conditions deteriorated. The shells kept flying in, and one of the makeshift theatres was hit. 'The ceiling has come down and Daddy says they won't be able to amputate any more. All is hopeless. I go to the kitchen. Everything is filthy, the water is disgusting and very scarce anyhow. We have almost none left. So no food, no gas, no electricity and now no water. And no hope. The mood is sinking.'

Morale had not been helped either when SS troops invaded the sanctity of the hospital. An orderly, Private Tom Bannister, thought his last moment had come.[3] 'They marched all of us outside and lined us up with hands on heads near the garage we were using as a mortuary. It looked as though this was it.' With their backs to the wall, it was hardly a time for humour, but the chap standing next to Bannister looked across and grinned. 'Well, there's one thing, Tom,' he said, indicating the mortuary, 'they won't have far to carry us.' But, thankfully, no firing squad appeared, no lorry pulled up with a machine gun mounted on the back. After an inspection, the relieved medics, a little surprised still to be alive, were dismissed back to their work. But the SS weren't finished. Para Reg Curtis, his leg shattered by a mortar shell, was lying at the top of the main stairway of the Tafelberg when there was a shuffling below him, a shouting of orders in German, and troops in grey came dashing at the double up towards him. 'A sinister-looking bod about twenty years old led the way and was coming right at me. I found myself looking straight down the barrel of his Schmeisser automatic, his trigger finger shaking like billy-o. He was glaring at me with red beady eyes. "Christ, this is it," I thought. I had heard of other wounded being shot up. But I didn't bat an eyelid. My luck was in, he passed me by, and with two other SS wallahs went into a room leading off the landing and started shooting out through a window.'

This was a direct contravention of the agreed articles of war, and the senior British medical officer, a colonel, came roaring up the stairs, cursing the Germans for firing their weapons from a clearly marked Red Cross building and violating its neutrality. He demanded they stop. This confrontation could have gone either way. 'The SS men looked defiant and sullen,' the watching Curtis recalled. 'They paced up and down, glaring at everyone, their fingers playing hesitantly over their automatics. But they obeyed, if reluctantly. Then they started scrounging for cigarettes, trying each man in turn. One came up to me and demanded "*Zigaretten?*" but though I had two hundred tucked under the blanket and had a half-smoked dog-end in my hand, I said, "No, mate," all innocently. He shrugged his shoulders and sloped off. After a short while, the SS troops were gone, and our own men were back in charge.'

It was strange to 'have the enemy in the building one minute, and quickly replaced by our own combat men the next', but that was the nature of this close-quarter battle. 'Huns captured our aid post and then lost it to our boys,' noted Eric Davies. 'More and more casualties being brought in, Germans too. I gave one a cigarette and told him to cheer up, but he looked forlorn. Unlike one of our chaps next to me. His fingers have been blown off but he is coolly smoking a fag held between the bloody stumps. Summed up the airborne soldier, I thought. Spirits are still high. We know that we are better than the enemy no matter what.'

The seeing-off of the SS troops was a boost to everyone's morale – and there was more food for the soul when a local minister called the Dutch civilians together for a religious pep talk. 'He says we owe it to the English to be brave and to carry on,' Anje noted. 'We have to do our very utmost. God will be with us in this hell. We return to our posts, cheered up a little bit.' Out of the blue, there was physical sustenance too. 'Suddenly, there is a shout. There are some sheep in the road outside. After a prolonged debate about whether doctors are allowed to take up weapons in these circumstances, one of them goes out and shoots two of the animals and they are brought inside to the kitchen. Soon the most delicious smell of roasting meat wafts through the Tafelberg and everybody really cheers up. We take plates of mutton to the patients, and it is touching to see their grateful faces. Some Tommies are so self-effacing they refuse the food. But we insist that they eat now, for who knows when the next time will be?' Finn, she noted with special pleasure, 'got most of the bones and is under the kitchen table with them'.

Fortified in body and soul, she went to find Ken, who had, she learned, been wounded. He was in a 'ward' upstairs. 'I go there and find many people I know. Ken is in a lot of pain but is terribly brave.' And so was she, for from that point on she was an active nurse and inspiration to the wounded. She downplayed her own role in her diary and insisted afterwards that the wounded were the real heroes. But they knew the value of her presence and remembered her contribution. Reg Curtis thought she was 'wonderful' and singled her out for mention in his Arnhem memoir as a key member of a nursing team that worked 'with grit and determination' and stretched themselves to the limit and beyond. He had a vision in his head of 'this very young-looking girl, floating by, carefully stepping over and around the wounded on the landing where I was'. He saw her bravely dashing downstairs to the front door with her brother to help bring in new casualties whenever they arrived, an increasingly frequent occurrence as, outside, the odds tipped even more in the Germans' favour. Another wounded soldier remembered how the young volunteers brightened up the whole place. He was struck by their cheerfulness, despite this terrible situation in which their own home town and their own homes were being blown apart. He felt 'among friends'.[4]

But, for Anje, in managing to conceal her true feelings of fear and horror from patients like him, there was a personal cost that she paid for the rest of her life. 'I was just a young girl caught in the middle. I couldn't really believe it was happening to me. A few days ago I'd been playing and full of hope that the war was nearly over. Now I was among the dead and wounded. I grew up so very quickly but it made a mark on my soul.' Some of the losses were personal bereavements, shocking to a teenager. 'My friend, Bytje, died last night,' she recorded about a girl she knew who'd been brought to the Tafelberg. 'A splinter hit her head and destroyed the skull. Her father stayed beside her until she died. Poor man. She was such a lovely girl and a good skater. Now we will never see her again. Another friend is here too and is severely wounded. A piece of shrapnel has gone right into her back. The doctors have given up hope. Both girls are seventeen, the same age as me.'

She did the rounds, helping where she could. 'I go to a Tommy who has lost both his hands, and I help him to smoke a cigarette. We talk about books, England and his home and we are away for a minute, out of this hell. For a while I sit in the cellar and listen to the shells and I know it is all in vain and hopeless. I am afraid all the time. I can't bear the noise any longer and the knowledge that every shell kills people. Upstairs I take water to two patients on stretchers. One of them says he is sorry to be such a nuisance and sorry that Oosterbeek has been so badly damaged. They keep on saying they are sorry for *me*. Not their own lives, but our lives, our village, our future is what they are worried about. Even in this mess. They are excellent chaps but the situation is getting worse by the minute. The English still say Monty is coming. Are they really so naïve to think we still believe that? Or do they just say it to comfort us? But I do wonder why Monty doesn't come to relieve these poor chaps of his who have been fighting for five days and five nights without sleep, food, water? They are so exhausted. It is too much. It makes me very cross.'

The next day, Sunday – a whole week since the airborne invasion began and her world had gone mad – she was woken by enormous explosions and her courage melted away again. 'I cry. I feel lost and alone and a little bit crazy. I don't want to die, not now, yet we are facing death. We could well be killed in the next hour or so and be buried underneath the rubble. Daddy is desperate too for he has nothing left to treat people with and he feels a great responsibility for them.' One of the army surgeons joined the casualties when a shell burst in the foyer and hurled him through the doors of what had been the hotel's dining room but was now the hospital's main ward. Curtis was scared too. 'Our men were still doing their damnedest outside but the Germans were slowly closing in, though they had to fight like mad to gain every inch of that bloody ground. Suddenly there was an almighty explosion in a room on my right, and men already wounded once, twice even, were hit again. Some were killed.'

From where he lay, next to a gaping hole that had once been a window, Curtis could see what was coming next. 'Further enemy reinforcements were mustering, powerful, long-barrelled SS tanks armed with armour-piercing shells. Occasionally, an airborne man would break cover to stalk the enemy, and would be met by shell bursts and machine-gun chattering.' He heard the squeak of tracks and then caught sight of a self-propelled gun trudging nearer. It stopped from time to time and its gun turret traversed ominously, seeking out a target. It blasted some anti-tank guns in the grounds, then turned its attention to the hotel building. 'It stopped 100 yards away. I went cold. The gun slewed round until its gargantuan barrel was pointing right at me. As it bellowed out, I shut my eyes. I don't know where the shell went exactly but I felt the draught as it came though a hole in the wall and sailed by.'

The Tafelberg shook to its foundations, and so did Curtis. 'The place was an absolute shambles, the floor littered with debris, blood and glass, plus the acrid smell of smoke and gun-cotton. I thought the entire building was going to tumble down. There were pitiful cries coming from a room that had taken the brunt of the attack and a medic came out cradling someone in his arms. I saw the medic falter, his eyes red, face drawn and dust covering his whole frame, which cried out with gross fatigue. Bracing himself, he picked his way through the forms on the floor. Unwittingly, his foot came in contact with an Airborne's hand. "Sorry, lad," I heard him say and the soldier on the floor muttered, "That's all right," before sinking into a coma. There was another resounding crash of bombs, followed by men's voices loudly cursing the Boches.' But those accusing voices were mistaken this time. A medic informed them that the last salvo had come from British guns – Second Army artillery was joining in all the way from Nijmegen. So that's all right then. Curtis breathed a sigh of relief. 'I thought they were Jerry shells, but they were ours!' he told himself, though whether excitedly or sarcastically was difficult to tell.

And, in truth, if men were encouraged by the thought that there were long-awaited reinforcements out there at last, it was not for long. Distant guns, however accurate, could make no difference now, with the Tafelberg surrounded and enemy tanks not miles but just feet away. The battle was lost, and, as those inside now realized, the only alternative to surrender was to prepare to die.

*

Anje's father chose life for her and for his patients, as did his British counterparts. 'Daddy goes with an English doctor to the German headquarters to seek an armistice,' she noted. 'He carries an enormous red cross flag and wears a red cross helmet and a white coat. I catch a glimpse of him as they leave. Aunt Anke is afraid that he won't come back. While they are away there is a terrible lot of shooting and we think he must have been hit. But then they all come back unhurt. They have had a terrible walk to the German headquarters but a truce has been agreed and for an hour there will be no shooting. This turns out to be nonsense as everything goes on as before and the Tafelberg is hit again and again.'

There is worse to come. 'Suddenly, the Germans are at the door. The monster has come back! I thought we were free and now we are occupied again, back under the German boot. The battle, the blood, the wounded, all the unbelievable courage, all the devotion, it has been for nothing. This was the worst moment of the war. Our British friends have to go and so do we. We say our goodbyes. I see Ken but all I can do is to squeeze his hand and smile.' She never knew his surname, never saw him or Stan again and had no idea what happened to them.

Inside the now-surrendered Tafelberg, the place teeming with German soldiers, this was a frenetic and frightening moment. Anje's immediate concern, as it was for all the other Dutch civilians down in the cellar, was what vengeance the SS might exact on them. She had been scared for days but, as fire licked round the Tafelberg and the hated *Moffen* took charge, she was petrified. 'We thought they might kill us all.' The survivors of the Tafelberg waited, fearing these could be their last moments. 'There is a lot of shouting and we are ordered upstairs to show our identity cards. There is panic amongst the men and the boys, lots of whom were in hiding from the Germans before all this started.' They trooped nervously upstairs to the foyer and stood anxiously at the bottom of the hotel's main staircase, waiting to see what would happen next. A local minister was with them and he stepped forward to ask permission to conduct a service. The Germans refused. Defiantly, he led everyone in a hymn anyway. 'Abide with me,' strained voices rang out, 'Fast falls the eventide,' sombre and uplifting at the same time. To Anje, to everyone, it was 'a deeply moving moment. This is our last time with our airborne friends. Even the artillery outside keeps silent. It is as if a little bit of heaven has come down into this war.'

Just down the road in the Schoonoord Hotel, Padre Pare was also seeking spiritual comfort for his flock, now in mortal danger too. It being Sunday, he was preparing a service. 'There was a piano, and a soldier started to tap out two hymn tunes. Suddenly there came the most tremendous crash outside and dust flew everywhere. The road outside was being shelled. An orderly had been hit by a piece of shrapnel, and was breathing his last. I laid my hand on his head, and commended his soul.' This was the start of a barrage that lasted all morning. There was also a German sniper firing in at the wounded from a building opposite. 'It was against the rules of war but no one could stop him. His bullets came in and made the patients squirm, but all we could do was keep our heads well down. A wounded RAF chap, who had baled out from his burning supply plane, was heard to state emphatically that he was an airman and had no desire to be in the Army, thank you very much.' Yet all thoughts of rescue had not gone. Knowing little if anything about events in the outside world, 'we still hoped the Second Army would come and relieve us. But in our hearts we knew that the situation was desperate. Casualties were still being brought in, and the water and food situation was going from bad to worse.'

Something had to give. That afternoon, by agreement, German medical staff arrived in white-painted ambulances to evacuate the most serious cases and take them to a proper hospital in Arnhem. The enemy medics invited the padre to go too, and he accepted. On the drive to the St Elizabeth hospital, he witnessed the calamity that had befallen the city. 'The road was littered with wrecked cars. Most of the houses we passed had their windows smashed, and some had been totally gutted.'

The St Elizabeth, at which he now arrived, had been commandeered by the Airborne at the start of the operation, but for most of the ensuing battle was in the middle of German-held territory. SS officers were prone to marching in and trying to throw their weight about. But it remained largely a neutral zone, an island of mercy, staffed by a mixture of British and Dutch doctors, a German surgeon, German nuns, Dutch and English nurses, some Resistance fighters and a group of voluntary Red Cross assistants. Here heroic operations were performed under the most trying of conditions. Sometimes, German sentries stood guard in the busy and over-stretched operating theatre itself but, if the first incision didn't send them packing, then the sight of the saw amputating limbs usually did. Pare toured its wards, jotting down the names of the wounded and offering words of comfort to each man. For all the misery and suffering there, he thought the place 'a paradise' compared with the 'hot corner' of the Schnoonord, to which he now returned. On the way back along those same rubble-filled roads, he saw, 'to my great dismay', more German tanks clanking their way towards Oosterbeek.

That evening, the sounds of battle outside were noisier than ever and, as he took evening service, he could hardly hear his own voice.

But he managed to make himself heard when he began to sing 'Abide with Me', and the wounded men joined in as best they could, or just lay listening. 'God of the helpless, O abide with me' – never, he concluded, were the words sung in a more appropriate setting. The text for his sermon was 'Take no thought for the morrow,' from St Matthew's Gospel, and he believed it brought much-needed comfort. As he bade the men goodnight and left, a man beside the door began to sing, in a thin, shaking voice. 'Just a song at twilight, when the lights are low/ And the flick'ring shadows softly come and go . . .' An Irish ballad steeped in sentiment, 'Love's Old Sweet Song' had brought an emotion-filled end to many a night round the piano at home or down at the pub. 'Tho' the heart be weary, sad the day and long/ Still to us at twilight comes Love's old sweet song.' Pare choked. 'It was so full of pathos and the memory of peace at home that I could barely keep back my tears.'

Back at the St Elizabeth, many of those recovering from their injuries saw clearly what was happening and were not prepared to let tomorrow take care of itself. One of these was Brigadier Gerald Lathbury, commander of 1 Para. He had been in the vanguard of Market Garden and fought hard to reach the bridge but had been turned back by fierce German resistance. Caught in mortar and sniper fire, he was wounded in the back on the second day of the operation. He was just a few hundred yards from the hospital at the time and carried there for treatment. His wound was not a major one, but there was no way back to his lines. From then on he was a reluctant spectator of the battle for Arnhem and Oosterbeek, trying to make sense of the noisy mayhem outside and what he could glean from talking to other casualties and the Dutch orderlies. He took the sensible precaution of concealing his high rank from the German nuns who cooked and cleaned, unsure of their loyalties. When SS officers toured the wards, he hastily took to his bed to stay out of their way. The last thing he wanted was to be deemed well enough to be shipped off to Germany as a prisoner of war. His debriefing of men still being brought in from the front line told him that things were going badly outside but that British forces were thought to be on the other side of the river, almost within reach. But it was no good waiting for them to get to him. 'I made my arrangements to go,' he noted. 'The hospital was no place to stay in.'[5]

It was one o'clock in the morning and drizzling with rain when he crept out into the unguarded hospital grounds on to the road and began walking as inconspicuously as possible in a north-westerly direction. 'There were fires everywhere and it was dangerously light in consequence. Crossed the railway carefully, crawling under about seven trains. Felt very naked walking through the edge of town as fires lighted up everything.' Then he was into the woods, grateful to be in the dark at last but having to plot his course with a compass through dense undergrowth. 'Fences a nuisance. Got tired very soon.' As it began to get light he could see around him scores of re-supply containers and parachutes, flown in at huge personal risk and loss of life by RAF pilots but to no useful purpose. He at least could make use of them and he picked up a tin of soup to have later. 'It was pouring with rain. Not sure where I was.' He rested up in the loft of a farm, too cold and wet to sleep.

In the morning the weather was fine and he pushed on. He passed houses and gardens and saw several dead Germans but no British. He also spotted, he noted rather proudly, as if writing up nature notes, 'two green woodpeckers, a red squirrel and a hedgehog'. Then, perhaps letting his guard slip in the glorious sunshine, he 'got rather careless and walked on top of a German ammunition dump and had a narrow shave with the sentry. Had to make a big detour. Getting very tired. Very few houses now. Chose one and decided to risk it. Struck very lucky. House full of evacuees, many speaking English. Was given food and wine. Found an escaped British soldier who had been brought out of Arnhem by the evacuees, wearing civilian clothes. What luck so far.'

*

Luck, however, seemed to have deserted Anje van Maanen. Back at the Tafelberg, she and the other Dutch civilians had spent a difficult and anxious last night. They had been informed by their German captors that they would have to leave the next morning. 'But we don't know where to go as our house is still in British hands.' When she woke, 'I am afraid what this day will bring. A lot of new misery I am sure.' Outside, there was no let-up in the battle, with the big guns of the Second Army a dozen miles away still belatedly joining in the artillery exchanges with the Germans. 'The noise is terrible. It has not been as bad as this before. We can't speak because of it. The Germans take away their patients and the British start to move out theirs too.' The wounded men, immobile as they were, confined to what passed for beds, seem not to have been told what was happening, perhaps to stop them panicking. They knew something was up by all the disturbance and activity downstairs, and during a lull in the shelling one optimistic Cockney ventured to Reg Curtis that 'Jerry's packed up and buggered off.' But then orderlies came to carry them out, and Curtis was aware that these medics were very quiet and looked distressed. 'You're going to the hospital in Arnhem,' he was told.

As he was carried out of the makeshift field hospital in the Tafelberg that had sheltered him for six days, he saw the bodies of Airborne and enemy lying where they had fallen. 'Jeeps and small vans were improvised as makeshift ambulances, anything with wheels that could get us away from this hell hole. Three of us stretcher cases were loaded onto a small open lorry. It was a rough ride along the shell-holed and litter-strewn roads and those of us with shattered bones cried out in pain until we came to a standstill at the St Elizabeth Hospital.' Other wounded had to walk that same route, a tough 2-mile slog for men with injuries, some carrying others on stretchers. One of them considered they must have looked a pitiful sight. 'We were battered, like the buildings around us. We were scruffy and dirty. Our uniforms were torn. We couldn't march with our heads high as we had done when we arrived here as liberators. But most of us still wore our red berets and we still felt proud of them. We had proved to the enemy that we weren't to be trifled with.'

The Dutch were about to be sent on their way too, Anje recalled, thrust out into the middle of what was still a battlefield. 'We are told we must leave, and a message is sent to the German headquarters to stop the firing, but it doesn't. Outside, just 20 yards from the Tafelberg is a German artillery officer with orders to blow the whole place up. He tells us the shelling is not going to stop and we must take a route through the garden and down the back streets. I don't know how we're expected to drive a car through a garden with seriously wounded people. But there is no other solution. A shell wrecks the kitchen. Fortunately, no one is hurt. Finn appears from under the table, grey with dust and wagging his tail. That dog is amazing!' The Dutch sat in the cellar while negotiations went on for their safe passage. 'There are more loud crashes and everything shakes and trembles. A man we know comes rushing down and tells us his sister, Corry, a nurse, has been killed. Oh no, it can't be possible. Just a little while ago she was sitting with me in the kitchen. When the latest attack came, five people were hit, three of them dead and two wounded. Corry immediately went to the wounded boys. And when the second attack came a shell splinter hit her. It is too awful for words. I hate God. We sit in the cellar feeling utterly miserable. I feel as if I have aged ten years since last Sunday.'

It was now made clear that there would be no ceasefire to evacuate the building safely. They would have to take their chances with the bombing and shelling outside, as would the remaining patients. Some of the Dutch occupants dithered but her father ordered Anje to leave. He would stay. The Tafelberg was his responsibility until the last of the wounded had gone. But she must go now. She feared she might never see him again. 'Everyone says goodbye. I am crying. I can't help it. I don't want to go outside and face possibly being killed. On the other hand I am desperate to get away and out of this mess. We go on our way, past people who can't make up their minds. I wave at the Tommies still left behind – and I never found out whether they came out of this mess alive. Aunt Anke and I make our way along a small corridor and have to step over a German corpse. We put our noses outside the door, into the open air – and sun! It seems ages since we saw the sun. Then machine-gun bullets hit the wall beside us and we disappear back inside. But we can't stay here. We must go.'

They tried again. 'We are a party of fourteen fugitives, and I walk in front carrying a long stick with a white handkerchief tied at the end. One of the women with us has a wounded foot and is still in her pyjamas. I wonder how she will manage. We creep to the wood, climbing across destroyed trees and branches and all sorts of rubbish. The shelling stops for a moment, then starts again and I fall flat on my face into a heap of manure. We set off again and follow a small path and soon we have left the Tafelberg behind.'

They walked through a destroyed landscape. 'The houses we come to are smouldering and those of people we know are deserted. Everything is in such a mess that I hardly recognize the farm where I went five days ago to collect bread. In the street, there are the remains of tanks and cars, and we have to climb and struggle our way through the rubble. The Germans we pass laugh at us. The dead and injured lie everywhere, and we realize our own lives are on the line too, that we could be killed at any point. The only sound that we hear is the thunder of artillery and machine guns targeting the Tafelberg.'

Then, to make matters even worse for Anje, Finn disappeared. He ran off and didn't come back. She searched desperately for him. He had been her source of comfort in the dark hours. 'I call and call for him.' He had to be somewhere in the rubble of battered streets and buildings. 'But no Finn appears, and we have to move on.' She never saw her beloved dog again and was devastated. His loss seemed to encapsulate everything she, her friends, her family and the British she so admired had endured in the debacle of the failed Arnhem mission.

And so the van Maanens – minus their father – trooped dejectedly away from Oosterbeek and their home. Anje's brother found two prams in an empty house and they bundled their belongings on top. It began to rain, hard, as if the misery in their hearts and the anguish of being refugees were not punishment enough. They made a forlorn sight. 'Aunt Anke wears a soaked dinner jacket on top of a summer dress. She has torn stockings and her hair falls around her head like bits of string. Paul is unshaven and unwashed. I had a new perm just the other day and now I look like a sheep. I wear Aunt Anke's raincoat, old shoes, socks with holes and a dress with a tear down from the middle to the hem, but I couldn't care less. There is more firing and we dive into some trenches but it is only the Germans firing at the Tafelberg. No danger for us now.'

A Dutch SS man they came across directed them to the town of

Apeldoorn, 20 miles away to the north, a long haul on foot. The route took them into the remains of Arnhem. It was another journey through hell. 'There are corpses everywhere. I think I see someone hiding behind a tree, but when I go and look I discover it is a dead farmer with black socks and clogs. At the viaduct we see another corpse sitting against a stone wall with an entirely black face. We see destroyed British guns and burnt-out trams and cars. The place is crowded with Germans, who scream abuse and laugh. We feel lost and scared. I meet two schoolfriends of mine and they tell us the town is empty. Everyone has been evacuated. On we go. I see a couple of Germans accompanying captured Tommies in their red berets. I smile at the Tommies but I don't say hello. The Germans won't allow it. Meanwhile, the German artillery is still firing at Oosterbeek and at the Tafelberg. "Daddy" groans a voice within me. When I look back I see aeroplanes over Oosterbeek, see them dive and fire, and then black smoke rises. That was our home . . .'

The family made its slow and sad way into the unknown, like tens of millions of other refugees turned out of their homes all over Europe in the terrible years of the war. 'We come to a farm where we find water, which we drink furiously for we are so thirsty. People are sorry for us and help us wherever they can. I begin to notice the silence. It is quiet again after all the thunder of bombardments in the past days. We are allowed to put our luggage on top of a cart with a very old horse in front of it. We trudge on, either walking or riding on top of the cart, our blankets pulled tightly round us against the rain and the cold. Aunt Anke worries about Daddy and so do I. She cries but I can't. I am too confused and upset to cry.'

Miraculously, he caught up with them. Red Cross cars were making their way past the long line of evacuees and she spotted the familiar faces of people from the Tafelberg. 'I wave my hands and they wave too. I look desperately for him. The last one has almost gone past when I catch sight of him in it. I scream like a madman and start to run. I get to him and hug and kiss him. He has driven past mines, been bombed and shot at, but he has made it, and all the patients too. We have never been so poor and never so rich. We have lost our village, our home and all things in it. But we have each other and we are alive. How happy we are. It really is a miracle he is with us and we are terribly grateful.'

The sounds of the battle still going on back at Oosterbeek began to recede as the miles went by and they neared Apeldoorn and safety. They stopped on high ground and looked back. In the distance, 'the sky is coloured red, the blood of many brave Airbornes who gave their lives for us. They always thought of us in this terrible week while we fought together against an enormous enemy, a great friendship is born, a tie which pulls us together. We will never forget those brave heroes. They may have lost the battle but, morally, they won it.'

*

The Schoonoord was virtually the last of the British field hospitals still operating with any degree of independence in Oosterbeek, even if it had German ambulances arriving to take away the most serious cases. George Pare picked his way around its crowded wards, fielding the same questions time and again: 'How's it going out there, Padre? Are the boys still sticking to it? When will we be relieved?' As a man of God he may have wanted to be truthful, but he couldn't crush the spirits of his questioners. 'I always gave optimistic but inaccurate replies,' he noted later. The wounded continued to flood in and, while the urgent cases were quickly transferred, the majority stayed, many of them desperately ill. Despite the numbers leaving, 'we never seemed to have any floor space,' he noted. The Germans behaved well, 'bringing us water, for which we were thankful. There was no interference with the medical work.' The once spick-and-span hotel was reduced to a terrible mess, but it continued to function as a hospital, Pare declared proudly.

It was a frightening situation, nonetheless, and the padre found himself trembling from time to time. 'That didn't matter as long as I could keep up the pretence of not being too worried. But the doctors had to retain absolutely steady hands and focused minds as their skilled fingers sought to bring back life to the nerves and sinews of damaged bodies. I could not praise these doctors and orderlies highly enough. Their cheerfulness – as well as that of the patients – was a continuous source of wonder to me.' Cheerfulness tipped over into unwarranted optimism. The growing crescendo of artillery noise from outside led to wild rumours among men in complete ignorance of what was happening beyond their walls and unaware that the relief operation they still clung on to in their minds was petering out. Some of the rumours were wonderfully elaborate – that, because, as everyone now knew, the bridge at Arnhem had been lost, Second Army sappers were at that very moment racing for the Lower Rhine to throw a Bailey bridge across just to the south of Oosterbeek. To fevered and desperate brains, such schemes seemed more than plausible – they were fact. 'We thought the legendary relieving force was almost upon us,' Pare recalled. 'We believed our liberators were even now on the other side of the river.'

And indeed some were, though they had then failed to cross in numbers that might make a difference. But eager imaginations conjured up British tanks giving Jerry hell, which was simply not true, because there wasn't any British armour within 10 miles. And while the idea of XXX Corps' big guns in action might be comforting, they were also life-threatening to friend and foe alike. Patients were moved away from the walls and windows and cautioned to lie flat on the floor at all times as lumps of plaster fell from the ceiling, along with cascades of glass splinters. 'But we were immensely cheered, believing that this was indeed the Second Army on its way, crossing the river even now. In the morning, we told ourselves, we would be free.'

That night, after settling the men down, the dog-tired and flagging padre was just about awake enough to see two figures in airborne smocks make their way into the Schoonoord from the inferno of shelling outside and seek out the commanding officer. 'I couldn't make out what they said, but I heard him wish them God-speed, and they left.' The hazy incident in the flickering candlelight passed from his mind as he fell into a deep sleep.

The next morning was Tuesday 26 September, and he awoke to a bright, clear dawn, feeling better. 'But immediately I could sense there was something different. What was it? Then I realized that it was unnaturally quiet.' Pare heaved himself up and went to join the regimental sergeant-major, who was standing by a window space. 'Hello, Padre,' the RSM said. 'Heard the news?' 'No,' replied Pare, looking out and seeing a group of German soldiers lolling casually in the road outside. 'What news?' 'They've gone!' said the RSM. 'Who's gone?' 'The Division, or what was left of them.' 'The Division! But surely all that noise last night was the Second Army crossing?' 'Afraid not, sir. Look for yourself. We are prisoners now. I don't know why, but the Army hasn't crossed over to us and our chaps have had to retreat to them instead.'

A stunned Pare shook his head in disbelief. 'I can't believe it either,' said the RSM bitterly, 'but it's true. They've gone. I never thought this could happen.' He shrugged his shoulders. Market Garden, the mission to end the war by Christmas and for which nearly 1,500 brave men gave their lives, had collapsed into a seven-letter word that until now had probably never crossed the mind of a single 1st Airborne soldier: retreat. How had it happened? What exactly had gone on in the last twenty-four hours?

13. Pulling Out

The dwindling British contingent inside the Oosterbeek perimeter was unconvinced by the local legend of the little Dutch boy who plugged a leaking dyke with his finger and saved his country from flood. They were discovering that stopping up the gaps in your defences was next to impossible against overwhelming forces. In those last days of resistance, the Germans probed relentlessly for weaknesses. When they found one, they pushed through it. Defenders had to be diverted from one weak wall to shore up an even weaker one. Tanks broke through in the north of the enclave and were marauding around inside the defences until reinforcements from the southern perimeter forced them back. For now. As one para officer put it, 'Our position was only partially restored. We were all right but we felt a bit draughty.'¹ Sapper Arthur Ayers was blunter. 'Our position looks hopeless. It is a week ago that we parachuted in here. It seems like a year now.' Waking from sleep, in that split second of uncertainty before his brain kicked in, he had forgotten where he was. 'Then I saw a hand hanging in front of my eyes. I reached out and touched it. It was dead cold. I crawled out from underneath the table where I'd been sleeping, to find a young paratrooper lying on top. He was naked from the waist up, a thick bandage around his chest. The centre of the bandage was bright red with his blood while his face was deathly white and his eyes shut. I felt sick.'

There seemed a new urgency to the German onslaught. For days they had chipped away, knowing they had time on their side against a weakening force of paras whose ammunition, supplies and manpower were running out. Now, with concerted mortar and machine-gun fire from three sides and massive King Tiger tanks loaded with incendiary shells on the move, it seemed as if they wanted to speed up the result by slicing the oblong enclave in two, right through the middle, and then strangling each half. Resistance was fierce from howitzers and the few remaining anti-tank guns. The para officer was amazed at the men's fighting spirit, even now. 'From as little as 50 yards, the guns were firing over open sights at these enormous enemy tanks. One by one our guns were knocked off, but they did enough damage to slow down the rampage. PIATs, gammon bombs, anything and everything, were used against those big brutes. As effective as anything was the hidden infantryman lying in wait with a howitzer to knock off their tracks.' The well-directed fire from XXX Corps' heavy artillery – 'beginning to get really busy in our support at last' – also helped repulse the attack. The German tanks pulled back; the British had held their ground. 'But we were left in a pretty sorry state.' The buildings in which the paras were holding out took a terrible pasting. The perimeter, defenders were forced to acknowledge, was 'doomed'.

Some of the men became downhearted. Sergeant Bob Quayle shared a trench with his mate Alf, and Alf had had enough. He was cleaning his Sten gun, wiping off the sand and grime with an old bed sheet, when he saw another purpose for the cloth in his hand. 'I think next time Jerry comes, I'll wave this sheet and give up,' he said out loud, his frustration directed as much at his own commanders as at the enemy. What particularly irked him was that no one ever told them what was happening. Were the guys at the bridge still holding on? They didn't know, though they had their suspicions. Where was XXX Corps? No idea. 'There's little point in carrying on,' he concluded. Quayle tended to agree. 'It had come to a point,' he recalled in his memoirs, 'where nothing seemed to be coordinated, no orders, no plans, just little pockets of men fighting their own little battles.' Yet when that next attack came, as it inevitably did, there was no question at all of putting that white sheet to the use the moaning Alf had mentioned. Quite the opposite, because, as Quayle also observed, when the chips were down, 'we were stubborn men who refused to give up.'

Two Tigers came into the open and advanced towards the trenches, followed by a hundred enemy infantry in extended order. It was a horrifying sight but, to a man, the paras – Alf included – rose from their foxholes. 'We discovered in North Africa and Italy that the Germans were not fond of fighting in the open,' Quayle explained, 'so we got out of our trenches and started to walk towards them. On my left I could see a dozen chaps on their feet and doing the same, advancing to meet the enemy.' It appeared suicidal – their chances of surviving this encounter were slim to zero. But this was fierce regimental pride and determination in action. 'There was iron discipline in the airborne forces,' Quayle wrote later, 'and it bred a comradeship that will never be bettered.' They lived to tell the tale, but only because of outside help. As they stepped forward, the faraway guns of XXX Corps opened up on the Germans. 'The air above us screamed with shells passing over. I hit the ground hard and cowered a little. The barrage burst and, happily for us, not one shell fell short. I looked up to see a mess, German tanks on fire and the infantry getting out of there as fast as they could. The artillery saved the day. We could not have held the enemy off on our own.'

Ron Kent also appreciated the assistance now coming in from the other side of the river. 'The artillery were doing a fine job, even if they sometimes dropped their shells mighty close to our front line.' And it wasn't just the high-explosive shells that were starting to pin the Germans back. 'Typhoons roared overhead discharging their rockets at targets on the ground.' He was elated and encouraged to the point of optimism. 'We felt that relief really was on its way to us.'

Ronald Gibson, a glider pilot now turned to his secondary role of soldier, must have longed to be back in the air rather than stuck here, not just on the ground but *in* it, for a whole week now. Behind him was what remained of divisional headquarters in what remained of the once glorious Hartenstein Hotel. In front of him in those final days of Market Garden was a thick wood of beech and oak saplings. There were trenches to the right and left of him, some occupied, some not. It had become, as one wag among them noted, like some grim version of musical chairs, except that it was the players who were diminishing rather than the places of refuge. When his trench was targeted by an enemy mortar, Gibson dashed for another one. 'I waited for the next shell to burst, then grabbed my rifle and sling and made a hop, skip and jump into another trench about 10 yards away.

It was occupied by a sergeant whose face I did not recognize. He mumbled some conventional epithet about the temperature of our surroundings. The next burst brought a splinter from a tree that tore a great hole in his back. I could see the jagged vent in his smock. He gave a scream and slumped into the corner of the pit. I shook him by the shoulder. He mumbled a few words and then died. I moved into another trench a little to the left.'

Gibson stayed alert, despite his lack of sleep. If he heard a rustle of leaves or a twig crackling, he was focused, cocking his rifle and placing his Mills bomb at the ready. It was nerve-wracking, waiting for the inevitable. They were a ragbag army by now, the remnants of many different units. 'There were two 6-pounders and their crews from the Border regiment, in the hedge was a Vickers gun manned by two parachutists and in the slit trenches were several men from other squadrons. We wore an odd assortment of garments, especially our headgear. One guy had an American helmet on,' another a Dutch railwayman's cap he'd found. Several wore scarves of parachute silk and green and brown camouflage nets knotted round their heads.' It was a far cry from the smartly turned-out warriors who had left England eight days earlier. He saw flame-throwing tanks prowling the edge of the perimeter and then hurl what looked like sheet lightning at a section of the line. He later learned that two of his closest friends had been roasted in their foxholes, burnt alive. Men were being picked off in other ways too. A Polish captain made his way to the Hartenstein for orders, dodging through shrubbery and sprinting across open ground. He threw himself down by a bush, only for the bottom branch to lift and three Germans reveal themselves with a machine gun pointed straight at him. '*Hände hoch*,' they cried, and he had no choice but to comply. While they stripped him of his weapons, he spotted a huge tank behind them camouflaged with branches. The enemy seemed to be everywhere.

Death was all around too. Gibson left his trench and wormed his way to a nearby copse to get some fresh pine branches to line his 'billet'. There he came across the remains of a young lieutenant, killed in an attack two days earlier. 'He was lying face downwards with his head buried in a clump of heather, his arms bent stiffly on the ground before him, as if he had been crawling.' Next to him was the body of a young German corporal, his knapsack wide open to reveal a lump of old brown bread and a rusty knife. The hungry Gibson reached out for the dead man's morsel. 'But when I touched it, it felt like damp rubber, so I let it lie.'

Trench by trench, line by line, they were being forced back. 'We were ordered to withdraw to a command post. There, our casualties were counted and proved very heavy. As we were sorting out the bandoliers and remaining Brens, the shelling began again and we withdrew again, to a row of houses. We dashed across by turns in small groups.' He found himself in the back room of a cottage, whose thatched roof and latticed windows reminded him of homes in the English countryside. Inside, smart chintz furnishings mingled with ammunition boxes. The remnants of snatched meals were scattered over the carpet. Four other glider pilots were already in occupation. One was a mate. 'I had last seen him across a table in a café in Leicester during a weekend leave. He looked very white, but still managed to grin. He was killed on the following day.'

An officer took charge, spreading out the depleted defences as best he could. Gibson was sent to man the house next door. The terrified Dutch family were still in residence. 'We could hear them down in the cellar as we stumbled about the house, piling the furniture against the windows. Beyond the houses directly opposite us I could see the glow of a big fire from a street on the edge of the German lines. We posted sentries, and I lay down in a corner and wrapped myself in a curtain and a rug, with a fur mat for a pillow. I felt cold and very tired after seven nights of almost ceaseless watch.' He had taken the opportunity of being indoors to smarten himself up. 'I found a mirror, and the first sight of my own face after seven days was disconcerting. I had a heavy stubble of beard, stained yellow from the sand of my trench. The remainder of my skin was a sickly grey colour, caused by lack of sleep and a diet of condensed rations. I washed off as much of the sand as I could and made a brave attempt to comb my hair.' But, despite getting spruced up, Gibson was feeling very low. He had not wanted to pull back from the trenches to take up a position in these houses. 'We'd stood firm in front of the wood for five days and it had seemed we would hold on there for ever. Withdrawing from there was a shock.' An even bigger shock awaited him, a withdrawal he had never contemplated for a second.

There was a hint of what was to come when, from his vantage point, Dick Ennis, another glider pilot, saw that a section of British troops were out in no-man's land uprooting a line of posts and knocking down the remains of a wire fence stretching alongside the road. It was a risky thing to do under fire, so this must be important. 'Perhaps it was so that when the Second Army reached us, its progress would not be impeded,' he guessed, wrongly. But here was that indomitable optimism that the airborne men seemed never quite to lose, however bad things got. It was exemplified again when Gibson took himself on a scouting tour around the immediate area. He climbed out through the broken French windows and sprinted across the lawn to the houses behind. Down in the cellar were half a dozen fellow glider pilots. His next call was on the house next door, where more mates from the Glider Pilot Regiment were holed up. As they took stock of their numbers and their remaining ammunition, he came to the conclusion that, even if the enemy managed to get past them, the houses could be knocked through to make a decent stronghold. They could hold out, he was confident of that.

In that positive frame of mind, he sat down to a late lunch of biscuits and boiled sweets, found in a discarded rucksack. 'We mixed them with the boiled potatoes and ate from dishes that had been left in the kitchen cupboard.' The semi-civilized meal, eaten from plates, was shattered by the barbaric roar of a mortar shell exploding. 'The remaining glass blew in from the French windows, and for a moment we were blinded by a cloud of black smoke. As it cleared I saw the dim figures of the others, crouched against the walls, their plates still on their knees. Outside was a hole.' Bombs fell for an hour, clipping the corner of the house next door. 'We returned to our stations at the window ledges and watched the street.' Then came the real bombshell.

It was the afternoon of Monday 25 September, the glider pilots recalled, when their senior officer was summoned away to a meeting. He returned at around 5 p.m. with what Gibson thought 'a very secretive expression' on his face. He closed the door, gathered every one around him in a corner and spoke in a whisper so that the Dutch family couldn't hear. 'We're pulling out tonight, over the river. The Second Army can't cross. We lost the bridge several days ago and our tanks can't pass the German guns to reach it. We are to assemble on a little patch of grass behind the garden at 21.15. We are to bring any surplus kit. We are to cover our boots with strips of blanket and rug. We are to follow white tapes down to the river. We are to retain our arms at any price. We should keep together.'

Gibson listened to the orders in a state of 'dazed surprise, almost shock'. Officially, this might be termed an orderly withdrawal because of an 'intolerable' military situation, but the men knew a retreat when they saw one. He felt let down. 'For nine days we had held to one belief – that the Second Army was coming through. We had heard rumours and more rumours of their steady advance to the river bank, of vast lines of tanks on the Nijmegen road, of lines of guns firing a barrage over our heads. When shells had burst through our window that very afternoon, we assumed they might be British, for the blast had blown from south to north, and it was from the south that we expected the Second Army. We had also watched a sortie of Typhoon fighters swooping down on the German lines and heard the rasping and booming of their rockets.' They had genuinely thought that, if they held on long enough, they would be relieved. Now they were being told to run.

Ron Kent, who had been one of the first airborne soldiers into the battle, his feet among the first to touch Dutch soil, was mortified by the decision to pull out. After his optimistic reaction to the increasing intervention of XXX Corps' big guns, it took him completely by surprise. 'For me and for many others, there was only one thought in our minds – survival so as to see the tanks of the Second Army cross the Rhine. There was never any question of us going to the relief. It would come to us and, when it did, we would have vindicated our presence in Oosterbeek. The real tragedy of Arnhem was that the men who fought and died there did so with a firm belief in our ultimate victory. When the end of our effort came, it was totally unexpected.' He would come to see this as a betrayal – and not just of the British troops who gave so much for so little. 'We also had the Dutch civilians to think about. With our arrival they had seen the end of German occupation. We should have stayed for their sake.'

When he and his men were called together to be told of the plan to evacuate the Oosterbeek perimeter, 'the let-down was tremendous. Holding on as we had done all these past days had been a complete and utter waste.' Back in the school building he had been defending, there were six corpses piled up in a back room. 'Was it all for nothing?' His nerve very nearly broke. 'I had a distinct inclination to cry at the futility of it all. I said as much to the officer in charge and I'm sure he thought I was cracking up. He told me quite harshly to pull myself together.' It was made clear that this was not every man for himself but an orderly withdrawal in platoon order. And silent. Boots and every bit of loose equipment were to be muffled. 'We were told that, if it came to it, we would fight our way to the river, but the hope was that it would not be necessary. Despite all that had happened to us, we were expected to go out in the same orderly fashion as we arrived.' Then, while a handful of sentries continued to man the windows and walls, everyone else was dismissed to make ready for this 'trip of deliverance'.

For Ronald Gibson, however, there was a last special task to perform, one that rubbed salt into a smarting wound. He was selected to go out on a joint patrol of soldiers and glider pilots to reconnoitre the gardens of a street on the northern edge of the enclave. They were to fire on sight or sound of any suspicious movement, but to avoid any stand-up fight. They were there strictly to keep up appearances. 'The purpose of the patrol was to give the Germans the impression that we were still active – in order to conceal from them that we were actually withdrawing that evening.' On that patrol, Gibson came across a distraught and dishevelled para sergeant hiding behind a bush outside one of the many burnt-out houses that had once been part of the airborne defence line. 'He stepped out into the open in a rather blundering way. His smock was torn and his face black with wood ash.' His manner was distracted, as if he had lost his composure and possibly his mind. '"Have you seen my boys?" he asked. "I left them on guard in the cellar." He walked past us and lumbered over the wall into the embers. In one corner he stirred a hole in the ash with the butt of his Sten gun, whistling and calling in a low voice: "Hey, Ted! Ted!" Then he moved to another corner and called again. For several minutes he stumbled around the inner walls. Finally he stepped back over the outer wall and was hidden again in the bushes.' If anyone ever doubted that the men of the Airborne had given their all, then here was proof. And for what?

*

Yet it is difficult to argue that the order to pull the boys out of Oosterbeek was anything other than the correct military decision. The anger of disappointed men willing to fight on was based on the notion that the Second Army could still make it and, as Ron Kent imagined, 'we would see our tanks and our troops sweeping through Oosterbeek and Arnhem and down into Germany.' But that was now out of the question. The Second Army wasn't going anywhere. German armour stood in its path miles short of Arnhem, whose bridge across the Lower Rhine was firmly in German hands and had been for several days. The possibility of crossing the river at some other point was a non-starter – as Horrocks must have realized when he came to the front line and stood with the Polish commander, Sosabowski, on the top of the church tower in the village of Driel and stared across the water at burning, ravaged Oosterbeek. A whole fleet of assault boats would be needed, hundreds of them, and they weren't in the plans. The mission had been to secure a road crossing for the express purpose of making a time-consuming wholesale water-borne assault unnecessary. Sosabowski could rail, as he did, with good reason, that boats should have been part of the contingency planning, but the plain fact was that they weren't because the whole point of Market Garden and the seizure of the Arnhem bridge was that they wouldn't be needed.

The Polish general was right that it would take a whole division crossing the Rhine to have any chance of winning the battle. He saw Horrocks's decision to ignore his advice at that contentious field conference and send in a single battalion, the Dorsets, as a weak-willed blunder by a commander who did not grasp the situation. In reality, Horrocks grasped all too well what was going on. There were simply no means of getting a whole division over, and even if he did, he reckoned he would need a further division of reinforcements to continue the drive into Germany and on to the Ruhr, which, after all, was the ultimate objective. Two facts had to be faced – that Market Garden could not succeed and that reinforcing the Oosterbeek perimeter was not feasible. He had no choice but to make the best of what had turned into a bad job and bring home as many of the lads as he could.

Ultimately, the decision to evacuate was down to Montgomery, as the field marshal acknowledged in his memoirs. At his mobile tactical headquarters outside the Belgian town of Leopoldburg, he received a signal from Urquhart on Monday with the starkest of sit-reps. 'Must warn you that unless physical contact is made with us early tomorrow, consider it unlikely we can hold out. All ranks now exhausted. Lack of rations, ammunition and weapons, with high officer casualty rate. Even slight enemy offensive action may cause complete disintegration. If this happens all will be ordered to break towards bridgehead rather than surrender. Have attempted our best and will do as long as possible.'

Monty was well informed by his own on-the-spot liaison officers. He would also have had Horrocks's reports, and it is clear that, as early as Friday, Horrocks was of the opinion that establishing a bridgehead across the Lower Rhine west of Arnhem was problematic without massive reinforcements and had passed that firm assessment up the line.[2] If the probes across the river by the Polish Brigade and the Dorsets had been unopposed then there might still have been a chance for a bigger operation, but the stiff opposition they encountered sealed the fate of any rescue mission. 'We could not make contact with them [1st Airborne, across the river in Oosterbeek] in sufficient strength to be of any help,' Monty wrote later, 'and I gave orders that the remnant of the division were to be withdrawn back over the Lower Rhine at Arnhem and into our lines.' Market Garden was Monty's brainchild and he now had no choice but to kill it off. He conferred with Dempsey, commander of the Second Army, and they agreed that the 1st Airborne should pull back across the Lower Rhine.

It would seem that the decision had virtually been taken before the Dorsets made their ill-fated night crossing. With them that night went a colonel from a different regiment carrying contingency plans and orders. He was dumped from an amphibious craft into the muddy water on the far side, waded ashore and then made his way through the fighting to the inside of the perimeter. As dawn was breaking, he reported to Urquhart's headquarters in the Hartenstein cellar and handed over a letter informing the general that the Second Army was abandoning its attempt to reinforce his bridgehead and giving him permission to withdraw his men back across the river when he saw fit. Urquhart took a little time to think through his limited options. Intelligence reports – backed by common sense – suggested that the Germans were building up to a major assault to annihilate the last pockets of resistance. It was time for 1st Airborne to cut its losses and leave while it still could. He called in his senior officers from the dug-outs and semi-derelict buildings they were grimly hanging on to, and they ducked their way through mortars and sniper bullets to his HQ for a 10.30 a.m. conference.

They were, Urquhart ordered, to prepare an evacuation for that night, under cover of darkness, starting in the north of the enclave and rolling down like the collapsing of a bag to the river bank, where boats from the far side would be waiting. The listening officers did not need to be told that this was the most difficult of military operations – withdrawal when interlocked with the enemy. The blueprint for what was designated Operation Berlin was the British withdrawal from Gallipoli in 1916, which, ironically, had been the only successful part of that military disaster. Urquhart's staff drew up a complex timetable. The route by which every single group would move and the time of every movement were to be planned to the last detail. Covering fire from the other side of the river had to be coordinated. Orders were to be passed down the line in the strictest of confidence. Copies of orders were to be memorized and destroyed. Any Dutch people still in the area were to be kept in the dark for fear of panicking them and giving the game away. The Polish contingent, dug in

nearest the river and freshest to the battle, would form the rearguard
– last in, last out. The first man, it was hoped, would be away at 2200
hours, but as for the last of the 2,500, nobody could say when. But at
least the end was in sight. Just one final water obstacle, the Lower
Rhine, to get over and what was left of the 1st Airborne Division
would be out of this hell-hole.

*

That morning, Dick Ennis recalled, an officer made his way from
trench to trench in that battered defence line around the Hartenstein to
brief the occupants. When he heard what was up, Ennis realized why
that wire fence out in no-man's land had had to come down. It wasn't
to allow the Second Army in, as he had fancied, 'but to facilitate *our*
exit'. The instructions were precise. 'We were to start moving off at
8.45 p.m. in sections of about a dozen men with a three-minute inter-
val between each section. The enemy were between us and the river.
We would have to creep through their lines. They must on no account
get the least suspicion that we were pulling out. It would be fatal if the
enemy caught us in the open. So that we could move unhampered, we
were to leave every article of equipment behind and carry only our
arms. Anything in our pockets which might rattle – such as loose
rounds of ammo or matches – was to be thrown away before we moved
off. The signal to start moving down to the river would be a Second
Army artillery barrage stretching all round the edge of our perimeter.
We were told that if any man had the misfortune to be captured, he
must on no account divulge that an evacuation was in progress.'

Ennis was not devastated, as Ron Kent was, by these unexpected
orders. 'So we were to pull out,' he noted. 'It was a new train of
thought. We had never considered such a proposal until now. It was
a nice thought. We might yet get out of this mess.' They discussed
between themselves the chances of covering the distance to the river
without being detected and decided they might just about do it. The
officer who had briefed them returned with a promised tin of cigarettes for them. 'We took one each and passed the tin on. This was our
lucky day – cigarettes and the prospect of a get-away. Mortars were

still being flung at us. It would be terrible luck to be hit now.' But between then and nightfall, luck ran out for another 120 of the defenders. By some awful irony, the body count that last day was huge, half as much again as on previous days. With the prospect of deliverance just hours away, the glider pilots alone lost thirty-two of their men. Phosphorous shells added to the dangers and an ammunition store exploded. No wonder that Kent remembered everyone being 'as nervous as kittens' in the run-up to H-hour. The Second Army shelling of the German lines that had once given him reassurance now seemed a threat to his survival. Was it getting too close for comfort? How awful to be knocked out at the very last minute, and by your own side! Major Ian Toler, commander of a glider pilot squadron, wondered 'if we will live to see the withdrawal', but then borrowed a razor and a smidgeon of soap and bucked himself up with a shave, 'because if we *are* getting out tonight we don't want the rest of the army to think we are tramps.'

There were nerves too about the action itself and how dangerous it would be, and with good reason. One man confessed that his knees shook at the prospect and he could not stop them, however hard he tried. Another considered the journey down to the Rhine and across to the other side 'extremely dicey'. He was not optimistic. 'We knew that Jerry was all around us with self-propelled guns, machine guns and heaven knows what, that snipers were in the woods right up to our front door and that there was an enemy battery which had the range of the strip of shoreline where we were to embark. We knew too that it was between a mile and a half and two miles down to the river, that the width of the escape route was only a few hundred yards and even that was not really clear of Germans.'[3]

As darkness fell after a long day marked by impatience, anxiety and a lot of enemy action, Ennis and his section collected up what sacking and parachute silk they could lay their hands on, tore them into strips and bound them round their boots. They blacked up their faces – as if that was necessary after not washing for a week, one man quipped. 'We buried our grenades and ammunition in the bottom of the trench, all except eight rounds which I left in the magazine of my Colt. It was not six o'clock and we were ready. The evacuation was to start at 8.45 p.m. but our section wouldn't be off until 9.30. There were three and a half hours to wait. Would they ever pass?' In pockets of Airborne from north of the Hartenstein down to the Oosterbeek church, men huddled for a last mug of tea and pooled their remaining emergency supplies of Horlicks tablets and chocolates for a farewell 'feast'. Sitting in the cellar of the Hartenstein itself, waiting for the off, Arthur Ayers looked at the dirt-caked faces around him. 'Lack of food and sleep, plus the constant attacks by the enemy, had taken its toll. Bloodshot eyes showed what they had been through. Some had bandages around their heads or on a limb, but their spirit was not broken. Whatever the future held, they would see it through.' He himself was worried. 'I couldn't swim. Supposing the boat I got on sank. My chances of survival would be very slim.'

Every few seconds the men glanced at the luminous hands of their watches glowing ghost-like in the dark. The time dragged. Each minute felt like an eternity. Ennis wondered if his watch had stopped. Would 8.45 ever come? 'Suddenly the artillery crashed into action' – the signal for the operation to begin – 'and shells screamed over our heads to tear up the ground in front of us. Tortured trees threw shattered branches about us while clods of soil rained on to our heads.' The first men were on the move, shadowy figures flitting through the night, hugging close to the walls of burning buildings, to assemble at the appointed place – a cabbage patch behind the Hartenstein. Passwords were whispered. The first sections departed into the night. Following their precise orders, Ennis and his section waited again as the next forty-five minutes ticked slowly away. His mind played tricks on him. Had the officer's briefing really happened? What if everyone else had gone and they were left behind? And then his mate Billy was shaking him out of his reverie and saying, 'Come on. Let's go.' This was it.

'I struggled out of the trench. A few other men appeared, their dirty, bearded faces lit up every few seconds by the flash from exploding shells, and we formed into our section. We stepped out on to the road, crossed it and entered trees behind the burnt-out relics of two houses. We followed a path, stumbling our way round craters and over fallen tree trunks. Before long we caught up with a long column of men as all the sections merged together into one long line. Soon we left the wood behind us and entered the centre of Oosterbeek. Practically every house was a mass of flames. We filed down a street, walking close to the houses where the pavement had once been, and passed a patrol of Germans – about eight or nine men. They crouched beside the front wall of a garden. They could not see either the beginning or the rear of our column and had no way of knowing how many of us there were. They did not start anything and nor did we. We just carried on, practically brushing against them as we passed by. They must have been petrified at first, but then they ran off among the burning houses.'

But clearly any hopes that the evacuation would go undetected were blown. 'We reached the end of the street and were once more in the country, moving through a hedge and into a field. Suddenly a flare went up and we fell frozen to the ground. In its light I saw a dead cow, lying on its back with its stiff legs stretching in the air. The flare flickered out and we carried on across ditches and through more hedges. Mortar shells exploded nearby, sending shrapnel purring through the air about us.' Toler, who fell into an open sewer and came out 'smelling like a polecat', then felt something hot on his neck but thought no more about it. The next day he found a shard of shrapnel in his smock.

And then they were there. Ennis could see the Lower Rhine, the river they had been trapped behind for so long. Barbed wire lined the top of a steep bank which led down to what passed for a beach. 'One of our men had been flung into the middle of the wire by a shell, and he called, "Please don't leave me, don't leave me here." Two of us went over to him, but he was dead. He'd lost both his legs. We scrambled under the wire and down the bank. There were now 12 yards of mud flats reaching towards the river's edge. We lay down flat in the mud. The beach was crowded with men all waiting their turn to be ferried across the river.'

Meanwhile, on his way out of Oosterbeek, Arthur Ayers was faced with a dilemma. As he progressed along the road to the river, he felt everything was going well. 'I blindly followed the man in front of me. The way was rough and I stumbled once or twice in invisible pot-holes, but I managed to keep a firm grip on his jacket. When we came to a divide in the road, one of the glider pilots who'd been given the job of marking the route stood waving a guiding hand in the direction we had to take. Suddenly, without any warning, the column in front of us was raked by Spandau fire. I heard shouts and screams from up ahead, and we all dived for shelter in the ditch. When the night became silent again, I crawled out and hurried after several figures I saw disappearing into the gloom. Then I caught sight of dark shapes lying very still in the road. They seemed beyond help, their hopes of crossing the river and getting back to England gone in a few seconds. Then I heard the voice. It was low, almost a whisper. "For God's sake, somebody help me."' There was a man lying in a ditch, one of the glider pilots. 'It's my face,' the voice whispered. 'I've been hit in the face.' 'Can you get up?' Ayers asked. 'Can you walk?' The man clambered up. 'I peered closely at his face and shuddered at the sight. It was a mass of blood, with two small slits for his eyes and a larger slit his mouth.' It was a wonder he could speak, but he managed to croak a whispered 'Please don't leave me.' Ayers knew that if he stopped to help he was almost certainly throwing away his chance of reaching the river and getting home.

Back in the area around the Hartenstein, Ron Kent was still in the cabbage patch, a backmarker. Mortars were screaming in and some of his men suspected that the Germans must have rumbled what was happening. Instinctively, some of them scratched shallow trenches in the earth with their hands. 'We waited as other units passed through us on their way to the river. Then all movement ceased and I sensed that something was wrong.

'I went down the line of waiting men lying flat on the ground and discovered that most of the company had moved off, leaving more than half of my platoon behind. It seemed we had missed the boat.' Kent made contact with another sergeant, and they decided not to wait for any more orders. They were going to make their way to the river with their men as best they could. They had been given no details of where the crossing point was, so their plan was to move south to where the river had to be. It was a pitch-black night and they were as good as blind. Suddenly, the sergeants saw red tracer shoot up into the sky ahead of them, from the other side of the river. That must be it. 'We got the men on their feet, telling them to hold on to the belt of the man in front and follow the leader to the river's edge. More by luck than judgement, we hit upon white tape that had been tied to trees to mark the route to the river bank.' They could hear heavy fighting to the side of them. One section had stumbled on a German machine-gun nest in a house in the woods and taken a number of casualties before eliminating it with a grenade attack.

*

Down at the beach, a mini-Dunkirk was under way, but it was a slow business and, as time went by, becoming every bit as dangerous as the original. To Ronald Gibson, standing in the moonlit queue, it seemed inconceivable that thousands of men could get away unobserved, and he was right. 'There came a succession of "plop, plop, plops" from a mortar battery in the wood, and the next moment a string of shells burst in the centre of the queue. There were screams and shouts for help. Several voices shouted "Scatter." Bodies crawled in all directions. An officer moved the queue about 50 yards downstream, but the next batch of shells fell accurately on the new position. The wounded who were able to crawled away, the others were carried by their mates. Two officers ran to the ditch and told us to push back. "Don't bunch, for Christ's sake!"'

The queue was moved a second time, and thinned to a narrower line.

'The men were passed forward in little groups. I must have wallowed in the ditch an hour or more before our turn came. Someone called from across the field. We ran across the slope of grass and clattered on to the shelving stones of the bank. A canvas assault boat with an outboard motor screwed to the stern and, manned by two Canadian sappers, was swinging against a groyne of stones that sloped into the water. We waded out and heaved ourselves over the side. The boat was pushed off from the groyne and a sapper jerked the engine-starter with a rope. The engine spluttered, chugged a few turns, then died. We twirled downstream in a fast current, drifting back to the bank. As we grounded, a voice shouted: "Why in hell's name don't you paddle with your rifles?" We dipped the butts in the river and did just that. The boat's head began to swing upstream. We passed mid-current. Suddenly the engine started with a jolt that flung us off our balance. The bows lifted and we raced across the final reach into the shadow of the dyke.'

Back on the other side, Ennis and his men were still waiting. They had been on the go for two and a half hours. It was midnight. Heavy rain began to fall, an added burden that later led Horrocks – a man who loved a good phrase – to bewail that 'even the gods were weeping at this grievous end to a gallant enterprise.'⁴ The men soldiered on. 'We lay in the soaking mud, wet through, and every few minutes a boat would pull in and take off a party of men – twelve to fifteen at a time.' There were supposedly thirty-seven boats in all, but some were lost and, though the twenty-one motorized ones could speed across in three minutes, they were liable to break down.⁵ Given the current, the ones depending on paddle-power required as many as four crewmen to get them across, thereby reducing the number of passengers they could take. The growing queue was patient, with a discipline that awed one leading Arnhem historian. 'Everyone took their turn, irrespective of rank. Urquhart and the other senior officers queued like everyone else. One brigadier showed some reluctance to cross until he was sure that all of his brigade had left but was persuaded that such honourable gestures were not practicable.'⁶ One veteran recalled the calming voice of a stalwart officer urging everyone not to panic and directing traffic with his arms as if on point duty in the middle of Oxford Circus.

Still Ennis waited. 'At two in the morning I was still among those waiting a turn. The beach seemed to be as crowded as ever, and now mortar shells were landing among us. I saw one of the boats hit as it left the shore, loaded to capacity, and heard the screams of drowning men.' Ennis could see that there were not enough boats to move everyone before daybreak. Life-or-death decisions had to be made. 'An officer called out that every man who could swim should get across as best as he was able, leaving the boats for wounded and non-swimmers. When we left England we were each given a Mae West inflatable lifebelt in case we ditched in the sea. On landing, I had untied mine, and I put it inside my smock. It was still there, and I pulled it out. I am a poor swimmer but the river was only about 500 yards wide and I reckoned that with the lifebelt I might be able to struggle to the far bank. I tore off my boots and steel helmet, inflated the Mae West and waded out into the water.'

But this was no easy stretch of water. It was cold and fast, with tracer and mortar shells flashing across the surface. 'As soon as my feet left the bottom, I felt the current catch me and swirl me along downstream. I was so exhausted that I could do little more than feebly struggle against it. I knew then that I would never reach the other bank. I was going to drown. Just when I had practically given myself up, a boat laden with men passed by me. I made one last effort, my fingers reached out and clawed at a rope. I hung on, while the men in the boat paddled with their rifle butts, fighting to beat the current. In that manner I was towed across until I was able to let go of the rope and crawl ashore. I tried to get on my feet, but my legs were unable to support me, and I crumpled into the mud, gasping for my breath.' Ennis eventually managed to stand up, only to throw himself flat again into the mud as machine-gun fire rattled around him. 'Don't worry, mate,' said a friendly voice. 'They're ours.'

The British soldier directed Ennis away from the bank, across a meadow, to a road. He had made it. The ordeal of Arnhem and Oosterbeek was over, and he was alive. He kept walking – rough going over gravel without the boots he'd jettisoned in the water. 'A chill wind was blowing, and our soaked clothes clung to our bodies, setting our teeth chattering.' Then he was at a farmyard and entering a large barn 'full of our men, all laughing and talking, a lot of them in various stages of undress. Tins of hot rum were thrust into our hands and we were given a thick round of bread on to which a steaming concoction of mixed vegetables was poured. We just couldn't believe it. We didn't have to share our ration. It was glorious! We had nearly forgotten how to eat – we just wolfed it down.' Outside, he saw the comforting shape of a British tank, pulled off the road. One of the crew was leaning out of the turret smoking a cigarette. 'You blokes just come from over there?' he asked, pointing in the direction of the river. 'Yes,' he was told. 'Been a bit sticky, hasn't it?' the tank crew-man observed. 'You're okay now though.'

For Ron Kent, however, things were far from okay as he lay in the teeming rain and cold north wind for hours, waiting for his chance to cross. 'Every now and then the area would be lit up by German flares, and we pressed our faces to the ground and prayed we would not be spotted. Occasional mortar bombs exploded in our midst and, from time to time, green tracer bullets criss-crossed as the Germans combed the area. At other times, they would arc across the river in answer to the heavy machine-gun fire from the other side that was trying to give us cover.' The waiting went on. He thought of his older brother, who had been in similar circumstances at Dunkirk. 'I had never felt so close to him as I did then.'

At last, as he edged closer to the water, his moment came. A boat manned by Canadian sappers pulled in, he waded into the icy water up to his knees and scrambled his men on board. They were across in min-utes and scrambling again, this time up the high walls of mud on the south bank. He was proud of himself. 'I had not discarded one item of equipment and my Sten gun was still in working order with a full mag-azine to snap into it if need arose.' But that need was behind him. What lay ahead, beckoning him, was a line of hurricane lamps planted in the ground, directing him and the 2,000-plus other evacuees to safety. Fig-ures appeared beside the track to urge them on with reassurances that it was 'only a few hundreds yards more'. In fact, it was a 2-mile slog to Driel. 'Along the way, a rumour told us of a hot meal, a blanket, ciga-rettes, chocolate and rum waiting for us. It sounded like the pot of gold at the end of the rainbow. I walked for what seemed hours, wet, tired and hungry and with my stomach still knotted with tension. Finally, I arrived at a farm and joined a long queue of several hundred other chaps waiting outside a barn to see if the fairytale would come true.'

It didn't. The frontmarkers like Dick Ennis had eaten to their heart's content, but by the time Kent got to the barn, shuddering with cold and fatigue, the hot food was gone and so had the blankets. All he got was a slice of dry bread, three cigarettes and a tot of rum – meagre reward for eight days of hell. This did nothing to alleviate his unhappiness at the outcome of his endeavours. 'I was still sick at heart at the failure of the operation.' Transport had been promised but that had vanished too, and he joined a stream of survivors slowly foot-slogging their way south down the road towards Nijmegen. But he was 'pleased as Punch' to be alive and free, when thousands of dead and captured comrades were not. He was tired physically and mentally, but the para spirit kicked back in. 'Endurance is a mental thing. Some have it, some don't. Endure and survive. Endure and survive. I threw back my head, took in great breaths of cool air and broke into the easy loping stride we had cultivated in training all the way to Elst.'

*

One of the luckiest crossings was made by Denis Longmate, one of that small band of Dorsets who had made it over from the south bank the night before and not fallen straight into enemy hands. He had got to Oosterbeek and taken up a defensive position inside the perimeter, only to be ordered out in the general evacuation. He'd been very fortunate to survive that first crossing. It seemed tempting providence to make the return trip so soon after. Back down at the river bank, he was climbing into a rescue boat when he slipped and fell in the river. He thought he was a goner. Those on board were pushing off from the side, desperate to get away as the evacuation stretched on towards dawn and the odds of the Germans crashing in to stop it increased. He gripped the side of the boat, 'hanging on for dear life', but they were about to leave him struggling – drowning – in the water when a sergeant took charge. 'We're not going till you're on,' he said, and made the men pull Longmate on board. 'I was in the water for seconds but it felt like a lifetime. I thought I was going to be left behind, to be shot or taken prisoner. It was such a relief to get on board. I bless that sergeant.'

On the other side, Longmate was overwhelmed by a sense of desolation. All around him, Airborne were meeting up with mates, reunited, happy to be alive. But there was no sign of any other Dorsets. 'As I walked down that road away from the river, the very same one I'd come down twenty-four hours earlier, I thought I was the only man of my regiment left. All the rest must have died. There was just me. I went into the old barn where we'd rested up on the way out. Nothing there, not a soul. I felt myself wondering if I was actually dead.' But he was alive and, as he now discovered, not alone. 'I got to the building in Driel that had been our company headquarters and went in. There was a glow of candlelight at the bottom of the stairs, faces, and a cheer went up. "It's Den! Good old Den! Well done!" There were about fifteen of them and though we were tired, cold and wet, we all had one thing in common – we had returned in one piece.' A Dorset officer, a young lieutenant they all knew, came to address them. He was injured, his arm was in a sling, but he was going back over the river to help complete the evacuation. He asked for volunteers to go with him. No one stepped forward, no one said a word. 'I don't blame you,' he said as he left. 'You've done your bit.'

But others were going back, among them Robert Talbot Watkins, the Methodist chaplain of 1 Para. He had done much of his work in the battle with the wounded and the dying, particularly at the casualty station in Kate ter Horst's house. When the evacuation was ordered, Urquhart had instructed – sensibly – that the wounded and the medics attending them would have to stay behind. No stretchers – the same order as there had been in the latter stages at Dunkirk. Nor would those being left behind be told in advance. But, since his casualty station was close to the river – half a mile at most – Watkins argued that the walking wounded should be given a chance as long as they did not slow down the able-bodied. This was agreed. With the evacuation just about to begin, he quietly broke the news to the medics in his casualty station and asked them to choose who should go.

'I specified that they should be men who physically had a chance of making it and who had enough reserves of spirit to be able to endure a trip which I expected to be opposed. They would have to be assembled and ready to move without fuss at 11.30 p.m. on the dot.' His 'flock' were there right on time, standing in the rain, some thirty of them. 'I was a bit taken aback by many of them. They looked such wrecks. There were even men with chest wounds, unable to hold themselves erect. I explained the plan. They would be divided into two sections, each in the charge of an orderly. They would move down the taped route. They would obey all orders. They would claim no privileges and were to claim no help from fit men or hinder the evacuation of fit men.' He warned them to expect to encounter fighting and that they might be safer staying where they were rather than trying to leave. 'I asked if anyone wished not to take the risk, but not one changed his mind.'

They moved off, each man holding the tail of the smock of the man in front. 'They were so slow and so weak that it seemed scarcely possible that many of them would get far. They started off in the middle of a column, but their snail's pace soon put them at the rear. By now the Germans had cottoned on that something was up and were putting down fire and putting up flares, and we had to get flat in the mud. Many of them must have suffered greatly but none complained and none gave up. I do not know how long it was before their turn came for the boats. There were some men on that evacuation beach that night who lost their heads. But not these walking wounded. They kept their discipline, and not a single one of them was lost on that crossing.' It helped that Watkins's insistence on the wounded getting no favoured treatment was generally ignored. There were many reports of fit troops standing to one side to let their injured comrades through first, whether they asked or not.

Now, something remarkable happened. Having brought his party of the lame and the halt over to safety, Watkins decided to go back for more. 'It was hare-brained,' he wrote in his memoirs, 'but I had the daft idea that what had come off once would come off again. I went back to the river and crossed over in a boat, with the notion of getting another lot out of that casualty station.' He soon saw the error of his ways. 'All sorts of stuff was flying about the river area, and I realized I was not going to get anyone else out. In fact, it was going to take some doing to get myself out.' Sunrise found him on the wrong side of the Rhine, along with upwards of 150 other Airborne for whom time had run out. The discipline so evident earlier began to crumble.

There were unfortunate scenes when a group of Poles from the rearguard arrived late and at a run, dashing out across what they thought was the deserted polder, over the mud flats and straight on board a boat that was pulling in. As it pulled away, they looked back to see fists being shaken at them by angry soldiers who had been lying low, waiting their turn, until the boat arrived and had now been pipped at the post. Now it was every man for himself. Men flung off their clothes and struck out for the far side. One soldier watched, helpless, as 'more and more heads were swallowed by the river, never to reappear.' Another saw German machine-gun fire rake the water and felt like crying as splashes from bullets surrounded bobbing heads until a direct hit notched up another dead man. The last boat shoved off at 5.30 in broad daylight and lost almost all its occupants to enemy fire. The order was given to end the evacuation.

On that far bank, Watkins considered his position. 'There were other Airbornes scattered about that polder, but it was no time for organized parties. Each man had to take his own chance. I had seen the swiftness of the river and how there were groynes at intervals to retain the banks. I worked my way upstream from groyne to groyne until I reached a reed bed. I lay up in those reeds all day and was lucky.' There was some movement nearby, which caused Watkins considerable alarm, but it turned out to be a Dutchman, a fellow fugitive. They decided to attempt the crossing together at dusk. The key, the other man advised him, was not to fight the current but go with it. 'We made our way upstream to under the railway viaduct, stripped off and went in. I never saw the Dutchman again and have no idea whether he made it. I got out some couple of miles down-stream and fell in with Canadian sappers, who told me I was mad – and very lucky.'

The evacuation had been a success – perhaps the best executed of all the military manoeuvres in the Arnhem debacle, given the speed with which it had to be planned and carried out and the appalling conditions. If the Germans had cottoned on earlier, there could have been a bloodbath on that open river bank. The precise numbers who got across were never certain – not least because the tellers counting heads on the south side were hampered by the rain rendering their notes unreadable. Ninety-five men were known to have died that night – shot, mortared or drowned – but between 2,400 and 2,500 were saved. That, though, left many thousands of mainly wounded Airborne still in Oosterbeek and Arnhem and consigned to a captivity they had tried their utmost to avoid.

14. Left Behind

In any fighting retreat, there has to be a rearguard, who risk being overrun or left behind. In the evacuation from Oosterbeek, that precarious role fell to the Polish Brigade, who had crossed over from the south bank two nights earlier and taken up defensive positions at the bottom end of the perimeter. Lieutenant Albert Smaczny was ordered by a retreating British officer, a major, to stay in place with his company of twenty men – all that was left of the thirty-six he had had when he arrived – until 12.30 a.m. at the earliest. He was to withdraw only on specific orders from the major, brought to him by a runner. Smaczny sensibly asked if one of his own men could go ahead with the major now, just to make sure that the message to withdraw got back to him and he and his men would not be left stranded. His request was refused. Not necessary, the major told him as he departed. He would come back for them himself if need be. As he watched the Englishmen slip away into the darkness, Smaczny was not happy that this was going to turn out well. He kept from his men his fear that what they had just been given was 'a virtual sentence of extermination'.[1]

As the hours rolled by and no messenger came, he worried. It was past midnight, and they'd seen the last of the British soldiers pass them en route to the evacuation beach some time ago. But he stuck to his orders, despite knowing that every minute he waited was precious time lost. Eventually, with the first vague hint of light in the sky, he sent out a scout to check on what was happening. The man came on a British command post, deserted except for some wounded and their orderlies, who were staying behind. The rest had left more than two hours ago, he was told. Discovering that, for whatever reason, he and his company had indeed been left in the lurch, Smaczny led them off to the river.[2]

As they neared the polder, they heard rifle fire and terrible screaming. Reaching the beach, they were in time to see the last boats leaving. There was now only one way over the water, and the lieu-tenant told those who felt up to it to swim. He opted to stay with the non-swimmers and those who could not face the dangerous waters. In the early morning light, one of his men saw what happened to bobbing heads out there, caught by the current or by bullets, and decided: 'I would rather die with a gun in my hand than drown.' With decisions made and the last of the swimmers either over on the other side or lost, a stillness settled over this reach of the Lower Rhine. The men now marooned on the wrong side, British and Polish alike, settled down where they were, concealed as best they could be on the flat and soggy meadowland. What would happen now? There was firing coming from the woods and from behind the dykes on either side, but the Germans made no attempt to advance or attack. An hour went by. No one moved. Then one British sol-dier rose to his feet and hung a white rag at the end of his rifle – until a furious sergeant crawled over and ordered him to put it down, 'or I'll shoot you'. The sergeant's action was a defiant gesture, pure Red Devil, but only delayed the inevitable. There was an exchange of fire. More casualties. Not long after, the senior British officer among them accepted that their position was hopeless and ordered the white flag to be raised again. German soldiers stepped from their defensive positions and came forward to disarm and take charge of their prisoners. Smaczny saw a chance of escape and edged his men away and back towards the woods. Two tanks emerged to stand in their way. At bayonet point, the remnants of the Oosterbeek redoubt were marched away, back into the smoking ruins of Oosterbeek and captivity.

Poles and British stuck together, despite German attempts to iso-late the Poles, some of whom they had already taken away and shot. Now an SS officer stopped the column of prisoners and demanded that the Poles step forward. Not a soul moved. The tense silence was broken by a British officer, who called out: 'Don't do it. We fought together and we'll go to prison camp together.' Another took off his red beret and put it on Smaczny's head before telling the fuming Ger-man officer, 'There are no Poles here.'

Such solidarity was a hallmark of the evacuation. Arthur Ayers had his chance to get away, but his headlong dash to the river came to a halt when a freshly wounded man, his face macerated by a mortar, pleaded for help. Ayers knew he was about to blow his chance of escaping, but he couldn't just turn away. 'As the man moaned in pain and grasped my arm for support, my mind was made up. "Of course I will help you," I said.' Years later, he had no regrets. 'I didn't even know what his name was, just that he was one of our men and he was wounded and needed help. I never thought of leaving him and saving myself. The thought didn't cross my mind. I just did what I believe any reasonable person would do. How can you leave a wounded man? Well, I couldn't.' The man, a glider pilot, had managed to stand, and Ayers, knowing that it was imperative to keep moving if they were to reach the river bank and the possibility of boarding a rescue boat, urged him to try walking, though there was still more than a mile to go. 'He moved one foot forward, then swayed, complaining of giddiness. I steadied him, put his arm around my shoulder and we staggered slowly along, looking like two old pals on their way home after a night on the beer.'

They came to some houses, now deserted, just as mortar shells started to fall, sending up showers of masonry and timber into the air. Ayers hauled his friend into a building to shelter. 'The front door opened to my push and I led him into the hall. Leaving him propped up against the wall, I struck a match and started to explore. Down some narrow stairs was a cellar, with a table and chairs and a large mattress. Tins of food and bottles of wine were stacked in a corner, a heart-warming sight. I fetched him down and we sat facing each other. "What's my face like?" he whispered. "Is it bad?" "No," I lied, but he didn't believe me. "I used to be quite good looking," he sighed. "Never had any trouble getting girlfriends."'

Ayers found water and a bowl and began to clean the man's face. 'He sat patiently as I carefully washed away the blood, wincing in pain when I touched an open wound. When I had finished, the wounds didn't look so bad but I realized he needed proper medical attention. I suggested we gave ourselves up to the enemy so he could be taken to hospital, but he wouldn't hear of it. "Not bloody likely," he said. I dined on tinned meat and fruit in syrup, washed down with a bottle of wine. He found it too painful to eat, but managed to drink some wine. Then we laid our weary bodies down on the mattress and tried to sleep.' It was ten thirty the next morning when Ayers woke. 'My companion seemed to be sleeping soundly, so I left him and went up the stairs. Suddenly I was conscious of activity and voices outside. I peeped through a window to see dozens of German soldiers walking along the road. A large truck pulled up and several men in field-grey uniforms jumped out, automatic weapons at the ready. My heart sank. It looked as though they were going to search the house. But then they formed up and marched off up the road, out of my sight.' His relief was momentary. This, he realized, was only a reprieve. 'It could be only a matter of time before the houses would be searched.'

Ayers scouted the house. He came to a window overlooking trees and a field. 'I heard shots and then saw half a dozen British paratroopers appear out of the trees, escorted by their captors. I made my way back to the cellar, where I found my companion sitting up. He tried to smile, but the effort was clearly very painful. The wounds on his face looked red and angry. I told him what I had seen and we debated our future. The decision we came to was to stay where we were and take a chance the houses would not be searched. After all, we had food and shelter and, besides, there was a chance that the Second Army would arrive in Arnhem at any moment and we would be relieved.' That incredible airborne optimism was undimmed even now.

The two airborne evaders lay in the house through Wednesday and Thursday, dozing mainly, and eating. 'My companion, who had kept very cheerful during this ordeal, despite the damage to his face, was now able to eat a little solid food. At mid-morning on Friday I made my usual trip upstairs to the window to look out. The road was quiet and deserted, but as I turned away I heard voices. English voices. They were singing "Roll out the Barrel", and my heart leaped. It had to be the Second Army. They'd got here at last.' His joy at the prospect of rescue, of going home, was short-lived. 'When I returned to the window and looked out I saw a column of dirty, dishevelled but still defiant paratroopers marching along the road, flanked by German soldiers. Some were bareheaded but others still proudly wearing their red berets. They looked very tired but far from disheartened. I watched until they passed out of sight, then returned to the cellar feeling hopeless and abandoned.'

That afternoon Ayers heard footsteps in the house above and was startled when a figure appeared at the top of the cellar stairs. 'It was a smartly dressed civilian. He stared down at us, a surprised look on his face, then turning hurriedly he disappeared back through the doorway. Uncertain if he was friend or foe, we decided to leave the house and find shelter elsewhere. We quickly packed the remaining tins of food in my haversack and prepared to leave. But it was too late. As we reached the foot of the stairs, I heard the sound of heavy boots and I looked up to see two German soldiers. 'They shouted at us and motioned with their rifles. I was a prisoner, something I had never visualized being. Part of me was pleased that my war was finished, though I was sad that I wouldn't be going home right away. But I presumed I would get there at some point, and perhaps sooner rather than later. We still thought the war would be over pretty shortly.' As the two men were led away to a jeep, they passed the man dressed in civilian clothes who was standing by the front door. 'He stared at us with no expression on his face. I stared back.' They were driven out of Oosterbeek, getting glimpses along the way of the devastation the battle had caused. 'The few civilians we passed turned and just stared, their expressionless faces showing nothing of the misery they must be feeling. I wondered if they blamed us for all this. Then we pulled into the grounds of the St Elizabeth Hospital on the outskirts of Arnhem, and my wounded companion was taken inside. This was the last I saw of him.'

In the back of the jeep, Ayers shared a tin of pears with one of his captors before being driven away. 'We were travelling through Arnhem itself now and I was hoping to get a view of the bridge, which, after all, was the main reason for us being here. But I never did.' On the edge of town, the jeep came to halt outside a large marquee. 'I was roughly pushed out by the guard, and that was when it really hit home to me. Like the many British troops in airborne smocks and red berets milling around there, I was a prisoner of war.'

*

In the hospitals and casualty stations, the hardest task was telling the wounded that the division had evacuated Oosterbeek without them, that the Second Army wasn't coming to rescue them and that, therefore, they were now destined to live behind barbed wire for the duration of the war, now certain to last beyond Christmas 1944 and, if the pessimists were to be believed, possibly beyond Christmas 1945 as well. There are indications in some accounts by the wounded that they may have been misled into thinking all was well so they would not panic at being left behind. One para recalled being specifically informed by a messenger sent from divisional headquarters on Sunday night that the Second Army had captured the bridge at Arnhem and that the Guards Armoured Division would be rolling into Oosterbeek the next morning. Others were told that the Polish Brigade had arrived with tanks. An officer excused the deception. 'We must keep the wounded quiet. They must not feel too anxious, so we tell them the big lie.'³ The truth, though, had to come out, and inside what had until a few hours ago been the perimeter, sick and injured men were now discovering what had happened in the night while they slept.

Fred Moore, with shrapnel wounds in his hand, leg and arm, was in the casualty station at Kate ter Horst's house down by the river in Oosterbeek, and it was here that he learned his fate from her. She had woken that morning in the cellar and been struck, as so many people were that day, by the incredible silence. It was so quiet that one Dutch civilian believed the world had ended and he was the sole survivor. Either that, or his eardrums must have shattered. Kate looked up through a hole and saw a German officer on her doorstep. Bravely, she went up to face him. Her old vicarage, she told the officer, housed hundreds of unarmed wounded soldiers, who needed immediate evacuation to hospital. He sent her back in to break the news. Down in the cellar, Moore remembered, 'she came in and said: "I'm afraid I have some bad news for you. Your comrades were evacuated across the river last night and the house is surrounded by Germans. An officer is waiting outside to speak to someone who is able to walk." I volunteered and, emerging from the front door, was confronted by this officer, who saluted and said in impeccable English, "Your people have withdrawn back to their lines. I congratulate you on your efforts but you are now our prisoners. Please accept these gifts." He gave me tins of cigarettes and chocolate, which obviously came from supply containers meant for us that had dropped outside our lines.'

Before transport arrived to take them to the hospital at Apeldoorn, the men whispered their goodbyes to Kate, whose ministrations had been such an inspiration. They were still positive, assuring her that this was a temporary setback, and 'the great Army will be here in a week's time!' Did they still believe it? Did she believe it? It seems just possible they did. Another Oosterbeek resident, fifteen-year-old Marie-Anne, with the British soldiers gone from her house too, was nonetheless convinced that they would be coming back over the Rhine 'very soon' and hung on to that belief until the end of October. As for the Airborne, many of the wounded did their best to avoid being declared fit to travel and flung on a train to Germany in the hope that the German lines would yet be overrun by a victorious Second Army. For now, though, it was time to go. Kate had one last act of kindness to perform when two of the patients told her they had no trousers. She dashed back inside to raid her husband's wardrobe for them, but as she came out a German officer stood in her way. 'Enough!' he barked at her, and his hostility was a warning of how much the situation had changed. She watched the line of Airborne as they trailed away. 'Any of them who can walk at all, must walk. Whoever has two legs to walk on must drag another along. And so they march forth. We hardly dare to look at them any more.'

At the Schoonoord Hotel, it fell to padre George Pare to tell the wounded men in his charge that the last fighting remnants of the airborne army had gone, leaving them behind. A sergeant-major confessed that he didn't have the nerve to break it to them. 'It's the worst news they will ever get,' he told Pare. 'You'll have to do it.' The padre, deeply depressed himself by this unexpected turn of events, had a heavy heart as he began his round of the wards. 'Everyone tried to take the calamity in good heart,' he recalled, 'but the news was very bitter.' He found it difficult to keep up a cheerful and positive pretence. In the end, 'I was relieved to finish the whole miserable business.' All of a sudden, there was new activity in the

Schoonoord, now that the long siege was over. The Germans arrived in large numbers and were cooperative, even the unpredictable SS. Ambulances rolled up to the front door to take the patients to hospital in Apeldoorn. Spirits began to rise. Going into captivity was not good, that was true, but, looked at another way, 'the battle was over and we were still alive. In the circumstances, that was a lot to be thankful for.'

One by one, the pockets of wounded dotted round the battlefield went the same way. Glider pilot Peter Clarke, who once trained as a medical orderly, had been running his own first-aid post close to the Hartenstein Hotel for several days, largely on his own. It was his 'little sanctuary giving comfort and kindness', and the task had focused his mind and eased his Christian conscience by keeping him from having to kill. He was offered the chance to escape on the evacuation, but declined. 'It crossed my mind that, as a trained glider pilot, I really ought to try and get back, but it seemed more important to be saving lives. I had four casualties to look after, and I wasn't going to clear off and leave them in the lurch.' The thing he most feared was an enemy attack on the house and a grenade coming hurtling in through the window. Instead, he heard German voices outside and opened the door to be greeted – 'very courteously, I must say' – by a German officer. 'I saw the casualties off and then I went "into the bag". My war was over but it was a relief to me that these chaps were going to be taken care of.' Afterwards, he doubted if his presence had been essential and that if he had chosen to join the retreat, those casualties would have been treated any differently. But, then again, 'giving comfort was as important as anything else in those last few hours, somebody just being there with them. That totally justified my staying.'

With that duty done, Clarke felt freed from any obligation. Taken to Apeldoorn and incarcerated in an old barracks that served as a temporary prisoner-of-war camp, he now saw no reason not to try to get home. The rumour was that they were to be shifted to Germany within days and, once across the border, escape would be harder. It was now or never. He and two other glider pilots stocked up on food – honey sandwiches – and pooled their resources. 'Our navigational equipment consisted of our service watches and one collar-stud compass, but no maps. We had in mind travelling north-west towards the Zuider Zee, but decided that we would put off formulating any definite plan until we were outside the wire.' It was a clear and moon-lit night as they crawled through high grass and under two rows of wire. How they managed to flee undetected was a small miracle 'because I remember looking back at the figure of a sentry silhouet-ted in the moonlight, who for some reason failed to see us. But then dogs were barking and guards shouting and we ran for fully fifteen minutes through the woods before stopping to recover breath.' The hue and cry stopped. They were on their way.

They slept the night in a woodman's hut, laid up there for most of the next day and set off impatiently – and foolishly – in the late after-noon. Until then they had moved only in the dark, but as they moved out now it was still light. They came to heathland and hid behind a screen of brushwood designed as a deer-stalker's hideout to plan their next move. 'Then we spotted a German officer and an NCO approaching the hide with a young woman' – he didn't speculate on what they might have been up to. 'They seemed quite unaware of our presence at first but it was too late for us to retreat back into the wood.' And that was that. 'We were back in the bag.' A lorry took them back to Apeldoorn, where they hadn't been missed. 'But the rumour that had set us off – that we were going to be taken into Ger-many – proved to be correct and we were soon bundled off into cattle trucks and shipped east.'

For those Airborne whose injuries left them unable to attempt an escape, defiance of their German captors had to come in other ways. Reg Curtis's leg was so badly smashed and infected that it would later have to be amputated. He had been in the casualty station at the Tafelberg when the Germans captured it, and taken to the St Eliza-beth Hospital in Arnhem. There, the word went round quickly that the division had withdrawn and 'the show was over.' Curtis was made aware of the scale of the disaster that had befallen Market Gar-den when he questioned a British Tommy with a bloody bandage round his head: 'What mob are you then?' The man replied, almost crying, 'The Dorsets. My lot were wiped out.' Yet Curtis remained on good form despite hearing grim stories like this and despite his leg being encased in a cast from crotch to toes and knowing that amputation was inevitable. He prayed it would be done by a British army surgeon – of which there were several at the St Elizabeth – rather than a German doctor, whose technique tended to be a crude guillotine cut rather than a measured trimming and shaping.

As he lay in bed, there was a commotion in the ward. A German general was coming to pay a visit, 'so we were hastily tidied up and bedding arranged ready for inspection. Eventually, through the doors at the end of the ward, half-a-dozen SS officers, uniforms in various shades of blue, blue-grey, field-grey, brown and black appeared. They were immaculately turned out, with brightly polished boots fit for a passing-out parade. At their head was the general, in a very pale blue uniform with loads of silver braid. He was wearing a monocle and was as square headed a true German as you could ever wish to meet. A few paces behind came members of the Gestapo, all in black with swastika armbands, belted gun-holsters, shoulder straps and peaked caps. The most sinister of them stood with his gloved hand resting on his waist and his thumb hooked in his belt.' This was a show of strength clearly intended to show the prisoners who was the master race. The procession was greeted with absolute silence – broken by 'the most beautiful raspberry I have ever heard vibrating from the far end of the ward'. The Germans stopped in their tracks at this clear display of derision and contempt. 'The general's left eyebrow twitched and the SS doctor in charge went pale. The other SS officers looked slightly sheepish, not knowing what to do. The Gestapo officers instinctively put a hand on their gun-holsters and turned to look in the direction the raspberry had come from. One undid his holster, and we could see the brown handle of his Luger pistol.'

It was a tense moment. Honour was at stake and might have been saved only at the expense of bloodshed. The general, fortunately, had the sense not to be wound up. After the pause, with dozens of eyes on him, waiting to see if he would retaliate, he carried on with his inspection before sweeping out of the ward with his entourage. The Gestapo officers stared icily at the patients before leaving too. Their departure was greeted by an outburst of raucous laughter from the beds and a volley of loudly expressed curses. The paras had shown they would not be cowed. 'We had had our entertainment,' wrote Curtis, 'and it was great to exercise the lungs after so much tension. I think it was the first time that a lot of us had laughed since we left England.'

★

The larger part of the men who flew and dropped into the Arnhem bridgehead ended their war in captivity. Of a force of 11,920 airborne troops, glider pilots and Poles who left England with such expectations of success, 6,525 became prisoners of war. That was never a pleasant experience, and in the final chaotic months of the war, when they became extremely vulnerable to Nazi vengeance, their lives were at great risk.[4] But the vast majority made it home in the end. In the meantime, the civilian population left behind in the Netherlands found their country – which remained under German occupation until May 1945 – had itself become a vast prison camp in which they were systematically starved and repressed. The failure of Market Garden had its greatest impact on them.

For the inhabitants of Arnhem and Oosterbeek in particular, the aftermath of the battle was the realization of their worst nightmare. For a few precious days, they had had the supreme joy of believing themselves free. Their misery now was in equal proportion. With the British gone, Kate ter Horst came out of the cellar of her once pretty house to a landscape she barely recognized. 'There are trenches everywhere, and out of every hole rises a grinning head under a German helmet, with jaws distorted in convulsive laughter as they call out in triumph to each other. Our garden has been shot to pieces. Branches of trees, dead men, parts of motor-cars, all are mixed up together.' She spread a cape across the naked corpse of a soldier before calling her children out of the cellar. They would be shocked soon enough by the sights they were to witness but at least she could spare them this horror in their own back garden. 'Good luck,' the airborne troops had told her when they were taken, 'and keep a stiff upper lip!' She would need every ounce of their good wishes for what lay ahead.

She found a handcart, fortunately undamaged in contrast to everything else around her. It had room for their rucksacks and blankets, and for a couple of the little ones to sit, legs dangling, alongside the baby's cradle. They set off, she and the two elder children pushing and pulling, up the hill and away from home. 'We walk with a white napkin tied to a stick. More and more refugees join around us, a long, sad stream. But, there is the sun, wind, fresh air and the billowing heather. We breathe deep, and our hearts are full of courage.'

In Arnhem itself, the Germans began a systematic purge of the town. As if Piet Huisman and his family had not endured enough, huddled in their cellar for a week, now they were expelled from the only place of security they knew. He recorded in his diary 'a new proclamation from the Germans – tomorrow at 8 a.m. everyone must leave. What will we do? No one wants to go, but an SS order declares that those who stay will be shot. There was a meeting to try to declare Arnhem an open city, but without success. We have to go! Staying alive is the most important thing now, so we gather up as much food as possible to take with us. We put what we can hide under the floor and in the attic and then say goodbye to our home.' He had no idea where they could go. They tagged on to a procession of refugees carrying white flags, hardly able to believe what was happening to them. 'We saw old people in ditches along the way. The sick from the hospital were being carried on litters and stretchers. SS tanks passed by, nearly hitting us.'

On the edge of Arnhem, on a hill just outside the city's northern boundary, Heleen Kernkamp, a nurse from Amsterdam who had been staying with friends in Arnhem when the fighting began, volunteered to help in an aid post for refugees which the Red Cross had hurriedly set up in a former school. She had known hardship in her life. Her father was a well-to-do businessman who had lost everything in the Wall Street Crash, reducing the family to poverty. But as she watched the wretched line of dispossessed persons coming towards her, 'a pitiable moving train of suffering', she had never seen such human misery. She could barely believe that a whole town was to be emptied – ninety thousand people in all. 'There were men, women and children carrying mattresses, blankets, suitcases, bulging sacks, whatever they could manage. Mothers had a baby in their arms and two or three other children at their sides, crying and wailing.' Seeing her nurse's uniform, they turned to her in their distress. 'Sister, I have been disabled for eight years and I can't walk.' 'Sister, my husband has been sent to Germany, I have five children and the sixth is due any moment.' 'Sister, where are we to go?' She had no answers and no solutions, no transport to summon up, no food to distribute. 'I was swamped by a feeling of misery so great I felt it would choke me. I hated the Germans, who were to blame for all this.' This bitterness would last a lifetime. Half a century later, she confessed that the sound of someone speaking German 'gives me a physical shock'.

She was told that the German explanation for the evacuation was that the British were about to carpet-bomb the town. She thought that unlikely. Later she concluded that the evacuation was a punishment, 'a retaliation by the Germans for the help and assistance the people of Arnhem and the Resistance gave to the British soldiers. The same goes for the comprehensive ransacking of the abandoned town during the months following the evacuation. The whole population was made to pay dearly.'

Her aid post was overwhelmed as Arnhem people poured in, queuing for hours to register their names and the addresses of friends who might take them in, and then waiting. There was no system in place to deal with them. They milled around, with nowhere to go. Her specific task was to run an infirmary for the sick, and soon she had four hundred of them – the old, infirm, cripples, invalids, those with terrible wounds from being caught in the fighting. 'The place swarmed with people crying and clutching each other and asking "When do we leave?" and "Where are we going?"' Her most vivid memory of this tidal wave of people washing up around her was 'the shuffling feet and eyes full of anguish'. The floors of her building were solid with people, while outside hundreds waited in the rain on the off-chance of getting in. Many were very scared, especially those who had come from Oosterbeek. 'It was very hard keeping them calm.' An air raid turned distress into terror. 'One woman clutched me with such tenacity that I could not pry myself loose from her to comfort all the others.' Heleen had nothing with which to nurse the really sick. 'We had to lay a totally paralysed man on a horse-rug on the bare floor, next to a woman who had just suffered a stroke, because we could do nothing else for them.' All anyone could do was wait, in the forlorn hope that some transport would turn up. 'Everything with wheels had been requisitioned by the Germans. We had nothing.'

In time, though, transport began to arrive, in dribs and drabs, first a private car, then a horse-drawn cart or two. The sick began to leave, packed on open carts and with no protection from the pouring rain, but away at last to Apeldoorn, where there was a hospital to receive them. Those who looked back could see that Arnhem was no longer theirs. Germans were ransacking private houses and hurling furniture and household effects through windows. With her hundreds of charges gone, Heleen joined teams who went down into the shattered town to search for anyone who'd stayed or been left behind. A house-to-house search uncovered eighteen people trapped in an air-raid shelter with a blocked entry. But moments of elation like that were rare as she tramped the dead streets, surrounded by destruction. Oosterbeek was the same. She went there secretly with a girl who was taking food to three British paratroopers hiding in the cellar of a heavily damaged house. 'One of them had a bullet wound in his arm which caused him much pain. Alas, I could not do much for him. As for the once peaceful village on the banks of the Rhine, with its pretty church, grand houses and well-tended gardens, it was now a mess of broken-down vehicles, weapons, clothes, empty tins and containers, rubble and glass. Not one house, she noted, was complete or undamaged.

Piet Huisman and his family, meanwhile, had managed to cling on within the Arnhem boundaries despite the German threats. They had been forced out of their own home, but not far away, on the edge of town, were the buildings and compound of what had been an agricultural and folklore museum. A shanty town was growing up there, to which the Germans must have decided to turn a blind eye. His family found a place in a barracks, among a display of antique Dutch sledges. The living was hard. 'There are ninety-three people in this one building,' he recorded in his diary, 'and we each have a two-and-a-half-metre space on the stone floor. It is very cold with no heat. Later we got some straw to lie on and found an old wood-stove for cooking. We don't have a lavatory so everybody goes outside in the woods. At night we take turns at guard duty in case of shells and firing. The Germans still say that if we dare to go home, they will shoot us on sight.' But a defiant Huisman did just that. He needn't have risked his life. When he got to his house, it had been ransacked. As he sneaked away, he was shot at, but the bullets narrowly missed him.

Life in the barracks and the camp spreading outside it continued in its hand-to-mouth way for more than a month. There were constant scares. The SS searched the camp for British paratroopers still evading capture – 'we have some hidden in the woods and others are in the tombs of a cemetery. We take them food every day.' One day, the German police came, selected twenty people for slave labour and took them away. Another day, a member of the Resistance who had been harbouring British evaders was captured and executed outside the barracks. All the men in the camp were made to watch as he was put up against a wall and shot.

Finally, the Germans moved in and closed down the camp and sent the Huismans and all the other occupants there away. Arnhem was now entirely sealed off, a ghost town. From that point, it was methodically and thoroughly plundered by special salvage detachments sent in by the Germans. These 'gangs of robbers', as Heleen called them, stripped every home and sent the spoils by train to Germany. What they didn't haul away, they vandalized. They used antique clocks for target practice and rubbed treacle between the strings of grand pianos. Sheets and clothes were torn to shreds. People who returned after the war found their homes had been used as stables and were strewn with horse manure. Many inhabitants who came back were struck by the absence of birds, as if nature itself had turned its back on these desolate ruins. The once busy and thriving Arnhem was 'a sombre, brooding place, full of horrors,' wrote one observer, 'a town of the dead. And no birds. It was deathly quiet. Even the sparrows had flown away.'[5]

★

One of the most tragic outcomes of the failed Arnhem expedition – sadder even than the 1,500 dead airborne combatants and the 6,500 who went into captivity – was that the people of the Netherlands, far from being freed, were made to suffer grievously for eight months until their liberation. They were left behind – in the lurch, some might say – as the focus of the Allied drive into Germany shifted southwards. Come the spring of 1945, an air and river assault would finally cross the Rhine, but 40 miles upstream from Arnhem. The due-east direction of this thrust bypassed the larger part of the Netherlands, leaving it firmly and oppressively in German hands for the duration of the war. Denied food supplies, close to twenty thousand people starved to death, and those who lived survived on foraged tulip bulbs and boiled nettles.

It always bewildered and impressed Arnhem veterans when they returned to the Netherlands for regular post-war reunions that Holland's misery was never held against them and their failed mission. At what became annual events of celebration, they were as fêted as they had been when they marched as liberators along the roads to Arnhem in September 1944. Yet, as one ex-paratrooper noted, 'We did not achieve our wartime objectives and lost the battle. In the process we destroyed their town and villages and forced the inhabitants to experience their "Winter of Hunger". Yet every time they greet us, nothing is too much trouble and their gratitude for our efforts has to be seen to be believed.' [6]

It could have been very different – thousands of lives saved and 5 million men, women and children spared the most terrible deprivation – if Market Garden had lived up to its promise. If the great airborne adventure had worked, if its optimistic masterplan had not been dogged by errors of judgement and thwarted by a determined and clever enemy, if the Second Army had swept all before it and crossed the intact bridge at Arnhem, then the misery the Dutch endured between September 1944 and May 1945 would have been avoided. The war might well have ended before Christmas, as so many hoped. But, as an American sports commentator used to say, 'If "ifs" and "buts" were candy and nuts, wouldn't it be a Merry Christmas?' Those words could well be Market Garden's epitaph.

15. Home is the Hero

Having escaped the Oosterbeek 'cauldron', Ron Kent was dousing himself with welcome hot water in a recently vacated German army barracks at Nijmegen. 'For the first time in nine days I stripped myself of every bit of clothing and dumped my torn and muddy clothing. I joined the others naked at the showers and let the water trickle over my aching limbs. Then I towelled myself vigorously as I walked back to a bed laid out with three blankets.' British jeeps, ambulances and trucks had carried the exhausted airborne survivors of the river crossing to a Dutch city with a bridge that had indeed been captured from the enemy – giving the whole Market Garden operation a semblance of success, despite the failure at Arnhem. Montgomery claimed a victory of sorts – that Nijmegen was as good a kick-off point for invading Hitler's Germany as Arnhem was. 'The fact that we shall not now have a crossing over the Lower Rhine will not affect the operations eastward against the Ruhr,' he argued. 'In fact, by giving up that bridgehead [at Arnhem] we shall now be able to keep more within ourselves and be less stretched.'[1]

He was clutching at straws. This assessment of the situation simply wasn't true. Montgomery's attempt to slip into Germany through the back door had been a bold one. To pretend now that failure didn't really matter was not only to diminish his own plan but to make a nonsense of the lives that had been lost trying to carry it out. Much had been sacrificed, but what had been gained? The field marshal's biographer, Nigel Hamilton, wrote a damning judgement of Market Garden. 'This so-called Rhine bridgehead [at Nijmegen] had not only been achieved at the cost of almost an entire British airborne division, it had also provided the Allies with a useless strip of low-lying land between the Waal and the Lower Rhine, the seizing of which used up the offensive capability of the Second Army.'

Not that such strategic thoughts were of immediate interest to the men back from the battlefield and now enjoying freedom and life itself. 'In a vast dining hall,' Kent recalled, 'we were waited on hand and foot and served a first-class hot meal. There were double helpings of good food, tea, chocolate, cigarettes and, to round off the meal, a glass of neat brandy. It was like Christmas.' Sleep came easily. No one seemed bothered to be in beds that a few nights before had held SS soldiers. 'I wriggled down between the blankets and slept, untroubled, for seven solid hours.' Afterwards, he felt so refreshed that he decided he should do something about his personal appearance, and he shaved off his beard and tidied up his bedraggled moustache. 'I looked at myself in a broken mirror. Apart from the wrinkles of tiredness about my eyes, I thought I looked little the worse for the past nine days' action.' But he felt older and wiser. 'I knew I would never be the same again.'

As men woke and pinched themselves that they really were alive, there was a frenzy to find old friends. With survivors from all units in this one building, there was now constant coming and going as men looked for their particular pals and sought news of those they could not locate. There were joyous reunions. Dick Ennis recalled sitting down to a breakfast of black bread and honey and noticing opposite him on the other side of the table 'a fellow who looked vaguely familiar. Suddenly it struck me – it was Billy!' The cheerful sapper he'd shared a trench with, eking out their last cigarettes, was alive after all! They'd last seen each other at the water's edge when Ennis had plunged in to swim across, leaving his mate behind to wait for a boat. 'We recognized each other at exactly the same time and jumped up, hanging on each other's neck and slapping each other's back.' But there was sadness too. Kent felt like a mother hen as he gathered his section around him and then went looking for those still absent. 'Some I knew I would not see again. But there were two or three others I wasn't sure about.'

A parade was called, and for an hour sergeants sorted out the various units, lined everyone up in ranks and called them to attention. Then the roll was called, a solemn and emotional moment, as the men of the 1st Airborne took on board the true extent of their losses. If the calling of a man's name was not answered, then a mark of absence was placed in the register. In the tense hush of that hall, the silences far outnumbered the responses of 'Here, Sergeant'. Kent recalled that the commonest such mark that day was 'Missing believed killed', followed by 'Wounded and POW'. His thoughts were with them, 'and with the civilians we had had to leave in Arnhem and Oosterbeek'.

Nijmegen was not a safe place. It was being strafed by enemy planes, and the road back to the Belgian border was cut off from time to time by determined enemy attacks. But none of this made much impression on men who had experienced Oosterbeek. 'We didn't let them bother us,' said Dick Ennis. 'We felt we had survived worse things and nothing could harm us now.' Then they travelled by lorry away from Nijmegen and down that narrow corridor the Second Army had so laboriously carved out. And though others might be critical of the Second Army's performance, all he could see were signs of its great endeavour. 'We were able to picture the magnificent struggle they had put up in their efforts to reach us. Every river and canal we crossed was spanned by a Bailey bridge. The roads were lined with the burnt-out wrecks of tanks and vehicles. At one point there was a whole enemy convoy lying wrecked in the ditches. It had been caught and strafed as it fled.'

On their way home, the Arnhem survivors were greeted as if they were victorious heroes rather than the rag-tag remnants of a beaten division. 'As we passed through towns like Grave and Eindhoven, great crowds lined the streets to cheer us. Food, fruit and cigarettes were thrown into our trucks as we passed by.' It was the same when they reached Brussels. One para sergeant, Bob Quayle, remembered crowds gathering at a pavement bar to buy beers for him and his mates. The drinks just kept coming. 'I think they were amazed at our capacity.'[2] He bought a bottle of cherry brandy to take home for his mother in the Isle of Man. 'It was still in the sideboard when she passed away fifty years later.' From Brussels they were flown home in the same Dakota transporters that had taken them into battle. 'We cheered when the English coast came in sight,' Ennis recalled. 'Soon the fields of old England were spread out beneath us. How quiet and peaceful they looked!' The reception when they landed at their own airfield was 'magnificent'. 'It made everything we had gone through seem worthwhile.' But, after the cheering was over, there was a reckoning. 'We came back to the same huts we had occupied before going on the operation. I sat on my bed. Everything looked the same as when I had left it. Two others came in and we just sat looking at one another – not speaking. Less than a fortnight before, twenty men had slept in this hut. Now there were three of us.' For survivors, guilt was never far away. He found himself with questions he could not answer then and never would. 'Why had we been spared to come back? Were we any better, either spiritually or bodily, than the men we had left behind? Were we the lucky ones? I cannot say.'

*

If words failed Dick Ennis, then it fell to Robert Watkins to find the right ones to try to bring comfort to those bereaved by the mission. The 1 Para chaplain returned to base at Grimsthorpe Castle, a sumptuous Vanbrugh pile in Lincolnshire. The place was 'tragically empty', he lamented. For two weeks, he had sad work to do – letters, lots of them, many by hand. 'I have no record of how many I wrote but this was a massive job. In the case of the known dead, I did hand-written letters for the whole brigade. For the missing and for those likely to be prisoners, I had to use typists, but we did include any known facts.' Then there were the kit and the personal effects of men dead or missing to be sympathetically dealt with. 'Every parcel was sorted through before it was dispatched in order to eliminate anything which next-of-kin would do better not to see.' Somewhere, one particular mother was now opening the next-of-kin letter that her soldier son, 21-year-old Ivor Rowbery, had written to her the night before Market Garden was launched, the one 'I hope you will never receive'.[3] But she did. He died on the first day of the battle, and all she had now were his last words to her, telling her how he was willing to die simply to protect 'my little world centred around you, Dad, everyone at home, my friends'. He begged her not to make herself ill with grief, which he suspected she would do. 'All I want is for you to remember me and feel proud of me. You were the best mother in the world. I never had much money but what I have is yours. Spend it on yourself or the children, not on me. Goodbye and thanks for everything. God bless you all, your unworthy son, Ivor.'

Watkins, the padre, threw himself into his work liaising with families like Ivor's and maybe even stretched it out a little. It had a secondary, private purpose – it helped him to come to terms with all he had experienced. He had brought out one group of walking wounded and then gone back across that treacherous river in a futile attempt to fetch more. He had had to swim for his life and his freedom. He felt the need to 'unwind', as he put it, a tame word for what today would probably be diagnosed as post-traumatic stress. He, like all those other men returning from the battlefront, was expected just to deal with the horrific films still running in his head, the nightly re-visits to experiences and sights he could never erase. The remedies were generally basic ones. 'This was a time,' Watkins wrote, 'when many people were the better for going out and getting roaring drunk.' This wasn't available to him. 'I do not drink, and I never touched Benzedrine pills. A lot of officers took them into battle, but I distrusted them. So it took me quite a while to stop living with the tension of the battle.'

On the surface, many of these men were unmarked. Family photographs of Bill Mollett, for example, on his return from Arnhem showed him lean and fit. But to nurse his mind and his emotions back to health, his thoughtful parents bought him a kitten, and this strapping paratrooper, a mature man of twenty-eight, carried the tiny creature about for weeks inside his smock. If this was a way of putting away all he had endured, all that fearful post-battle baggage, and reconnecting with a gentler world, then it was simple but effective therapy. Denis Longmate, aged eighty-seven now, is still troubled by memories. He was one of that small cohort of Dorsets who fought their way over to Oosterbeek from the south side of the river, the only section of the relieving Second Army ever to reach their target and join the fighting. By then, though, it was too little too late and, within thirty-six hours, he was on his way back and lucky to be alive. He never forgot. 'I still see that scene on the river – bodies floating past me, screams for help. These were my friends . . .' His voice tailed off into silence as he remembered. He still goes to reunions. 'I have to, I just have to, to pay my respects, to visit their graves. Yes, I cry. I'm not ashamed of that. I shed a tear for my friends. It's very sad, very poignant.' A huge question hangs in the air. Was it worth it? 'I'm proud of what the Dorsets, my regiment, did, and I'm proud of my role. But we suffered huge losses and achieved nothing. We felt that even at the time.' But the stark reality that the sacrifice of so many lives was to no positive end did not make him angry or resentful. It just made him sadder and the losses more, not less, poignant.

*

It must be said that, in the immediate aftermath, Arnhem was spun as close to a victory as a defeat can be. In that sense, it was Dunkirk Mk II. Ron Kent remembered the adulation in the press, 'making us out to be heroes of an epic in the annals of British arms. Perhaps the finest tribute we received was from the *Daily Mail*, which stated that we were "worthy of our fathers and examples to our sons".' He liked that but thought it went too far. 'Our fathers fought in the Great War and their ordeals were far worse and more prolonged than anything we had to undergo.' He was being modest. Putting aside the limited success of the mission, what mattered was the courage, the comradeship and the incredible fighting spirit the British soldiers had shown. Even the enemy, magnanimous in victory, acknowledged it. A German war reporter paid tribute in a radio broadcast to 'these hardy fellows, the pick of the bunch' and their stubborn fight. 'They are of all sorts – blacksmiths, bus conductors and students. When they are captured they smile, and if they are wounded they hide their pain.'[4] A Dutch journalist, speaking on the BBC, pledged that his countrymen 'will proudly guard your dead as if they were the deeply mourned sons of our own people. The word "heroes" has been heard so often during this long and grim war that it is in danger of growing trite. But here it takes tangible shape, before the eyes of our people, who stand in awe and bare their heads.'[5]

In Britain, the praise heaped on the warriors of Arnhem was fulsome with ringing phrases: 'a tremendous feat of arms', 'a gallant stand', 'an immortal story', 'British valour in the hell that was Arnhem'. A writer for the Army Bureau of Current Affairs was simply reflecting the national mood when he wrote, 'Arnhem has left in history a record which those who come after must strain every ounce of courage and endurance they possess even to equal.' Others looked to past victories for comparisons. Montgomery's assertion that 'In the years ahead, it will be a great thing for a man to be able to say "I fought at Arnhem,"' had echoes, which cannot have been accidental, of Shakespeare's Henry V at Agincourt.

As for the mission itself, the word 'defeat' was struck from the lexicon, just as the 'retreat' across the river had been presented as a more neutral 'evacuation'. Newspaper reports spoke of a 'lack of complete success', as if Operation Market Garden had nearly made it, but not quite. 'Four-fifths successful,' said *The Times*, and its correspondent quoted a staff officer as saying that the battles at Arnhem and Oosterbeek should be considered 'not as a brilliant failure but as an expensive success'. Official sources took the same line. Almost immediately, Arnhem was being presented as a near triumph. In *The War Illustrated*, a veteran commentator and retired general told the magazine's mass readership that the airborne landings 'accomplished enough to have made the heavy sacrifices entailed more than worth while. We now know how near we came to complete success and, but for the weather, it probably would have been achieved.'

The courage of those who took part was enough for everyone to overlook the fact that the assault force took two thirds casualties and failed in its primary objective. After Monty met and debriefed Urquhart, the field marshal wrote a letter for him to pass on to the men of the Airborne Division. It was rhetoric worthy of the occasion as he delivered his unambiguous 'appreciation of what you all did at Arnhem for the Allied cause. I want to express to you my own admiration, and the admiration of us all in 21 Army Group, for the magnificent spirit that your division displayed in battle against great odds on the north bank of the Lower Rhine in Holland. There is no shadow of doubt that, had you failed, operations elsewhere would have been gravely compromised. You did not fail, and all is well elsewhere. All

Britain will say to you, "You did your best. You all did your duty; and we are proud of you." In the annals of the British Army there are many glorious deeds. In our Army we have always drawn great strengths and inspiration from past traditions, and endeavoured to live up to the high standards of those who have gone before. But there can be few episodes more glorious than the epic of Arnhem, and those that follow after will find it hard to live up to the standards that you have set. So long as we have in the armies of the British empire officers and men who will do as you have done, then we can indeed look forward with complete confidence to the future.'

The supreme allied commander, Eisenhower, also wrote to Urquhart in praise of the 'courage, fortitude and skill' of his 'gallant band of men'. 'In this war there has been no single performance by any unit that has more greatly inspired me or more highly excited my admiration.' In their actions at Arnhem and Oosterbeek, the Airborne had, he declared, 'contributed effectively to the success of operations to the southward of its own battleground'. In the House of Commons, a sonorous Winston Churchill made the same point. Drawing on his stirring 'never in the field of human conflict' style of oratory, he proclaimed that 'the cost has been heavy, the casualties in a single division have been grievous; but for those who mourn there is at least the consolation that the sacrifice was not needlessly demanded nor given without results. The delay caused to the enemy's advance upon Nijmegen enabled their British and American comrades in the other two airborne divisions, and the British 2nd Army, to secure intact the vitally important bridges and to form a strong bridgehead over the main stream of the Rhine at Nijmegen. "Not in vain" may be the pride of those who have survived and the epitaph of those who fell.'

'Not in vain.' What this oratorical flourish disguised was that the failure of Market Garden to meet its objective was a setback. The hard thing to swallow for the British people and the Allied armies – the disappointment that flowed from the Arnhem debacle – was that there was going to be no quick end to the war. The Germans had retreated through France and Belgium at an astonishing pace, like a defeated army on the run. The performance of those SS divisions at Arnhem was the beginning of the fight back. The Reich would stand its ground to the bitter end. All of this the politicians and the generals tried – quite rightly, some might say, in the middle of a war, with morale at stake – to conceal.

The problem was that their words transforming failure into success rang hollow. Churchill exulted in 'the largest airborne operation ever conceived or executed' and how it had helped achieve 'a further all-important forward bound in the north'. Except that it hadn't. That 'forward bound' was into a cul-de-sac. Leaders and generals are apt to dismiss as ill informed or just plain wrong the views of the rank and file, deprived of the bigger picture. What would they know? But Leo Heaps, who fought at Arnhem and lost – and knew that he had lost because he endured months of imprisonment as a result – had no qualms in describing the Arnhem he experienced as 'that disastrous hiccup in the liberation of Europe'. There is every reason to think he was right.

Yet, in the immediate aftermath, it was now the consensus view that capturing the bridge at Nijmegen had been the key objective of Market Garden and therefore the important contribution of the Airborne Division had been in keeping the Germans tied up at Arnhem and Oosterbeek while that bridge 10 miles south was secured. 'Your losses have been very heavy,' a seemingly sorrowful Horrocks wrote to Urquhart, 'but in your fighting north of the Lower Rhine, you contained a large number of German reserves and prevented any reinforcements from moving down towards Nijmegen, [which] gave us time to secure those vital bridges.' Browning wrote in similar vein. 'Without the action of the 1st Airborne Division in tying up, pinning down and destroying in large numbers the German forces in the Arnhem area, the capture of the bridges at Nijmegen would have been quite impossible.' It is hard, reading the correspondence and the speeches sixty-five years later, not to conclude that the military establishment was suffering from collective – and convenient – amnesia. Hadn't Arnhem been the principal objective, so that the Second Army could make its dash to the Ruhr? That was certainly what those thousands of paratroopers and glider pilots holed up in Arnhem and Oosterbeek and waiting for the promised deliverance had believed, and it was why many had given their lives and even more their freedom. But in the aftermath, there seemed to be a total unwillingness to recognize that the Second Army had failed to deliver and, as a result, the brave men of Arnhem had been cut off behind enemy lines and sacrificed.

Arnhem was a defeat. There can be no doubt about that. And there were recriminations. The Allied high command, in need of a scapegoat, vented their exasperation on the Polish general, Sosabowski, for supposedly lacking zeal. His vociferous and justifiable complaints about the operation were used in evidence against him, and he was fired. Browning was exonerated of any blame but was never promoted again. Horrocks, though, went from strength to strength, untainted by any criticism. His XXX Corps finally reached the Rhine in March 1945 after a fierce and costly battle for the Reichswald forest, which would never have been necessary if the Arnhem 'left hook' into Germany had been pulled off six months earlier. As for Montgomery, his reputation took a huge knock, not least with the Americans, whom he disliked and who disliked him in return. In his memoirs, published fourteen years later, he admitted mistakes and 'bitter disappointment', but in such a way that, characteristically, he shifted the blame on to others. He put up a raft of excuses and explanations or, as he put it, 'reasons why we did not gain complete success at Arnhem'. He blamed himself for not insisting that the drop zones were closer to the bridge – not as humble a *mea culpa* as it sounded, because everyone knew that this had been the RAF's call, not his – but, otherwise, it was primarily Eisenhower who was at fault for being half-hearted and hedging his bets and under-equipping him with men and materials. And then there was the weather, which 'turned against us after the first day. But weather is always an uncertain factor, in war and peace. This uncertainty we all accepted. It could only have been offset, and the operation made a certainty, by allotting additional resources to the project, so that it became an Allied and not merely a British project.' In other words, if Montgomery was to be believed, even the problems created by the weather were down to the American supreme commander.

*

But in this defeat on the banks of the Lower Rhine, there was also victory for the Airborne at Arnhem, and a notable one at that. The courage of the men who fought it, who endured and who gave up only when ordered to, was a magnificent triumph of the spirit. A reporter welcoming some of the exhausted men back listened to their stories of ceaseless enemy attacks with flame-throwers, tanks and self-propelled guns firing high-explosive and armour-piercing shells, but what truly amazed him was when they added: 'When can we go back? We have to go back to get the rest of our chaps out.'[6] He concluded rightly that 'they were beaten in body but not in spirit.' A para sergeant-major spoke for the entire division when he wrote – in an anonymous memoir entitled simply 'I was there'[7]– that 'I am proud to have fought at the Battle of Arnhem, not just to have been there but to have been side by side with men of courage and determination, so many of whom did not come back.'

Lieutenant Bruce Davis was an American airman who went on the Arnhem mission as a ground observer, tasked to scout locations for a US air force signals operation behind the German lines. Instead he was caught up in the fighting. American servicemen did not always rate their British allies, but his report when he got home was an extraordinary encomium. 'Courage was commonplace and heroism was the rule not the exception,' he wrote, not about himself – because 'I was badly scared a great deal of the time' – but about the British companions he found himself fighting next to. 'I saw men who were hungry, exhausted, hopelessly outnumbered, men who by all the rules of war could have gladly surrendered and had it all over with, men who were shelled until they should have been hopeless psychopaths, and through it all they laughed, sang and died, and kept fighting because they were told this battle would shorten the war. They absorbed everything – mortars, tanks, S-P guns, machine guns – everything in the book, and kept coming up for more. The German infantry was scared of the Red Berets and would not attack without the help of armour or big guns. There was constant evidence that they gave Jerry the fright of his life. And the amazing thing about the British was that they carried on with the light-hearted abandon of a Sunday-school class on their first spring picnic. What I learned from the Arnhem operation was that men born and bred as free men have a great strength and willpower, which they never suspect until they need it.'[8]

★

A good number of those brave men were still having to call on their reserves of strength and willpower. Not everyone had escaped across the river or gone into captivity. There were an unknown number of airborne men on the loose and in hiding in that German-held area of woods, heaths and farmland north of the Lower Rhine. This was the postscript to the Battle of Arnhem: the continuing fight to survive and stay free long after it was over. They would trickle back to their own lines over the next weeks, some individually, others in groups organized by the Dutch Resistance. Some would lie low, protected by brave local families but in constant danger of discovery or betrayal, for more than six months, and not get home until the Netherlands was finally liberated and the war was very nearly over. The hundreds who made their way home in the months after Arnhem knew that they owed their survival and their salvation to the Dutch. Glider pilot Alan Kettley not only escaped – first from a moving train heading into Germany and then across the Waal to his own lines – he also went back on undercover missions to help others to come out. But he felt his bravery was eclipsed by the courage of the Dutch underground movement. 'If any of us had been captured, it was a POW camp. But for the Dutch it meant they and their families would be shot and their houses burnt down. The Dutch resistance, the Dutch civilians, were the real heroes.'

But so too were the evaders, and every one of them had an incredible story to tell. The first to get home was Major Eric Mackay, who had fought so determinedly to hold the school building at the Arnhem bridge until forced to surrender. His escape was surprisingly easy, even though it was from inside Germany. His captors had quickly spirited him away with the remnants of his company to a transit camp south-east of Arnhem and just over the border in the town of Emmrich. He dropped out of a window and on to a street.

With three others, he hiked back over the Dutch border and made for the Rhine, where they stole a small boat. 'It had no rudder and just one oar but once we got into mid stream there was a good current running.' They came to the major fork in the river, where the right channel became the Lower Rhine and flowed towards Arnhem and the left-hand one was the Waal and would take them to Nijmegen. The river was so wide here they almost got lost as well as nearly run down by a massive barge. Then Mackay saw the familiar shape of a large bridge ahead. Was it Arnhem? Had they taken a wrong turn and been swept back to where they started? To his relief, it was the Nijmegen bridge they were approaching, all too recently secured by the Allies. He heard a voice say, 'Halt! Who goes there?' and he knew he had made it. He had been so quick he was back behind his own lines even before the evacuation from Oosterbeek was ordered, let alone carried out.

For others, however, getting home was proving much harder. Major Tony Hibbert, another of the heroes of the fighting at the bridge, had been captured hiding in a coal shed in the wreckage of Arnhem and was on board an open 3-tonner lorry and en route to Germany when he grabbed his chance to escape. 'There were thirty of us, mostly officers, crammed in with two old Luftwaffe guards armed with pistols and rifles. There was a third guard with a Schmeisser sitting on the front mudguard. We continued giving V-signs to the Dutch as well as the odd German, and every time we did this the corporal on the mudguard lost his temper and stopped the lorry to tell us he'd shoot us if we did it again. But we carried on, because every time we stopped it took some time for the lorry to build up speed again. That was our opportunity.' He jumped over the side. 'I hit the road hard and there was lots of blood, but nothing seemed broken.'

There was pandemonium. A fellow escaper was downed by the corporal's machine gun as he climbed over a wall, but Hibbert had luck on his side and was away. 'I made a dash for the nearest side-turning, zigzagging to avoid the bullets, and crashed straight through a wooden fence. Then I zipped through half a dozen gardens and decided to go to ground. I covered myself with logs in a small garden hut and listened to the weapons still firing in the streets and the shouts of the search party.' He would discover much later that his escape had been costly. 'The corporal with the Schmeisser had completely lost his head and turned his gun on the back of the lorry, killing Tony Cotterill [a British war reporter] and another, and wounding eight more. He was threatening to kill the others when a German officer who was passing managed to get matters under control. It's something that's been very much on my conscience ever since.'

Unaware of these developments at the time, Hibbert waited until it was dark and headed away from the town and into the countryside, planning to seek help. 'After I'd gone 2 or 3 miles I found a small, isolated farmhouse. I pulled hard at the bell and tapped on the window, and eventually a very suspicious man stuck his head out and shone a torch on me. I was wearing a groundsheet and my face was covered in blood and bruises, so the glimpse he'd had of me can't have been very reassuring. It soon became clear he wasn't going to let me in, and I left. I was told later that he thought I was a German deserter. When he heard the next day that I was a bona fide Englishman he burst into tears and spent the rest of the day bicycling about looking for me.' But, through another farmer, the major did make contact with the Underground and was sheltered for three weeks with a family in the town of Ede. He discovered he was one of numerous escapers in the area, including half a dozen officers of his brigade. 'We formed a new Brigade headquarters in a butcher's shop in Ede. Every morning, dressed in an odd assortment of civilian clothes, we met in the back room to prepare plans for a mass escape.'

Among those officers was Brigadier Lathbury, commander of 1 Parachute Brigade, who had slipped away from the St Elizabeth Hospital to avoid being sent to Germany. After a miserable time spent 'skulking' in a hut in the woods, he'd fallen on his feet when he was secretly billeted in the large country house belonging to a 'most charming' countess. She and her husband had no fewer than sixty refugees in and around their country pile. But no one could tell the brigadier what was happening with the fighting, though he had a bad (and correct) feeling that the bridgehead at Oosterbeek had been abandoned. There were rumours (also correct) that the focus of the main Allied thrust had shifted away from Arnhem. If that was the case, then a quick sortie to escape over the river would not be possible. 'It began to look as though we might have to wait here for weeks, possibly until our own troops arrived.' (The latter was wishful thinking, though a lot of the evaders believed it.) Another strong rumour was that the Germans, who were already rounding up any young people they could find for war work, were going to evacuate all the villages. There was a lot to worry about.

But, amid the tension and the boredom and the constant fear of discovery, at least there was the consolation of comrades in the area, all biding their time while plans were hatched to get them home. Lathbury was moved again, this time by car and with a fellow officer he knew. 'We had bandages put round our heads and liberally sprinkled with red ink. We passed several parties of Germans marching alongside the road, but there was no other traffic. The driver said the only danger was our Typhoons and I was relieved when the journey came to an end.' He was now in Ede, where he could link up with more senior men on the run for those meetings in the butcher's shop. Here it was safe enough to walk the streets, albeit discreetly, although fellow evader Digby Tatham-Warter – the major who had flamboyantly strolled around Arnhem at the height of the fighting with an umbrella – was so bold as to offer his services to help push a German staff car out of a ditch. Tatham-Warter was liaising with the Resistance and moving between pockets of hidden British soldiers to keep them informed on plans to escape.

The weeks were slipping by. Lathbury thought there might be a chance of a Lysander sneaking in to fly him and other ranking officers whose experience might be useful back at Division headquarters out, but this never happened. And time could well be running out. 'Germans are taking over houses here and there is a fear of evacuation hanging over us. We are told that at Amersfoort and Apeldoorn the Germans have started a reign of terror – making all men between seventeen and fifty dig defences and shooting objectors. I hope to God that doesn't happen here.' But an escape plan was cooking – codename Pegasus – whose secret ingredient was a private telephone line belonging to a Dutch electricity company which, unbeknownst to the Germans, ran alongside the power cable and linked directly to Nijmegen. The escape committee could speak directly to Second Army headquarters to plan a route down to the river, where boats would be ready. In all, there were 130 men waiting. 'We were determined to go out as a fighting patrol,' Hibbert recalled, 'and arranged over this telephone line to have weapons and uniforms parachuted to us near Ede.'

*

On 22 October – five weeks after the Battle of Arnhem had ended – Pegasus was on. The hidden men who would join the escape were carefully brought together, converging on a wooded area near the river, close to the village of Renkum. They came in small parties, some on foot and some by bicycle, with Dutch guides. 'Digby T is doing wonderful work,' Lathbury noted. He said goodbye to the Dutch family who had been sheltering him and then, with Tatham-Warter, he cycled 6 miles to the assembly area. 'We passed many German troops and it gave one a nasty feeling to think that we might be stopped at any moment. There was one particularly unpleasant-looking SS man who seemed to look right through me.' The rendezvous was in a thick pine wood, where men were arriving throughout the day. 'They were organized into platoons and sections under officers and NCOs, since what lay ahead was a difficult night move through enemy lines. Order and control were essential. An added difficulty was that many of the men were unfit and weak through shortage of food and exercise or, like me, were recovering from wounds. All of us had some portion of uniform with us so that we should be treated as soldiers in the event of capture. Most of us were armed.'

The distance from the assembly point to the river was 3 miles and, given the difficult nature of the terrain, three hours were allowed so as to be at the river at midnight. As it got dark and the 9 p.m. start time approached, one party of men had yet to arrive. They were coming from the far side of Arnhem, a difficult 10-mile drive through

German lines. 'It seemed impossible that they could ever reach us, without detection. However, at about 8.30 p.m. there were loud noises of motor vehicles approaching, followed by shouting in English. I felt sure that we would be discovered at any moment since there was a German battery position just a quarter to half a mile away. But all remained quiet.'

In charge of that particular party was Tony Hibbert, who had gone out from Ede to round them up.⁹ 'We travelled in two magnificent old charcoal-burning lorries, open and with sides about 2 feet high. As we were all in British uniforms, it seemed unwise to sit boldly upright and we lay down in two layers with potato sacks on top. It was rough on those at the bottom as the lorries had few, if any, springs. No wonder there was some reluctance to volunteer for the bottom layer.' The journey was not without incident. They passed through two German checkpoints before stopping in a clearing in the woods. 'I went round to the back and said, "Everybody out, and keep bloody quiet because there are Germans all round here." Needless to say, as they climbed out, there was a certain amount of "Fuck you," "Christ, watch out," "Prison camp would be better than this!" Just then, a German cycle patrol came along with a lot of tinkling of bicycle bells and cries for us to get out of the way. The troops politely stood to one side and allowed them to pass. The German patrol didn't seem to notice a thing!'

With all now present, the escape could get under way. 'We formed up into a column in single file,' Lathbury recalled. 'It was pitch dark and one could hardly see more than a few feet. Part of the journey was through thick woods, and extremely difficult. Those of us at the rear found it very difficult to keep up. Everyone was frightened of getting lost and, eventually, a rope was passed back and we all held on to it.' Silence had been ordained, 'but we seemed to make the most shattering noise'. The trickiest manoeuvre was crossing a road near some houses and going through a gate into the meadows near the river. 'Our boots made a terrible noise on the tarmac, but still nothing happened. A slight moon began to shine through the clouds and additional light came from some burning buildings in the village of Renkum, just as we were passing through the enemy's forward defences.' Hibbert was astonished that they weren't detected. 'We were climbing over hedges and dropping down ditches about 8 feet deep and up the other side. The Germans must have heard us, and probably did see us, but maybe they felt that anyone who was making that amount of noise must be one of their own patrols. Either that, or there were so many of us that they felt the sensible thing to do was to keep quiet, because if they started shooting they would probably get shot at even harder.'

Ahead now was the river, half a mile or so away. They dropped to their knees and crawled over the meadow, stopping frequently while the way was scouted. Nerves were frayed, Lathbury recalled. Discipline wavered a little. Word from the front of the column was that lights were flashing from nearby German positions, and a ripple of apprehension went down the line that they had been discovered. Men braced themselves for an ambush on this last lap to the river. 'Firing broke out in front and we all expected the worst. It turned out that our leading patrol had encountered a German reconnaissance patrol who had fired at them but then withdrawn. After a very nervous five minutes we hit the river and, almost immediately, British guns opened up from the other side with tracer, as arranged. It was midnight. We flashed back the agreed light signal across the water. Nothing happened. No boats. No sign of movement. We waited for an awful twenty minutes.' Lathbury felt he had been here before. 'As one who was on the beaches of Dunkirk I am convinced that there is nothing more demoralizing than waiting to be taken off from the wrong side of a water obstacle.'

What had gone wrong? Had they come to the wrong spot on the river bank? Should they move position? Upstream or downstream? How long did they dare to wait out there in the open before pulling out and taking cover? These were anxious moments. Then, 'out of the darkness, we heard a cheerful, confident American voice hailing us. His boats were a quarter of a mile downstream. The relief was indescribable as we moved down the river bank in complete but cheerful disorder. Half an hour later the last boat was across, and not a sound from the enemy.' They had made it. Six weeks since dropping from the sky behind German lines, they were at last back on their own side. For Hibbert, the joy of escape was marred by an accident. 'We were ferried away from the river bank by jeeps, and I volunteered to sit on the front bonnet to guide the driver as, of course, there were no lights. We were going fairly fast when we went slap into another jeep coming from the opposite direction. If I hadn't moved my legs in time, they would have been chopped off at the knee. As it was, I did a triple somersault, landed in the road and bust my leg, and spent the next five months in hospital. A thoroughly unsatisfactory battle ended in a thoroughly unsatisfying anti-climax.' An impressive military career was cut short, and he was subsequently invalided out of the army.

★

Hibbert's accident apart, Pegasus was a success, which was why it was repeated a month later for another batch of evaders, but this time with disastrous consequences. The Germans were on the alert, the evaders ran into ambushes and were captured, killed or scattered. Almost none got over the river. No one should ever underestimate how difficult it was for the Arnhem survivors to get out of enemy-occupied territory and back to their own lines. There were heroic individual escapes in the months to come, but many of those in hiding had to stay that way until the war was virtually over. Lieutenant Eric Davis was one of them. His legs were shot up at Oosterbeek and he had gone into German custody while being treated at the field hospital in the Tafelberg Hotel. He could barely walk, and his fellow patients at Apeldoorn urged him to accept his fate as a prisoner of war. He refused to listen. 'I'll be drinking beer in London while they're caged up in Germany,' he told himself. Put on a train for Germany, 'I had an altercation with the guards about the war and was darned nearly brained with a rifle butt. Felt I was still fighting the war and determined to escape now. There is no doubt I am still feeling very aggressive.'

He rolled himself out through the window of the moving train. 'Made a good landing beside the railway track just clear of the turning wheels. The train stopped quickly and the track was searched. I rolled down the embankment and lay doggo in the grass. There was a bit of shooting into the shadows but then the train moved off. I'd done it. I'd escaped.' He moved on, ploughing across marshy fields and through ditches, trying not to think what the filthy water was doing to his already festering wounds. He broke into a barn and fell asleep, and was discovered by the friendly farmer next day. He was in good hands, though his rescuer was cagey at first. 'It seems the Huns have been running around in our uniforms asking for help and when given it shooting and burning.' Soon he was with the Resistance, and totally dependent on them. His legs had packed up on him completely and he had to be carried or tugged along on a bicycle. He was lodged with a family and laid up in bed for weeks to get better. The risks his hosts were taking troubled him greatly. 'The penalty for helping the likes of me is death.'

It was late November before he left them. His legs were better, and it was time, he decided, 'to try to get back and fight another day'. He moved to another family living closer to the Rhine but there was to be no quick resolution. He was still there on 9 December, his twenty-sixth birthday, which they celebrated with a party that had unexpected and uninvited guests. 'The eldest daughter and I were playing "Silver Threads among the Gold" on the piano when some Germans knocked on the door. They had heard the music and asked to come in and sit and listen. We just kept on playing. There was nothing else I could do except sweat a little.' By this point, the botching of Pegasus II had caused all organized escapes to be stopped. Christmas – the one by which the war was supposed to be over – beckoned and Davis was still a long way from home. On Boxing Day, the lieutenant got the most unseasonal of gifts. The condition of his right leg had been deteriorating over the weeks and needed an operation to save it. A Dutch surgeon was found and, at a safe house – surrounded by armed Resistance fighters in case the Germans arrived – Davis climbed on to the kitchen table, was given a spinal injection and waited to be carved up. 'The doctor opened my leg from the back of my knee to my rump. His anatomy book lay by my side and gradually got covered with bloody finger marks. He could not find one end of a broken nerve because a bullet had severed it at an angle and taken quite a section out. He insisted on showing me the problem with a mirror but I told him to just find the end and join it up, and we would worry about getting my leg straight afterwards. The end was found, my knee bent up at an angle of 90 degrees and the nerve sutured. Three hours after starting, the doctor sewed me up and we all had a drink. I felt quite bucked because I didn't pass out once!' The surgery left him immobilized. Escape was out of the question.

As 1945 began, conditions worsened in the Netherlands. Food was scarce, crackdowns by the Gestapo more frequent. There were executions. One of Davis's doctors was arrested, so too was a female courier carrying a letter to him about escape plans, though thankfully it wasn't found on her, despite a strip-search. The net seemed to be closing in on him. 'Life here is getting vicious,' he wrote in his diary. 'Everyone is edgy.' The house was raided at one in the morning but, luckily, he was tucked up in his special hiding place and was not found. Then, on 19 March came the news he had been waiting for. He was to prepare for the first leg of his journey home. 'Cycle to Apeldoorn; had my hair cut in civilian barber shop, next to Huns there doing the same thing. Arrive at a house known as the Submarine Base because of its hidden tunnels and chamber. It is a collecting and transit place for people like me. Padre Bill Pare is one of those here.' A few days later, the Germans pounced. 'It was a lightning raid and I had no time to go underground and hide, so I just sit in the garden and act the Dutchman. Exciting, but got away with it.'

His journey stalled. A crossing was on, then it was off. In the first week of April there was news that Canadian forces were close by. 'However, the Underground will not help us to get to them because it would be too dangerous. They say we must wait, but I decide I'm going to move without them.' He set out with five others. 'The Boche seem to be everywhere. They are retreating and in a nasty mood.' He headed for Apeldoorn, where the Canadians were reported to be on the town outskirts. 'Started off well enough but then three of our party decided the roads were too dangerous and returned to their old farm hideout. Travelling on foot was too slow so the remaining three of us stole bikes. During this, one went missing and so we were down to two. There are Germans everywhere.

Can't get away from them.' When they got to Apeldoorn, a massive battle was going on. 'Shells, mortars, machine guns and small arms and searchlights flashing in the sky. We left the bikes and clambered over some railings into some parkland. We were almost run down by a wild boar the size of a donkey and then walked into a Hun sentry. We ran for it, back into the woods.' For the next forty-eight hours they dodged German troops, at one point lying face down in a gutter as a platoon marched by.

'*16 April 1945*. Did a foot recce to the canal that runs through Apeldoorn, with the Canadians on the other side of it. I decided to sleep tonight and swim the canal tomorrow night. *17 April 1945*. This morning discovered the Canadians had crossed the canal during the night, so swim not necessary. The Boche are beating it – getting out of town in quick time. Walk down the street into Canadian territory – FREE at last!'

*

Two weeks later, Hitler was dead in his bunker, and a week after that Germany surrendered. Now was the time for the very last of the Arnhem survivors – the prisoners of war – to make the long trek home too. It is difficult to give an overall verdict on how the Airborne fared in captivity, because each man served his time in his own way. Many were upset and ashamed when they had to surrender and may never have exorcised those feelings. They felt tainted in some way, their reputations blemished. Some undoubtedly felt they had been abandoned, and resented it. But if they suffered recriminations in this way, they did so alone. There was, it appears, no collective breast-beating among the Airborne. Signaller Leo Hall recalled that 'neither in the hospitals nor in the stalags was there any desire to discuss the battle or its outcome. The subjects were never raised. There was no introspective brooding at all.' He himself remained positive. 'I didn't take the defeat badly and I'm glad about that. For me it was a kind of victory. I'd been tested and had come through it all with something to spare, and in doing so I'd let nobody down.'

Airborne *esprit de corps* seems to have remained strong and gave a fillip to the thousands of other British prisoners of war the Airborne now mingled with, largely in Stalag XIB at Fallingbostel in northern Germany. Longstanding inmates there, some of whom had been in captivity since Dunkirk, remembered the men from Arnhem marching through the camp gates led by the ramrod figure of Regimental Sergeant-Major John Lord with all the swagger of the guardsman he had been before joining the paras. One prisoner of war remembered Lord 'snapping a salute which would not have been out of place at Pirbright or Caterham. We found ourselves instinctively standing to attention. The impression on the Germans was incredible.'[10] The compound was overcrowded and in a state of near-chaos, but Lord took charge and, as best as anyone could in those awful conditions, imposed airborne discipline and standards of dress and behaviour. Few dared cross his fearsome personality and rough tongue. He had his work cut out. James Sims was appalled by the attitudes he encountered in the camp. 'There was no mucking-in spirit. It was just dog eat dog and the weakest to the wall.' He remembered bitter arguments and fist fights breaking out over the smallest of disagreements, and brawls between men of different regiments.

And now these men were coming home. They had gone to Arnhem one Sunday with hopes of being back in the pub by the weekend. After eight months of incarceration when they were half-starved, poorly treated, demoralized and never sure they would ever see home again, they were flying in from camps in conquered Germany. Wives were waiting. After a whirlwind romance that began in a Woolworth's tea bar, eighteen-year-old Lola Ayers had married her airborne sapper husband Arthur a fortnight or so before he flew to Arnhem. On her own admission, they didn't know very much about each other. They hadn't had time. And then he had gone back to his unit, and she had heard not a word from him or about him from the beginning of September until sometime in October, when an official letter came saying he was missing in action in north-west Europe. She had had no idea if he was alive or dead. She was living with his parents through this terrible time of not knowing, and sharing the agonies with his mother. 'She was finding it very difficult because he was an only child. She was very, very worried.' Lola got on with her work in the ATS. 'I didn't really know what else to do.'

Their Christmas present that year was a card from Arthur telling them he was a prisoner of war. It came from Stalag 4B in eastern Germany and was addressed to 'Mrs A. Ayers' with a 'jun' [for Junior] tacked on the end of the name to signify his wife rather than his mother. 'My own darling wife,' she read. 'Just a few lines, sweetheart, to let you know I am OK and well. I am waiting patiently for that day to come, darling, when we will make up for all this time we have been parted.' Lola was thrilled. 'It was such a joy to know that he was alive.' Behind the barbed wire, he was comforted, too, by the letters he got from home. 'They gave me a wonderful feeling as I absorbed line after line of their neat handwriting,' he recorded in his diary. 'I felt close to them. Each scrap of news was treasured in my memory, to be remembered again in the days to come.'

He released himself, slipping away from a column of British prisoners as they were forced by the Germans to march away from the advancing Allied front. He stayed hidden and was liberated by American troops. There was no chance to telegram to say he was coming home. 'He just arrived in the middle of the night,' Lola recalled. It was a low-key reunion, as so many were. Returning prisoners and their loved ones could be like strangers, made awkward rather than emotional by long absence. 'I asked if he wanted anything and he said yes, a tin of condensed milk! He wanted to spoon it out and eat it straight away. He looked like a skeleton – about 7 stone. We were just so relieved to have him back.' For Arthur, the moment had huge significance. 'Walking back into the arms of my wife signalled the end of the war' – and of the Arnhem operation – 'for me. I got back on with my life. I don't think I was affected by what I'd seen and done. I just did my duty, as everybody else was doing.'

Ron Brooker hobbled home from his eight months as a prisoner after being shot in a failed escape attempt. There was a disappointment awaiting him. 'I'd had a girlfriend from the time I was at school, and though I'd never even kissed her, she was my girlfriend. While I was a prisoner I'd been working out how much money I was saving and that I'd be able to buy a bed, furniture, crockery, things like that.

I was planning for the future. After I got home I went round to her house and I said, "Look, Joan, I'm not messing about, I'm hoping to get married," and she said, "So am I, I'm getting married tomorrow." And she did. She married a Canadian soldier!' But, that setback apart, getting home and being reunited with his family was marvellous. 'My mum was over the moon, and it was all really an emotional reunion because Dad was home on leave too. All of the brothers survived the war.' As for the Arnhem experience, however hard it had been, however many mates he had lost, however many horrors he had witnessed, 'they were some of the happiest days of my life. I still think it was all well worth doing. I'm proud of my contribution. The best times of my life but, obviously, some of the saddest and frightening times as well. But I wouldn't have missed Arnhem for the world.'

For Dutch civilians caught up in the battle, Arnhem would also be a highlight of their lives, and unforgettable in more ways than one. Nurse Heleen Kernkamp's daughter, Marga, remembered being out walking with her mother many years afterwards when some planes flew low overhead. 'She ran for cover behind a wall.' Survivors like her rarely talked about their experiences, but Heleen wrote hers down as a way, daughter Marga explained, 'to get rid of them from her soul'. It was only when Marga read her mother's account that she grasped the enormity of what the older woman had seen and done. 'She was a hero, and we, her children, never knew it. When I read her diary, I did not even recognize her. I saw that what she did among all that suffering and death was incredible. As a nurse, she was needed, and she thrived on that. It was a crazy, dangerous time, an incredible challenge that she passed with flying colours. But she never had the chance to live on the edge like that again. Arnhem was her high point. She never bettered it. She went on to become a well-known writer and translator and won awards for her work, but she never felt she achieved again what she achieved at Arnhem, and I think she regretted that.'

Back in England, Andy Milbourne would have Arnhem hanging over him for the rest of his life. He had permanent mementoes – both arms cut off below the elbow and an empty eye socket. He'd been firing a heavy machine gun from the back of a jeep, covering the retreat from Arnhem to the Oosterbeek perimeter, and took a direct hit from a mortar. An appalling time followed in a German-run hospital, where his arms were amputated. He managed several months in Stalag XIB at Fallingbostel, but his wounds were so severe that he was repatriated in a prisoner exchange early in 1945. He had left the camp with the words of an old mate ringing in his ears – 'What's your mother going to say?' He was about to find out. As he sat in a Red Cross ambulance driving him to his home in Alnwick, 30 miles north of Newcastle, the reunion with his mother was not the only reason for the gnawing feeling in the pit of his stomach. He was feeling angry and sorry for himself. In Germany, he had had months to think about the future of a working man with no hands. He'd been noted as a boy for his long fingers – 'piano fingers' someone had said. 'Given to me by God, now taken away by a mere mortal,' he told himself, with real bitterness. 'Now what? Who's going to employ me?' In his head, he had written himself off after a child at the railway station had stared in fascinated horror at his empty eye socket and a woman in a pub had been hysterical at the sight of his missing arms. But now, as the ambulance drew up outside number 12 St George's Crescent, the moment had come to face his loved ones. He was angry when the driver sounded the horn, hating the attention that was being drawn to him. 'Why the hell didn't they have a fanfare of blasted trumpeters too? Then the whole street could turn out to gawk at the armless and one-eyed freak.' The ambulance doors opened and there was his father with a broad smile on his face and offering to lift him down. 'Get out of the way!' snapped the young Milbourne. 'Do you think I am that bloody helpless?' The older man looked hurt then walked away, calling behind him to his son, 'Carry on, soldier!'

'I jumped down and made my own way to the door, where two of my aunties were standing. "Here comes the hero," one of them said. They tried to keep their eyes on my face, but instinctively they looked to where my hands should have been hanging. Both began hugging me, but I had nothing to hug them back with except a pair of flapping, empty sleeves.' His mother grabbed him next, 'and kissed me until I thought I would faint. I could have screamed and, if someone hadn't given me a cigarette, I'm sure I would have done.' A table was groaning with food and a cake with 'Welcome home' iced on it. He sat down and his mother offered a morsel to his mouth. 'Now don't be shy,' she said. 'I've done this before when you were a baby!', and he was mortified. 'Those words were said in all sincerity and with a mother's true love for her son. But was I to be fed like this for the rest of my days? Was I to be washed, shaved, then taken for a nice walk? Was I to have those intimate parts of my body touched by her hands as she had had to do when I was little? And would my father always be on hand every time I wanted to urinate?' He looked around the circle of concerned family faces. 'As I met their gaze, one by one they dropped their eyes, and pretended that they were not paying me the slightest attention.' Milbourne erupted. 'Take all this food away,' he roared. 'I don't want it.'

He stomped off to the pub, joined by his father. The ale helped. 'Here was my escape from reality. This was the way to dodge one's problems. With a few pints of wallop inside of me, I couldn't care less who looked at me. Let them look. The great paratrooper who used to throw a nifty dart with the best of them couldn't even lift his own pint of beer. So what? I might be able to use my toes.' But the notion that people were feeling sorry for him, especially his own family, was a terrible torture, a blow to his pride that would take a long time to soften. And then there was Peggy, the girl he was semi-engaged to. She was serving with the ATS but would soon be back on leave. He was terrified of the reunion. 'I lay awake for hours at night wondering what she would say or do when she saw me. When I eventually fell asleep, I would dream of her. In those dreams, I had hands.'

He went to meet her at the station and, as she came to greet him, neither of them knew what to do. 'I couldn't very well get hold of her as I wanted to, so rather awkwardly I offered to kiss her. We gave each other a little peck, and then just stood for a while studying one another.' Then, guided by his father, it was back to the Milbourne house, where his mother instantly whisked Peggy away. 'I think she wanted to warn her that I was not myself and not to take any notice of me, to let me get on with whatever I was doing and, most of all, not try to help. I don't know for sure that this was the gist of their conversation but I suspected it was, because mother had been coming in for a lot of abuse from me. Every time she made to help me, I would start raving at her. My temper was foul.' When he and Peggy were on their own, conversation was stilted. 'So I decided to force the question – were we still going to get married? I said to her, "Peggy, have you ever thought of the drawbacks which are bound to confront a man like myself?"' She was silent for a minute or two, which the anger inside Milbourne instantly interpreted as the rejection he had expected. Then she came back at him. 'You think you're licked, don't you? You think that you're a social outcast because you've lost your hands. Because of your wounds, you're not going to be married. I suppose it would hurt your pride to have a mere woman helping you.'

Milbourne was stung. Before Peggy went back to her unit, they rowed all the time but, as he later acknowledged, she made him get a grip of himself and the self-pity that was gnawing away at him. 'Her tongue, plus my mother's cooking, had me making a fighting comeback.' It took a while – and a whole lot of binge-drinking with his mates – before this happened. He was fitted with prosthetic arms. He married Peggy. He made a life for himself. Defying his disability, he found work after the war, including an extraordinary period when he worked down a coal mine. When this came to the attention of a Labour MP and newspaper stories were written about him, he became something of a celebrity and an inspiration. He wrote his memoirs, which were published in the fifties to great acclaim. One holder of the Victoria Cross hailed his 'courage in its highest form, moral as well as physical' and another saw him as 'a symbol of man's triumph over the worst possible afflictions'. In many ways, Milbourne's endurance, suffering and courage epitomized the Battle of Arnhem and the incredibly brave men who fought it. Militarily, it was a defeat, but not for the human spirit. Fittingly, Milbourne dedicated his writings to his fellow soldiers. 'To those who fell and to all who survived, whether whole in mind or body,' he wrote, 'Thank you, gentlemen, for the honour of your company.' Amen to that.

This Arnhem narrative began in the Netherlands with the seventeen-year-old Anje van Maanen and her dog on the peaceful banks of the Lower Rhine. 'We had no idea what was to happen over the coming days' – that those green meadows were soon to be a blood-soaked battlefield and a graveyard. With what Anje saw and experienced, she was forced to grow up from girl to woman in a week. To her go the final words that sum up that battle for survival in Arnhem and Oosterbeek in September 1944: 'I shall never forget the terror, fear, and death but also the wonderful friendships. The bravery of the British was incredible. The way the Dutch people helped them also made me so proud. The sacrifice will never be forgotten and nor will the way people conducted themselves amidst the horror. That was truly the triumph of Arnhem.'

Notes

Chapter 1: 'Where are the Tommies!'

1 Private memoir and JN interview, 2010.
2 Anje van Maanen – private diary, and JN interview, 2010. This day-by-day account was written in September 1945, exactly a year after the events she described, as a way of trying to come to terms with the horrors she had experienced and which still haunted her dreams.
3 Private memoir by Heleen Kernkamp-Biegel. Airborne Assault, Imperial War Museum, Duxford, and JN interview with her daughter Marga, 2010.
4 The Netherlands consists of twelve provinces, only two of which are known as Holland (north and south), the name by which the whole country is often erroneously called. Arnhem was in Gelderland. Ironically, the city of Geldern, from which the province took its name, was (and is) in Germany.
5 Sir Alistair Horne in *Monty, the Lonely Leader*. Macmillan, 1994.
6 *The Tommies are Coming. Diary of an Oosterbeek Girl*. Surname unknown. Airborne Museum, Oosterbeek. Copy lodged at Airborne Assault, Imperial War Museum, Duxford.
7 *Arnhem Spearhead*, by James Sims. Imperial War Museum, 1978, and Sphere Books, 1989.
8 The use (or misuse) of the words 'paras' and 'paratroopers' can still cause fighting to break out in the ranks. In the text, we have opted for the generic definition where necessary, for ease of reading.
9 *The Memoirs of Field Marshal Montgomery*. Collins, 1958, and Pen and Sword Military, 2010.
10 Alan Kettley, Official intelligence debrief, October 1944 (Airborne Assault, Imperial War Museum, Duxford), and JN interview, 2010.
11 In his memoirs, Montgomery gave a succinct summary of Market Garden. 'My plan was to drive hard for the Rhine across all river and canal

obstacles and to seize a bridgehead beyond the Rhine before the enemy reorganized sufficiently to stop us. The essential feature was the laying of a "carpet" of airborne forces across the five major water obstacles which existed on the general axis of the main road through Eindhoven to Uden, Grave, Nijmegen, and thence to Arnhem. XXX Corps was then to operate along the axis of the "carpet", link up with the 1st British Airborne Division in the Arnhem area and establish a bridgehead over the Neder Rijn north of that place. Second Army was then to establish itself in the general area between Arnhem and the Zuider Zee, facing east, so as to be able to develop operations against the northern flank of the Ruhr.'

12 Major Toler. Diary. Provided by Major Mike Peters, Army Air Corps.

13 Private memoir. Airborne Assault, Imperial War Museum, Duxford.

14 Quoted in *Monty: The Field-Marshal*, by Nigel Hamilton. Sceptre, 1986.

15 *Lease of Life*, by Andrew Milbourne. Transworld, 1955.

16 Private Les Davison, Royal Army Medical Corps. Private memoir. Box 45, RAMC Archive, Keogh Barracks, Hampshire.

17 Letter by Ivor Rowbery, Airborne Assault, Imperial War Museum, Duxford.

Chapter 2: 'A Piece of Cake'

1 Quoted in *Men of the Red Beret: There Shall be Wings. The RAF 1918 to the Present*, by Max Arthur. Hutchinson, 1990.

2 Alan Kettley: see Chapter 1, note 10.

3 Reg Curtis, *Tafelberg*. BN1 Publishing, and JN interviews, 2010.

4 Apart from the shame and ridicule, this was a court-martial offence.

5 There were different symbols for specific units.

6 'Market' was the codename for the airlift part of the operation and 'Garden' the codename for the land operation. Hence the operation as a whole was 'Market Garden'.

7 Quoted in *Arnhem*, by Lloyd Clark. Headline, 2009.

8 Ted Mordecai. Private memoir. Airborne Ordnance at Arnhem, Airborne Assault, Imperial War Museum, Duxford.

9 *It Never Snows in September*, by Robert Kershaw. Ian Allan, 2009.

10 Ron Brooker's account in *Tribute* edited by Philip Sidnell. The Military & Aviation Book Society, London, 2002, and JN interview, June 2010.

11 Peter Clarke. Private memoir, and JN interview, 2010.

Chapter 3: 'Home by the Weekend'

1 *Cloud over Arnhem*, by Kate ter Horst. Allan Wingate, London, 1959.

2 P. H. Huisman. Private memoir. Airborne Assault, Imperial War Museum, Duxford.

3 Private memoir. *Target Mike One*, and JN interview, 2010.

4 *Down to Earth*. Private memoir by Fred Moore. Airborne Assault, Imperial War Museum, Duxford.

5 *Nine Days*, by Ronald Gibson. Arthur Stockwell, 1956. The authors are grateful to his daughter, Candy, for permission to quote from it.

6 Eric Webbley. Private memoir. Courtesy of his widow and Niall Cherry of Warton, Lancs.

Chapter 4: 'Are We on Overtime Now?'

1 Projector Infantry Anti-Tank.

2 Or 'Woah Mohammed!', as some paras recalled the cry.

3 Private memoir from www.paradata.org.uk

4 Lt. Pat Barnett. Private memoir. Airborne Assault, Imperial War Museum, Duxford.

5 Major Eric Mackay. Private memoir. Airborne Assault, Imperial War Museum, Duxford.

Chapter 5: Stopped in Their Tracks

1 Private memoir. Airborne Assault, Imperial War Museum, Duxford.

2 The story of the Tafelberg field hospital is told in fuller detail in Chapter 12.

3 Robert Quayle. Private memoir. Airborne Assault, Imperial War Museum, Duxford.

4 Private memoir. Provided by Steve McLoughlin, 4th Parachute Squadron RE website.

5 Private memoir. Airborne Assault, Imperial War Museum, Duxford.

6 4th Para Squadron Royal Engineers, Official War Diaries.

7 Major Daniel Webber. Private memoir. Airborne Assault, Imperial War Museum, Duxford.

8 *Capture at Arnhem*, by Harry Roberts, Windrush Press, 1999.

9 Private memoir. The authors are grateful to his nephew John Merry for providing a copy.

10 Private memoir. 'The Further Side of the Arnhem Bridge.' Provided by David Brook of the Glider Pilot Regiment Association.

11 The badly wounded Roberts subsequently went into captivity when the field hospital he was in was taken over by the Germans. He survived his time in a prisoner-of-war camp and returned home relatively unscathed.

12 The main body of Polish paratroopers should have been arriving, too, but they were grounded by bad weather in eastern England. Their armour was on gliders that took off on schedule from airfields further south, where the weather was better. See Chapter 11.

13 Quoted in Poles Apart, by George Cholewczynski. Greenhill Books, 1993.

Chapter 6: 'If You Knows a Better 'Ole'

1 It was so well known that it was the basis of a stage play and two comic films, one starring Syd Chaplin.

Chapter 7: 'He was Engaged on a Very Important Airborne Mission'

1 JN interview, 2010.

2 Major Powell, quoted in *Green On!*, by Arie-Jan van Hees (see note 8 below). Despite the hilarity of the moment, the major thought there was method in this apparent madness. He wrote: 'The content of supply drops had to be pre-packed to a standard formula with everything that might be wanted in the course of a battle. Red berets were a valuable psychological weapon, and the Boche had learned to hate the sight

of them. Everyone dropped with his beret tucked into a pocket, but some were lost. Probably only the one container of berets was included in the whole supply drop and it was just our luck to happen on it.'

3 They were members of the Royal Army Service Corps.

4 The details of KG374's last flight are recorded in comprehensive investigations by i) Karel Margry in *After the Battle* magazine, number 96, published in 1997, and ii) Phil Rodgers in 'An Arnhem Survivor' in *Britain at War* magazine, September 2008. The authors are indebted to these writers for being allowed to draw on their exemplary work.

5 Now rarely used, it was a shortened version of 'Lord love me'.

6 According to the squadron operations log, though other sources claim half the load was ammunition.

7 Flight-Lieutenant Stanley Lee, quoted in Karel Margry, op. cit.

8 The authors are indebted to Arie-Jan van Hees, who compiled many of these accounts in his excellent book *Green On! A Detailed Survey of the British Parachute Re-supply Sorties during Operation Market Garden 18–25 September 1944*. Private publication. ISBN 90–806808–2–6.

9 He would later become a general.

10 JN interview, 2010.

11 Van Hees, op. cit.

12 JN interview, 2010.

13 The smart London suburb where he was born.

14 His story is taken from his memoirs (*Six of the Best*. Robson Books, 1984), as reproduced in Van Hees, op. cit.

15 What effect this had on the German prisoners, who, as we have seen, were corralled there, is unknown.

Chapter 8: At the Bridge – A Desperate Battle for Survival

1 Anon., *I Was There*. Airborne Assault, Imperial War Museum, Duxford.

Chapter 9: Hands in the Air . . . But Heads Held High

1 Anon., *I Was There*. Airborne Assault, Imperial War Museum, Duxford.

Chapter 10: In the Mood . . . to Fight until We Drop

1 This is an amalgamation of slightly different versions by Ennis and Webbley.
2 Private memoir. Airborne Assault, Imperial War Museum, Duxford.
3 Major Ian Toler.
4 To the British, it was known as Ovaltine.

Chapter 11: A Long, Long Way from Warsaw

1 Private memoir and JN interview, 2010. The authors are grateful to Kazic
   Szmid's son, Andrzej, for providing his father's life story.
2 Some sources put the number of Poles deported to Siberia at 1.7 million,
   of whom only 400,000 are thought to have survived.
3 All in all, 115,000 Poles left the Soviet Union in this way, according to
   Polish sources.
4 For information about the Polish Brigade, the authors are indebted to
   George Cholewczynski and his encyclopaedic book, *Poles Apart*.
5 Tarrant Rush in Dorset and Keevil in Wiltshire.
6 Private memoir. Airborne Assault, Imperial War Museum, Duxford, and
   JN interview with his son, Philip Mollett, 2010.
7 Interview for Second World War Experience Centre, Leeds, and JN interview, July 2010.
8 Lloyd Clark, senior lecturer in war studies at the Royal Military Acad-
   emy, Sandhurst, in *Arnhem: Jumping the Rhine*. Headline, 2009.
9 Afterwards, the British generals would blame unexpected resistance and
   difficult terrain for their tardiness, but there were others who felt the
   column was never advanced with sufficient urgency.

Chapter 12: Chaos and Compassion in No man's Land

1 Revd Chignell, padre of the glider pilots. Private diary. Museum of Army
   Chaplaincy.
2 See Pegasus archive: http://www.pegasusarchive.org/arnhem/graeme_
   warrack.htm

3 Niall Cherry, *Red Berets and Red Crosses*, R. N. Sigmund, 1998.
4 Jo Johanson.
5 Personal memoir. Airborne Assault, Imperial War Museum, Duxford.

Chapter 13: Pulling Out

1 Revd R. T. Watkins, 1 Para chaplain. Private memoir. Museum of Army Chaplaincy.
2 See Hamilton, op. cit. A liaison officer who visited the front reported that Horrocks believed such a bridgehead 'difficult with present resources'.
3 Revd Chignell.
4 Quoted in Clark, op. cit.
5 By the end of the evacuation, only two were still operational.
6 Martin Middlebrook in *Arnhem 1944: The Airborne Battle*. Penguin, 1995.

Chapter 14: Left Behind

1 Quoted in Cholewczynski, op. cit.
2 Charitably, he did not rail against this, simply wondering if the runner had been killed or had lost his way – which was entirely possible in the circumstances. It did cross his mind, however, that the rearguard had been 'written off'. What is most puzzling about this incident is why the English officer refused to take a Polish runner along with him.
3 *Cloud over Arnhem*, by Kate ter Horst. Allan Wingate, 1959.
4 See Nichol and Rennell, op. cit.
5 Quoted in Heleen Kernkamp's memoirs.
6 Kazic Szmid.

Chapter 15: Home is the Hero

1 Memo to the Chief of the Imperial General Staff, quoted in Hamilton, op. cit.
2 Bob Quayle.

3 See Chapter 1, note 17.

4 *War Illustrated* magazine, October 1944.

5 Dutch writer Johan Fabricus. Broadcast on the BBC Home Service, 27 September 1944.

6 *The Times*, 28 September 1944.

7 Lodged at Airborne Assault, Imperial War Museum, Duxford.

8 Airborne Assault, Imperial War Museum, Duxford.

9 How many were in the party is disputed. Lathbury says thirty; Hibbert, sixty.

10 Quoted in Nichol and Rennell, op. cit.

Bibliography

Arthur, Max, *Men of the Red Beret: There Shall be Wings. The RAF 1918 to the Present*, Hutchinson, 1990

Bentley, Stewart W. Jr, *Orange Blood, Silver Wings*, AuthorHouse, 2007

Buist, Luuk, Reinders, Philip and Maassen, Geert, *The Royal Air Force at Arnhem*, Airborne Museum, Oosterbeek, 2005

Cherry, Niall, *Red Berets and Red Crosses*, R. N. Sigmund, 1998

Cholewczynski, George, *Poles Apart – Polish Airborne at the Battle of Arnhem*, Greenhill Books, 1993

Churchill, Winston, *Triumph and Tragedy*, Penguin, 2005

Clark, Lloyd, *Arnhem: Jumping the Rhine*, Headline, 2009

Curtis, Reg, *Tafelberg*, BN1 Publishing, 2009

Gibson, Ronald, *Nine Days*, Arthur Stockwell, 1956

Hamilton, Nigel, *Monty: The Field-Marshal*, Sceptre, 1986

Kershaw, Robert, *It Never Snows in September*, Ian Allan, 2009

Mackie, Alastair, *Some of the People All of the Time*, Book Guild Publishing, 2006

Middlebrook, Martin, *Arnhem 1944: The Airborne Battle*, Penguin, 1995

Milbourne, Andrew, *Lease of Life*, Transworld, 1955

Montgomery, Field Marshal, *Memoirs*, Pen & Sword Military, 2010

Morrison, Alexander, *Silent Invader*, Airlife Classic, 1999

O'Reilly, John, *From Delhi to Arnhem*, Thornton Publishing, 2009

Peters, Mike and Buist, Luuk, *Glider Pilots at Arnhem*, Pen & Sword Military, 2009

Ryan, Cornelius, *A Bridge Too Far*, Hodder, 2007

Sidnell, Peter (ed.), *Tribute – Combat Experiences of the Military and Aviation Book Society*, Military and Aviation Book Society, 2002

Sims, James, *Arnhem Spearhead*, Imperial War Museum, 1978, and Sphere Books, 1989

Smith, Claude, *History of the Glider Pilot Regiment*, Pen & Sword Military, 2007

Ter Horst, Kate A., *Cloud over Arnhem*, Allan Wingate, 1959

Van Hees, Arie-Jan, *Green On! A Detailed Survey of the British Parachute Re-supply Sorties during Operation Market Garden 18–25 September 1944*, Private publication, 2007

Index

'nfd' indicates that there are no further details.

JOHN NICHOL & TONY RENNELL

HOME RUN
ESCAPE FROM NAZI EUROPE

The dramatic story of Allied evaders behind enemy lines in World War Two.

They were the few: the stranded soldiers and shot-down airmen who evaded capture in Nazi-occupied Europe and had just one goal – to get back to Britain and to safety. On the run, hunted and desperate, their lives hung constantly in the balance – find the secret escape routes and you might get home, trust the wrong person and the feared Gestapo would scoop you up. A concentration camp, or worse, would be your fate. This is the incredible story of the band of British heroes who made that elusive home run… and those who did not.

'Humanity shines through. A sensitive account of the best and worst of human behaviour' *Daily Telegraph*

JOHN NICHOL & TONY RENNELL

THE LAST ESCAPE
THE UNTOLD STORY OF ALLIED PRISONERS OF WAR IN GERMANY
1944-45

Hundreds of thousands of British and American servicemen were held as POWs in camps across Nazi Germany by the time of the Normandy landings in June 1944. As winter settled across Europe and the Allied advance threatened German borders, prisoners were moved away from liberating forces. The POWs were forced to march hundreds of miles in appalling conditions. Hundreds died of disease, starvation and exhaustion. Yet when the war was over those who survived found their extraordinary tale was largely ignored and forgotten.

The Last Escape brings the survivors' amazing stories to light telling one of the most courageous and brutal tales of the final months of the Second World War.

'Packed with first-hand testimony and impressive scholarship but with all the pace of a novel, this is a superb memorial of those Allied heroes who thought – wrongly – that for them the war was over' Andrew Roberts

TAIL-END CHARLIES
THE LAST BATTLES OF THE BOMBER WAR 1944-45

Night after night they flew through the flak and packs of enemy fighters to drop the bombs that helped demolish the Third Reich – and they died in their tens of thousands. The airmen of RAF's Bomber Command were heroes who defied Hitler in the early days of the war and continued to sacrifice themselves to shatter the enemy right to the end of the conflict. But with war over they were forgotten, some of their actions seen as crimes.

Tail-End Charlies tells the astonishing and deeply moving stories of the controversial last battles in the skies above Germany, through the eyewitness accounts of the many forgotten heroes who fought them.

'Compelling, powerful, gripping and revealing' *Daily Mail*

JOHN NICHOL & TONY RENNELL

MEDIC: Saving Lives - from Dunkirk to Afghanistan

'Awe-inspiring stories, astonishingly heroic actions, gripping and extraordinary' *Daily Mail*

Doctors, nurses, medics and stretcher-bearers go where the bullets are thickest, through bomb alleys and minefields, ducking mortars and rockets, wherever someone is injured and the cry for assistance goes up. Their job is to put themselves in the heart of danger – to run into battle to rescue the wounded and to risk their own lives to save the dying.

This is the story of those brave men – and, increasingly, women – who go to war armed with bandages not bombs, scalpels not swords, and put saving life above taking life. Many have died in the process, the ultimate sacrifice for others, to ensure that when the cry of 'Medic!' is heard, it will be answered. Regardless of the cost.

From the beaches of Dunkirk to the desert towns of Afghanistan, there can be no nobler cause.

'Moving, inspiring, superbly told. The hellishness of war was never more stark' Andrew Roberts, *Daily Telegraph*

He just wanted a decent book to read ...

Not too much to ask, is it? It was in 1935 when Allen Lane, Managing Director of Bodley Head Publishers, stood on a platform at Exeter railway station looking for something good to read on his journey back to London. His choice was limited to popular magazines and poor-quality paperbacks – the same choice faced every day by the vast majority of readers, few of whom could afford hardbacks. Lane's disappointment and subsequent anger at the range of books generally available led him to found a company – and change the world.

'We believed in the existence in this country of a vast reading public for intelligent books at a low price, and staked everything on it'
Sir Allen Lane, 1902–1970, founder of Penguin Books

The quality paperback had arrived – and not just in bookshops. Lane was adamant that his Penguins should appear in chain stores and tobacconists, and should cost no more than a packet of cigarettes.

Reading habits (and cigarette prices) have changed since 1935, but Penguin still believes in publishing the best books for everybody to enjoy. We still believe that good design costs no more than bad design, and we still believe that quality books published passionately and responsibly make the world a better place.

So wherever you see the little bird – whether it's on a piece of prize-winning literary fiction or a celebrity autobiography, political tour de force or historical masterpiece, a serial-killer thriller, reference book, world classic or a piece of pure escapism – you can bet that it represents the very best that the genre has to offer.

Whatever you like to read – trust Penguin.